THE BATTLE FOR THE AMERICAN MIND

THE BATTLE FOR THE AMERICAN MIND

A Brief History of a Nation's Thought

CARL J. RICHARD

ROWMAN & LITTLEFIELD PUBLISHERS, INC.
Lanham • Boulder • New York • Toronto • Oxford

ROWMAN & LITTLEFIELD PUBLISHERS, INC.

Published in the United States of America
by Rowman & Littlefield Publishers, Inc.
A wholly owned subsidary of The Rowman & Littlefield Publishing Group, Inc.
4501 Forbes Boulevard, Suite 200, Lanham, Maryland 20706
www.rowmanlittlefield.com

PO Box 317
Oxford
OX2 9RU, UK

British Library Cataloguing in Publication Information Available

Library of Congress Cataloging-in-Publication Data

Richard, Carl J.
    The battle for the American mind: a brief history of a nation's thought / Carl J.
Richard
        p. cm.
    Includes bibliographical references and index.
    ISBN 0-7425-3435-9 (alk. paper)
    1. Philosophy, American—History. 2. National characteristics, American.
3. United States—Intellectual life.
    I. Title.
    E169.1 .R563 2004
    973—dc22

                                                            2004004029

Printed in the United States of America

∞™ The paper used in this publication meets the minimum requirements of
American National Standard for Information Sciences—Permanence of Paper for
Printed Library Materials, ANSI/NISO Z39.48-1992.

For my precious Debbie—my wife, my best friend,
and the greatest of God's many gifts to me

"When Aristotle was asked, 'What is a friend?' he replied,
'One soul dwelling in two bodies.'"

—Diogenes Laertius, *Lives of Eminent Philosophers*

"You were the ax upon my belt and the bow in my weak
hand; the sword within my sheath, the shield that covered me
in battle; my happiest robe, the finest clothes I ever wore, the
ones that made me look best in the eyes of the world. That is
what you were; that is what you'll always be."

—Gilgamesh to his friend Enkidu, *Epic of Gilgamesh*

CONTENTS

Unit IV: The Age of Confusion

PREFACE

This brief history of American thought is not a monograph, a work intended for specialists, but a broader work, designed for general readers. Indeed, specialists will inevitably complain that I have addressed their own fields too briefly and too simplistically. Historical research has become so specialized that the subject of nearly every paragraph in this book now constitutes a field of study unto itself, each with its own particular set of controversies. Thus, writing a book of broad scope today is like sending a row of slow-moving ducks past a line of well-trained marksmen in a shooting gallery.

Because this work is intended for general readers, I have committed one of the greatest acts of heresy that can be committed in the modern historical profession: I have omitted all discussion of historiography. Nothing seems to fascinate modern historians so much as their own disputes, whether they concern truly significant matters or largely meaningless minutia. While there is certainly a place for historiography, it is not in works for general readers, whose interest in history far outweighs their interest in historians. For this reason also, I have streamlined the notes, so that they merely indicate to readers where they might find corroboration for the facts presented, rather than showcase historiographical disputes.

Some will complain about the fact that only three of this book's nine chapters concern the period since the Civil War, and only one the last sixty years. I can only answer that the need for brevity forced me to make some difficult choices. One of these decisions was to highlight the early, formative years of American thought, the periods in which Americans first struggled to adapt their inherited intellectual traditions to a unique context. The decision to focus on early, precedent-setting adaptations of tradition necessitated the devotion of considerable attention to the traditions themselves. Although the United States is a young nation, most of its early immigrants brought with them a culture firmly rooted in a Western civilization whose origins lay in ancient Israel and Greece. This means that one cannot understand the history of American thought without a comprehension of Christian theology and various Greek concepts, including popular sovereignty, natural law, and mixed government. While the United States has certainly produced many great minds since the Civil War, an even larger portion of their thought than that of their ancestors was inevitably derivative. It is not the fault of late nineteenth- and twentieth-century intellectuals that they appeared late in the timeline of Western thought, but it is a fact that must be faced by a historian attempting to write a brief history of American thought. I hope I may be forgiven if I have favored discussion of the foundation over that of the superstructure, however truly remarkable the latter. Indeed, the need for brevity has forced me to delete many fascinating stories from every period in the history of American thought to focus on dominant trends.

Complete objectivity is impossible for any historian. For instance, I am aware that my Christian background has profoundly influenced my perspective on American intellectual history. Therefore, my goal has not been objectivity as much as it has been to present the ideas of every individual accurately and fairly, regardless of whether or not I agree with them. It is my sincere hope that I have achieved that goal.

Four beloved and respected colleagues, James H. Dormon, Dolores Egger Labbe, John Robert Moore, and Matthew Schott, all gave generously of their time and energy to read an early version of this manuscript and to make valuable suggestions regarding its improvement. My general editors, Mary Carpenter and Laura Gottlieb, were, as always, bastions of support, encouragement, and wisdom. My copyeditors, Cheryl Hoffman, David Hoffman, and Lawrence Paulson, devoted their considerable skills to the improvement of the book.

Although the overarching themes of this book and many of its conclusions are entirely my own, my choice of subject matter was profoundly influenced by the brilliant lectures and writings of Paul K. Conkin, my mentor at Vanderbilt University in the 1980s. Perhaps more important, Professor Conkin conveyed to me and to numerous other students both the joy of working with ideas and the need for integrity in the search for truth. He never refrained from expressing an opinion merely because it was unfashionable or might displease the powerful. As a result, he won the admiration of students of diverse backgrounds and ideologies and inspired them with a determination to tell the historical truth, as they saw it, without regard to the consequences.

Some passages in chapters 3 and 4 of this book were taken from *The Founders and the Classics: Greece, Rome, and the American Enlightenment,* by Carl J. Richard (copyright 1994 by the President and Fellows of Harvard College. Reprinted by permission of Harvard University Press). I would like to reiterate my thanks to the many people whose suggestions improved those passages: Lance Banning, James Broussard, Senator Robert C. Byrd, Joyce Chaplin, Paul K. Conkin, Jack P. Greene, Ann Hawthorne, Forrest McDonald, Thomas McGinn, Samuel T. McSeveney, Meyer Reinhold, Jennifer Tolbert Roberts, James Williams, and Susan Ford Wiltshire.

INTRODUCTION:
THE THREE PHILOSOPHIES

The premise of this book is that there have been three philosophies—or worldviews, or zeitgeists, or faiths, if one prefers—in the history of the Western world, and that each of these philosophies has dominated American thought at one time or another. The first of these Western philosophies, theism, is God-centered. Because theists hold that humans are innately flawed in their reason and morals, a flaw that Christian theists term "original sin," they deny the possibility of lasting social and moral progress in the earthly world. Considering this life nothing more than a small passageway to the real and eternal world, theists trust that God will lead humans into an otherworldly utopia. Progress is an instrument of God and is restricted to His world. Mentally and morally stunted by original sin, humans move in circles in the temporal world, constantly repeating the same errors. Western theism is largely divided into three religions—Judaism, Christianity, and Islam—and each of these is subdivided according to variations in doctrine and practice.

The second philosophy, humanism, is human-centered. Humanists reject the theist contention that humans are innately depraved. Hence humanists believe in the possibility of lasting earthly progress, a fortunate circumstance since the orthodox humanist either denies or de-emphasizes the existence of a utopian afterlife. Humanists may be divided into two subcategories. Members of the first subcategory, exemplified by Epicurus, argue that the infant's mind is a blank slate on which his environment writes. The thought and behavior of the individual are entirely the product of his environment, including his family, his culture, and the vast number of other external stimuli that bombard him. Thus, if humans can use reason to manipulate their own environments or, better yet, the environments of their uncorrupted children, they can eliminate depravity. Moral and social progress will then accompany scientific and technological progress. Of course, Epicurean humanists are themselves divided over the question of which policies and institutions (systems of environmental manipulation) contribute most to such progress. For instance, while liberal humanists favor religious toleration, representative government, and free enterprise, Marxist-Leninist humanists endorse the elimination of religion, totalitarian government, and state ownership of the means of production on behalf of workers. Members of the second subcategory of humanists reject both the theist view that humans are innately selfish and the Epicurean claim that they are innately neutral. These humanists, exemplified by Plato, hold that humans are innately good. But even Platonic humanists have tended to emphasize that a proper education (environmental manipulation) is required to transform the child's innate tendency toward goodness into genuine virtue.

The third philosophy, skepticism, is uncentered. Like theists, skeptics consider humans incapable of achieving lasting social and moral progress in this world. But skeptics also deny the existence of any other world. Skeptics may also be divided into two subcategories: those, like Friedrich Nietzsche, who believe that lasting social and moral progress are impossible because of humans' animalistic instinct for aggression, and those, like William James, who consider it impossible because of the limitations of human reason. In short, the orthodox theist has faith in God but not in man, the orthodox humanist has faith in man but not necessarily in God, and the orthodox skeptic has faith in neither.

The existence of a fourth philosophy, called agnosticism, has been suggested but is doubtful. Agnostics deny having any opinion concerning God, the universe, and human nature, claiming that such questions cannot be answered satisfactorily. But no agnostic has ever stood the test of a close scrutiny. What I wish to suggest is that all humans develop basic assumptions regarding reality, if only as a psychological defense mechanism. The very act of living requires so many decisions that humans would soon exhaust themselves if they stopped at each decision to examine their basic assumptions concerning reality. However tenuous and mutable, assumptions concerning the basic issues of life are both universal and essential. At any rate, even if this philosophy of no philosophy called agnosticism exists, nothing more can be said about it. We have examined the shell and found nothing inside. Just as no building can exist without a foundation, no philosophy can exist without basic assumptions.

Of course, there are a great many alternative methods of categorizing Western philosophies. Categories and concepts are artificial human constructs, tools designed to reduce the vast totality of reality to some meaning. If reality is an ocean filled with fish, categories and concepts are the nets that humans construct to catch some of these fish. The larger the portion of reality a category or concept captures (explains), the greater its utility. But no conceptual net has ever caught all of the fish. Furthermore, many people adopt elements of more than one philosophy simultaneously. But I would argue that, in such cases, one of the philosophies is dominant, the other recessive. Finally, the degree of faith that binds an individual to his dominant philosophy varies considerably.

Although each of the three philosophies has existed, to some degree, throughout Western history, each has enjoyed its own epoch of dominance. Theism is the most ancient of the philosophies. In the first century A.D. the ethical monotheism of the ancient Hebrews gave rise to Christianity, which eventually became the predominant form of theism in the West.

Two sharp blows knocked Christian theism off its pedestal. The first was wealth. Wealth is the nemesis of theism (and skepticism), because economic progress often breeds optimism regarding social and moral progress, thereby creating the perception of independence from God and distracting attention from preparation for the afterlife. The revival of European trade with the Asian and Near Eastern civilizations as a result of the Crusades (1095–1291) combined with agricultural innovations to produce the first surge of Western wealth. Expanded by New World discoveries, Western commerce ultimately provided the capital for the Industrial Revolution, which increased wealth still further.

The second factor that caused the decline of Christian theism in the West was the scientific revolution of the sixteenth and seventeenth centuries, which culminated in the work of Isaac Newton. Enthusiastic supporters of the eighteenth-century movement called the Enlightenment deduced from the physical laws of Newton and the other scientists the existence of laws governing human affairs. They believed that once these laws of politics, economics, literature, and the arts were uncovered, moral and social progress would surely follow scientific and technological progress. The age of humanism had arrived.

Theism was, to some extent, co-opted by humanism. For instance, it is more apt to speak of Thomas Jefferson as a theistic humanist than as a humanistic theist. Although Jefferson possessed a fervent belief in God, his God was much like the kindly uncle who rarely interferes. By the antebellum period even formerly orthodox Christian denominations had tacitly discarded the crucial doctrine of original sin in their quest for progress through social reform. Meanwhile, though rebelling against the cold rationalism of Epicurean humanism, the transcendentalists embraced Platonic humanism, seeking progress through intuition. They argued that humans were innately good but were generally corrupted by civilization. Hence the individual needed to shut out the clamor of society and listen to his own "inner voice."

The late nineteenth and early twentieth centuries witnessed the eclipse of humanism by skepticism. Westerners were plagued by growing doubts concerning human rationality, the value of science in ascertaining transcendent truth, and the possibility of moral and social progress. By hypothesizing a common ancestry for humans and animals, Charles Darwin's theory of natural selection seemed to refute the humanist contention that reason formed the basis of human thought and action. Sigmund Freud located the source of human behavior in biological drives rooted in the subconscious. Furthermore, modern physicists' encroachments on the supposedly ageless laws of Newton, at both the micro and macro levels, raised doubts about the very idea of objective knowledge. Other developments, such as the carnage of the U.S. Civil War and World War I and the social problems created by industrialization, mass immigration, and the Great Depression, raised further doubts concerning human rationality and potential for progress. The age of skepticism had arrived.

Today we live in the age of confusion. Sizable numbers of adherents of each of the three philosophies coexist in the tolerant West. In the United States the post–World War II period witnessed a resurgence of humanism as a result of the nation's victory over economic depression and the Axis powers and its uncontested command of the global economy. Many Americans sincerely believed that economic growth would eventually solve all social problems. The contests of the 1960s represented an internal struggle between the two branches of humanism. The "radicals," Platonic humanists who were convinced of the possibility of progress through intuitive spirituality, battled the Epicurean humanist "establishment," which sought progress through rational materialism. But large numbers of Catholics, fundamentalist Protestants, and other orthodox theists remain, and skepticism has experienced its own resurgence in recent years. An unprecedented number of Americans are pessimistic about social progress.

The existence of large numbers of theists, humanists, and skeptics in the same society has resulted in a "culture war," waged in schools, newspapers, art galleries, and voting booths. The struggle has been particularly passionate because the differences between combatants are fundamental. Big business can compromise with big labor, ethnic and racial groups can compromise, and the genders generally do compromise by necessity, but how can orthodox theists, humanists, and skeptics compromise, when the very core of their thought is irreconcilable?

It is my contention that assumptions about God, the universe, and human nature form the basis of human thought and action. Thus, faith, defined as the belief in propositions that cannot be proven by reason and experience, lies at the core of thought and action, even for humanists and skeptics. In their epic battle for the

American mind the three broad faiths of theism, humanism, and skepticism, each manifested in a variety of somewhat contradictory forms, have dramatically influenced the course of the nation's history.

I have cast my conceptual net. Now it is time to clean the fish.

I

THE AGE OF THEISM

1

THE PROTESTANT REFORMATION: THE CRUCIBLE OF AMERICAN THEISM

The oldest of the three Western philosophies is theism, which originated in the ethical monotheism of the ancient Hebrews. In contradiction to the largely nonethical polytheism of the surrounding peoples, the Hebrews advanced the belief in an omniscient, omnipotent God who had created the universe and who demanded ethical behavior from humans in addition to rituals and sacrifices. Their prophets also proclaimed the coming of the Messiah, who would rule the world with justice.

These teachings paved the way for Christianity. The apostle Paul's doctrine of justification (salvation) by faith in Christ, rather than through adherence to Mosaic law, allowed the religion to spread rapidly among the gentiles of the Roman Empire. By the fourth century A.D., Christianity had gone from being the victim of Roman persecution to an integral part of the Roman establishment. Transformed by its new status as the state religion of the Roman Empire and by various doctrinal innovations, the Roman Catholic Church had become the only acknowledged Christian church in all of Western Europe by the early medieval period.

In the sixteenth century Protestants rebelled against some of these doctrinal innovations. Protestantism not only provided the principal motivation for the settlement of the American colonies but also became the dominant religious influence in the United States, a continuous factor in its historical and cultural development. Represented in American life from the outset, each of the three branches of Protestantism continues to play an important role in shaping American theism even today.

CORRUPTION IN THE LATE
MEDIEVAL CATHOLIC HIERARCHY

The Catholic Church brought meaning to the lives of people amid the poverty and brutality of the Middle Ages and gave them the priceless hope of a bright future in a better world. The pious spirit of the age was perhaps expressed best in Francis of Assisi's famous prayer:

> Lord, make me an instrument of your peace.
> Where there is hatred, let me sow love;
> Where there is injury, pardon;
> Where there is doubt, faith;
> Where there is despair, hope;
> Where there is darkness, light;
> Where there is sadness, joy.
> O Divine Master, grant that I may not so much seek
> To be consoled as to console;
> To be understood as to understand;
> To be loved as to love.
> For it is in giving that we receive;
> It is in pardoning that we are pardoned;
> It is in dying that we are born to eternal life.[1]

Ironically, it was the church's very success that caused its division. The money of the faithful poured into church coffers and corrupted its hierarchy, leading to the sale of indulgences, which, in turn, produced the Protestant Reformation.

By the sixteenth century the hierarchy of the Roman Catholic Church had become extremely wealthy and corrupt. Many bishops hired substitutes to perform their duties while they resided in more pleasant locations. As late as 1560 seventy Italian bishops lived in Rome rather than in their appointed sees. Bishops and popes routinely sold church offices or gave them to relatives (sometimes to illegitimate sons), and sold exemptions from marriage-related and other church laws. Pope Leo X, of the Medici family, squandered money on wars, carnivals, and gambling.[2]

Popes began to sell indulgences, certificates of absolution for an individual's sins. The sale of indulgences was based on the "treasury of merit" theory, the belief that the surplus goodness of Jesus, Mary, and the saints could be purchased from the pope and applied to one's own sins or to those of one's relatives to reduce the time spent in purgatory, a place where some sinners suffered before entering heaven. (The belief in purgatory was well established by the fifth century, though it had not existed in the first century and had little or no scriptural support.) This papal power stemmed largely from the pope's status as successor to Peter, whom Jesus had granted the authority to loose or bind sins (Matt. 16:18–19), but also partly from the papal collection of relics that were believed to confer grace. Of dubious origin, the papal relics allegedly included part of Moses's burning bush, the chains that shackled Paul, and the napkin Veronica used to wash the face of Jesus during the Crucifixion.[3]

Initially, popes had granted indulgences only to participants in the Crusades and to financial supporters of them. But by the late fifteenth century popes were sometimes even granting to princes the right to sell indulgences, based on their own relic collections. Those who viewed these relics and made an appropriate contribution received indulgences that reduced their sentences in purgatory by nearly two million years. The advantage of indulgences as a source of revenue was that since no one but God really knew the length of an individual's purgatorial sentence, there was an almost unlimited demand for them.[4]

Indulgences provided the funds for the construction of many cathedrals, monasteries, and hospitals, and even for purely secular projects like the building of bridges. Finally, as part of an effort to raise money to rebuild St. Peter's Basilica, by then dilapidated, Pope Leo X dispatched indulgence salesmen throughout Europe. Considered the greatest architectural work of the Renaissance, the basilica was partly designed by Michelangelo. Thus did the Renaissance help produce the Reformation.[5]

The pope's best indulgence salesman in Germany was Johann Tetzel, who almost certainly would be a used-car dealer or a politician were he alive today. Tetzel was a master at convincing the poor that by purchasing an indulgence from him they could save either themselves or deceased loved ones from the horrors of purgatory, which he described in graphic detail. He preached: "Listen to the voices of your dear relatives and friends, beseeching you and saying, 'Pity us, pity us. We are in dire torment from which you can redeem us for a pittance.' . . . Hear the father saying to his son, the mother to her daughter, 'We bore you, nourished you, brought you up, left you our fortunes, and you are so cruel and hard that now you are not willing for so little to set us free. Will you let us lie in flames? Will you delay our promised glory?' Remember that you are able to release them; for:

> As soon as the coin in the coffer rings,
> The soul from purgatory springs."[6]

MARTIN LUTHER (1483–1546)

It was Tetzel who infuriated the German monk Martin Luther into unintentionally inaugurating the Protestant Reformation. Although Tetzel did not sell indulgences in Luther's Saxony, he preached near enough that residents could travel to hear him. They reported Tetzel's claim that indulgences could even absolve the sins of a man who had violated Mary, the Mother of God.[7]

In 1517, on the eve of All Saints' Day, when indulgences were scheduled to be sold, Luther nailed the "Ninety-five Theses" to his church door at Wittenberg. The theses, propositions that Luther was prepared to defend in a debate, constituted a spirited attack on the sale of indulgences and on the papal authority undergirding the practice. Luther argued that the pope had no power to remit sins, only the authority to confirm their remittance by God. He added that since penance could not be given to those already dead, including those in purgatory, their sins could not be remitted. Indulgences were uncertain to save even the living, and anyone who repented of his sins was forgiven without need of them. There was no treasury of merit, since Christ granted His saving power freely. Christians should spend their money on their own necessities and on alms for the poor before purchasing indulgences. Priests should spend more time preaching the Word of God and less time selling indulgences. Finally, the sale of indulgences undermined respect for the pope, since Christians understandably asked, first, why the pope did not liberate the tormented souls of purgatory for the sake of love, rather than demanding money for it, and, second, why he did not use his own money to build St. Peter's, rather than that of "indigent believers." Indulgences might even cause the damnation of souls if they produced complacency. Luther's act probably would have come to nothing if printers had not printed the theses in German without Luther's consent, so that they were widely read and discussed.[8]

Thereafter, the increasing celebrity of Luther and his theses forced the monk to clarify the beliefs that had been gradually coalescing in his mind since 1513, when he had begun lecturing on the Psalms. In the few years after Luther presented his theses he formulated four principal doctrines. Luther claimed that these doctrines represented a return to the theology of the early Christian church, as best expressed by the apostle Paul.[9]

The first doctrine was predestination. This doctrine did not mean, as some have mischaracterized it, that the elect (those whom God has saved) could commit any evil act and still go to heaven. That is not how the theory worked. The elect would necessarily consist of good Christians, possessed of the Holy Spirit. The question was merely one of cause and effect. Believers in free will (including most late medieval Catholics) claimed that faith and good works caused one's salvation; conversely, Luther and other predestinarians argued that grace (God's saving power) caused a person's faith and good works.[10]

Since grace transformed the individual will, placing it into harmony with God's through the power of the Holy Spirit, it was wrong to think of grace as "compulsion," since that term refers to an operation undertaken against an individual's will. Nor did predestination diminish human dignity in any way. Though the elect could not claim credit for fashioning their own virtuous souls, such souls were still laudable. One did not scorn a beautiful statue because it did not create itself. Why, then, should one scorn a virtuous soul for not forming itself? Virtue, however derived, was inherently beautiful, vice inherently ugly. Unredeemed sinners, though no more responsible for their sinful natures, which were the product of original sin, than the redeemed were responsible for God's decision to bestow redeeming grace upon them, nevertheless possessed bad natures deserving of a bad end.[11]

Like Paul (Rom. 9:20–23), Luther countered the argument that predestination was unjust by denying that humans possessed the wisdom and experience to sit in judgment of an omnipotent God. Luther wrote regarding the seeming injustice of God:

> You may be worried that it is hard to defend the mercy and equity of God in damning the undeserving, that is, ungodly persons, who, being born in ungodliness, can by no means avoid being ungodly, and staying so, and being damned, but are compelled by natural necessity to sin and perish; as Paul says: "We were all the children of wrath, even as others" [Eph. 2:3], created such by God Himself from a seed that had been corrupted by the sin of the one man, Adam. But here God must be reverenced and held in awe, as being most merciful to those whom He justifies and saves in their own utter unworthiness; and we must show some measure of deference to His divine wisdom by believing Him just when He seems to be unjust. If His justice were such as could be adjudged just by human reckoning, it clearly would not be Divine; it would in no way differ from human justice. But inasmuch as He is the one true God, wholly incomprehensible and inaccessible to man's understanding, it is reasonable, indeed inevitable, that His justice also should be incomprehensible.

Just as the "light of nature" (human reason) had once held it unjust "for the good to be afflicted and the bad to prosper" in this earthly life, but had been superseded by the "light of grace" (the revelation of the Gospels), which had revealed that the godly would be rewarded and the evil punished in an eternal afterlife, so one day the "light of glory" granted in the afterlife would supersede the light of grace and make clear God's justice. Luther accepted predestination on the scriptural authority of Paul's epistles and trusted that the light of glory would one day solve the puzzle of how to reconcile it with God's justice. While it is true that, in 1530, Luther united with other German Protestants to endorse the Augsburg Confession, which assumed as official Lutheran doctrine the logically problematic position that the saved were predestined to be saved but the damned were not predestined to be damned, Luther's own, earlier writings had clearly advanced the doctrine expressed above, a doctrine similar to John Calvin's so-called double predestination.[12]

The second of Luther's doctrines was justification by "faith alone." If God had predestined some to be saved and others to be damned—some to be granted redeeming grace and others to be left to their own sinful natures—the obvious question was: How could an individual tell whether or not he was a member of the elect? Luther's answer was that faith in Jesus Christ was the only certain indication of grace. While the performance of good works was an unavoidable consequence of faith, it was not necessarily proof of salvation. In other words, while anyone who possessed real faith would necessarily perform good works, a person might perform good works without possessing faith. For instance, some people performed good works purely in the hope of receiving praise or a material reward.[13]

By faith, Luther meant an emotional, life-transforming attachment to Christ, not a mere intellectual belief. Transformed by the Holy Spirit, members of the elect would be filled with faith in their own salvation through Christ's death and resurrection, which would inevitably produce an overflow of gratitude and love that would, in turn, surely manifest itself in good works. Luther wrote: "When God in His sheer mercy and without any merit of mine has given me such unspeakable riches, shall I not then freely, joyously, wholeheartedly, unprompted do everything that I know will please Him? I will give myself as a sort of Christ to my neighbor as Christ gave Himself for me." He explained: "Faith is a living, restless thing. It cannot be inoperative. We are not saved by works; but if there be no works, there must be something amiss with faith." Anyone who failed to perform good works obviously lacked real faith. But the works themselves were only an incidental effect of grace, the external by-product of an internal transformation. Absent from the faith that produced them they could never glorify God. Indeed, an individual's very attempt to present his good works to God as meriting salvation corrupted them into damning symbols of arrogance.[14]

But even the predestined action of the Holy Spirit that instilled faith in an individual did not obliterate the effect of original sin. Grace merely began a lifelong struggle within the saved individual between his preexisting, sinful desires, the product of Adam's fall, and his new love of the good, the result of Jesus's death and resurrection. Luther wrote: "Therefore this alien righteousness, instilled in us without our works by grace alone . . . is set opposite original sin, likewise alien, which we acquire with our works by birth alone. Christ daily drives out the old Adam more and more in accordance with the extent to which faith and knowledge of Christ grow. For alien righteousness is not instilled all at once, but it begins, makes progress, and is finally perfected at the end through death." Yet God, in His mercy, ignored the remaining sin: "Grace is sufficient to enable us to be accounted entirely and completely righteous in God's sight. . . . He pays no regard to our remaining sins and does not judge them." By contrast, Luther wrote, the damned were deprived of this inner struggle, since original sin worked virtually unobstructed within them.[15]

Luther's doctrine of justification by faith alone contradicted the Catholic Church's emphasis on both faith and good works (as well as the partaking of the sacraments). Reiterating Paul's emphasis on the utterly unmerited nature of grace (Rom. 11:6), Luther argued indignantly that the late medieval church sought to render Christ's death and resurrection meaningless by placing the burden on the individual to save himself. Had not Christ freed Christians from the yoke of Mosaic law, according to Paul? Was not the Catholic Church's emphasis on works an attempt to restore that dreadful enslavement to law? (This was not a fair characterization of Catholic theology. Desiderius Erasmus and other late medieval believers in free will hardly considered Christ's death and resurrection meaningless. On the contrary, they believed it had been essential to the salvation of all humanity. They argued that

Christ's awesome sacrifice was a necessary, though insufficient, condition for each individual's salvation. If he so willed, the individual could deny the precious gift of grace through disbelief or inattention to good works. While Erasmus claimed that the damned rejected the gift of grace, Luther suggested that the gift had never been given to them—thus necessitating his defense of divine justice.)[16]

Furthermore, Luther argued that, "strictly speaking, there are but two sacraments in the church of God: baptism and the Lord's Supper, since we find in these alone a sign divinely instituted, and here alone the promise of the forgiveness of sins." An individual's partaking of the sacraments, like his other works, was not a sure sign (much less a cause) of his salvation, though any true believer would want to celebrate God's promise of salvation through participation in them. (Luther fervently endorsed matrimony and clerical ordination but did not consider them sacraments, since they did not relate to God's promise of salvation.)[17]

Luther had reached the doctrine of justification by faith through a personal spiritual crisis. Terrified by the image of "Christ the Judge," Luther had pursued every Catholic method of placating God: sacraments, pilgrimages, prayers to Mary and the saints for intercession on his behalf, fasting, and other, more severe forms of self-denial. When in Rome, Luther had visited many shrines, catacombs, and basilicas and had climbed "Pilate's Stairs" on his hands and knees to free both himself and his grandfather from the rigors of purgatory. At the monastery he had cast off his blankets and had nearly frozen to death. He had prayed to twenty-one patron saints, three for each day of the week. Above all, he had annoyed his fellow monks by the frequency and triviality of his confessions, on one occasion taking as long as six hours to recount his sins. The Catholic Church had taught that God's forgiveness must come through confession, but before one could confess each sin one must first recognize and remember it. Luther had been certain that corrupt humans constantly engaged in selfish thoughts and actions without even recognizing it, and what was unrecognized as sin could hardly be remembered and confessed. Johannes von Staupitz, the monastery's superior, had become so exasperated by one of Luther's marathon confessions that he had exclaimed: "Man, God is not angry with you! You are angry with God! . . . Look here, if you expect Christ to forgive you, come in with something to forgive—parricide, blasphemy, adultery—instead of all these peccadilloes!" Luther later recalled: "Though I lived as a monk without reproach, I felt that I was a sinner before God with an extremely disturbed conscience. I could not believe that He was placated by my satisfaction. I did not love, yes, I hated the righteous God who punishes sinners." Luther had begun to resent God for demanding the impossible: righteousness from beings inherently unable to be righteous. When presiding at his first mass, Luther had nearly been paralyzed with fear at the thought of his unworthiness to stand before God.[18]

But Luther's reading of the Psalms and the writings of Paul and Augustine had changed that. He had been particularly impressed by the manner in which both the psalmist and Augustine had looked solely to God's promise of salvation, finding no hope in themselves whatsoever. Luther recalled, "I felt that I was altogether born again and had entered paradise itself through open gates." Paul (Rom. 3:20; 5:20) taught Luther to see the commandments in a new light. Luther wrote: "They are intended to teach man to know himself, that through them he may recognize his inability to do good and may despair of his own ability. . . . For example, the commandment, 'You shall not covet' is a command which proves us all to be sinners, for no one can avoid coveting no matter how much he may struggle against it." Similarly, the Sermon on the Mount, with its instruction to love one's enemies (Matt. 5:44), was "too hard that anyone should fulfill it." Sinners like Luther must be reduced to such despair before they could abandon the arrogant position of attempting to save themselves and simply accept God's gift of grace. Once the sinner accepted the good news that Christ had freed him from the yoke of the law, his joy would be boundless. Luther concluded:

> I frankly confess that, for myself, even if it could be, I should not want free-will to be given me, nor anything to be left in my own hands to enable me to endeavor after salvation; not merely because in [the] face of so many dangers and adversities and assaults of devils, I could not stand

my ground and hold fast my 'free-will' (for one devil is stronger than all men, and on these terms no man could be saved); but because, even were there no dangers, adversities, or devils, I should still be forced to labor with no guarantee of success and to beat my fists at the air. If I lived and worked to all eternity, my conscience would never reach comfortable certainty as to how much it must do to satisfy God. Whatever work I had done, there would still be a nagging doubt as to whether it pleased God, or whether He required something more. The experience of all who seek righteousness by works proves that; and I learned it well enough myself over a period of many years, to my own great hurt. But now that God has taken my salvation out of the control of my own will, and put it under the control of His, and promised to save me, not according to my work or running, but according to His own grace and mercy, I have the comfortable certainty that . . . no devils or opposition can break Him or pluck me from Him.[19]

Luther's third doctrine was termed *sola scriptura*, Latin for "scripture alone." If faith was the only sure sign of membership in the elect, the next logical question was: How does one know what to believe? Luther's answer was that the Bible was the only infallible source of knowledge about God. By contrast, the Catholic Church claimed that both the Bible and church teachings were infallible sources of knowledge. Luther considered this approach dangerous and blasphemous. He wrote: "These adulators put the pope above Scripture and say that he cannot err. In this case Scripture perishes, and nothing is left in the Church save the word of man." Luther urged: "Let us turn our eyes and devote our minds purely and simply to that alone which Christ Himself instituted. . . . The word of God is prior to all else." Luther criticized all contemporary church practices that lacked biblical sanction and that conflicted with the simplicity of the early Christian church, including the intercession of Mary and the saints, the use of relics, masses for the dead, and abstention from meat on selected days. Attacking the mania for pilgrimages in which he himself had once participated, he added, "The true Christian pilgrimage is not to Rome or Compostela, but to the prophets, the psalms, and the Gospels."[20]

Luther's fourth doctrine was the "priesthood of all believers." If the Bible was the sole infallible source of knowledge about God, the next logical question was: Who should interpret Scripture? Luther's answer was that each believer must interpret the Bible for himself. By contrast, Catholic theologians like Thomas Aquinas had long taught that the Catholic Church was the proper interpreter of Scripture, not only because its leaders were inspired and because doctrinal unity was essential to social harmony, but also because interpretation of Scripture was too complicated for the masses. By contrast, Luther wrote: "All of us alike are priests . . . and we have the same authority in regard to the Word and the sacraments, although no one has the right to administer them without the consent of the members of his church, or by the call of the majority." Every believer was a priest. The only difference lay in "the office of preaching, and even this with our consent." Although all were priests, all could not have the time, education, and training to help the laity in the task of interpretation. But, though a trained ministry was vital, the clergy should be servants, as Paul called them, not tyrannical masters. No priest could deny the forgiveness of God or make it conditional on the performance of a penance. Luther advocated allowing the laity to drink from the chalice of wine at the Eucharist as well as to eat the bread (a reform adopted by the Catholic Church only in recent times), since the laity were priests as well. Although Luther retained genuflections and vestments, he translated the liturgy from Latin into the vernacular German, added more scriptural and instructional material to it, and instituted congregational singing. He viewed the liturgy not as a means of mystifying and overawing the people but as an opportunity to instruct them and to solicit their participation in the Word.[21]

Indeed, it was Luther's belief in the priesthood of all believers that led him to attack monasticism and clerical celibacy. The former monk believed that monks were arrogant elitists who engaged in a futile and blasphemous quest for moral perfection. Ironically, the hermetic lifestyle to which they falsely ascribed uncommon holiness actually constituted an abdication of responsibility. There should not be two classes of Christians, one considered holier than the other. Rather, every honest occupation, every "calling," was equally holy in God's eyes. It is here that we begin to see the "Protestant work ethic," the belief that work could serve as a form of prayer.[22]

At first Luther expected support from Pope Leo X in his attempt to reform the church, since the pope himself had condemned the excesses of the indulgence salesmen. Indeed, Tetzel was forced to retire to a monastery, after being publicly rebuked for his extravagant lifestyle and his two illegitimate children, a blow that drove the Dominican priest into a state of depression that ultimately killed him. (Luther wrote him a kind letter, but it did little good.) But the pope was alarmed by Luther's questioning of the Catholic Church's authority and his blistering assaults on its doctrines. By 1520 Luther was so disgusted with Rome that he was comparing it with Babylon and predicting that if the pope attempted to reform the church he would be poisoned. Luther called the Catholic Church, once the holiest of all, "the most licentious den of thieves, the most shameless of all brothels, the kingdom of sin, death, and hell." He concluded, "It is so bad even the Antichrist himself, if he should come, could think of nothing to add to its wickedness." In January 1521, after Luther refused to recant his doctrines, the pope excommunicated him.[23]

Luther's prince, Frederick, the Elector of Saxony (who had once sold many indulgences, based on his own, massive relic collection), then arranged for Luther to stay at Wartburg Castle, where Luther grew a beard and assumed the identity of a knight. The dark castle, which Luther called "my Patmos" (after the apostle John's island of exile), was abandoned except for a warden, two serving boys, and a few scores of noisy bats and owls, which Luther's feverish imagination identified as demons. While hidden away, Luther wrote nearly a dozen tracts and translated the Greek New Testament into German (1522), leaving a lasting effect on the language. The excellent diction, rich and exuberant vocabulary, earthiness, and profundity of Luther's Bible, complete with Old Testament by 1534, were unparalleled, influencing numerous later translations in other languages.[24]

Meanwhile, four wars with France and several more with the Turks prevented the Catholic Holy Roman Emperor Charles V

from suppressing Protestantism as he wished. In the 1540s wars be-
tween the German states ensued, with some princes converting to
Protestantism as an excuse to seize church property. In 1555 the
Diet of Augsburg allowed each German prince to choose between
Catholicism and Lutheranism as the official religion of his king-
dom, an uneasy agreement similar to that reached by Swiss
Catholic and Protestant cantons in the 1520s. Protestantism had
not only survived but had even prospered.[25]

THE RISE OF THE "RADICAL PROTESTANTS"

But Luther was unable to control the forces he had unleashed.
Numerous "Radical Protestant" sects arose, some of which were
nearly as hostile to Luther's doctrines as to Catholic theology. As
early as the 1520s three men from the nearby village of Zwickau
enraged Luther by claiming to be prophets who received direct
revelations from God. Though the trio's advocacy of violence
against "the ungodly" was unusual, their belief in direct revelation
foreshadowed the rise of some of the small Anabaptist sects of
Switzerland, Austria, Germany, Moravia, Bohemia, Italy, the
Netherlands, and England, as well as the emergence of other radical denominations. Belief in God's direct revelation to the laity
was as repugnant to Luther as the doctrine of church infallibility,
since any pretense to present revelation, whether claimed by commoners or by bishops' councils, could be used to undermine the
past revelation contained in Scripture, which Luther considered
the only true source of knowledge about God.[26]

Luther also compared Anabaptists' complete (and, in his
mind, irresponsible) withdrawal from secular society with that of
Catholic monks, arguing that both stemmed from a blasphemous
belief in the perfectibility of humans. Indeed, it was true that some
Anabaptists emphasized the power of the Holy Spirit over the lin-
gering effects of original sin and favored prophetic fervor over education in the selection of ministers.[27]

Unlike Luther, the Anabaptists also believed in free will and
in justification by both faith and works. They argued that baptism
was proper only for adults, since it was an outward sign of an in-

ner conversion that was impossible for infants. (Like Catholics, Luther advocated infant baptism, since children must be snatched from Satan quickly. He was hardly disturbed by the passivity of the baptized child, which only served to reinforce his conception of human powerlessness before God.)[28]

The Anabaptists were sacramentarians, whose argument that Christ was present only in spirit at the Eucharist contradicted not only Catholic transubstantiation (the belief that the physical body and blood of Christ miraculously replaced the bread and wine at the Eucharist) but also Lutheran consubstantiation (the belief that the bread and wine coexisted with the body and blood of Christ in the same space, since God was everywhere). Luther rebuked the Anabaptists for their literalism in prohibiting graven images even of Jesus while taking a metaphorical view of Jesus's eucharistic statement, "This is my body."[29]

The Anabaptists also renounced oaths (heeding the prohibitions of Matt. 5:34–37 and James 5:12), office holding, and violence of any kind. Some rejected the belief in separable souls for the belief in a purely material resurrection; hence, an individual "slept" and was conscious of nothing between his death and Judgment Day. Most radically, many Anabaptists advocated a separation of the church from the inherently evil state for the sake of the purity of the church. Some Anabaptists believed in the imminent approach of the apocalypse, and some practiced socialism. Other Radical Protestant sects dispensed with clergy, preaching from Scripture, the Eucharist, and the doctrine of the Holy Trinity entirely.[30]

Radical Protestants suffered intense persecution at the hands of other Protestants and of Catholics. Out of a total population of thirty thousand, as many as five thousand Anabaptists and other Radical Protestants were burned to death, decapitated, or drowned between 1525 and 1618. Only scattered pockets of Anabaptists remained.[31]

JOHN CALVIN (1509-1564)

Written by the French Protestant John Calvin, *Institutes of the Christian Religion* (1536) had the greatest impact of any work in spreading Luther's "Center Protestant" (or "Reformed") theology. Calvin never claimed any originality; his role was essentially that of a popularizer. Calvin was even more forceful than Luther in advancing the doctrine of predestination, flatly denying that the human will could reject God's gift of grace. Those who appeared to backslide had never received grace in the first place. Calvin cited the apostle John regarding some apparent backsliders (1 John 2:19): "They went out from us, but they were not of us; for if they had been of us, they would have remained with us." To the argument that predestination was unfair, Calvin asked in reply, "Would we have the power of God so limited as to be unable to do more than our mind can comprehend?" Why should one expect an omnipotent God to conform to the ideas of limited, self-interested humans? Just as Groucho Marx would not belong to any club that would accept him as a member, predestinarians would not worship any God so limited that they could fully understand His ways.[32]

Calvin also advanced Luther's doctrine that faith was the only certain sign of salvation. While it was true that Paul had not used the word "alone" when referring to justification by faith, his sharp contrast between Christian justification by faith and Jewish justification by works left no doubt that he denied that good works indicated membership in the elect. Furthermore, like Luther, Calvin maintained that though members of the elect were regenerated by faith, they did not cease to be plagued by fleeting moments of doubt and sin: "When we say that faith must be certain and secure, we certainly speak not of an assurance which is never affected by doubt, nor a security which anxiety never assails." He continued, "All writers of sound judgment agree in this, that in the regenerate man, there is still a spring of evil which is perceptibly sending forth desires that allure and stimulate him to sin." Indeed, Calvin claimed, "The seething spring of sin is so deep and abundant that vices are always bubbling up from it to bespatter and stain what is otherwise pure." He criticized those Anabaptists who argued that regenerate Christians had "the Spirit for their guide, and under his agency never err." Calvin maintained only Luther's two sacraments, baptism and the Eucharist (though he held to a sacramentarian view of the Eucharist), and, like Luther, viewed them as symbols, rather than causes, of salvation.[33]

Calvin agreed with Luther that the Holy Spirit acted upon the individual believer as he read Scripture, the sole infallible source of knowledge about God. Calvin wrote, "Our conviction of the truth of the Scripture must be derived from a higher source than human conjectures, judgments, or reasons; namely, the secret testimony of the Spirit." Christians believed Scripture "not like miserable men, whose minds are enslaved by superstition, but because we feel a divine energy living and breathing in it—an energy which we are drawn and animated to obey, willingly, indeed, and knowingly, but more vividly and effectually than could be done by human will or knowledge." Hence the leaders of the Catholic Church could not be considered infallible when they contradicted the Word. Calvin criticized the papacy for having added its own erroneous teachings to biblical doctrines, thereby "pouring sour wine into good." He criticized the hierarchy for continuing to use the Latin Vulgate Bible after Lorenzo Valla and Desiderius Erasmus had shown its text was "corrupted in innumerable places."[34]

Finally, Calvin also affirmed the Lutheran doctrine of the "priesthood of all believers," claiming that the individual believer possessed as certain an access to the Holy Spirit as did the church hierarchy. For this reason Calvin, like Luther, attacked clerical celibacy and monasticism, practices that separated clergy from laity. Indeed, the most significant difference between Calvin and Luther was that Calvin carried the doctrine of the priesthood of all believers further than Luther himself was willing to carry it. Although in theory Luther argued that the individual believer had the authority to interpret Scripture for himself, in practice Luther considered a hierarchical clergy necessary to assist the uneducated masses in interpretation and to maintain order. Calvin, on the other hand, supported a presbyterian church structure in which lay elders joined with pastors to form the congregation's judiciary, an influential system he introduced while a pastor in Geneva. Some Calvinists even adopted the congregationalism of the Anabaptists, a system in which each individual congregation appointed its own minister and set its own doctrine. Calvin maintained that neither "acuteness of understanding" nor a "liberal education in the schools" was necessary to "grasp spiritual teaching." Nothing was worse "than excluding the body of the people from the common doctrine, as if they were a herd of pigs." Kings and aristocrats throughout Europe were horrified by Calvin's religious republicanism, fearing it would encourage political republicanism.[35]

THE SPREAD OF PROTESTANTISM

Protestantism spread swiftly. Most of northwestern Europe converted to Protestantism, while most of southwestern Europe remained Catholic. Whether climate or ethnicity (northwestern Europe was more Germanic, southwestern Europe more Latin) was the greater factor in this division remains a matter of dispute.[36]

Clearer are the critical roles that the growth of literacy, the invention of the printing press, and the production of cheap paper played in the transmission of Protestantism. Educated in universities, a large portion of the rising urban middle class was attracted to Protestantism by its vernacular Bibles, its simplified liturgy, and its emphasis on congregational participation. Hundreds of inexpensive Protestant tracts were so widely read (even in Rome itself), though banned, that Luther soon concluded, "Printing is God's latest and best work to spread the true religion throughout the world." The printing press was one of the chief reasons the Protestant Reformation succeeded where past "heretical" movements with similar ideas had failed.[37]

To these factors may be added others. The Great Schism in the Catholic Church (1378–1417), produced by rival claimants to the papacy, who excommunicated each other's followers, had dramatically undermined the church's authority at a time of great theological speculation. The church issued no clear statement concerning justification in the millennium between the Second Council of Orange (529) and the Council of Trent (1545). As a result, considerable confusion developed regarding church teachings. Since it became difficult to separate essential doctrines from mere opinions, many Catholics did not consider Luther's teachings heretical at first. Furthermore, Renaissance scholars' emphasis on direct contact with ancient texts undermined Catholic reliance on the intervening traditions. A growing number of theologians put aside the Vulgate Bible to study Scripture in its original Hebrew and Greek languages and rediscovered the real Augustine through a haze of false texts, misleading fragments, and spurious commentaries, two developments Luther considered as providential as the invention of the printing press. Finally, an embryonic nationalism contributed to the success of the Reformation. Germans like Luther, Swiss like Zwingli, and Frenchmen like Calvin all resented Italian control of the papacy and the resultant redistribution of wealth from northern Europe to Italy.[38]

THE ENGLISH REFORMATION

England plotted a distinctive middle course through the swirling controversy. In 1521, only four years after Luther nailed the Ninety-five Theses to his church door, Pope Clement VII gave King Henry VIII (1509–1547) the title "Defender of the Faith" for his scathing attacks upon Luther and his theology in the *Defense of the Seven Sacraments*. By 1527, however, Henry VIII was desperately seeking either an annulment of his marriage with Catherine of Aragon or a divorce, since their marriage had not produced a male heir (only the daughter later vilified by Protestants as "Bloody Mary"). If Henry died without a male heir, he feared there might be civil war in England over the succession. Anxious to avoid offending Catherine's nephew, Charles V, who, as the king of Spain and the ruler of the Netherlands and the Holy Roman Emperor, was the most powerful man in Europe, the pope delayed the annulment hearings for seven years. This infuriated Henry, who felt that his past service to Rome deserved a better reward. In January 1533, after learning that his mistress Anne Boleyn was pregnant, Henry secretly married her. In March the English Parliament prohibited legal appeals to Rome, vesting the power of dispensation in the archbishop of Canterbury. Two months later the new archbishop, Thomas Cranmer, persuaded the Convocation of the Clergy to annul

Henry's marriage to Catherine. On June 1 Anne Boleyn was crowned queen of England. Three months later Princess Elizabeth was born.[39]

In 1534 Parliament recognized the king as the head of the Church of England, in effect breaking completely with the Roman Catholic Church. As the head of the newly independent Church of England (or Anglican Church), Henry appointed bishops and collected church revenues. He also dissolved many monasteries, confiscated land previously held by the Catholic Church, and sold it to the English gentry, thereby solidifying their support and raising revenue in a single stroke. Still largely Catholic in thought, however, Henry refused an alliance with the Lutherans of northern Europe when they insisted he adopt their theology. Though Henry's Anglican Church maintained only three of the Catholic sacraments (baptism, the Eucharist, and penance), it retained most of the church's rituals and doctrines, including transubstantiation, clerical celibacy, prayers for the dead, and justification by both faith and works, as well as its hierarchical structure. Even today the Anglican Church is often referred to as "Catholic, but without the pope."[40]

As a result of Henry's middle course, two broad categories of dissenters formed in England: a group of Catholics (like the ill-fated Thomas More) unwilling to recognize the king as head of the church, and a growing number of Protestants (mostly Calvinists) angered by his maintenance of Catholic doctrines, rituals, and hierarchical structure.

Following the brief reigns of the Protestant Edward VI and the Catholic Mary Tudor, Henry VIII's daughter Elizabeth I (1558–1603) returned England to her father's middle course. Although the Thirty-Nine Articles of Faith (1571) imposed by Elizabeth's Anglican clergy granted a few important concessions to Calvinists, such as the elimination of the veneration of saints and of clerical celibacy and descriptions of the will and the nature of the Eucharist that were vague enough to accommodate the Calvinists' predestinarian and sacramentarian views, they retained the other elements of Catholicism previously noted.[41]

But James I (1603–1625) and Charles I (1625–1649) were far less tolerant of Calvinists than Elizabeth. Though King James authorized a famous biblical translation that evoked the fervent admiration of English Calvinists, he had little patience with those who supported a presbyterian or congregationalist church polity. Noting the connection between religious and political republicanism, James I muttered, "No bishop, no king." If the common people could appoint their own ministers, would they not wish to appoint their own political leaders as well? James said of the Protestant dissenters, "I shall make them conform themselves or I will harry them out of the land, or else do worse." Charles I harried even larger numbers out of the land through a combination of unconstitutional taxes and religious persecution. The ultimate result of Charles I's attempt at absolutism was the English Civil War (1642–1646), which produced chaos, violence, and a military dictatorship under Oliver Cromwell, thereby causing still larger numbers to leave the land. Many of the harried fled to England's new American colonies.[42]

NOTES

1. George Appleton, ed., *The Oxford Book of Prayer* (Oxford: Oxford University Press, 1985), 75.

2. "A Plea for the Reform of Germany," 1437, in *The Portable Medieval Reader*, ed. Mary Martin McLaughlin and James Bruce Ross (New York: Viking Press, 1949), 311–17; Steven Ozment, *The Age of Reform, 1250–1550: An Intellectual and Religious History of Late Medieval and Reformation Europe* (New Haven, Conn.: Yale University Press, 1980), 196, 399; Roland Bainton, *Here I Stand: A Life of Martin Luther* (New York: Abingdon-Cokesbury Press, 1950), 21, 196.

3. Bainton, *Here I Stand*, 46–48, 72, 74–76, 117, 296; Augustine, *The City of God*, trans. Marcus Dods (New York: Modern Library, 1950), 784, 795; Robin Lane Fox, *Pagans and Christians* (New York: Alfred A. Knopf, 1987), 412. 2 Maccabees 12:45 states: "Wherefore he made the propitiation for them that had died, and that they might be released from their sin." But Jews and Protestants do not recognize 2 Maccabbees as part of the Scriptures.

4. Bainton, *Here I Stand*, 69–71.

5. Bainton, *Here I Stand*, 74–75.

6. Bainton, *Here I Stand*, 78–80; Ozment, *Age of Reform*, 251.

7. Bainton, *Here I Stand*, 76–80.

8. Martin Luther, *The Ninety-five Theses*, 1517, in *Martin Luther: Selections from His Writings*, ed. John Dillenberger (Garden City, N.Y.: Doubleday, 1961), 490–500; Bainton, *Here I Stand*, 80–84.

9. Bainton, *Here I Stand*, 60–68; Ozment, *Age of Reform*, 232, 235, 243, 292, 294.

10. Martin Luther, "Preface to the Epistle of St. Paul to the Romans," 1522, in *Martin Luther*, ed. Dillenberger, 23–25, 32; Martin Luther, *The Bondage of the Will*, 1525, in *Martin Luther*, ed. Dillenberger, 181; Martin Luther, *Theses for Heidelberg Disputation*, 1518, in *Martin Luther*, ed. Dillenberger, 502.

11. Luther, *Bondage of the Will*, 182.

12. Luther, *Bondage of the Will*, 200–2; Erwin L. Leuker, ed., *Lutheran Cyclopedia*, 2d ed. (St. Louis, Mo.: Concordia, 1975), 499, 632.

13. Martin Luther, "Preface to the New Testament," 1522, in *Martin Luther*, ed. Dillenberger, 18; Luther, "Preface to Romans," 20–22; Martin Luther, *The Freedom of a Christian*, 1520, in *Martin Luther*, ed. Dillenberger, 56, 62, 68; Luther, *Theses for Heidelberg Disputation*, 503; Bainton, *Here I Stand*, 254.

14. Luther, "Preface to Romans," 21–22; Bainton, *Here I Stand*, 230–31, 332.

15. Luther, "Preface to Romans," 23; Martin Luther, *Two Kinds of Righteousness*, 1519, in *Martin Luther*, ed. Dillenberger, 88.

16. Luther, *Bondage of the Will*, 175, 203; Ozment, *Age of Reform*, 297.

17. Martin Luther, *Pagan Servitude of the Church*, 1520, in *Martin Luther*, ed. Dillenberger, 279, 326, 351, 357; Bainton, *Here I Stand*, 137, 139.

18. Martin Luther, "Preface to the Complete Edition of Luther's Latin Writings," 1545, in *Martin Luther*, ed. Dillenberger, 11; Bainton, *Here I Stand*, 30, 38, 41, 45, 49–51, 54–55.

19. Luther, "Preface to Latin Writings,"11; Luther, *Freedom of a Christian*, 57; Luther, *Bondage of the Will*, 199; Bainton, *Here I Stand*, 46, 58–59; Ozment, *Age of Reform*, 243; Alister McGrath, *The Intellectual Origins of the European Reformation* (Oxford: Basil Blackwell, 1987), 119.

20. Luther, *Pagan Servitude of the Church*, 271, 274, 310; Bainton, *Here I Stand*, 89–90, 98, 117, 155, 224, 296, 367.

21. Luther, *Freedom of a Christian*, 65; Luther, *Pagan Servitude of the Church*, 263, 322, 345, 349; Bainton, *Here I Stand*, 89, 138, 140, 259, 273–74, 340–49; Mark U. Edwards Jr., *Luther's Last Battles: Politics and Polemics, 1531–1546* (Ithaca, N.Y.: Cornell University Press, 1983), 72; McGrath, *Intellectual Origins of the European Reformation*, 124.

22. Bainton, *Here I Stand*, 155, 200–1, 233–35.

23. Luther, "Preface to Latin Writings," 5, 10; Luther, *Freedom of a Christian*, 46; Bainton, *Here I Stand*, 105.

24. Bainton, *Here I Stand*, 193–98, 326–29, 384–85.

25. Ozment, *Age of Reform*, 253–59, 338.

26. Bainton, *Here I Stand*, 208, 257, 261; Ozment, *Age of Reform*, 345.

27. Ozment, *Age of Reform*, 269.

28. Bainton, *Here I Stand*, 142, 259–60; Ozment, *Age of Reform*, 263, 331, 346.

29. Bainton, *Here I Stand*, 139–40, 258.

30. Bainton, *Here I Stand*, 259–60, 375; Ozment, *Age of Reform*, 330–31, 345, 348; George Huntston Williams, *The Radical Reformation* (Philadelphia: Westminster, 1962), xxv–xxxi, 46, 91, 149, 172, 174, 204, 299, 303, 323, 325, 337–38, 403, 506, 519, 617, 853–56, 865.

31. Ozment, *Age of Reform*, 332, 347.

32. John Calvin, *Institutes of the Christian Religion*, trans. Henry Beveridge, 2 vols. (Grand Rapids, Mich.: William B. Eerdmans, 1970), vol. 1, 73, 466, 478; vol. 2, 88, 229, 246–47; McGrath, *Intellectual Origins of the European Reformation*, 54.

33. Calvin, *Institutes*, vol. 1, 469–71, 484, 516, 519; vol. 2, 513, 557, 563, 626, 635–36, 638, 647; William J. Bouwsma, *John Calvin: A Sixteenth-Century Portrait* (Oxford: Oxford University Press, 1988), 36.

34. Calvin, *Institutes*, vol. 1, 71–73; vol. 2, 398; Bouwsma, *John Calvin*, 43, 118.

35. Calvin, *Institutes*, vol. 2, 317, 325, 396; Bouwsma, *John Calvin*, 60–61, 199, 226–27; Ozment, *Age of Reform*, 363, 367.

36. For an excellent map delineating the spread of the various forms of Protestantism, see Ozment, *Age of Reform*, 373.

37. Bainton, *Here I Stand*, 111, 115, 120–23, 295, 305; Ozment, *Age of Reform*, 98, 201–3, 210–11, 294.

38. McGrath, *Intellectual Origins of the European Reformation*, 14–16, 24–25, 40–42, 46, 129–34, 137, 175–88, 202.

39. G. R. Elton, *Reform and Reformation: England, 1509–1558* (Cambridge, Mass.: Harvard University Press, 1977), 75–76; Pierre Crabites, *Clement VII and Henry VIII* (London: Routledge, 1936), 5–10; A. G. Dickens, *The English Reformation* (New York: Schocken Books, 1964), 105–7.

40. Dickens, *English Reformation*, 118–19, 123–24, 142, 160, 165, 175–78, 185, 191, 329; Ozment, *Age of Reform*, 395.

41. Dickens, *English Reformation*, 200, 202–3, 206, 210, 213, 220, 245–53, 264–66, 295, 302–4, 312; Ozment, *Age of Reform*, 395.

42. Derek Hirst, *Authority and Conflict: England, 1603–1658* (Cambridge, Mass.: Harvard University Press, 1986), 99.

2

EARLY AMERICAN PROTESTANTISM

It has been estimated that 75 percent of the American colonists were "Center (or Reformed) Protestants," in the tradition of Luther and Calvin. They far outnumbered "Radical Protestants," such as the Amish and the Mennonites, who followed in the tradition of the Anabaptists, and "Conservative Protestants," such as what would later be termed "high-church Anglicans," not to mention the relatively small number of Catholics and Jews who lived in the colonies. Many came to America, at least in part, to escape intense religious persecution in Europe, often at the hands of the Church of England, which not only defrocked hundreds of congregationalist Calvinist ministers but also imprisoned dissenters and seriously infringed their rights to inheritance, marriage, and even work. Not surprisingly, the dissenters themselves were hardly modern libertarians; their desire for freedom to practice their own religions rarely implied a belief in the separation of church and state. Even the few colonists who advocated the separation of church and state and complete religious toleration, in imitation of the early Christian church before Constantine, did so for the sake of religious purity, not individual rights. Even so, the American colonies, with the notable exception of the early Puritan colonies of New England, possessed a greater degree of religious toleration than any other society in the world. While Americans often had to pay taxes to support their colony's established church (generally the majority church) and had to obey Christian blue laws (instituted more for social order than for the salvation of souls), they were generally free to practice their own religions. Far from representing a decline in religious fervor, the growth of even greater toleration in the eighteenth century was the product of a religious revival movement that also helped cause the American Revolution.[1]

THE NEW ENGLAND COLONIES

The first European settlers in New England were Separatists, not Puritans. While both groups adhered to the same Calvinist theology, they favored different tactics. Puritans wished to remain within the Church of England in order to purify it. By contrast, Separatists wanted to separate completely from the church, which they considered a corrupting influence beyond the hope of reform.

The Pilgrims

In 1608 a band of Separatists immigrated from Scrooby, a town in northern England, to Amsterdam, to escape the persecution of the English king James I. The following year they moved to Leyden.[2]

In 1619 the Separatists, later dubbed "Pilgrims," left the Netherlands to establish a colony in America. Having received assurances that James I would not persecute them in America, the Pilgrims decided to settle at Jamestown, the first permanent English colony, which had been established in 1607. In July 1620, thirty-five Separatists journeyed to Southampton, England. On September 6 they piled into the *Mayflower* with a larger group of colonists. Aware of the potentially lethal nature of the voyage and of the difficult adjustments that awaited them, the 102 "saints and strangers" sailed for Virginia. Although storms drove them far off course, so that they landed in what is now Massachusetts, the arduous voyage cost them only one life, an unusually low casualty figure.[3]

Since these squatters established Plymouth Colony outside the jurisdiction of any colonial government (some believe they intentionally "drove themselves off course"), the forty-one adult males drafted and signed the Mayflower Compact on November 11, 1620. The Mayflower Compact was a covenant, based on the numerous covenants of Puritan and Separatist communities in England. It was not a constitution; it did not specify Plymouth Colony's form of government. Nevertheless, under the agreement, the Pilgrims not only consented to obey God's law but also pledged to obey the laws made by leaders of their own choosing. Hence the Mayflower Compact set a precedent for the written constitutions that soon followed.[4]

Though Plymouth Colony possessed only seven thousand settlers when it merged with the much larger colony of Massachusetts in 1691, Plymouth's fame, secured by its early settlement and by William Bradford's remarkable account, *Of Plymouth Plantation*, greatly exceeded its size. Governor of the colony for thirty-three years, Bradford could have been the sole proprietor of Plymouth had he wished, but he surrendered his patent rights to the colony's freemen.[5]

The Puritans

In 1629 the English king Charles I issued a charter to the Massachusetts Bay Company. Fortunately for the company, the king's lawyers forgot to include the usual provision that the company's headquarters must remain in London. Taking advantage of the omission, the Puritan stockholders of the company moved the headquarters with them to America, out of the reach of royal authority, thereby making the colony self-governing.[6]

The Puritans' Massachusetts expedition (1630) consisted of an armada of seven ships, followed closely by another ten vessels, and over one thousand settlers, including an unusually high percentage of university graduates. John Winthrop resigned a powerful post as county justice of the peace to lead the expedition. Having caught the Puritan fever while at Cambridge University, Winthrop believed that the Church of England was still worth saving. But this conclusion created what historian Edmund S. Morgan called the "Puritan dilemma": how to save the church without being corrupted by it—in broader terms, how to live in this impure world without being corrupted by it. Winthrop explained his answer to that question in a sermon ("A Model of Christian Charity") aboard the *Arbella*, en route to Massachusetts. The answer was to build a "city upon a hill," a model community so pure that England and its state church would have no choice but to admire and emulate it. Winthrop and the Puritans decided that the only way to save England was by leaving it. Since all of their direct efforts at reform in England had failed, leaving such iniquity that they feared for their own children's souls, they would launch a flank attack against corruption. As Morgan put it, "Winthrop knew that in England he was not tall enough to do anything effective for the cause of God against the towering ungodliness of King Charles, but, in New England, Charles would cast a small shadow indeed, and Winthrop would be the giant."[7]

Contrary to popular myth, the Puritans did not believe that they could construct a perfect society. Their Calvinist theology taught that humans were so depraved that they could not save themselves, much less build a utopia. The idea of an earthly utopia was blasphemous. Only God's grace could save humans, and heaven was the only utopia. The Puritans merely sought to form a purer society. Indeed, to show the world that their intent in emigrating to America was to purify, and not to renounce, the Church of England (as the Separatists had), the Puritans issued a statement before they sailed, avowing their affection for the church and denying that they were "of those that dreame of perfection in this world." This is not to say that individual Puritans, intoxicated by the excitement of their mission and emboldened by the idea of a new start, did not approach utopianism on occasion. But their theology invariably reasserted itself, leading them to the conclusion that as much as humans might delude themselves, they could never escape original sin by fleeing to the fresh air of a New World, for wherever they journeyed they would carry it with them, like a stowaway, in the very depths of their hearts. However dormant the virus of original sin might lie, it would eventually arise and strike hardest at those who strove the hardest to ignore it. A real "New World" was impossible until the afterlife, when the "Old Adam" within each Christian would no longer exist. The Puritans understood that they could have some degree of success in suppressing theft but not greed; adultery but not lust; murder but not hatred.[8]

Based on their belief in spiritual equality, the Puritans established a political system that was radically egalitarian for its day. While it is true that the Puritans sometimes asserted that their government was not a democracy but a theocracy, that claim was intended to mollify contemporaries alarmed by their radical egalitarianism. The Puritan claim to theocracy actually signified little: Many governments claim to govern according to God's will; the real question is, who is the ultimate interpreter of God's will? Since the vast majority of adult males could vote in the elections of seventeenth-century Massachusetts, seventeenth-century Massachusetts must rank as one of the most democratic societies of its day. The only other evidence that has been presented for the claim that the Puritans were undemocratic is the fact that some wealthy men were continually reelected to office. But no society has ever made a habit of electing poor men to high office. Few can afford to leave their jobs to campaign. In what democracy, from ancient Athens to the modern United States, have the same people *not* been continually reelected? It is not the individuals a democracy elects that make it a democracy. It is majority rule. Furthermore, some modern Americans confuse democracy, or majority rule, with libertarianism, a high regard for individual liberty. But institutional protections of individual liberty, such as the U.S. Bill of Rights, are invariably undemocratic, since they involve limiting the ability of the majority to legislate. In short, the Puritans were highly egalitarian for their day, but not libertarian.[9]

In seventeenth-century Massachusetts the governor and both branches of the colonial legislature (the General Court) were elected annually by all adult male church members, who constituted over two-thirds of the colony's adult males in 1637—a degree of democracy not seen since Athens in the fifth century B.C. In addition, the requirement of church membership was not rigorously upheld; men of certified good character could vote without it, and the loss of church membership did not result in the loss of the franchise.[10]

In an age in which local government played a much larger role in citizens' lives than it does today, Massachusetts's town governments were direct democracies. The selectmen who sat on the town councils were elected annually (sometimes semiannually). The selectmen merely set the agenda for the town meeting. Citizens voted directly on town ordinances. Puritan New England's direct democracy was far more participatory than the modern representative system.[11]

Each Puritan colony also possessed its own compact, a written constitution approved and signed by every adult male. Consensual and consensus-driven, Puritan governments were among the most stable of the tumultuous seventeenth century.[12]

The Puritans' political egalitarianism arose from a belief in spiritual equality, which also manifested itself in their congregationalist church polity and in their public schools. Each Puritan congregation had the power to elect and remove ministers and to approve or excommunicate members by a simple majority vote. The Puritans established the first public schools in America, so that all children could learn to read the Bible. Parents could be punished for neglecting their children's education. In 1636 the Puritans established Harvard College, the first institution of higher learning in what is now the United States. Its original purpose was to train ministers—not only in theology, but also in logic, rhetoric, and science. It was not uncommon for Puritan ministers to study ten or twelve hours a day and to sacrifice their health in the production of massive tomes. The Puritans believed that while human reason was limited, it should be used to its fullest extent in deducing God's truth from both Scripture and nature. The Puritans wanted to chasten reason, not annihilate it.[13]

The Puritans extended their egalitarianism into economics as well. At the outset, they distributed land roughly equally among the adult males, although some political leaders, other men of prestige, and larger families received more than others. In addition, New England recognized the property rights of women to a greater extent than the other colonies. Widows were guaranteed at least one-third of their husbands' land, whether the husbands willed it or not. Husbands could not dispose of certain of their wives' possessions, such as clothing. Wives exercised a veto power over the sale of houses and land. Indeed, some women even owned taverns. In their recognition of these rights the Puritans followed John Calvin, who had insisted that women were spiritually equal to men.[14]

The Puritans could not escape the hierarchical mind-set of the seventeenth century entirely, of course. They believed that the wealthy, the well-born, and the well-educated had both the right and the duty to lead the commoners in both church and state affairs, though the commoners sometimes chafed under their leadership.

But if one compares the Puritans with their contemporaries, the only sensible comparison, the radical nature of their egalitarianism becomes apparent. Certainly their contemporaries thought so. Even their Presbyterian brethren, fellow Calvinists who were themselves considered radical because of their support for a less hierarchical church polity, were shocked and appalled by the degree to which the New England Puritans had established a democracy (hence the need for the Puritans to emphasize the stabilizing influence of theocracy).[15]

Neither were the Puritans as "puritanical" as is often alleged. The modern stereotype of the Puritans as "kill-joys in tall-crowned hats, whose main occupation was to prevent each other from having any fun" is, like most stereotypes, a gross exaggeration. Those Puritans who could afford it wore crimson waistcoats and fine cloaks, not the dark, dismal outfits generally portrayed in modern films about the Puritans. They played musical instruments, enjoyed secular music, told jokes, and drank beer, wine, and rum. The Puritans noted that Jesus's first miracle was the conversion of water into wine (John 2:3–11). The pious Puritan minister John Cotton wrote that wine was "to be drunk with a cheerful heart." Drinking was legal, but public drunkenness was illegal, because it led to fighting, cursing, and fornication, with detrimental effects on society. The Puritans considered sex a natural, healthy, and enjoyable part of marriage, essential to the satisfaction of innate desires that might otherwise be manifested in bestiality or some other form of perversion. For this reason, the First

Church of Boston expelled a man for denying his wife sexual intercourse for two years. To the Puritans, all earthly pleasures were gifts of God and, as such, were good when enjoyed moderately, responsibly, and gratefully.[16]

The Puritan conception of earthly pleasures was the product of a long Christian tradition. Augustine urged Christians to show gratitude for earthly pleasures, not to despise them. He wrote: "Suppose, brethren, a man should make a ring for his betrothed, and she should love the ring more wholeheartedly than the betrothed who made it for her. . . . Certainly, let her love his gift. But, if she should say, 'The ring is enough—I do not want to see his face again,' what would we say of her? . . . The pledge is given her by the betrothed just that, in his pledge, he himself may be loved. God, then, has given you all these things. Love Him who made them." The proper response to God's gift of earthly pleasures was neither contempt for them nor the abuse of them but love and gratitude toward their divine provider. Similarly, Martin Luther wrote, "I have no use for cranks who despise music, because it is a gift of God. Music drives away the Devil and makes people happy; they forget thereby all wrath, unchastity, arrogance, and the like." Luther declared concerning music, which he considered second only to the Word of God, "He who does not consider this an inexpressible miracle of the Lord is truly a clod and is not worthy to be considered a man." Like most of his fellow Germans, Luther loved beer, which he often quaffed from his favorite mug. Although Calvin disliked excessive displays of wealth, denounced dancing because it led to fornication, and opposed vulgar language and drunkenness, he also called wine "a very healthy food," cited Jesus's conversion of water into wine, quoted Psalm 104:15 ("wine that maketh glad the heart of man"), opposed celibacy as "against nature," and urged a moderate lifestyle, "neither too lavish nor sordidly parsimonious." Having noted that God had given humans "a superabundance of good things," including food, drink, art, music, and sex, he called the ascetic's contempt for such benefits "profanation and sacrilege." Particularly fond of wine, the Frenchman emphasized, "It is permissible to use wine not only for necessity, but also to make us merry." Similarly, sex within marriage was permissible not only for reproductive purposes but for pleasure as well. Calvin warned, "The contempt which believers should train themselves to feel for the present life must not be of a kind to beget hatred of it or ingratitude to God." Calvin opposed the extremes of monastic self-denial and unrestricted hedonism with equal fervor.[17]

Indeed, in their belief that wealth was sometimes a sign of God's favor, many Puritans surpassed the early church in their acceptance of materialism. Both Jesus and Paul instructed Christians to seek the reward for their virtue in the next life, expecting only persecution in this world. Augustine taught that God acted mysteriously, granting both prosperity and hardship to both good and evil individuals and nations. Hence neither prosperity nor hardship denoted divine favor or disfavor. Yet, ignoring these cautionary pronouncements, medieval Christians nervously sought signs of God's pleasure or displeasure in earthly life for centuries. Peace, prosperity, and good harvests were widely interpreted as tokens of God's approval, droughts, epidemics, and other disasters as signs of His disapproval. Magistrates typically called for days of thanksgiving in response to the former, days of fasting in response to the latter. Perhaps as a result of this alternative tradition, Calvin expressed greater ambivalence about wealth than previous theologians. On the one hand, he wrote, "Adversity is a sign of God's absence, prosperity of His presence." On the other hand, he sometimes noted that the elect suffered while the wicked prospered. Furthermore, while prosperity might be a sign of God's favor, wealth must be regarded warily, since it frequently led to "pride, pomp, scorn of God, cruelty, fraud, and everything of the kind; and then it brings bodily delights and pleasures, so that man is wholly brutalized." Calvin criticized merchants and denounced ostentation.[18]

Similarly ambivalent, most Puritans were careful not to equate earthly success with salvation but generally welcomed it as something more than mere luck. Indeed, they hoped their prosperity would convince others that "the New England Way" was God's way. Yet they worried, simultaneously, that wealth might be a temptation from Satan. While most Puritans refused to see wealth as inherently evil, few looked upon success with complacency.

Their ambivalence was understandable, since the relationship be-tween piety and earthly success is exceedingly complex. While the characteristics generally associated with piety—frugality, disci-pline, hard work, kindness to others—can (and, in the Puritans' case, did) yield earthly rewards, in other instances piety has elicited persecution. The same piety that might produce wealth in New England might attract persecution in Old England.[19]

Much of the prudery falsely attributed to the Puritans is ac-tually Victorian in origin. For instance, seventeenth-century New England court records often included earthy language. Yet when the same records were reproduced in the nineteenth century, Vic-torian editors frequently excised such passages. Similarly, it was not until the nineteenth century that lascivious passages from the Greek and Latin poets were expunged from schoolbooks. The Pu-ritans disapproved of such passages but retained them.[20]

Like most people of their day, the Puritans were intolerant. They did not tolerate ideas and practices they considered harmful to their mission. Puritans had suffered extreme hardships (storms at sea, disease, hunger, snowstorms, the attacks of Native American tribes, backbreaking toil) and had given their lives to build the "city upon a hill," and their survivors believed it must be protected at all costs. But, like Calvin, the Puritans viewed punishment as the last resort when dealing with recalcitrant people. Winthrop spent much of his time as governor attempting to persuade people to give up their "heresies," or at least not to preach them. Punish-ments were inflicted only after great deliberation, since it was con-sidered as grievous a sin to punish acts God did not consider sin-ful as to allow those He abhorred. When punishment was judged necessary, it was generally inflicted by the will of the community as a whole, not as the private vendetta of an elite. One reason the people did not reelect Winthrop one year (1634) was that they considered him too lenient. (They chose the harsher Thomas Dudley to replace him.) The Puritans emphasized shame over physical pain in the selection of punishments. The same principle was applied to the education of children, as Calvin had recom-mended. (Calvin had criticized the "immoderate harshness" and "lash-loving executioners" then common in grammar school classrooms.) Even at the end of the seventeenth century, the Puritan sage Cotton Mather wrote that he used shame to punish his children (though punishment was seldom necessary). He reminded them that God's eyes were upon them. For good behavior he held out the ultimate reward: to be taught something.[21]

To the Puritans, church and state were two aspects of the same unity, the purpose of which was to accomplish God's will. They were two horses pulling the same carriage. The carriage could not be pulled by the church alone, if the state rebelled and pulled in the opposite direction. Although, by custom, ministers never sought public office in Puritan New England (unlike in the modern United States), all citizens were required to pay local taxes to support the church and to attend church services, as in most of the other colonies and in the mother country. No church was allowed in Massachusetts without the consent of the General Court. Citizens might be fined for speaking disrespectfully of ministers. The idea of the separation of church and state was still very new and held by very few.[22]

The notion that church and state were partners in the salvation of souls had originated in the fourth century, when Constantine's conversion transformed the Christian Church from a victim of the Roman establishment into an important part of it. Augustine supported Christian emperors' suppression of heresy, noting that the ancient Israelites had used force to advance the Word of God. Aquinas defended the execution of heretics, arguing that they were worse than pagans, since they corrupted the faith. The medieval church had sometimes joined with the state in launching inquisitions against heretics, pogroms against Jews, and crusades against Muslims. Nor had the heretics themselves been libertarians; nearly all had sought merely to substitute their own dogmas for their opponents' as the recipients of state support. Protestants had hardly been more tolerant than Catholics. In his early years Luther supported the expulsion of heretics (Radical Protestants) from his principality and, in his later years, Jews from all of Europe. Calvin endorsed the execution of the famous heretic Michael Servetus. He argued concerning the pastor and the ruler: "Their responsibilities should be so joined that each helps rather than impedes the other. . . . If we permit the profligate and corrupt to come here to practice their lewdness, will we not necessarily become debauched and totally corrupt with them?"[23]

In each instance the assumption had been that the salvation of eternal souls easily outweighed any injury done to mortal bodies. Medieval and early modern people were deeply preoccupied with thoughts of the fate that awaited them at the end of their very short lives. It would hardly be considered a friendly act for political leaders to allow heretics to continue espousing errors that leaders believed threatened both the heretics' own immortal souls and those of their listeners. Added to the fear of hell was the almost universally perceived need for social unity. Society could not be unified and could not pursue a common purpose without common beliefs regarding a matter as important as religion. Hence, in the Puritans' day, every government in Europe expelled or executed heretics.[24]

By examining the three most famous cases of Puritan intolerance one may come to a clearer understanding of the Puritans. The first case was that of Roger Williams. Upon his arrival in Massachusetts in 1631, the Reverend Williams's commitment to separatism was so great that he would not even take a position as pastor of the Boston congregation unless the congregation publicly declared their repentance for having had communion with the churches of England while they lived there. Although Winthrop liked Williams personally, he rebuked him for self-righteousness. Williams migrated to Plymouth but proved too much of a Separatist even for the Pilgrims. He complained publicly and bitterly when church members who had visited England and had attended Anglican services there were not expelled upon returning to Plymouth. He also complained that the unregenerate (those who had not had a conversion, or rebirth, experience) were treated with the same respect as the regenerate. The kindhearted William Bradford called Williams "a man godly and zealous, having many precious parts, but very unsettled in judgment" and possessing "strange opinions." When Plymouth rejected him, Williams returned to Massachusetts, where he continued preaching his extreme brand of separatism and refused to stop. He taught that the godly should never pray with the ungodly, even if the latter was a spouse. His own congregation removed him in 1635. When Williams grew even more vociferous, the General Court tried him and banished him to England. Fearing for Williams's safety in England, Winthrop suggested that he escape to Narragansett Bay. The General Court did nothing to stop Williams from creating his own colony in Rhode Island, with the help of Native American tribesmen, in 1636.[25]

Williams's actions after fleeing to Rhode Island reveal why the Puritans considered him so grave a threat to their mission. In his ever-increasing zeal for church purity Williams soon excluded everyone but his wife from communion. Williams wrote letters to Winthrop, urging him to come to Rhode Island: "Abstract your-selfe with a holy violence from the Dung heape of this Earth." But Williams failed to understand what Winthrop and the Puritans had known all along: that total abstraction from the material world was impossible.[26]

Winthrop waged a lifelong war against the two extremes of exclusion and inclusion that he believed threatened the Puritan mission. The Puritan must live in the world and accept some human fallibility, contrary to Williams's separatism, but he must not accept all beliefs as equally valid. Hence Winthrop dissuaded the Puritan minister George Phillips of Watertown from preaching that the Roman Catholic Church was a "true church." Winthrop could not accept Catholic beliefs. While Catholics may quarrel with Winthrop's doctrinal boundaries, it is certain that every church must have such boundaries if it is to be anything more than a social club. Conversely, Winthrop then persuaded John Masters to hold communion with fellow layman Richard Brown. Masters had refused to hold communion with Brown, because Brown would not abandon Phillips's original position of tolerance toward the Catholic Church. Realizing that the Puritans' zeal made them more apt to fall into the error of excessive exclusion, leading to schism, than excessive inclusion, leading to moral relativism, Winthrop devoted most of his considerable energy to combating separatism.[27]

Winthrop's dilemma was hardly new. Although Augustine fervently denounced heresies he considered lethal to the church, he opposed the extremism of the Donatists, who refused to recognize those bishops they considered impure. While the Donatists considered the battle between good and evil strictly a struggle between good and evil people, Augustine considered it largely (though not entirely) a struggle within each individual. The souls of even the best Christians were battlegrounds in the ancient war between original sin and the Holy Spirit. Calvin agreed, warning ministers against overzealousness:

> Whenever we must criticize vices, we should remember to begin with ourselves, so that, recalling our own weaknesses, we are temperate toward others. . . . Since all men are somewhat beclouded with ignorance, either we must leave no church remaining, or we must condone delusion in those matters which can go unknown without harm to the sum of religion and without loss of salvation. . . .Pretending zeal, some are always fulminating and forget that they are men; they show no sign of friendliness but exude only bitterness. . . . Terrifying sinners so inhumanely, without any sign of anguish or sympathy, they make God's Word seem insulting and distasteful.

Yet Calvin noted that other ministers were too inclusive, flattering their congregations and ignoring "the most serious iniquities." But Calvin (like Winthrop) considered excessive zeal the greater vice of his day: "By nature, we are almost all too irritable, and Satan pushes us to inhumane rigor under the pretext of strictness. As a result, wretched men, denied forgiveness, are swallowed up by grief and despair." Puritans like Winthrop understood that perfection could never exist in this world—even within a small number of God's elect—and must be expected only in the next life. While Puritans considered themselves better than most other people outwardly, their habit of intense introspection led them to doubt that they were much better inwardly.[28]

But if Williams's brand of religious separatism had no future, his political separatism—his belief in the separation of church and state—had a glorious one. Williams advocated the separation of church and state because he feared that state power would corrupt the church. Williams opposed mandatory church attendance not out of concern for individual rights, but because the regenerate might be corrupted by the unregenerate who would be required to attend services. He argued that it was impossible to convert anyone by force and that Jesus, though the Son of God, had never used force to convert anyone. Williams proposed returning to the tolerance of the early church before it had been corrupted by the state power Constantine had bestowed upon it. Williams was supremely confident that the Holy Spirit could not only defend Christianity but advance Christian truth, without state aid. He wondered if it was a lack of faith in the Holy Spirit that caused the Puritans to stop short in their quest to re-create the early church. Was it not strange that the Puritans should make intolerance the only exception to their general project of substituting the purer practices of the early church for the intervening Catholic tradition? Here Williams struck a nerve. As he well knew, the Puritans agreed with him that the decline of the church had begun with Constantine, who had corrupted it with wealth, power, and prestige.[29]

Williams hoped that the separation of church and state would end the civil wars, massacres, and crusades falsely waged in God's name, though he was hardly a complete pacifist or libertarian. (He supported defensive wars, the death penalty in a few cases, and the public identification and disarming of suspicious Catholics.) Williams's Rhode Island welcomed all immigrants, even Jews and Muslims.[30]

A second famous example of Puritan intolerance is the case of Anne Hutchinson, the Puritan daughter of an Anglican parson. In 1634 Anne and William Hutchinson, a middle-aged couple, landed in Massachusetts. Winthrop, who lived across the street from the Hutchinsons, described William, an affluent clothing merchant, as "wholly guided by his wife." William's reliance on Anne was understandable, since, by Winthrop's own admission, she was an intelligent and courageous woman. Indeed, it was Anne who had convinced her husband to follow the magnetic John Cotton to New England. Anne soon achieved popularity in Boston for her kindness in nursing women through their illnesses.[31]

The trouble began between 1635 and 1637 when Anne held regular sessions, attended by as many as sixty women and twenty men, in which she eloquently expounded on Cotton's sermons. Unfortunately, she also expanded on them, going well beyond Cotton's meaning (and orthodox Christianity) to revive antinomianism, the old Gnostic belief that the union between the Holy Spirit and members of the elect was so complete that the elect stood above the injunctions of biblical law and had no need for good works as evidence of grace (though Anne herself was hardly deficient in works). While the Protestant reformers had argued that not everyone who performed good works had grace, they had insisted with equal fervency that grace could not be present without producing good works. Thus, while good works could not provide the believer with a positive assurance of grace, they were certainly necessary to have any assurance at all. Considering this doctrine essential to the maintenance of a moral society, both the reformers and their Puritan heirs looked with horror on those who would banish moral responsibility from theology. Furthermore, Hutchinson informed her friends that all of Massachusetts's ministers except for Cotton and John Wheelwright (a distant relative of Hutchinson's) were unfit to preach the New Testament because they preached "a covenant of works." The implication was that all of the colony's ministers were damned except for these favored two. Wheelwright was equally rash in speaking of his clerical brethren. Anne and her followers began proselytizing newcomers to the colony.[32]

Alarmed, Winthrop persuaded the people to remove Governor Henry Vane and other Hutchinson supporters from office. Like most other religious dissenters of the day, Vane was no champion of religious liberty; he merely contended that Hutchinson's antinomian doctrine was alone true and deserving of state support.[33]

In 1637 the General Court tried Hutchinson for heresy. On the verge of acquittal, she ignored Winthrop's sign to be silent and proudly proclaimed that the Holy Spirit had directly revealed to her, while in England, that she must come to New England and suffer persecution, but that God would deliver her like the prophet Daniel. She then warned the court: "If you go on this course you begin you will bring a curse upon you and your posterity. And the mouth of the Lord hath spoken it."[34]

Although there was a definite element of sexism at Anne's trial (Winthrop remarked that her preaching sessions were not "fitting for your sex"), and though her conviction reaffirmed clerical authority, historians who emphasize these factors miss the real point of Hutchinson's trial. Not only did the Puritans consider antinomianism a repudiation of the orthodox Christian doctrine of original sin (which held that grace did not cure humans of sin completely) and the doctrine of direct revelation a blasphemous contradiction of the Protestant doctrine of *sola scriptura*, they also worried that the doctrine of direct revelation threatened the very existence of any church. How could church doctrines based on the authority of Scripture be maintained if any member was free to claim, at any time, that he had received a divine revelation that contradicted them? As a result, even most of Hutchinson's followers became disturbed by the implications of her doctrines and abandoned her. (Cotton had never subscribed to them, and even Wheelwright would not go as far as Hutchinson.) Winthrop concluded regarding Hutchinson, "She walked by such a rule as cannot stand with the peace of any State; for such bottomless revelations . . . if they be allowed in one thing, must be admitted a rule in all things; for being above reason and Scripture, they are not subject to control." The fear of social chaos was so great in a new society like Massachusetts that only two members of the General Court voted for Hutchinson's acquittal (with one abstention). She and some of her followers were banished; others were fined, disarmed, and disfranchised.[35]

By far the most famous example of Puritan intolerance was the Salem witch trials. In 1692 Salem Village (later called Danvers) hanged nineteen people convicted of witchcraft. Another man was pressed to death with heavy stones when he refused to utter a plea. (An English law provided for such a practice as a means of forcing a plea of guilty or not guilty from a defendant who remained silent.) More than one hundred people were jailed to await punishment. The mass hysteria that produced this state of affairs was begun by two young girls, nine and eleven years of age, who shouted odd things, went into convulsions, tossed burning logs around the house, and had visions. Under intense questioning, the girls finally identified three old women as their tormentors. One of the women, a West Indian practitioner of voodoo, confessed to witchcraft, volubly and in great detail. The odd behavior then spread to seven or eight other girls, age twelve to nineteen, and even a few adults. They charged others with various forms of witchcraft, including the pinching and biting of victims from afar. One man even said that another was preventing him from emptying his bladder, thereby causing him excruciating pain. As in all witch hunts, people rushed to incriminate one another in order to avoid being incriminated. The accusers later recanted, and nothing like it happened again in New England.[36]

But it is not true that the Salem witch trials exemplify the Puritan mind. The witch hunt was largely confined to a single small town long notorious for the intensity of its factionalism. Salem Village was so bitterly divided that its congregation appointed and dismissed four ministers and hired a fifth in a nine-year period. It is surely no coincidence that the pattern of accusation mirrored the chief division in the village. Nearly all of the accusers lived in the poorer, agricultural, western portion of the village, nearly all the accused in the more prosperous, commercial, eastern part. Even the terrible carnage of the witch hunt hardly dampened the villagers' love of strife. In 1695 a seventeen-member commission of outside dignitaries whom the villagers had asked to resolve yet another internal dispute rebuked the community, as had so many outsiders in the past, for its fractiousness. Ignoring the rebuke, the party that received the decision it favored nevertheless complained that the commission had not used the language they wanted in expressing that decision. Ironically, "Salem" is an anglicized form of the Hebrew word *shalom*, meaning "peace."[37]

Far from being a manifestation of Puritan theology, the witch trials were finally ended by the direct and organized intervention of the principal Puritan ministers of Massachusetts, led by Increase Mather. Though Mather believed in witches, like nearly everyone else of his era—indeed, some people *did* attempt to practice witchcraft—he declared, "It were better that ten suspected witches should escape than that one innocent person should be condemned." He noted that the court was violating Puritan practice by convicting people on the basis of "spectral evidence" (visions). Such visions might well have been produced by Satan, seeking to harm innocent people. Mather also faulted the court for not placing enough emphasis on determining the credibility of witnesses. Based on such arguments, Governor William Phips prohibited any further imprisonment or trials for witchcraft, dissolved the court, and freed the prisoners. There were several witch-hunting episodes in other colonies, and "witches" continued to be executed in Europe into the eighteenth century.[38]

In fact, the Salem witch trials actually contradicted a growing trend toward toleration in Puritan New England. As early as the 1640s it was becoming clear to American Puritans that their model community, their "city on a hill," had not purified the Anglican Church. Even English Puritans had begun pressuring New England Puritans to tolerate religious dissenters. New England Puritans felt betrayed by the sudden willingness of their English brethren to tolerate erroneous doctrines. The truth is that English Puritans were a minority who had everything to gain from toleration, while American Puritans, a solid majority in New England, felt they had nothing to gain from it. The obvious failure of their mission greatly demoralized New England Puritans.[39]

Another reason for the gradual growth of toleration in New England was the death of the first generation of Puritan leaders. Between 1647 and 1652, three of the most influential Puritan leaders, Thomas Hooker, John Winthrop, and John Cotton, died. Some Puritans recalled tearfully that when Winthrop was temporarily ousted as governor of Massachusetts in 1634, the people demanded an audit of public finances in order to determine whether Winthrop had stolen any funds. The audit revealed that Winthrop had often spent his own money on the colony. Second-generation Puritans considered themselves unworthy to succeed such leaders, heroes who had braved so many dangers and suffered so many hardships to build a community out of nothing. The second generation blamed themselves for the failure of the mission. Though they had been baptized as infants, few came forward to proclaim that they had had a conversion experience, an act necessary for full church membership. Since only the children of full members could be baptized, the number of baptisms dropped dramatically. Grandparents who were full church members were horrified that their grandchildren could not be baptized because their children had not become full members. In Dedham, Massachusetts, for example, the percentage of babies baptized plummeted from 80 to 40 percent. In 1662, a synod suggested the "Half-Way Covenant," which extended baptism to the children of baptized but unregenerate parents. In other words, partial members were allowed to transmit that partial membership to their children. Strongly supported by most of the clergy, the Half-Way Covenant eventually overcame the fierce resistance of the more zealous laity.[40]

The third reason for the growth of tolerance was an increase in wealth produced by commerce. The constant subdivision of New England's rocky soil among heirs made it impossible for a growing number of New Englanders to earn a living from agriculture. As a result, the Puritans turned increasingly to the sea. Made from vast tracts of virgin timber and sailing from fine harbors, New England ships carried large quantities of fish, furs, horses, grain, beef, pork, masts, and naval stores to the West Indies, the Canary Islands, Newfoundland, England, and the other American colonies. In return New Englanders imported tobacco, sugar, and cloth. Commercial towns like Marblehead, Salem Town, Ipswich, and Charlestown arose beside Boston. Wealthy New England merchants grew increasingly resentful of Puritan restrictions on displays of wealth. Ministers complained increasingly of powdered wigs, lavish weddings, drunkenness, gambling, and ornate clothing and furniture. As trade and wealth advanced, a pious society united in pursuit of a religious mission was dissolving into a collection of quarrelsome economic interests.[41]

Finally, the English monarchs William and Mary imposed tolerance on the New England colonies. In 1691, three years after deposing James II in the Glorious Revolution, William and Mary imposed a new royal charter on Massachusetts. The new charter replaced Massachusetts's religious qualification for voting with a property qualification. Little changed in practice; the property qualification was too small to disfranchise many, and the Puritans had already been tolerating small Anglican, Baptist, and Quaker congregations for nearly twenty years. But the act was significant symbolically. It undermined the vision of Massachusetts as an exclusive community with a common religious identity and mission.[42]

THE MIDDLE COLONIES

Center Protestantism predominated in colonial New York as well as in New England. The largest church in New York, which had been a Dutch colony called the "New Netherlands" until an English fleet seized the colony in 1664, was a Calvinist denomination called the Dutch Reformed Church. The English continued the Dutch policy of toleration, which had attracted Huguenots (French Calvinists), Mennonites, Lutherans, Presbyterians, Quakers, and Sephardic Jews to the colony. The English even allowed Dutch settlements to assign their church taxes to the Dutch Reformed Church, a reform of the usual religious establishment, in which the official church of each colony (usually the Church of England) received all of the funds set aside for that purpose.[43]

The Quakers, the largest of the Radical Protestant denominations, established their chief refuge from persecution in Pennsylvania. In 1652 George Fox, a shoemaker and shepherd in northern England, established the Quaker sect, as the Society of Friends was called in ridicule (because it was said that Friends "quaked" with emotion when inspired). The Quakers believed in God's direct revelation to individual believers. The emphasis on direct revelation rather than the interpretation of Scripture caused them to stress education less than the Puritans. Indeed, Quakers often complained of the vanity caused by excessive erudition. The belief in direct revelation also caused the Quakers to dispense with formal ministers and sacraments, though a body of "Public Friends" did arise to constitute an informal clergy. Quakers held no services, only meetings, at which anyone who felt inspired could speak.

They did not consider meetinghouses any more sacred than other buildings. The absence of a formal clergy and the resultant meeting format gave women religious equality. Quakers refused to take their hats off to their "betters" (even to the king) or to use titles like "mister" (a title derived from "master," then reserved for aristocrats), because they believed that all people were equal in God's eyes. They also used "thee" and "thou" rather than the more formal "you." They wore simple, gray, homespun clothes. As a result of the Quaker belief in the separation of church and state, they refused to pay taxes to support the Anglican Church. They refused to take oaths, both for scriptural reasons and because they disliked the implication that they were not equally honest at all times and places. This practice created problems in English courts and prevented Quakers from holding office, since the Test Act demanded that all officeholders take an oath against the Catholic doctrine of transubstantiation. Considering all violence sinful, the Quakers refused to serve in the British Army.[44]

Accounting each of these practices bizarre and dangerous, if not downright seditious, many Britons became further alarmed when followers of the Quaker charismatic James Naylor hailed him as Christ. Oliver Cromwell imprisoned three thousand Quakers, and the Restoration monarchs jailed another fifteen thousand. By 1700 forty thousand Quakers had fled to the New World (half of those to Pennsylvania), while fifty thousand remained in Britain.[45]

In 1661 seventeen-year-old William Penn was expelled from Oxford University for organizing prayer meetings that conflicted with high-church Anglicanism. Deeply disturbed, Penn's father, the wealthy merchant and landowner Sir William Penn, sent him to study in France. When young William returned, he participated in a few battles and considered a military career, but his father vetoed the idea. Ironically, the best surviving portrait of Penn, painted in this period of his life, depicts the future pacifist in a suit of armor. While managing his large estate in Ireland, young William attended a Quaker meeting and was converted to the faith. In 1681, eleven years after Sir William's death, Charles II granted his son the proprietorship of Pennsylvania in payment of the father's £16,000 loan to the king. Penn himself stayed in the colony only twenty-two months. As the result of a lavish lifestyle, he spent time in an English debtor's prison.[46]

Pennsylvania's government was fairly democratic and extremely tolerant. Property owners (nearly all adult males in early Pennsylvania) elected both branches of the assembly. The governor, who was appointed by Penn, had no veto power, though the generally absent Penn did. There was no tax-supported church, though the English government forced Penn to prohibit Catholics and Jews from voting or holding office. Pennsylvania's policy of tolerance stemmed from the Quaker belief in the separation of church and state, a policy based on concern for the church, not for individual rights. Like Roger Williams, Quakers believed that state power corrupted churches.[47]

Tolerance attracted immigrants from a variety of denominations, a variety that encouraged further tolerance. By 1776 there were twelve denominations in Pennsylvania. There were even thousands of Catholic and Jewish colonists.[48]

Far from being an indication of religious apathy, Quaker tolerance for other sects was accompanied by a strict discipline within the Quaker sect. As the historian Jack Marietta put it, "Quaker discipline governed a Friend's life from birth to death: the Society registered his birth, oversaw his religious and secular education, approved his choice of spouse, and buried him 'decently, orderly, and publicly.'" Migration, or even prolonged travel, required the approval of the congregation. At monthly meetings, the congregation took up complaints against the behavior of members. Members judged to be at fault had to write out a confession condemning their own actions, which was then posted or circulated. The church prohibited marriages with non-Quakers. Marriages were approved only after two investigators determined that neither potential spouse possessed any unabsolved violations of discipline, previous engagements or commitments, or objecting parents.[49]

Furthermore, even in Quaker Pennsylvania the legislature took it upon itself to pass traditional blue laws that prohibited cursing, creating a clamor, and selling liquor to Native Americans, and that banned plays, cards, dice, lotteries, "or such like enticing, vain, and evil Sports and Games." Such laws were considered secular, not religious, since they were thought vital to civic order. To Quakers, the separation of church and state meant the strict separation of institutions, not the intellectual separation of religion from governance, a separation they would have considered neither possible nor desirable.[50]

THE SOUTHERN COLONIES

Despite the economic motives that played a large role in the settlement of the southern colonies, most southerners were no less devoted to Center Protestantism than their counterparts in New England and the middle colonies. The first permanent English colony in America, Jamestown, was established by the Company of Virginia in 1607. Sir Edwin Sandys, a major figure in the company, had studied in Calvinist Geneva after graduating from Puritan-dominated Cambridge University. Jamestown's settlers began the construction of a church the first day they landed. Though Anglican, most southerners were theologically closer to the Calvinism of the Puritans than to the near Catholicism that soon prevailed among the Anglican hierarchy. Their blue laws were similar to those of the other colonies. These laws mandated church attendance; imposed stiff fines for gambling, blasphemy, and drunkenness; prescribed whipping for disrespect to clergy and tongue-boring for blasphemy (death for the third offense); and confiscated the property of citizens excommunicated for consorting with prostitutes. It is indicative of the piety of the era, and of the general desire for social order, that Virginia used this strict code as an advertisement for settlers in London. The chief leader of the colony, Captain John Smith, was a Puritan who had a favorable opinion of both Puritan Massachusetts and Separatist Plymouth. Even in Maryland, established as a Catholic refuge from Anglican persecution, Protestants outnumbered Catholics from the start. In the South, as in Puritan New England, congregationalism generally prevailed; lay boards often appointed their own ministers.[51]

Partly by necessity and partly by philosophy, American Anglicans possessed simpler churches, communion tables, and vestments than their En-glish counterparts. No Anglican bishopric was ever created in America. Since apathetic royal governors were expected to regulate the Church of England in America before the 1670s, the church hierarchy exerted little control over American congregations. Thereafter, the colonies were placed under the authority of the bishop of London, who was equally neglectful.[52]

Religious toleration was greater in the southern colonies than in early New England. With the encouragement of Maryland's Catholic proprietor, Lord Baltimore, the colony's legislature passed the first toleration act in the New World in 1649. The act granted religious freedom to all Trinitarian Christians. Religious toleration in South Carolina was more complete than in any other colony except Rhode Island and Pennsylvania. North Carolina was similarly tolerant, though the initial requirement of oaths prevented its Quaker population from seeking office. In Georgia, the last of the thirteen colonies, all were tolerated except Catholics. While dissenters had to join Anglicans in paying fairly low taxes to support Anglican churches throughout the South, most of the support that sustained these churches came from the Society for the Propagation of the Gospel in Foreign Parts, an organization founded by Thomas Bray in England in 1701.[53]

THE GREAT AWAKENING

Origins

In the 1730s and 1740s the colonies were rocked by a religious revival movement that became known as the Great Awakening. It was, in part, a reaction against the increasing commercialization of the economy and the rise of humanism, developments discussed in chapter 3. The emotional brand of religion associated with the Great Awakening began in the 1690s among Lutheran and Moravian pietists in Germany. From there it reached the pulpit of Theodorus Frelinghuysen, a Dutch Reformed minister in New

Jersey, in the 1720s. By the 1730s it had spread to the Presbyterians of New Jersey and Pennsylvania, led by William Tennent, who established the famous "log college" of Neshaminy Creek, Pennsylvania, for the training of Presbyterian revivalist ministers. Tennent's pupils went on to establish small academies of their own.[54]

Jonathan Edwards (1703–1758)

Meanwhile, the "Little Awakening" occurred in Northampton, Massachusetts. In 1729 young Jonathan Edwards replaced his maternal grandfather, Solomon Stoddard, as pastor of the town's Congregationalist (Puritan) church. Building on Stoddard's mild form of revivalism, Edwards launched his own revival in 1734–1735, hammering home the message that anyone could die at any time, so all had better be prepared. Edwards believed that a loving pastor should warn his congregation of hell just as he would warn them if their houses were burning. Edwards considered such a warning all the more necessary at a time when humanists were either de-emphasizing or dismissing the threat of eternal punishment. Edwards' oratorical power came not from gyrations or from a loud voice but from vivid words, a sincere delivery, and relentless logic. Especially popular with the young people for his prayer groups and his advocacy of singing in worship services, Edwards doubled the size of his congregation, necessitating the construction of a new meetinghouse. Edwards's own house replaced the local tavern as the favorite meeting place of the youth.[55]

It is a shame that so many editors of anthologies choose such sermons as "Sinners in the Hands of an Angry God" (1741) as their selection from Edwards—and sometimes excise the concluding five paragraphs of the sermon, in which Edwards emphasized God's mercy in forgiving sinners who repented and put their faith in Christ. Even in their complete and undistorted form, such popular sermons reveal far less of the subtlety and profundity of Edwards's thought than do his theological works. In his elegant treatise *The Nature of True Virtue*, Edwards defined true virtue as the love of God, which was equivalent to "benevolence to being in general." However beneficial to society, most acts that were called virtuous were not truly so, since they were based not in a love of all being but in benevolence toward only a part of being—toward oneself, or one's family and friends, or even one's nation. To love others merely because they returned that love was natural but essentially selfish. By drawing the circle of benevolence well short of all being, those who were virtuous only in a conventional sense might actually foster division and disrupt the harmony of minds in the universe. Anything short of benevolence to all being (though not necessarily an equal love of each being) arose from the illusion of independence from all being (God). Since true virtue ran against the current of humans' natural inclination to selfishness, it was possible only when the Holy Spirit touched the elect.[56]

Similarly, in *A Treatise Concerning Religious Affections* (1746), Edwards argued that "natural man" was so mired in self-love that a true love of God could only come through the Holy Spirit, an infusion of God Himself. Such an infusion was the only means by which an individual could perceive the true beauty and excellence of God and, hence, the only force that could elicit that love of Him and His creation that natural man could experience only faintly. Natural man was like one who could not appreciate the sweetness of honey because he lacked the sense of taste. In such a case all attempts at instruction were ultimately futile unless taste buds could be implanted from the outside. True love of God could never arise from self-love, the central emotion of natural man. A real Christian wanted God glorified because he loved God, but why did he love Him? The "first cause" lay outside the Christian, in God: both in the innate beauty and excellence that inspired love and in the infusion of the Holy Spirit that permitted the ability to perceive that innate beauty and excellence. When properly perceived, God's beauty and excellence were irresistible. Edwards noted that some natural men masquerading as Christians rejoiced in Scripture because it showed how important *they* were, as the objects of Jesus's sacrifice. Or else they loved attracting attention by discussing their spiritual experiences far more than they loved either the experiences themselves or the One responsible for them. Edwards concluded, "If they saw only a little of the sinfulness and vileness of their own hearts, and their deformity, in the midst of their best duties and their best affections, it would knock their affections on the head; because their affections are built upon self, their self-knowledge would destroy them."[57]

Generally considered America's greatest theologian, Edwards defended predestination better than Calvin himself in such works as *The Justice of God in the Damnation of Sinners* (1746) and *Freedom of the Will* (1754). Edwards claimed that since God was worthy of infinite love, honor, and obedience, sin was worthy of infinite punishment, yet God, in His mercy, chose to save some sinners. Even though humans were not ultimately responsible for their own selfish natures, the product of original sin, God still held them accountable. Far be it from humans to criticize the injustice of such a policy when they themselves practiced it every day, holding people who wronged them accountable for their actions, even though the wrongdoers had not created their own evil personalities: "How common is it for persons, when they look on themselves greatly injured by another, to inveigh against him, and aggravate his baseness, by saying, 'He is a man of most perverse spirit; he is naturally of a selfish, niggardly, or proud and haughty temper; he is one of a base and vile disposition.' And yet men's natural corrupt dispositions are mentioned for them, with respect to their sins against God, as if they rendered them blameless." Humans constantly praised or blamed individuals for their good or bad characters, though the individuals had not selected their own attributes. The selfish nature of all humans, though not self-caused, left all worthy of a bad fate. God was the only self-caused being. Edwards agreed with Augustine that what one loved determined choice, but choice did not determine what one loved. Believers in free will confused the individual's real power to choose with a nonexistent power to determine the inclinations that ultimately produced those choices.[58]

Like Augustine, Edwards defined evil not as a substance in itself but as mere privation of the good—which is to say, privation of God. After Adam's fall, God withdrew most of His substance from the world. Though humans still possessed a small amount of God's substance, they were largely bereft of it and, hence, were corrupt. Though caused by privation, sin assumed the active form of selfishness. Yet God, in His mercy, had decided to save some humans through an infusion of Himself (the Holy Spirit). To Edwards, God was an overflowing fountain of goodness continually directing His own flow. All humans received a very small amount at birth, but only some received the second, saving portion (though even this portion left much emptiness in the vessel). Although sin was a deficiency, it was necessary to highlight the glory of goodness (God). Hence hell was necessary, since the eternal contrast between good and evil was necessary.[59]

Edwards contended that free will was a mere euphemism for chance. If not from God, the "first determination of the will must be merely contingent or by chance. It could not have any antecedent act of the will to determine it." In order to retain human responsibility, advocates of the doctrine of free will had been forced to dissociate choice from character, preferences, all reasons for choosing one option over another, since any such reason would be an external factor beyond the chooser's control. Hence these theologians had no choice but to define free will as chance; one was free only when nothing determined choice. When they had to say that a given individual not only wanted the object of his choice but wanted to want it, they were forced to realize that this solved nothing: Why did he want to want it? The search for a first cause led either to God or to chance. But predestination was "in no respect more inconsistent with liberty than mere chance or contingence." Edwards explained:

> For if the determination of the will be from blind, undesigning chance, it is no more from the agent himself, or from the will itself, than if we suppose, in the case, a wise divine disposal by permission. . . . It would have been very unfit that God should have left it to mere chance whether man should fall or no. For chance, if there should be any such thing, is undesigning and blind. And certainly it is more fit that an event of so great importance, and which is attended with such an infinite train of consequences, should be disposed and ordered by infinite wisdom, than that it should be left to blind chance.

Indeed, Edwards noted that the very notion of real chance was inconsistent with the idea of an omniscient and omnipotent God.

An omniscient and omnipotent God's decision to allow the completely foreknown consequences of "chance" to occur involved an approval of those results that invalidated the very idea of chance in any meaningful sense. If a person has complete foreknowledge of the precise outcome of every roll of a dice and has the power to allow or disallow each roll, the results cannot be considered accidental but are clearly determined by his presumably thoughtful decision of which rolls to allow.[60]

Like his Puritan forebears, Edwards sought a balance between reason and emotion. But while seventeenth-century Puritans, living in an age of religious zeal, had naturally considered undisciplined emotion the chief threat to true religion, Edwards, living in the increasingly humanistic eighteenth century, just as naturally perceived a greater threat in the deification of reason. As a result, Edwards was far more willing to countenance displays of emotion (so long as they bred no heresies) in order to revive the pulse of what he considered a dying religion.[61]

George Whitefield (1714–1770)

But it was the young Anglican minister George Whitefield, Oxford graduate and son of an English tavern proprietress, who brought the Great Awakening to its peak. Inspired by Edwards's account of the revival in Northampton, Whitefield sought to save souls throughout Britain and the American colonies. Like his friend John Wesley, whose Methodist followers are discussed in chapter 6, Whitefield despised the cold rationalism that was then seeping into his church. Replacing the logical and theological Puritan style with a more direct and dramatic simplicity, he successfully appealed to popular emotions.[62]

Whitefield's first stop on his grand tour of the American colonies in 1739–1740 was Philadelphia, where he was the guest of Benjamin Franklin, for whose unorthodox soul he often prayed. (Though Franklin doubted the divinity of Jesus, he frequently donated money to Christian churches and hosted visiting preachers because he liked the social effects of Christianity.) Whitefield whipped the six thousand to eight thousand Philadelphians who came to see his outdoor sermons into a frenzy. Even Franklin found him irresistible. Although Franklin did not intend to give anything for Whitefield's cause, a Georgia orphanage, because he thought it better to find homes for the orphans in Philadelphia, Franklin found himself donating his copper coins in the first collection plate, his silver coins in the second, and finally emptying his pocket, gold coins and all, into the third. Another Philadelphian, having heard of Whitefield's persuasive powers, had taken care not to bring any money with him, lest he be tempted to give it all away. But Whitefield so overwhelmed the man that he begged a friend to lend him the money to contribute. The friend, who was indeed a Friend (a Quaker), must have been the only person in Philadelphia unmoved by Whitefield, for he replied sternly, "At any other time, Friend Hopkinson, I would lend to thee freely; but not now, for thee seems to be out of thy right senses."[63]

Franklin aptly summarized Whitefield's impact on Philadelphia: "From being thoughtless or indifferent about religion, it seemed as if all the world were growing religious, so that one could not walk thro' the town in an evening without hearing psalms sung in different families of every street." Many years later, on hearing of Whitefield's death, Franklin wrote: "I knew him intimately upwards of thirty years. His Integrity, Disinterestedness, and indefatigable Zeal in prosecuting every good Work I have never seen equaled, I shall never see exceeded."[64]

After leaving Pennsylvania, Whitefield journeyed to Georgia, then moved northward, like a conquering general, blazing a trail through the colonies. Some who had not been to church in years came out to see him. In New Brunswick, New Jersey, seven thousand people heard Whitefield. By the time Whitefield reached Massachusetts, the Reverend Benjamin Coleman noted that the people were ready to receive him as "an angel of God and Messenger of Jesus Christ." Whitefield addressed four thousand people in a Boston meeting house. Another twenty thousand citizens, the largest crowd that had ever been assembled in America, thronged the Boston Common to hear him. The crowd wept when Whitefield spoke of his imminent departure. Edwards then hosted him at his Northampton church. Whitefield was so beloved that even

Calvinists were willing to consider the appointment of an Anglican bishop over America in the 1760s if Whitefield were selected
as the bishop. Numerous itinerant preachers toured the colonies in
imitation of the revivalist.[65]

Though Whitefield was an Anglican minister, he frequently
criticized his own church, whose leaders opposed revivalism.
Whitefield was, in many ways, more Calvinist than high-church
Anglican. He believed in predestination. He recommended Puritan books. He urged clergymen to stress the need for a conversion
experience. Though he never criticized the theory of apostolic
succession popular among the hierarchy of his church, he placed
no emphasis on it, considering the ordinations of other denominations as legitimate as those of his own. A profound ecumenicist,
Whitefield angered the dogmatists of his church by declaring,
"Oh, that the partition-wall were broken down and we all with
one heart and mind could glorify our common Lord and Saviour
Jesus Christ!" He recalled, "I bless God, the partition-wall of big-
otry and sect-religion was soon broken down in my heart; for as
soon as the love of God was shed abroad in my soul, I loved all of
whatsoever denomination who loved the Lord Jesus in sincerity of
heart." As a result of the Anglican hierarchy's resistance to the
Great Awakening, it was the Congregationalist and Presbyterian
churches that attracted most of the largely lower- and lower-
middle-class "New Lights" who attended the revivals, while the
Church of England attracted many of the largely affluent "Old
Lights" who shunned them.[66]

Effects of the Great Awakening

The Great Awakening had several important effects on American society. The first was the establishment of colleges. As late as
1740, there were only three colleges in the American colonies.
Harvard College (Cambridge, Massachusetts, 1636) had been established for the training of Congregationalist ministers. The College of William and Mary (Williamsburg, Virginia, 1693) had been
established for the training of Anglican ministers. Yale College
(New Haven, Connecticut, 1701) had been established for Con-

necticut Puritans who believed that Harvard had become too unorthodox. As a result of the Great Awakening, the Presbyterians now established the College of New Jersey (Princeton, 1746), the Anglicans King's College (Columbia, 1754), the Baptists the College of Rhode Island (Brown, 1764), the Dutch Reformed Church Queen's College (Rutgers, 1766), and the Congregationalists Dartmouth College (1769, originally for Native Americans). Only Franklin's College of Philadelphia (the University of Pennsylvania, 1751) was nondenominational, though dominated by Anglicans and Presbyterians. Many of the Founding Fathers, including James Madison and Alexander Hamilton, were trained in these new institutions.[67]

The second effect of the Great Awakening was the further growth of religious toleration. The Great Awakening created divisions within the denominations. While Old Lights disapproved of the emotionalism of the revivalist preachers, New Lights considered "rational religion" as cold and dead as a corpse. The Great Awakening also produced schisms by undermining the authority of the regular clergy. Some itinerants, like William Tennent (*The Dangers of an Unconverted Ministry*, 1740), preached that only a conversion experience, not theological knowledge, qualified one to be a minister. When a Dutch Reformed minister asked itinerant Johann Bernhard Van Dieren for his license to preach, Van Dieren raised a newly purchased Bible and said that was his license. As Old Lights and New Lights within each denomination struggled against each other, they reached out to their counterparts in other denominations for support. In the process they realized that they had more in common with similarly inclined elements of other denominations than they had with the opposing elements within their own.[68]

As a result, an ecumenical spirit grew. Whitefield was far from being its only proponent. Samuel Davies, the Presbyterian pastor of Hanover County, Virginia, expressed this new spirit: "I care but little whether Men go to Heaven from The Church of England, or Presbyterian, if they do but go there." By 1760, although the New England colonies still harbored tax-supported churches, each congregation could assign its taxes to support its own ministers. In Virginia the Revolutionary War created a need for unity among

patriots, which resulted in the displacement of the Anglican establishment, first by a multidenominational establishment and, finally
in 1786, by the end of all state support for churches. In Philadelphia a large meeting hall was built to accommodate visiting
preachers of all faiths.[69]

A third effect of the Great Awakening was the inauguration of
a century-long process by which large numbers of African Americans converted to the Christian religion. A whole range of factors,
such as linguistic and cultural differences, the shortage of clergy, and
the opposition of masters, had delayed the large-scale Christianiza-
tion of slaves for over a century. Dismissive of slaves' aptitude for religion and fearful that biblical egalitarianism would spur rebellion,
slaveholders resisted clerical efforts to convert their slaves to Christianity until the Great Awakening, when Anglican, Presbyterian,
and Baptist ministers in the South made the conversion of slaves a
high priority. Fortunately for their task, African religions had already imparted to slaves the belief in direct emotional contact with
a personal God and in divine rewards and punishments in an afterlife.[70]

Samuel Davies devoted much of his time to teaching slaves
to read religious works and Isaac Watts's hymns, copies of which
were donated by English benefactors, including John and Charles
Wesley. Once Davies wrote concerning the slaves, whose singing
of hymns in his kitchen awakened him at two or three in the
morning, "A torrent of sacred harmony poured into my cham-
ber and carried my mind away to Heaven." The mild-mannered
Presbyterian reserved his most severe rebukes for slaveholders
who denied their slaves religion and a basic education, blaming
Anglo-American defeats in the French and Indian War on such
sinfulness.[71]

Though limited in its effect, Davies's and other ministers' emphasis on the Christian obligations of planters toward their slaves
was responsible for the growth of paternalism, a sense of duty that,
however condescending, served to reduce the harshness of slavery.
Though rare, there were a few instances in which churches disci-
plined or expelled masters for mistreating their slaves. Some
churches recognized slave marriages when governments would

not and urged masters not to separate families. But while Christianity improved slavery, slavery did not improve Christianity. Rather, slavery taught Christian masters brutality, Christian slaves theft and deceit. Power corrupts, and so does powerlessness.[72]

While it is true that the preachers whom slave owners directed to proselytize their slaves stressed those biblical passages that commanded humility and obedience to masters, it is also true that African Americans, like so many previous peoples, seized Christianity from their oppressors and made it their own, thereby converting a potential source of weakness into a source of strength. Christian slaves possessed their own ministers, some licensed, some unlicensed, who often played as great a role in the conversion of slaves as did white pastors. Some slaves met after work each day to pray and sing. Others defied irreligious masters by attending revival meetings against orders. At secret services in houses or in the woods slave preachers risked severe punishment by emphasizing such themes as the Israelites' exodus from slavery in Egypt. Though the Bible taught some slaves to turn their attention to the next life, where their only solace awaited, it taught others to resist tyranny by flight or rebellion. Nearly every major nineteenth-century slave rebellion can be traced to a significant religious influence. In 1800 the slave minister Martin recruited supporters for his brother Gabriel's revolt near Richmond by citing the Book of Exodus. Denmark Vesey and the other plotters of the 1822 Charleston rebellion used Scripture to win supporters among fellow members of the city's African Methodist Church. Nat Turner, the leader of the famous 1831 rebellion in Southampton, Virginia, was a Baptist minister who believed that God directed him. African Americans came to Christianity on their own terms, not as the result of indoctrination. Even the few masters who cared enough to mandate church attendance for their slaves could not force them to adopt Christian beliefs, much less to pass those beliefs down to their children for generations after slavery was abolished.[73]

Indeed, far from being victims of mental conditioning, African Americans exerted a lasting influence on American religion and culture. Slave spirituals transformed American music, both religious

and secular. The simple piety, perseverance, and profound love of
God manifested by slaves even occasionally melted the hearts of
masters. One slave named Morte reduced his master's family and
friends to tears by preaching to them of *their* enslavement to sin. In
the end, the pupils taught the teachers. Much like early Christians
meeting under the shadow of Roman persecution, and, ironically,
much like their masters' own Puritan ancestors meeting under the
shadow of Anglican persecution, the slaves met in secret to practice
a purer, more authentically Christian religion than that of their
masters, whose pride and prosperity often blinded them to the biblical message that Christianity belongs most to the poor, the persecuted, and the downtrodden. The historian Albert J. Raboteau was
correct in stating that African Americans transformed their religion
from a potential source of social control into "a source of economic
cooperation, an arena for political activity, a sponsor of education,
and a refuge in a hostile white world." Raboteau concluded, "That
some slaves maintained their identity as persons, despite a system
bent on reducing them to a subhuman level, was certainly due in
part to their religious life."[74]

More than any other single force, slave religion contributed to
the creation of an African American community, which made survival psychologically possible. Indeed, the most effective melting
pot in America may have been that in which Africans from a variety of different ethnic, linguistic, and religious origins fused their
cultures and added new elements to form a new community and
culture.[75]

Finally, the Great Awakening revived throughout America
both the Puritan fear of corruption and the Puritan belief in a collective mission to form a purer society. When the parliamentary
taxes of the 1760s reawakened among the descendants of those
who had fled religious persecution the belief that England was
hopelessly corrupt, it was plain to many Americans that they must
resist—not merely to defend their natural rights of life, liberty, and
property, but to save their very souls. While Old Light ministers
(including most Anglican ministers, two-thirds of whom returned
to England during the Revolutionary War) generally remained
loyal to Britain, New Light ministers, the "black regiment," were

among the first, the most ardent, and the most influential of patriots. These ministers were crucial to preparing the American public for independence, in an age when rebellion was considered the darkest act of villainy and rebels were summarily hanged. Thomas Jefferson noted that sermons advocating resistance to British tyranny ran through Virginia "like a shock of electricity." John Todd, who had served as chief assistant to the now deceased Davies, led Virginia Presbyterians in support of the patriot movement, while John Witherspoon, president of the College of New Jersey, attempted to rally Pennsylvania Presbyterians. Previously pacifistic, Virginia Baptists rallied to the patriot cause, enlisting as soldiers and sending preachers to the army camps.[76]

These Calvinist dissenters felt that they were fighting against the Anglican establishment, a form of "popery," as well as against the corrupt Parliament. Many Protestants feared that the Quebec Act, which granted religious toleration and territory in the Ohio River valley to French Canadian Catholics, was merely a prelude to papal repression in the American colonies.[77]

The revival of these Puritan fears was accompanied by the revival of the Puritan sense of mission. The religious mission of the Puritans to turn New England into the world's incubator for a purer Protestantism was slowly being transformed into the political mission of all Americans to turn the United States into the world's incubator for republicanism.[78]

But evangelical Protestantism was not the only source of the fear of corruption and of the missionary spirit that produced the American Revolution. Taught in every American grammar school and college, classical republicanism was equally concerned with the duty to resist tyranny as a source of corruption. Steeped in a Greco-Roman literature whose perpetual theme was the steady encroachment of tyranny upon liberty, the Founding Fathers of the United States became virtually obsessed with spotting the early warning signs of impending tyranny so that they might avoid the fate of their classical heroes. They learned from the political horror stories of ancient Greek and Roman historians that liberty was as precarious as it was precious—precarious because cunning individuals were constantly conspiring against it, precious because virtue could not survive its demise. Tyranny was the worst fate not so much because it deprived one of liberty as because it deprived one of virtue. The corrupting effects of living in tyranny—the dehumanizing sycophancy and the degrading collaboration necessary to avoid the tyrant's bad graces—were more abhorrent and disgusting than the oppression itself. The founders feared that if the cunning prime ministers of Britain could ever convince the American public to accept even the smallest unconstitutional tax, Americans would eventually lose not only the power, but the very will, to resist. Americans would then be no more than slaves, subject to the whims of distant masters. To stay within the British Empire would be to witness the recreation of that horrifying degradation and depravity that the historian Tacitus had so vividly described in imperial Rome. But to leave the empire and start anew would be to embrace the exciting possibility of creating a society so elevated and virtuous as to inspire future Plutarchs to immortalize the nation. The fear of witnessing another Roman Empire was as essential to producing the revolution as the hope of creating another Roman republic. As Jefferson astutely noted in the Declaration of Independence, humans are not, by nature, rebels. Only genuine fear of the dire consequences of persisting in their current situation, joined with real hope in the possibility of achieving a better fate, can inspire people to disrupt their lives and undertake the arduous sacrifices and hazard the frightful dangers characteristic of revolutions.[79]

While it is generally true that upper- and upper-middle-class Americans, who constituted a large proportion of college graduates, were heavily influenced by classical republicanism, while lower-middle- and lower-class Americans were heavily influenced by the Great Awakening, the two influences merged in the minds of many Americans. Hence it is often impossible for the historian to determine whether an individual patriot's fear of corruption and hope of creating a better society stemmed more from Protestant sermons or from classical histories. Rightly called the "Father of the American Revolution" for his able leadership of the Boston Sons of Liberty, Samuel Adams had been energized by the Great Awakening while a student at Harvard in the 1730s. By the 1760s,

long before most other Americans, Adams had come to the conclusion that America must separate from Britain in order to escape
its corruption. His dream was to construct a "Christian Sparta," a
nation that would combine Christian piety with republican frugality, self-discipline, courage, and patriotism. Patrick Henry re-
portedly claimed that he was "first taught what an orator should
be" by his favorite minister, Samuel Davies, whose extemporane-
ous style Henry employed with great effect. Henry adopted a
sober manner of dress uncommon to his aristocratic class and became deeply preoccupied with fostering Christian virtue in society. As the historian Rhys Isaac aptly put it, Henry was considered
the greatest orator of his day because he was able to "communicate in popular [revivalist] style the passion for a world reshaped in
truly moral order that lay at the heart of both the religious revolution of the evangelicals and the political revolution of the patriots." Yet Henry had also received a rigorous classical training from
his father and, as an adult, made it a rule to read Livy's *History of
Rome* in the original Latin each year. In his famous Stamp Act
Speech, Henry compared King George III with Julius Caesar and
hinted that the king might suffer the same fate.[80]

While both evangelical Protestantism and classical republicanism were traditional, communal, and animated by moral concerns,
a third ideology that contributed to the American Revolution, subsequently called "liberalism," looked more to the future than to the
past and concerned itself more with individual rights and contractual obligations than with moral duties. Although liberalism, a form
of Epicurean humanism, is discussed in chapter 3, suffice it to say
here that even this ideology, which conflicted somewhat with its
fellow contributors to the Revolution, often melded with them in
the minds of patriots. The influential sermons of patriot ministers
generally appealed to natural rights as well as to the need to escape
British corruption.[81]

The marriage between evangelical Protestantism and its secular
partners, classical republicanism and liberalism, was somewhat uneasy,
since their values and goals conflicted in some ways. But the offspring
they produced, the United States of America, was, in the words of
John Adams, a "spirited infant."[82]

NOTES

1. William G. McLoughlin, *Revivals, Awakenings, and Reform: An Essay on Religion and Social Change in America, 1607–1977* (Chicago: University of Chicago Press, 1978), 45; Emery Battis, *Saints and Sectaries: Anne Hutchinson and the Antinomian Controversy in the Massachusetts Bay Colony* (Chapel Hill: University of North Carolina Press, 1962), 9; Edmund S. Morgan, *Roger Williams: The Church and the State* (New York: Harcourt-Brace, 1967), 67.

2. William Bradford, *Of Plymouth Plantation, 1620–1647* (New York: Random House, 1981), xii–xiii, 17.

3. Bradford, *Of Plymouth Plantation*, 23–26, 50; Edmund S. Morgan, *The Puritan Dilemma: The Story of John Winthrop* (Boston: Little, Brown, 1958), 30–31.

4. Bradford, *Of Plymouth Plantation*, 68, 83–84; William Warren Sweet, *Religion in Colonial America* (New York: Scribner, 1943), 78; Paul K. Conkin, *The Uneasy Center: Reformed Christianity in Antebellum America* (Chapel Hill: University of North Carolina Press, 1995), 36.

5. Bradford, *Of Plymouth Plantation*, xiii–xiv.

6. Morgan, *Puritan Dilemma*, 46.

7. Morgan, *Puritan Dilemma*, 7, 30–31, 43, 51, 55, 69–70.

8. Morgan, *Puritan Dilemma*, 18, 52–53.

9. Morgan, *Puritan Dilemma*, 94.

10. Battis, *Saints and Sectaries*, 256; Paul K. Conkin, *Puritans and Pragmatists: Eight Eminent American Thinkers* (Bloomington: Indiana University Press, 1968), 19.

11. Kenneth A. Lockridge, *A New England Town: The First Hundred Years* (New York: W. W. Norton, 1970), 38–42; Battis, *Saints and Sectaries*, 67.

12. Perry Miller, *The New England Mind*, 2 vols. (New York: Macmillan, 1939; Cambridge, Mass.: Harvard University Press, 1953), vol. 1, 409, 413.

13. Miller, *New England Mind*, vol. 1, 21, 71, 88, 439, 448; Morgan, *Puritan Dilemma*, 71; John Demos, *A Little Commonwealth: Family Life in Plymouth Colony* (Oxford: Oxford University Press, 1970), 104–5; Emory Elliott, *Power and the Pulpit in Puritan New England* (Princeton, N.J.: Princeton University Press, 1975), 47.

14. Lockridge, *New England Town*, 70–73; Demos, *Little Commonwealth*, 85–86, 88–90; William J. Bouwsma, *John Calvin: A Sixteenth-Century Portrait* (Oxford: Oxford University Press, 1988), 138.

15. T. H. Breen, *Puritans and Adventurers: Change and Persistence in Early America* (Oxford: Oxford University Press, 1980), 22.

16. Miller, *New England Mind*, vol. 1, 34, 60–61; vol. 2, 94; A. G. Dickens, *The English Reformation* (New York: Schocken Books, 1964), 319; Edmund S. Morgan, "The Puritans and Sex," *New England Quarterly* 15 (December 1942): 592–93.

17. Peter Brown, *Augustine of Hippo: A Biography* (Berkeley: University of California Press, 1967), 326; Roland H. Bainton, *Here I Stand: A Life of Martin Luther* (New York: Abingdon-Cokesbury Press, 1950), 295, 298, 341, 343; John Calvin, *Institutes of*

the Christian Religion, trans. Henry Beveridge, 2 vols. (Grand Rapids, Mich.: Eerdmans, 1970), vol. 2, 27, 32–33; Bouwsma, *John Calvin*, 51–52, 55–56, 60, 89, 134–37.

18. Augustine, *The City of God*, trans. Marcus Dods (New York: Modern Library, 1950), 10; Bouwsma, *John Calvin*, 51, 96, 170–71, 196–97.

19. Miller, *New England Mind*, vol. 1, 39, 474; vol. 2, 5; Morgan, *Roger Williams*, 82, 107–8; Conkin, *Puritans and Pragmatists*, 31.

20. Mark Morford, "Early American School Editions of Ovid," *Classical Journal* 78 (winter 1982–1983): 152–53.

21. Morgan, *Puritan Dilemma*, 79–81, 98–100, 104–13; Steven Ozment, *The Age of Reform, 1250–1550: An Intellectual and Religious History of Late Medieval and Reformation Europe* (New Haven, Conn.: Yale University Press, 1980), 367–68; Bouwsma, *John Calvin*, 89–90; Kenneth Silverman, *The Life and Times of Cotton Mather* (New York: Harper & Row, 1984), 265–66.

22. Conkin, *Uneasy Center*, 52; Morgan, *Puritan Dilemma*, 71; Morgan, *Roger Williams*, 63, 75.

23. Brown, *Augustine of Hippo*, 234, 237, 241; Frederick B. Artz, *The Mind of the Middle Ages, A.D. 200–1500: An Historical Survey*, 3d ed. (New York: Alfred A. Knopf, 1962), 269a; Jacob von Konigshofen, "The Cremation of the Strasbourg Jewry," in *The Portable Medieval Reader*, ed. Mary Martin McLaughlin and James Bruce Ross (New York: Viking Press, 1949), 174; Bernard Gui, "The Waldensian Heretics," in *The Portable Medieval Reader*, ed. McLaughlin and Ross, 215; Jeffry Burton Russell, *A History of Medieval Christianity: Prophecy and Order* (New York: Thomas Y. Crowell, 1968), 153–57; Ozment, *Age of Reform*, 14, 371; Mark U. Edwards Jr., *Luther's Last Battles: Politics and Polemics, 1531–1546* (Ithaca, N.Y.: Cornell University Press, 1983), 137; Bainton, *Here I Stand*, 314, 379; Bouwsma, *John Calvin*, 211, 217–18.

24. Miller, *New England Mind*, vol. 1, 457.

25. Morgan, *Puritan Dilemma*, 116–29; *Roger Williams*, 31; Bradford, *Of Plymouth Plantation*, 286.

26. Morgan, *Puritan Dilemma*, 130–31.

27. Morgan, *Puritan Dilemma*, 98–100.

28. Brown, *Augustine of Hippo*, 213–14, 224–28, 243–44; Bouwsma, *John Calvin*, 218, 223, 229; Sacvan Bercovitch, *The American Jeremiad* (Madison: University of Wisconsin Press, 1978), 52.

29. Morgan, *Roger Williams*, 96, 98, 112, 118; Roger Williams, "A Brief Discourse Concerning the Name Heathen, Commonly Given to the Indians," 1645, in *The American Intellectual Tradition*, 3d ed., 2 vols., ed. Charles Capper and David A. Hollinger (Oxford: Oxford University Press, 1997), vol. 1, 45; Miller, *New England Mind*, vol. 1, 467.

30. Morgan, *Roger Williams*, 121–23, 137.

31. Battis, *Saints and Sectaries*, 5–6, 11, 14–15, 84; Morgan, *Puritan Dilemma*, 134.

32. Battis, *Saints and Sectaries*, 44, 55, 91, 101, 115, 143, 165; Henry Chadwick, *The Early Church* (Baltimore: Penguin Books, 1969), 34; Morgan, *Puritan Dilemma*, 140.

33. Battis, *Saints and Sectaries*, 153, 158.

34. Bettis, *Saints and Sectaries*, 202–4.

35. Bettis, *Saints and Sectaries*, 184, 187–88, 208, 210–11, 286; Thomas Hutchinson, *The History of the Colony and Province of Massachusetts Bay* (Boston: Thomas and John Fleet, 1767), vol. 2, 366; Miller, *New England Mind*, vol. 2, 60.

36. Paul Boyer and Stephen Nissenbaum, *Salem Possessed: The Social Origins of Witchcraft* (Cambridge, Mass.: Harvard University Press, 1974), 1–9, 17.

37. Boyer and Nissenbaum, *Salem Possessed*, 35, 51, 61, 66, 69–70, 74–75.

38. Boyer and Nissenbaum, *Salem Possessed*, 9, 16–20, 74; Miller, *New England Mind*, vol. 2, 194; John Putnam Demos, *Entertaining Satan: Witchcraft and the Culture of Early New England* (Oxford: Oxford University Press, 1982), 9, 12; Jon Butler, *Awash in a Sea of Faith: Christianizing the American People* (Cambridge, Mass.: Harvard University Press, 1990), 9, 22, 29.

39. Miller, *New England Mind*, vol. 1, 75; vol. 2, 9.

40. Miller, *New England Mind*, vol. 1, 471; vol. 2, 3, 11, 94, 100, 105; Morgan, *Puritan Dilemma*, 114, 205; Lockridge, *New England Town*, 33–36.

41. Lockridge, *New England Town*, 80–82, 91, 94; Boyer and Nissenbaum, *Salem Possessed*, 86, 94; Miller, *New England Mind*, vol. 2, 306–7, 314, 321.

42. Perry Miller, *Errand into the Wilderness* (Cambridge, Mass.: Harvard University Press, 1956), 151–52; *New England Mind*, vol. 2, 129; Lockridge, *New England Town*, 88; Conkin, *Puritans and Pragmatists*, 21.

43. Randall Balmer, *A Perfect Babel of Confusion: Dutch Religion and English Culture in the Middle Colonies* (Oxford: Oxford University Press, 1989), vii, 3–4; Sweet, *Religion in Colonial America*, 35–38.

44. E. Digby Baltzell, *Puritan Boston and Quaker Philadelphia: Two Protestant Ethics and the Spirit of Class Authority and Leadership* (New York: Free Press, 1979), 84–86, 101–5; Melvin B. Endy Jr., *William Penn and Early Quakerism* (Princeton, N.J.: Princeton University Press, 1973), 59–60 n. 14; Butler, *Awash in a Sea of Faith*, 119; Sweet, *Religion in Colonial America*, 77–78, 147.

45. Baltzell, *Puritan Boston and Quaker Philadelphia*, 88–89; Sweet, *Religion in Colonial America*, 100–101.

46. Baltzell, *Puritan Boston and Quaker Philadelphia*, 113–14.

47. Endy, *William Penn and Early Quakerism*, 351–52.

48. Baltzell, *Puritan Boston and Quaker Philadelphia*, 117–18; Sweet, *Religion in Colonial America*, 163.

49. Jack D. Marietta, *The Reformation of American Quakerism, 1748–1783* (Philadelphia: University of Pennsylvania Press, 1984), 4–5, 56–57.

50. Edwin B. Bronner, *William Penn's "Holy Experiment": The Founding of Pennsylvania, 1681–1701* (Westport, Conn.: Greenwood, 1978), 38.

51. Frederick Woolverton, *Colonial Anglicanism in North America* (Detroit: Wayne State University Press, 1984), 37, 41, 64; Miller, *Errand into the Wilderness*, 105–6, 108; Butler, *Awash in a Sea of Faith*, 38–39; Sweet, *Religion in Colonial America*, 33; Conkin, *Uneasy Center*, 43, 47.

52. Woolverton, *Colonial Anglicanism in North America*, 52–53, 84, 232; Conkin, *Uneasy Center*, 43, 47.

53. Woolverton, *Colonial Anglicanism in North America*, 22, 87, 136, 157, 171.

54. Patricia J. Tracy, *Jonathan Edwards, Pastor: Religion and Society in Eighteenth-Century Northampton* (New York: Hill & Wang, 1979), 87; George William Pilcher, *Samuel Davies: Apostle of Dissent in Colonial Virginia* (Knoxville: University of Tennessee Press, 1971), 20–21; Butler, *Awash in a Sea of Faith*, 34; Conkin, *Uneasy Center*, 54, 58.

55. Tracy, *Jonathan Edwards, Pastor*, 3, 11, 71, 79–80, 111–13, 133; Conkin, *Puritans and Pragmatists*, 53, 55.

56. Jonathan Edwards, *The Nature of True Virtue* (Ann Arbor: University of Michigan Press, 1960), 3, 14, 18–23, 26, 47–54; Tracy, *Jonathan Edwards, Pastor*, 133–34; Douglas J. Elwood, *The Philosophical Theology of Jonathan Edwards* (New York: Columbia University Press, 1960), 65.

57. Jonathan Edwards, *A Treatise Concerning Religious Affections*, 1746, in *The American Intellectual Tradition*, ed. Capper and Hollinger, vol. 1, 77, 80, 84–88.

58. Jonathan Edwards, *The Justice of God in the Damnation of Sinners*, 1746, in *The American Intellectual Tradition*, ed. Capper and Hollinger, vol. 1, 67–68; Jonathan Edwards, *Freedom of the Will*, ed. Arnold S. Kaufman and William K. Frankina (New York: Bobbs-Merrill, 1969); Brown, *Augustine of Hippo*, 373.

59. Elwood, *Philosophical Theology of Jonathan Edwards*, 29, 69, 77–78, 85, 92, 125, 145–47, 153.

60. Edwards, *Justice of God in the Damnation of Sinners*, vol. 1, 69–70; Conkin, *Uneasy Center*, 94.

61. Miller, *New England Mind*, vol. 1, 261; Elwood, *Philosophical Theology of Jonathan Edwards*, 141; Boyer and Nissenbaum, *Salem Possessed*, 27–29.

62. Woolverton, *Colonial Anglicanism in North America*, 190–91, 198.

63. Benjamin Franklin, *Benjamin Franklin: The Autobiography and Other Writings*, ed. L. Jesse Lemisch (New York: Penguin Books, 1961), 117–20; Balmer, *Perfect Babel of Confusion*, 121.

64. Franklin, *Benjamin Franklin*, 337; Woolverton, *Colonial Anglicanism in North America*, 198.

65. Woolverton, *Colonial Anglicanism in North America*, 191, 194–96, 200; Balmer, *Perfect Babel of Confusion*, 123; John C. Miller, *Sam Adams: Pioneer in Propaganda* (Stanford, Calif.: Stanford University Press, 1936), 6.

66. Woolverton, *Colonial Anglicanism in North America*, 189–91; Balmer, *Perfect Babel of Confusion*, 138–39; Henry F. May, *The Enlightenment in America* (Oxford: Oxford University Press, 1976), 91–93.

67. Elliott, *Power and the Pulpit in Puritan New England*, 47; Lawrence A. Cremin, *American Education: The Colonial Experience, 1607–1783* (New York: Harper & Row, 1970), 175, 321; Sheldon D. Cohen, *A History of Colonial Education, 1607–1776* (New York: Wiley, 1974), 98, 166; Conkin, *Uneasy Center*, 57; Baltzell, *Puritan Boston and Quaker Philadelphia*, 163; Merrill D. Peterson, *James Madison: A Biography in His*

Own Words (New York: Harper & Row, 1974), 16, 18; James Thomas Flexner, *The Young Hamilton: A Biography* (Boston: Little, Brown, 1978), 47.

68. Balmer, *Perfect Babel of Confusion*, 125, 134; Conkin, *The Uneasy Center*, 55; Butler, *Awash in a Sea of Faith*, 180; Cremin, *American Education*, 322.

69. Pilcher, *Samuel Davies*, 56; Conkin, *Puritans and Pragmatists*, 25; Rhys Isaac, *The Transformation of Virginia, 1740–1790* (Chapel Hill: University of North Carolina Press, 1982), 279, 281–82; Edwin S. Gaustad, *Faith of Our Fathers: Religion and the New Nation* (San Francisco: Harper & Row, 1987), 41; Franklin, *Benjamin Franklin*, 117.

70. Albert J. Raboteau, *Slave Religion: The "Invisible Institution" in the Antebellum South* (Oxford: Oxford University Press, 1978), 100, 103, 107, 127–31, 272; Butler, *Awash in a Sea of Faith*, 133, 161.

71. Pilcher, *Samuel Davies*, ix, 108, 111–14.

72. Raboteau, *Slave Religion*, 171, 183, 228, 295–96, 299–300; Butler, *Awash in a Sea of Faith*, 143.

73. Raboteau, *Slave Religion*, ix, 124–25, 133, 146–47, 163, 177, 214–15, 222, 251, 294, 318; Butler, *Awash in a Sea of Faith*, 135, 143, 156.

74. Raboteau, *Slave Religion*, ix, 148, 214–18, 221–22, 307, 317–18.

75. John W. Blassingame, *The Slave Community: Plantation Life in the Antebellum South* (Oxford: Oxford University Press, 1972), 66–75.

76. Butler, *Awash in a Sea of Faith*, 203–4; May, *Enlightenment in America*, 91–93; Pilcher, *Samuel Davies*, 98; Isaac, *Transformation of Virginia*, 170–71, 261.

77. May, *Enlightenment in America*, 160; Isaac, *Transformation of Virginia*, 197, 246.

78. See, for example, Thomas Paine, *Common Sense* (New York: Wiley, 1942), 42.

79. For a fuller discussion see Carl J. Richard, *The Founders and the Classics: Greece, Rome, and the American Enlightenment* (Cambridge, Mass.: Harvard University Press, 1994), 85–122.

80. Miller, *Sam Adams*, 6, 85, 228–29; Meyer Reinhold, *Classica Americana: The Greek and Roman Heritage in the United States* (Detroit: Wayne State University Press, 1984), 157; Pilcher, *Samuel Davies*, 83; Isaac, *Transformation of Virginia*, 269. For reference to the classical influence on Henry see Richard, *Founders and the Classics*, 31, 35, 91.

81. Bercovitch, *American Jeremiad*, 125.

82. John Adams to H. Niles, January 14, 1818, in *The Life and Works of John Adams*, ed. Charles Francis Adams (Boston: Little, Brown, 1850–1856), vol. 10, 275.

II

THE AGE OF HUMANISM

3

THE RISE OF MODERN HUMANISM

While theism provided the principal motivation for the colonization of America, shaped the culture of the American colonies, and helped cause the American Revolution, humanism provided the psychological basis for the new nation's political and economic theories and institutions during the early republican and antebellum periods. Indeed, humanism transformed American Christianity itself, undermining belief in the crucial doctrine of original sin and inspiring confidence in the possibility of lasting social and moral progress.

Humanism's rise to ascendancy in the modern West was a gradual process. Above all, the philosophy owed its triumph to scientific achievements that raised many people's estimate of the human potential. Startling advances in knowledge of the universe, when combined with the unprecedented prosperity fostered by revolutions in the commercial, financial, and technological realms, seemed to provide ample evidence that humans were rational creatures, capable of almost unlimited progress. Evidence of scientific and technological progress led many to assume that social and moral progress would follow, though there is no logical relationship between the two.

THE SCIENTIFIC REVOLUTION

The eighteenth-century humanist movement that the Germans first termed "the Enlightenment" was a product of the scientific revolution of the two previous centuries. The scientific revolution forever changed the manner in which Westerners, including Americans, viewed themselves and the world.

Nicolaus Copernicus (1473–1543)

Polish astronomer Nicolaus Copernicus published *On the Revolutions of the Heavenly Spheres* in 1543. In this work Copernicus advanced the heliocentric theory, which held that the earth rotated once per day and revolved around the sun once per year. The heliocentric theory directly challenged the dominant geocentric theory of the second-century Greek astronomer Claudius Ptolemy, which held that the earth was at the center of the universe and every other celestial body revolved around it. According to the medieval followers of Ptolemy, angels moved the nine "crystalline orbs" which encased the sun, the moon, the stars, and the five known planets around the earth.[1]

Contrary to popular belief, it was not superior observation that led Copernicus and many of the other great scientists of the age to their discoveries. On the contrary, basic observation seemed (and still seems) to support the geocentric theory and to contradict the heliocentric theory. The sun appears to move around the earth; the earth does not appear to move at all. In truth, Copernicus's theory arose from purely aesthetic considerations. The only way geocentrists could make their theory conform to the positions of planets in the night sky was by claiming that the planets followed hundreds of "epicycles," smaller orbits within their larger orbit around the earth. With the inclusion of epicycles, geocentric theory fit observation fairly well. But because Copernicus was a Platonist who felt strongly that the universe must possess an elegant simplicity, he could not believe that this ugly and complicated system of orbits within orbits represented reality. It was his own subjective association of simplicity with beauty and beauty with divinity, not superior observation, that led him to the heliocentric theory.[2]

Copernicus had first become acquainted with the heliocentric theory while studying at the University of Padua in northern Italy, the most important center of the scientific revolution. There he learned of the ancient Greek astronomer Aristarchus, who had advanced the theory in the third century B.C. Applying mathematics to Aristarchus's theory, Copernicus was able to eliminate the need for most epicycles. Copernicus was unable to eliminate them all, however, because he hypothesized a circular orbit for the planets, since he considered the circle a perfect form.[3]

Tycho Brahe (1546–1601) and Johannes Kepler (1571–1630)

Although Danish astronomer Tycho Brahe spent most of his career attempting to disprove the heliocentric theory, in the process he developed a series of new observation techniques that allowed him to compile the most accurate astronomical data ever collected up to his time. Ironically, Brahe's systematic observation of the skies called attention to phenomena that created doubts concerning the unchanging perfection of the heavens, the central premise of the geocentrists. These phenomena included the appearance of a new star (1572–1574) and the arrival of comets that charged through crystalline orbs as though they did not exist (1577–1596).[4]

When Brahe died in 1601, his data fell into the hands of his former assistant, Johannes Kepler, a devoted Copernican. Applying his own excellent mathematical skills to Brahe's data, Kepler deduced that the orbit of the planets around the sun formed an ellipse, with the sun as its focus. Kepler's three laws of planetary motion, published in a book called *On the Motion of Mars* (1609), completely eliminated the need for epicycles. Almost literally a sun-worshiper, Kepler wrote that the sun was the body "who alone appears, by virtue of his dignity and power, suited" to move the planets in their orbits—a statement only slightly more mystical than Copernicus's own depiction of the sun. Kepler also attempted to ascertain the "music of the planets" from Brahe's data and to translate it into musical notes.[5]

Many still refused to believe the heliocentric theory, because it raised questions that could not then be answered. If the earth was rotating and revolving at such a rapid rate, why didn't humans feel any movement? If the earth revolved around the sun, why was there no parallax—why did the stars maintain their positions relative to one another in the night sky? What caused the earth to rotate and revolve? While geocentric theorists answered difficult questions by resorting to supernatural explanations (e.g., angels moved the celestial bodies), heliocentric theorists could not produce naturalistic explanations with the same ease. Copernicus had actually answered the second question correctly: There was no parallax because the stars were so far away, and the earth's orbit was so minute by comparison, that the stars' positions relative to one another in the sky varied too little to be measured. But nobody believed this theory, since the distances necessary for such an effect were simply "astronomical." Copernicus's answer to the third question, that "rotation is natural to a sphere," explained nothing and satisfied no one. The questions that plagued the heliocentric theory would have to be answered—that is, the modern physics of Galileo and Newton would have to replace the medieval physics based on the theories of Aristotle—before the heliocentric theory could replace the geocentric theory.[6]

Galileo Galilei (1564–1642)

Florentine astronomer Galileo improved the telescope and was the first to turn it toward the skies. With this wondrous new invention Galileo discovered new stars, craters and mountains on the moon, spots moving across the sun, and moons orbiting Jupiter. Since these observations violated the medieval doctrine of the purity and stasis of the heavens, many of Galileo's opponents (including some of his own colleagues at the University of Padua) refused to look into his telescope. Nevertheless, the accessibility of the telescope probably did more to popularize the heliocentric theory than the astronomers' publications, which required uncommon mathematical skills of their readers.[7]

Equally important, Galileo developed several laws of dynamics. One law stated that objects dropped an equal distance from the ground would accelerate uniformly. In a vacuum, if a cannonball and a feather are dropped from the same height at the same time, they will hit the ground at the same moment. But the most important of Galileo's laws of dynamics is the law of inertia: The tendency of objects is to remain in the same state of rest or motion, until moved by a force; objects moved by a force will continue to travel in a straight line until opposed by another force. That is how modern nations are able to send unmanned spacecraft to distant planets: In the vacuum of space, without any force (like friction) to resist the spacecraft, their inertia continues to move them. They will travel forever until resisted by a force. The only reason that a baseball does not travel forever when struck by a bat is that the friction produced by the air molecules it strikes slows and eventually stops its horizontal motion, while gravity stops its vertical motion. Rest is no more "natural" for any object than motion; an object will continue to do whatever it is doing until affected by a force. By contrast, medieval physics maintained that rest was the "natural state" of all objects. Only motion had to be explained.[8]

As with Copernicus and Kepler, Galileo's triumph was one of superior imagination, not superior observation. To propose his laws of dynamics, Galileo had to envision a vacuum, a perfect Euclidean world without such complications as the friction of air molecules. Observation favored his opponents. In practice, when does a feather dropped from the same height as a cannonball ever hit the ground at the same time?

Galileo's *Dialogues on the Two Chief Systems of the World* (1632) tied his physics to Copernican astronomy in a general assault on medieval science. Galileo wrote that the universe was a book written by God in the language of mathematics. It remained only for the deists of the eighteenth century to ask: What does the Author do when He has finished His book? If the book is perfect, He has no need of revision. The belief in a mechanistic universe governed entirely by mathematical laws was slowly taking shape.[9]

Isaac Newton (1642–1727)

It was Isaac Newton who answered all of the nagging questions concerning the heliocentric theory. It is inertia that prevents our feeling the motion of the earth. Since we travel at precisely the same speed as the planet on which we stand, we do not sense any movement. It is gravity that keeps the planets revolving in an orderly fashion. The planets are attracted to the sun by the force of gravity, which helps determine their orbits. It is inertia that keeps the planets rotating in an orderly fashion. They continue to spin as they did when first captured by the sun's gravity.[10]

Although others had hypothesized the existence of gravity, Newton was the first to declare that gravity was universal. Every object in the universe is attracted to every other object by the force of gravity. Newton even provided a formula (Gravity = 1/distance between the objects squared) to calculate the exact force of gravity between any two objects. Yet, like his predecessors, Newton was hardly a modern rationalist. He studied alchemy, the conjuring of angels, and biblical prophecy avidly. Although Newton came to most of his conclusions in the 1660s, his concern over a few vexing anomalies delayed the publication of *Principia Mathematica* until 1687, when his friend and fellow astronomer Edmund Halley finally convinced him to publish.[11]

Newton's work was significant for three reasons. First, by solving the problems that plagued the heliocentric theory, he convinced the Western world of its validity. Universal gravity not only explained what moved the planets but also accounted for the minor but troubling deviations in the planets' orbits: Their mutual attraction affected their course. Second, Newton demonstrated the superiority of Francis Bacon's inductive "scientific method," which combined reason (hypothesis) with experimentation in an unending cycle. René Descartes and the French scientists had advocated the use of reason alone, an approach that might be acceptable for mathematics but is dangerous for medicine and most other sciences. Third, Newton demonstrated that the whole universe, both the heavens and the earth, existed under a single set of laws discoverable by humans.[12]

In the wake of Newton's discovery of the physical laws governing the universe there was a massive effort to uncover the laws believed to govern human affairs, such as politics, economics, law, architecture, and literature. If, as Newtonian physics seemed to show, a rational God had created a universe that operated according to mathematical laws, would He not have formulated laws governing human affairs as well? And if humans could use their reason to discover the mathematical laws governing the physical universe, why not the laws governing their own affairs? After all, it was primarily through the gift of reason that humans were connected with God. The whole concept of laws of politics and economics was predicated on the notion that humans were rational and, therefore, consistent and predictable. The scientific revolution, which culminated in Newton, was the mother of the Enlightenment.

THE COMMERCIAL, FINANCIAL, AND TECHNOLOGICAL REVOLUTIONS

But the Enlightenment was not the child of a single parent. While European scientists expanded human knowledge of the universe, European merchants expanded the Western economy, another development crucial to the transition from medieval theism to modern humanism. Commercial, financial, and technological progress was even more gradual than the advancement of scientific knowledge. (In spite of prevailing conventions, it is perhaps more accurate to speak of all of these movements as evolutions than as revolutions.)

A host of agricultural reforms beginning in the tenth century, such as the three-field system (in which each field lay fallow once every three years to restore nutrients to the soil), the heavy plow, the tandem harness, the horseshoe, the windmill, and the rediscovered watermill, increased food production. Food production also expanded when the seminomadic tribes on the fringes of western Europe settled down to agriculture and stopped raiding the farms of others. Larger food surpluses spurred trade, which increased the size of cities and the middle class of merchants and artisans who inhabited them. The growth of trade also led to the proliferation of currencies and the rise of a sophisticated banking system.[13]

The Crusades (1095–1291) furthered the process. While attempting to recapture the Holy Lands from the Muslims, Crusaders learned the value of Indonesian spices for preserving and enhancing monotonous or smelly food, Chinese silks for rough skins, Indian drugs for aching flesh, Arab perfumes for unbathed bodies, Tibetan gems for unadorned hands, and Persian draperies and rugs for gloomy castles. Upon their return to western Europe the Crusaders spread the desire for these items throughout the region. Northern Italians obtained the items from Arab traders, who were part of a vast caravan system that stretched across the Near East and the Asian hinterlands to India, Indonesia, and China, and sold them to the merchants of northern Europe via a growing network of roads. The revival of trade with the eastern world spurred shipbuilding and banking and broadened the western European middle class.[14]

Christopher Columbus's voyage to the Americas in 1492 further increased trade and wealth. Colonies, sometimes financed by joint-stock companies, supplied Europe with new raw materials and markets. Gold and silver poured into Europe from Spain's Latin American colonies, increasing aggregate wealth, though creating hardship (through inflation) for some Europeans. The increased trade among Europe, Asia, Africa, and the Pacific islands that resulted from other European expeditions had a similar effect in promoting European prosperity.[15]

Finally, in the mid-eighteenth century Britain's agricultural revolution provided the capital and surplus labor force for the Industrial Revolution. Crop rotation, combined with improvements in planting, hoeing, and animal breeding, produced a 43 percent increase in the agricultural output of Britain during the century. By providing sufficient food for a rapidly expanding population with the same number of laborers, the agricultural revolution freed other workers for employment in the new factories of the late eighteenth and early nineteenth centuries. The Industrial Revolution, discussed later, produced even greater wealth. As previously observed, wealth is the natural fertilizer of humanism, attracting attention to the pleasures of this world and distracting it from preparation for the afterlife.[16]

THE REVIVAL OF CLASSICAL HUMANISM

The Return of the Stoic Theory of Natural Law

Ironically, the scientific, commercial, financial, and technological revolutions that created the modern world did so partly by setting the stage for the revival of two ancient philosophies, Stoicism and Epicureanism. The near unanimous agreement of eighteenth-century philosophers regarding the ability of humans to fully comprehend natural law, a universal code of ethics equally applicable to all individuals and societies, regardless of time and culture, represented both a dramatic break from the Christian belief in original sin and a return to classical humanism. While the Stoic belief that humans must utilize both reason and intuition to comprehend natural law generally prevailed over the Epicurean belief in reason alone, eighteenth-century American leaders rejected Stoic fatalism for the Epicurean belief in free will.

The germ of natural law theory may be found in the writings of Plato. In Plato's *Meno* (77c–78b), Socrates argued that humans were innately good, possessing a knowledge of right and wrong gained by the soul prior to its binding with the body, rather than through reason (logic) acting upon sensory experience. In fact, in Plato's *Phaedo* (63c–68b), Socrates explained that sensory experience was actually an "obstacle" to knowledge. Socrates stated, "And the best sort of thinking occurs when the soul is not disturbed by any of these things—not by hearing, or sight, or pain, or pleasure—when she leaves the body and is alone and, doing her best to avoid any form of contact with it, reaches out to grasp what is truly real."

While Aristotle also believed in natural law (*Rhetoric*, 1.1375a.25–b.1–8), he contended that humans must use their reason to deduce it from experience. In the first book of the *Politics* he claimed regarding the citizen: "Justice, which is his salvation, belongs to the polis; for justice, which is the determination of what is just, is an ordering of the political association." Virtue was not the product of Plato's innate ideas but the result of rational training by the polis (city-state). The argument concerning whether humans obtained knowledge (including moral knowledge) intuitively ("from the inside out"), as Plato alleged, or through reason acting on experience ("from the outside in"), as Aristotle argued, so divided philosophers for millennia that Ralph Waldo Emerson once claimed that every man was a follower of either Plato or Aristotle.[17]

Epicurus (Diogenes Laertius, *Lives of the Eminent Philosophers*, 10.122–135) supported Aristotle's position on this issue. He claimed: "It is wise, however, to evaluate all these things by measuring one against another and discovering what is beneficial and what is harmful. For sometimes we consider good to be evil and also the opposite." Reason acting upon experience, not intuition, led humans to moral truth.

The Stoics assumed a middle position between Plato and Aristotle concerning the proper method of comprehending natural law. While the Stoics believed that natural law was imbedded in human nature through a sort of intuition, they claimed that humans could access it only with the help of reason acting upon sensory information. As Maryanne Cline Horowitz aptly summarized this aspect of Stoic philosophy: "They believed that the mind is born predisposed to certain ideas which are not yet consciously held. These ideas are evoked and developed through the stimulus of sense impressions and the development of reason." Cicero, the eclectic first-century B.C. Roman statesman and philosopher who agreed with the Stoics concerning natural law, wrote regarding nature and man:

> It is true that she gave him a mind capable of receiving every virtue, and implanted at birth and without instruction some small intimations of the greatest truths, and thus, as it were, laid the foundation for education and instilled into those faculties which the mind already had what may be called the germs of virtue. But of virtue itself she merely furnished the rudiments; nothing more. Therefore it is our task (and when I say 'our' I mean that it is the task of art) to supplement those mere beginnings by searching out the further developments which were implicit in them, until what we seek is fully attained.

Cicero used the two analogies of sparks and seeds to clarify his position. At one point he stated that human souls were all sparks temporarily separated from the Great Flame (the World Soul), but that a spark might be extinguished by a bad upbringing. At another time he argued that the seeds of virtue manifested themselves in the social nature of humans, in their "gregarious impulses" (*Laws*, 26.4). Similarly, the first-century Roman Stoic Seneca claimed, "Every living thing possessed of reason is inactive if not first stirred by some external impression; then the impulse comes, and finally assent confirms the impulse" (*Epistles*, 49.11). Regarding virtue he wrote, "Nature could not teach us this directly; she has given us the seeds of knowledge, but not knowledge itself." He added, "Even in the best of men, before you refine them by instruction, there is but the stuff of virtue, not virtue itself" (120.4–8). The Stoics believed that humans possessed the requisite experience to trigger innate impulses by about age seven.[18]

Though Paul and the early Christians accepted the concept of natural law, their belief in original sin left them far more pessimistic than the classical philosophers concerning the ability of humans to fully understand it, either through reason or intuition ("conscience"). Paul (Rom. 2:14–15) and Augustine held that while both reason and intuition still acted as guides to ethics, both had been so badly damaged by the fall of Adam as to become insufficient for the task. Paul wrote: "Now we see through a glass, darkly" (1 Cor. 13:12). Augustine declared: "Reason itself is clearly proven to be mutable, now struggling to arrive at truth, now ceasing to struggle, sometimes reaching it and sometimes not. . . . Unless the will is freed by the grace of God from the bondage through which it has become a slave of sin, and unless it obtains aid in conquering its vices, mortal men cannot live rightly and piously." Humans were unable to lead ethical lives without Scripture to teach them true morality and without the infusion of God's grace to help them to adhere to it.[19]

The theory of natural law persisted through the Middle Ages, though it was still subordinate to the revealed law, which now included church teachings in addition to Scripture. Although Thomas Aquinas, following the lead of Aristotle, emphasized reason and experience to the exclusion of intuition (unlike Paul and Augustine, who were influenced more by Plato), Aquinas agreed with his Christian forebears that original sin had rendered human reason insufficient for the attainment of true virtue. Humans could obtain the essential "theological virtues" of faith and love by the power of God alone through grace. Scripture and church teachings were superior to natural law as a guide to ethics, for two reasons. First, as the product of God's direct revelation, revealed law was a clearer expression of His will than natural law, which required the employment of greater deductive powers. Aquinas wrote: "On account of the uncertainty of human judgment, especially on contingent and particular matters, different people form different judgments on human acts; whence also different and contrary laws result. In order, therefore, that man may know without any doubt what he ought to do and what he ought to avoid, it was necessary for man to be directed in his proper acts by a law given by God, for it is certain that such a law cannot err." Second, revealed law was a broader, more inclusive representation of God's will than that natural law that humans could deduce from the operation of their flawed reason on their limited experience.[20]

Though restricting the category of revealed law to Scripture alone, the Protestant reformers agreed with Aquinas that original sin rendered revealed law superior to natural law as a guide to ethics. Luther concluded that while revelation did not contradict reason, it certainly transcended it. Even those moral tenets that sinful humans might deduce from nature without the aid of revelation they could hardly follow without the aid of the Holy Spirit. Luther wrote, "No one keeps God's law from his heart; nor can he do so; for to be averse to goodness and prone to evil are traits found in all men." The instruction of Scripture and the inspiration of the Spirit were essential to true virtue. John Calvin agreed. He compared Scripture to a pair of spectacles that allowed humans to see "the true God clearly." While God could be seen in nature as well, He could not be seen as clearly. Calvin contended:

> The mind of man has been so completely estranged from God's righteousness that it conceives, desires, and undertakes only that which is impious, perverted, foul, impure, and infamous. . . . Although there is still some residue of intelligence and judgment as well as will, we can-

> not call a mind sound which is both weak and immersed in darkness.
> . . . Since reason, by which man discerns between good and evil, and
> by which he understands and judges, is a natural gift, it cannot be en-
> tirely destroyed; but partly weakened and partly corrupted, a shapeless
> ruin is all that remains. . . . The testimony of the Spirit is superior to
> reason.

Reason alone would not necessarily have deduced from nature all
of the Ten Commandments. Furthermore, Calvin noted that Plato
had been naive in assuming that to know the good was to do the
good—that virtue required only wisdom. That simplistic formulation overlooked the importance of willpower, which only the
Holy Spirit could supply. (Plato himself had been forced to concede the importance of willpower on occasion. In the *Symposium*
(216) there is a touching scene in which the conniving dema-
gogue Alcibiades, thoroughly intoxicated and overwhelmed by
emotion, tells Socrates, his former teacher, that he knows what is
right but cannot ever seem to do it.)[21]

Writing in the aftermath of the bloody English Civil War,
seventeenth-century English monarchist Thomas Hobbes raised
doubts similar to those raised by the theologians concerning the
ability of humans to understand natural law. Hobbes questioned
the existence of intuition and the reliability of reason. The infinite variety of interpretations of natural law seemed a recipe for
perpetual conflict. Claiming some special ability to deduce the
vaporous law, aristocrats incited the common people to rebellion,
producing chaos and violence. Hobbes contended: "Good and
evil are names that signify our appetites and aversions which in
different tempers, customs, and doctrines of men are different. . .
. Nay, the same man in divers times differs from himself, and one
time praises—that is, calls good—what another time he dispraises
and calls evil; from whence arises disputes, controversies, and at
last war." The proper path for humans was to submit themselves
to the laws of their rulers in public matters, as Paul had commanded (Rom. 13:1–4), and to revealed law in dealing with one
another. Both government statutes and the Scriptures were clearer
than natural law, which relied too much on the flawed faculty of
reason.[22]

Not until the mid-seventeenth century did the gradual changes wrought by the scientific, commercial, financial, and technological revolutions begin the slow process of reversing centuries of Christian pessimism concerning human nature and social progress. In refuting Hobbes and the other monarchists, modern republicans in England and France revived classical optimism concerning the ability of humans to understand natural law, while also contributing a revolutionary emphasis on the natural rights of individuals, a deduction from natural law rarely pursued by the ancients. The Huguenots first summarized these natural rights as the right to life, liberty, and property. Algernon Sidney appealed to ancient English liberties and to the existing legal system, as though they somehow comprehended all of natural law. The product of an "ultimate reason," natural law was universal, rooted in the human conscience, and "above all passion, void of desire and fear, lust and anger." Sidney suggested that humans could make certain inferences from the common characteristics of all organized societies, adding that certain legal axioms were as obvious as Euclidean geometry. Sidney trusted Parliament, as the true representative of the people, to define natural law. John Locke, the most influential of the English republicans, wrote that a nation's laws "are only so far right as they are founded on the Law of Nature, by which they are to be regulated and interpreted." He added, "The Law of Nature stands as an Eternal Rule to all Men, legislators as well as others." He argued that men did not surrender their natural rights to government when forming the social contract, only their prerogative of enforcing natural law. If government threatened natural rights, its citizens were morally obligated to uphold natural law by opposing the government that violated it. Since such citizens resisted tyranny on behalf of law, they were in no sense rebels.[23]

Locke assumed a clear Epicurean position concerning the proper method of comprehending natural law. In his influential *Essay Concerning Human Understanding* (1690) Locke contended that an infant's mind was a "white paper, void of all characters, without any ideas"—or, to use the term coined by the Epicurean Pierre Gassendi in 1655, often mistakenly attributed to Locke, a *tabula rasa* ("blank slate")—filled only by his experience.[24]

Some rationalists seized on Locke's doctrine as the key to progress. If there was no original sin, no innate human depravity, it was possible to train children to be completely virtuous. Social and moral progress could then accompany scientific and technological progress. Bolstered by the triumph of Newton's scientific method, which combined reason and experience, Epicurean humanism grew in popularity, providing a rationalist tinge even to those who followed the Stoics in accepting the existence of intuition.

Fueled by the work of Newton and Locke, the eighteenth-century passion for discovering laws extended well beyond the physical and moral universes. Eighteenth-century Europeans hoped to deduce and apply the laws they assumed governed every aspect of human affairs. The Age of Reason had arrived. The poetry of Alexander Pope was almost maddening in its regularity and symmetry. In his early satires Jonathan Swift lampooned religious hysteria. Similarly, the essays of Joseph Addison and Richard Steele employed humor to attack superstitions, as well as to assault such irrational social practices as dueling. Plays were written according to the "laws of drama" that had been deduced from Aristotle's writings. Neoclassical architects adapted the symmetrical, columned and domed buildings of the Greeks and Romans to eighteenth-century needs and tastes. Adam Smith discovered "the law of supply and demand." The influential Dutch commentator Enrich de Vattel attempted to apply the principles of natural law to international trade and communications. Jeremy Bentham (1748–1832) advanced "utilitarianism," the doctrine that societies should rationally design all of their laws and institutions in order to produce "the greatest happiness of the greatest number." Reason, not custom, should prevail in law.[25]

The founders of the United States had access to every level of this Western discourse on natural law. They frequently quoted the Stoics in support of the theory. The founders generally derived their Stoicism not from the Greek philosophers Zeno and Epictetus but from the works of the two ill-fated Roman statesmen Cicero and Seneca and from the Roman historians. As early as 1759 John Adams exhorted himself, in his diary: "Labour to get distinct

Ideas of Law, Right, Wrong, Justice, Equity. Search for them in your own mind, in Roman, grecian, French, English Treatises of natural, civil, common, Statute Law. . . . Study Seneca, Cicero, and all other good moral Writers." In the 1760s Samuel Adams praised the British constitution, then threatened by parliamentary measures, as founded "On the Law of God and the Law of Nature," as interpreted by Cicero and the Stoics. Near the end of his life, Thomas Jefferson wrote regarding the Declaration of Independence, "All its authority rests, then, on the harmonizing sentiments of the day, whether expressed in conversation, in letters, in printed essays, or in the elementary books of public right, [such] as Aristotle, Cicero, Locke, Sidney, etc."[26]

Typical was James Wilson's admiration for Cicero, who had been part skeptic and part Epicurean, but fully Stoic on the issue of natural law. In a 1790 lecture to law students at the College of Philadelphia, part of a series attended by President George Washington, Vice President John Adams, Secretary of State Thomas Jefferson, and many other dignitaries, Wilson contended that humans possessed a sort of intuition, variously called "conscience" or "moral sense," that led them to the right moral conclusions. Wilson asserted, "Morality, like mathematicks, has its intuitive truths, without which we cannot make a single step in our reasonings upon the subject." He then quoted Cicero, "What nation, what species of man is there which does not have, without teaching, some sort of foreknowledge, that is, a certain image of the thing conceived beforehand by the mind, without which nothing can be understood, investigated, or discussed?" Wilson again quoted Cicero on natural law: "It is, indeed, a true law, conformable to nature, diffused among all men, unchangeable, eternal. By its commands, it calls men to their duty; by its prohibitions, it deters them from vice. To diminish, to alter, much more to abolish this law, is a vain attempt. Neither by the senate, nor by the people, can its powerful obligation be dissolved. It requires no interpreter or commentator. It is not one law at Rome, another at Athens; one law now, another hereafter: it is the same eternal and immutable law, given at all times and to all nations." An intuitive understanding of natural law was implanted by God, its "author and promulgator." Wilson quoted Cicero: "That first and final law, they used to say, is the mind of God, who forces or prohibits everything by reason." Humans' innate moral sense was evident in their universal need for community.[27]

Even Benjamin Rush and Thomas Paine, two prominent critics of the Greek and Latin language requirements in the schools, cited Cicero in support of natural law theory. Rush quoted the Roman statesman and philosopher: "This, my lords, is not a written but an innate law. We have not been taught it by the learned; we have not received it from our ancestors; we have not taken it from books; it is derived from nature and stamped in invisible characters upon our very frame. It was not conveyed to us by instruction but wrought into our constitution. It is the dictate of instinct." Paine was impressed by Cicero's arguments for the use of "right reason" in religion, for a rational God, and for natural law. In 1804 Paine claimed: "In Cicero we see that vast superiority of the mind, that sublimity of right reasoning and justness of ideas, which man acquires, not by studying bibles and testaments, and the theology of schools built thereon, but by studying the creator in the immensity and unchangeable order of his creation, and the immutability of his law." He quoted the Roman, "There cannot be one law now, and another hereafter; but the same eternal immutable law comprehends all nations, at all times, under one common master and governor of all—God." Paine then used this doctrine to assault the belief that God had propounded two very different sets of laws, one vested in the Old Testament, the other in the New Testament.[28]

Most of the founders shared the Stoic belief that both intuition and reason were necessary to understand natural law. Often citing Cicero, they spoke of the existence of a "moral sense," a term for intuition popularized by eighteenth-century Scottish philosophers. Having read and copied the Stoics long before he became familiar with Scottish moral philosophy, Jefferson believed that everyone possessed a "moral sense" that God had implanted in humans to ensure the preservation of their race. Not everyone listened to his moral sense; a plowman might decide a moral case better than a professor, if the professor were "led astray by artificial rules." But if people listened to their moral sense, they would find that it revealed the same things to each of them. Thus, Jefferson wrote that ethics should be taught at the University of Virginia as "moral obligations . . . in which all sects agree," and praised the Quakers for rallying around their common ethics, rather than fragmenting over theological points. Similarly, John Adams, like his hero, Cicero, found proof for the existence of God in the self-evident nature of certain truths. He argued: "The human Understanding is a revelation from its Maker which can never be disputed or doubted. There can be no Scepticism, Pyrrhonism, or Incredulity, or Infidelity here. No prophecies, no Miracles are necessary to prove this celestial communication. This revelation has made it certain that two and one make three; that one is not three; nor can three be one." Like Cicero, Adams also based his belief in an afterlife upon the supposed universality of that belief. In 1816 he contended: "All Nations, known in History, or in Travels, have hoped, believed, and expected a future and better State. The Maker of the Universe, the Cause of all Things, whether we call it Fate or Chance or God, has inspired this Hope." To Adams, the apparent universality of certain beliefs implied interconnection with a universal mind. Using a circular logic, many eighteenth-century intellectuals deduced a common God from the existence of universal laws, both physical and moral, and the existence of universal laws from a common God.[29]

Yet the founders also denied that the moral sense could be awakened without the aid of reason and experience. When witnessing examples of virtue in their daily lives, children instinctively recognized its inherent beauty and sought to reproduce it. Conversely, children who rarely experienced virtuous behavior could not develop their moral sense to its full potential. Jefferson used an enlightening analogy to explain this Stoic concept of the moral sense: "The moral sense, or conscience, is as much a part of a man as his leg or arm. It may be strengthened by exercise, as may any particular limb of the body. . . . In this branch, therefore, read good books, because they will encourage as well as direct your feelings." Such "good books" included Xenophon's *Memorabilia of Socrates*, Cicero's philosophical writings, Roman emperor and Stoic Marcus Aurelius's *Meditations*, and Seneca's essays. But at times Jefferson did not seem to appreciate the implication of this analogy: that any faculty that requires exercise can be considered neither infallible nor equally possessed by all.[30]

James Wilson agreed that both intuition and reason were necessary to comprehend natural law. In the same law lectures in which Wilson quoted Cicero repeatedly concerning intuition, he referred to "the divine law, as discovered by reason and the moral sense," and added, "We discover [the will of God] by our conscience, by our reason, and by the Holy Scriptures." Although Wilson emphasized intuition, he refused to exempt reason from a role in uncovering natural law. He concluded: "The cases that require reasoning are few, compared with those that require none; and a man may be very honest and virtuous, who cannot reason, and who knows not what demonstration means. . . . Our instincts are no other than the oracles of eternal wisdom; our conscience, in particular, is the voice of God within us." Odd that "the voice of God" should be silent in "a few cases." But most of the founders felt little need to elucidate the precise relationship between reason and intuition, perhaps because they possessed such an optimistic view of the powers of reason and the senses that they considered this road to knowledge as likely to end in success as the path of intuition.[31]

Nowhere is this optimism better exemplified than in Benjamin Franklin's famous quest for moral perfection, a struggle amusingly recounted in his autobiography. Franklin drafted a list of the thirteen virtues he considered worthy of acquisition. Each week he attempted to master a different virtue by trying to get through the period without committing any infraction against it. Franklin believed that such training would eventually render the virtues a matter of habit and allow him to achieve moral perfection. When Franklin abandoned the plan, it was not because he had arrived at the conclusion that moral perfection was impossible, but because he had decided that it might not be all that it was cracked up to be: If he were morally perfect, people might envy him. Franklin and many of the other founders rejected the traditional Christian doctrine of original sin for a Stoic theory of human nature that employed both intuition and reason as engines of unlimited progress.[32]

Yet the social implications that modern humanists like these founders drew from the Stoic conception of human nature were quite different from those drawn by the Stoics themselves. The Stoics had chosen to interpret their theory somewhat pessimistically. They had viewed the world as a place of pain and suffering in which only a fortunate few—those whose "seeds" of innate goodness were properly cultivated by capable gardeners—were destined to achieve any peace of mind, and that in solitude. But the scientific and economic developments of the early modern period led eighteenth-century philosophers to more optimistic conclusions. Within their own lifetimes, they could see tangible gains in human knowledge of the universe and in material wealth. By contrast, the lifestyle of the ancients had changed little from one generation to the next, in part as a result of the Greeks' notorious disdain for applied science. The Greeks had considered social progress of any kind unusual and ephemeral.[33]

The Revival of the Stoic Conception of the Nature and Purpose of Virtue

In addition to its theory of human nature, Stoicism also contributed much to the founders' conception of the nature and purpose of virtue. Influenced by Cicero, Seneca, and the Roman historians, as well as by modern philosophers influenced by the Stoics, the founders perceived the nature of virtue partly, and the purpose of virtue largely, in Stoic terms. Even George Washington, who was unphilosophical by nature, imbibed Stoicism at an early age. The Fairfaxes, whom Washington considered his second family, read Marcus Aurelius and the other Stoics. At the age of seventeen, Washington read Sir Roger L'Estrange's English translation of Seneca's principal dialogues. As the historian Samuel Eliot Morrison noted, "The mere chapter headings are the moral axioms that Washington followed through life." Partly as a result of their Stoicism, the founders equated virtue with frugality, simplicity, temperance, fortitude, love of liberty, selflessness, and honor.[34]

In emphasizing virtue's earthly over its heavenly rewards, many of the leading founders proved more classical than Christian, more humanist than theist. In 1787 Thomas Jefferson assured his nephew regarding his examination of religious questions: "If it ends in the belief that there is no god, you will find incitements to virtue in the comfort and pleasantness you feel in its exercise, and the love of others which it will procure you." Since virtue brought the earthly rewards of self-respect and the respect of others, it was nothing more than wisdom, vice nothing more than folly, an optimistic equation that ignored the fact that society's response to individual integrity is sometimes hatred and persecution, not love and admiration.[35]

The founders considered fame, virtue's greatest reward, a praiseworthy end. John Adams expressed the common view when, as a young man, he inscribed in his diary this line from Tacitus, "Contemptu Famae, contemni Virtutem," which Adams translated as, "A Contempt of Fame generally begets or accompanies a Contempt of Virtue." The founders' emphasis on fame as the principal reward of virtue was incompatible with the traditional Christian emphasis on the need for humility and on the relative insignificance of this world when set against the tremendous importance of the eternal afterlife.[36]

The founders were never fully classical, however. They retained enough Christian modesty to regard the full-fledged egotism of their own Greek and Roman heroes with embarrassment. Hence John Adams was at pains to defend Cicero against the charge of vanity, a quality that no Roman would have considered a vice. Similarly, Benjamin Franklin audaciously paired Socrates with Jesus as the two great models of humility. Whatever Socrates's virtues, humility had never been one of them. The gleeful arrogance with which the Athenian philosopher had enticed his opponents into admissions of inconsistency had persuaded few Athenians to consider him a humble truth-seeker. However eloquent and frank his final speech to the Athenian jury, its arrogance had probably contributed substantially to his death sentence. During the penalty phase of his trial, Socrates had suggested that, far from punishing him, Athens should honor him with free meals for the rest of his life, like an Olympic victor, for agreeing to serve as its "gadfly" (*Apology of Socrates*, 36d1–37d1). Some jurors who had voted to acquit him then voted for the death penalty.[37]

The Return of Epicureanism

Epicureanism was equally crucial to the founders' thought. Thomas Jefferson's favorite philosopher was Epicurus. In 1816 Jefferson termed the Epicurean philosophy "the most rational system remaining of the philosophy of the ancients, as frugal of vicious indulgence, and fruitful of virtue as the hyperbolic extravagancies of rival sects." In an 1819 letter, having stated that the doctrines of Epicurus contained "everything rational in moral philosophy which Greece and Rome have left us," Jefferson summarized these doctrines:

> The Universe eternal. . . . Matter and Void alone. . . . Gods, an order of beings next superior to man, enjoying in their sphere their own felicities; but not meddling with the concerns of the scale of beings below them. . . . Happiness the aim of life. Virtue the foundation of happiness. Utility the test of virtue. . . . The *summum bonum* ["ultimate good"] is to be not pained in body, nor troubled in mind. . . . To procure tranquillity of mind we must avoid desire and fear, the two principal diseases of the mind. Man is a free agent. Virtue consists in: 1. Prudence. 2. Temperance. 3. Fortitude. 4. Justice. To which are opposed, 1. Folly. 2. Desire. 3. Fear. 4. Deceit.[38]

Although Jefferson adopted the Stoic belief in intuition and found comfort in the Stoic emphasis on the patient endurance of misfortune, he vehemently disapproved of certain aspects of Stoicism. He rejected the Stoics' doctrine of a separable soul and their fatalism and was angered by their misrepresentation of the Epicurean philosophy as mere hedonism. In 1819 Jefferson argued: "Epictetus, indeed, has given us what was good of the Stoics; all beyond, of their dogmas, being hypocrisy and grimace. Their great crime was in their calumnies of Epicurus and misrepresentations of his doctrines; in which we lament to see the candid character of Cicero engaging as an accomplice."[39]

However much the other founders accepted the Stoic misrepresentation of Epicureanism as mere "hedonism," they shared Jefferson's preference for the Epicurean doctrine of free will over Stoic (and Calvinist) determinism. In his beloved Bill for Establishing Religious Freedom (1779), Jefferson had emphasized free will, writing, "Almighty God hath created the mind free . . . [and] being lord of both body and mind, yet chose not to propagate it by coercions on either, as was in his Almighty power to do, *but to extend it by its influence on reason alone.*" (The Virginia Senate deleted the italicized clause.) In a clearer attack on Calvinism in 1823, Jefferson wrote to a sympathetic John Adams: "I can never join Calvin in addressing his god. . . . If ever man worshipped a false god, he did. The being described in his 5 points is not the God whom you and I acknowledge and adore, the Creator and benevolent governor of the world; but a daemon of malignant spirit. It would be more pardonable to believe in no god at all, than to blaspheme him by the atrocious attributes of Calvin." In the previous year Jefferson had caricatured the "5 points of Calvin" as: "1. That there are three Gods [a reference to the Holy Trinity]. 2. That good works, or the love of our neighbor, are nothing. 3. That faith is everything, and the more incomprehensible the proposition, the more merit in its faith. 4. That reason in religion is of unlawful use. 5. That God, from the beginning, elected certain individuals to be saved, and certain others to be damned; and that no crimes of the former can damn them; no virtues of the latter save." Unfortunately, Jefferson substituted such ridicule and distortion of Calvinist theology for a rational explanation of the sense in which the human will could be free. Like so many others of his era, Jefferson never made the feeblest attempt to define free will, much less to reconcile it with the limitations imposed by the physical world, biological inheritance, society, culture, family, and individual personality. Nevertheless, John Adams adopted the free will position as well. In 1813 he penned a caricature of Calvin as unfair as Jefferson's. Benjamin Franklin dismissed predestination as an absurd belief. While Adams, Franklin, and Washington all saw the hand of "Providence" behind both the physical laws of the universe and grand historical developments, such as the American Revolution and the ratification of the U.S. Constitution, all denied it extended to the determination of individual salvation.[40]

Furthermore, although the founders differed from Epicurus in accepting the Stoic doctrine of intuition, they shared Epicurus's emphasis upon reason. Jefferson considered reason and intuition the two guides that God had implanted in humans for the preservation of the race. While both reason and intuition were humanity's ethical guides, reason alone was the guide for theology and metaphysics. In 1814 Jefferson claimed, "Dispute as long as we will on religious tenets, our reason at last must decide, as it is the only oracle which God has given us to determine between what really comes from Him and the phantasms of a disordered or deluded imagination." Although reason had to act on information provided by the senses, Jefferson was equally convinced of their reliability. In 1820 he declared, "A single sense may indeed be sometimes deceived, but rarely, and never all our senses together." Hence Jefferson regarded religious liberty as crucial, for if men were free to think as they chose, reason would surely lead them in the same direction. In 1813 he asserted, "If thinking men would have the courage to think for themselves, and to speak what they think, it would be found that they do not differ in religious opinions as much as is supposed." What would such "thinking men" believe? They would believe in a Creator, not on the basis of a superstitious acceptance of revelation, but on the basis of the intricate design of the universe. Although Jefferson's Epicurean argument for the existence of God differed fundamentally from Adams's Stoic argument concerning the existence of intuitive truths, both rejected faith in revelation.[41]

Because of their disdain for supernatural explanations, men like Thomas Jefferson had to alter Christianity in order to retain some form of it. Although Jefferson's favorite ethical philosopher was Jesus, it was Jesus viewed through an Epicurean lens. Taking his cue from a book called *Jesus and Socrates Compared*, written by his friend Joseph Priestley (the discoverer of oxygen), Jefferson frequently made the same comparison. He contended that the doctrines of both Socrates and Jesus had been corrupted. Plato had used "the name of Socrates to cover the whimsies of his own brain," and his dialogues were "libels on Socrates." Hence Xenophon's *Memorabilia of Socrates* was the only source for the unadulterated philosophy of Socrates.[42]

The doctrines of Jesus, on the other hand, had been corrupted by his inept and superstitious biographers (the Gospel writers), by conniving Platonists, and by illogical Calvinists. This corruption was tragic, Jefferson lamented, because, "Had the doctrines of Jesus been preached always as pure as they came from his lips, the whole civilized world would now have been Christian." Jefferson contended concerning Jesus that "fragments only of what he did deliver have come to us mutilated, misstated, and often unintelligible," and complained of "the follies, the falsehoods, and the charlatanisms" that the Gospel writers had foisted upon him. Jefferson trusted, however, that "the dawn of reason and freedom of thought in the United States" would tear down "the artificial scaffolding" erected by these biographers. He concluded, "And the day will come when the mystical generation of Jesus by the supreme being as his father in the womb of a virgin will be classed with the fable of the generation of Minerva in the brain of Jupiter."[43]

Worse yet, Platonists, intent on establishing and maintaining power for a dissolute class of priests, had afterwards engrafted onto Christianity the "sophisms" of that pernicious philosopher. After reading Plato's *Republic* in 1814, Jefferson subjected John Adams to this diatribe:

> While wading thro' the whimsies, the puerilities, and unintelligible jargon of this work, I laid it down often to ask myself how it could have been that the world should have so long consented to give reputation to such nonsense as this? . . . In truth, he [Plato] is one of the race of genuine Sophists, who has escaped the oblivion of his brethren, first by the elegance of his diction, but chiefly by the adoption and incorporation of his whimsies into the body of artificial Christianity. His foggy mind is forever presenting the semblances of objects which, half seen thro' a mist, can be defined neither in form or dimension. Yet this which should have consigned him to early oblivion really procured him immortality of fame and reverence. The Christian priesthood, finding the doctrines of Jesus leveled to every understanding, and too plain to need explanation, saw in the mysticisms of Plato, materials with which they might build an artificial system which might, from its indistinctness, admit everlasting controversy, give employment to their order, and introduce it to profit, power, and pre-eminence. The doctrines which flowed from the lips of Jesus himself are within the comprehension of a child; but thousands of volumes have not yet explained the Platonisms engrafted on them: and for the obvious reason that nonsense can never be explained.

Jefferson concluded that it was such Platonists, appealing to mystical and absurd doctrines like the Holy Trinity in their effort to establish their individual sects as the national religions of the United States and Great Britain, who were slandering him and Priestley for their religious opinions. But Jefferson hoped that Christians would not, in the end, "give up morals for mysteries, and Jesus for Plato."[44]

Finally, Jefferson believed that Calvinists had further obscured matters by adding the absurd doctrine of predestination to the Christian baggage. Jefferson wrote that if he were to establish a new sect, his fundamental principle "would be the reverse of Calvin's, that we are saved by our good works which are within our power, and not by our faith which is not within our power."[45]

In short, Jefferson concluded that both Jesus and Socrates had been Epicureans like himself. In 1820 he wrote dogmatically: "To speak of an immaterial soul or god is to say there is no soul or god; it is to be an atheist. Jesus taught none of it." Jesus had been a materialist: "He told us indeed that 'God is a spirit,' but he has not defined what a spirit is, nor said that it is not matter. And the ancient fathers, generally, if not universally, held it to be matter." Similarly, in 1824 Jefferson contended that Jesus had taught that the resurrection was purely material. On this point Jefferson was only partially Epicurean: Although Epicurus, like Jefferson, denied the existence of a separable soul, he also denied the existence of an afterlife, maintaining that death was nothingness. This is one of the few areas in which Jefferson's Christianity got the better of his Epicureanism. Jefferson also rejected the view that Jesus had held any pretensions to supernatural powers. In 1803 Jefferson wrote, "I am a Christian, in the only sense in which he wished any one to be; sincerely attached to his doctrines, in preference to all others; ascribing to himself every human excellence; and believing he never claimed any other." The Logos ("the Word") that had been with God from the beginning, as related in the first chapter of John, did not refer to Jesus, but to "reason." In the same fashion, Jefferson speculated that the daemon ("divine entity") that Socrates claimed spoke to him was also reason: "He was too wise to believe, and too honest to pretend, that he had real and familiar converse with a superior and invisible being. He probably considered the suggestions of his conscience, or reason, as revelations, or inspirations from the Supreme mind, bestowed, on important occasions, by a special superintending providence."[46]

Jefferson was so displeased with the Bible that he cut and pasted it to form one of his own. Shorn of the Old Testament, all miracles, and all references to Jesus's divinity, Jefferson's tiny volume, which he entitled "The Life and Morals of Jesus," emphasized the ethical teachings of the Sermon on the Mount. As the historian Edwin S. Gaustad noted regarding the Jefferson Bible: "When Jesus performed a miracle in connection with some teaching, the teaching survived, the miracle did not." Teachings that were apocalyptic in nature (e.g., Mark 13) held no interest whatever for Jefferson, who called the Book of Revelation "the ravings of a Maniac." The Jefferson Bible ended, "There laid they Jesus, and rolled a great stone to the door of the sepulchre, and departed." While Jefferson believed in a general resurrection on Judgment Day, he did not believe that Jesus Himself had risen from the dead.[47]

Jefferson based his belief in the afterlife on the view that it was necessary for the validation of justice, since virtue was not always rewarded in this life (a recognition curiously absent from some of his writings on the earthly rewards of virtue). Jefferson assumed, contrary to orthodox Christianity, that some people truly *deserved* immortality, an assumption based on his rejection of original sin for a Stoic conception of human nature. Of course, once Jefferson denied the existence of original sin, there remained no need for Jesus's atonement for that sin. Jesus had merely been a superlative ethical philosopher who had told humans what they needed to do to merit salvation on their own.[48]

How was Jefferson able to extract the true Epicurean meaning of the doctrines of Jesus and Socrates from their corrupt texts—to separate the diamonds from the dunghill, as he put it? Through the use of "reason," of course. In 1813 Jefferson explained how one might compose an accurate account of the teachings of Jesus, an operation he called "obvious and easy": "We must reduce our volume to the simple evangelists, select, even from them, the very words only of Jesus, paring off the Amphibologisms into which they have been led by forgetting often, or not understanding what had fallen from him, by giving their own misconceptions as his dicta, and expressing unintelligibly for others what they had not understood themselves. There will be found remaining the most sublime and benevolent code of morals which has ever been offered to man." In 1820 Jefferson contended that he was trying to "rescue His [Jesus's] character." He wrote regarding Jesus's perfect morals (as manifested in "humility, innocence, and simplicity of manners, neglect of riches, [and] absence of worldly honors"): "These could not be the invention of the grovelling authors who relate them. They are far beyond the powers of their feeble minds." True, even after completing the distillation process, one was left with some objectionable passages, but these might be explained by Jesus's need to escape the clutches of bloodthirsty priests. Jefferson then performed the same operation on Socrates, paring away the same fatty tissue with the same scalpel (reason) to reach the same Epicurean heart: "When, therefore, Plato puts into his mouth such paralogisms, such quibbles on words, and sophisms as a schoolboy would be ashamed of, we conclude they were the whimsies of Plato's own foggy brain and acquit Socrates of puerilities so unlike his character."[49]

Jefferson ignored conflicting evidence. John clearly intended the Logos to signify Jesus. He concluded his discussion of the Logos with, "And the Word became flesh and dwelt among us" (John 1:14), and followed this with a narrative of Jesus's life. In addition, both Plato and Xenophon related prominent instances in which Socrates demonstrated faith in the oracle of Delphi. In Plato's *Apology of Socrates* (20d–21b) Socrates stated that it was faith in the oracle that had launched him on his mission to examine others, leading ultimately to his trial and execution. When the oracle, a priestess who served as the voice of Apollo, had declared that Socrates was the wisest man in the world, the statement had seemed so odd to the philosopher that he had been determined to discover what the god really meant. The Athenian did not doubt for a moment that Apollo spoke through the oracle. In Xenophon's *Memorabilia* (3.1.5–7), a work Jefferson highly recommended, Socrates urged Xenophon to seek the oracle's advice before embarking on his ill-fated Persian expedition. Socrates's faith in the oracle proves that he believed in divine intervention in human affairs, contrary to the doctrines of Epicurus, and that he may well have believed that a god spoke directly to him. Central to the works that contain them, these famous passages could hardly have escaped Jefferson's notice.[50]

Why did Jefferson ignore these conspicuous passages? The answer seems to lie in his desire to "save Jesus's character"—and Socrates's as well. Enamored of their ethics (particularly Jesus's), an ethics that possessed a warmth and sense of benevolence absent from Epicureanism, Jefferson was determined that their metaphysics should match his own Epicurean metaphysics. In this way alone could he feel comfortable in defending their ethics against the onslaughts of materialist detractors.

In an anguished letter to his love interest, Maria Cosway, Jefferson included a touching dialogue between his head and his heart. His head was clearly Epicurean, contending: "The art of life is the art of avoiding pain. . . . The most effectual means of being secure against pain is to retire within ourselves. . . . For nothing is ours which another may deprive us of. Hence the inestimable value of intellectual pleasures. Ever in our power, always leading us to something new, never cloying, we ride sublime above the concerns of this mortal world, contemplating truth and nature, matter and motion, the laws which bind up our existence, and that eternal being who made and bound them up by these laws." But Jefferson's heart informed his head that happiness was not "the mere absence of pain" and that the warmth of friendship was a necessary comfort in life. Here we catch a glimpse of the reason why Jefferson's Christianity, with its emphasis on loving others, was as necessary to his emotional health as Greek philosophy, which merely taught the avoidance of self-injury and the injury of others. But Jefferson was too much the rationalist to surrender complete control of his head to his heart. Instead, he twisted and contorted the two to make them compatible. Jefferson was a true "heretic" in the original sense of the Greek word: "one who picks and chooses" those elements of a philosophical system that he likes, discarding the others.[51]

Ironically, Jefferson's reconciliation of Epicureanism and Christianity required an immense leap of faith from this leading figure of the Age of Reason. In order to satisfy his intense desire to retain some form of Christianity, the supreme rationalist had to betray reason itself—to discard the only historical record available concerning Jesus, the New Testament—and turn to a faith built purely on imagination and devoid of any empirical support.

THE COMPLEX RELIGIOUS BELIEFS
OF THE LEADING FOUNDERS

While the intricacies of Jefferson's theology were unique, most of the other leading founders shared its essential elements. These elements included a strong faith in a remote God; a belief in an afterlife of rewards and punishments; justification by good works; a fervent belief that religion and morality, defined largely (though not entirely) in Christian terms, was vital to the survival of a republic; a belief in free will; a reverence for Jesus as the greatest ethical philosopher in history; and a rejection of Jesus's divinity.

Benjamin Franklin possessed a genuine belief in God and even urged daily prayer at the Constitutional Convention. He once stated his beliefs: "I believe in one God, Creator of the Universe. That he governs the World by his Providence. That he ought to be worshipped. That the Soul of Man is immortal, and will be treated with Justice in another Life, respect[ing] its Conduct in this." But, however genuine his belief in God, Franklin frequently emphasized the social utility of faith: "Think how great a proportion of Mankind consists of weak and ignorant Men and Women, and of inexperienc'd Youth of both Sexes, who have need of the Motives of Religion to restrain them from Vice, to support their Virtue, and retain them in the Practice of it till it becomes habitual, which is the great Point for its Security." Furthermore, Franklin contended that Jesus had given humanity the best system of morals "the World ever saw," though His system had "received various corrupting changes." He added that while he doubted the divinity of Jesus, he did not mind others so believing, since it would make them more likely to follow Jesus's exquisite moral teachings. Franklin stopped attending Presbyterian services after 1735, when he became disgruntled with what he considered his minister's overemphasis on theology, an emphasis that conflicted with Franklin's view that faith was unnecessary to salvation except insofar as it bolstered virtue, the true path to both earthly and heavenly rewards. He proposed changes in the Anglican Book of Common Prayer, including abbreviating the Apostles' Creed and revising the Lord's Prayer.[52]

James Madison wrote that belief in an omnipotent God was "essential to the moral order of the World & to the happiness of man." Yet, despite the fact that he had attended a Presbyterian college and had read extensively in theology, the reticent Madison never left any indication that he believed in the divinity of Jesus, whose name is singularly absent from Madison's few religious references. Madison rarely referred to religion except to note its social utility or to plead for religious toleration.[53]

George Washington's views were similar to those of Jefferson, Franklin, and Madison. Though Washington was a lifelong Anglican/Episcopalian and acknowledged that an inscrutable Providence governed the destiny of nations in support of human liberty, he referred to God as "the Grand Architect of the Universe," "Governor of the Universe," "Higher Cause," "Great Ruler of Events," "All Wise Creator," and "the Supreme Dispenser of all Good"—distant, impersonal formulations more similar in style to the Stoic World Soul than to the highly personal Judeo-Christian God. Washington called religion and morality "the foundation of the fabric . . . [the] great Pillars of human happiness, [the] firmest props of the duties of Men and citizens." But references to Jesus are as rare in his writings as in those of Madison.[54]

John Adams initially wanted to become a minister but realized that his unorthodox opinions would get him into trouble. Adams wrote, "The Christian Religion as I understand it is the best," teaching natural law, the Golden Rule, and love of neighbor. He attended Congregationalist services. During the American Revolution Adams wrote: "It is religion and morality alone which can establish the principles upon which freedom can securely

stand. The only foundation of a free constitution is pure virtue."
But, like Jefferson, Adams considered the Holy Trinity a corruption of early Christianity and emphasized ethics over theology. He
believed that all religions possessed some truth: "I wish societies
were formed in India, China, and Turkey to send us gratis translations of their Sacred Books; one good turn deserves another." He
opposed the evangelical enthusiasm of John Wesley, saying that the
heart must be "controuled by the dominion of the head." He even
told his son, John Quincy, that the Christian doctrine that the creator of the world had been crucified was blasphemous, thereby
eliciting from his orthodox son a spirited rebuttal.[55]

Rather than completely rejecting theism, the founders interwove Christianity with classical philosophy. Under the shadow of
new scientific theories that appeared to reduce the universe to a
set of mathematical laws, many of the founders could no longer
accept the traditional Christian belief in direct divine intervention
in the world. They required "proofs" for the existence of God and
the afterlife, as well as earthly rewards for virtue, in case the afterlife proved an illusion.

But the psychological need to retain some elements of Christianity proved just as strong, for three reasons. First, like the early
Christian converts of the Roman Empire, the founders preferred
the warmth and benevolence of Christianity to the cold obligations of classical philosophy. After reminding his Epicurean head of
the numerous times in which the head had chosen safety over aiding those in need, Thomas Jefferson's Christian heart concluded,
"In short, my friend, as far as my recollection serves me, I do not
know that I ever did a good thing on your suggestion, or a dirty
one without it." After expressing admiration for *The Golden Verses
of Pythagoras*, with its maxims on the sanctity of oaths, the respect
due to parents, affection for friends, and connection to mankind,
John Adams nevertheless added, "How dark, mean, and meagre are
these Golden Verses, however celebrated and really curious, in
comparison with the Sermon on the Mount and the Psalms of
David or the Decalogue!" Second, the doctrine of the resurrection
and utopian afterlife provided tremendous comfort. Epicureanism
denied the existence of an afterlife, and the Stoic afterlife (reinte-

gration into the World Soul) was much too abstract for most people's taste. By reinterpreting Christianity in a classical light, the founders expected to have their cake of earthly progress and eat it in heaven. Finally, the reconciliation of Christianity with classical humanism served a vital emotional function. It saved the founders from the painful necessity of completely abandoning the religion of their ancestors and their countrymen.[56]

The founders were not the first to use classical ideas to satisfy the unique philosophical needs of their day. Just as Augustine had placed carefully selected elements of Platonism in the service of Christian theism, and just as the scholastics had done the same with Aristotle, so eighteenth-century intellectuals in both Europe and America used classical texts to support a version of humanism whose emphasis on progress and individual rights was distinctly modern.

NOTES

1. Thomas S. Kuhn, *The Copernican Revolution: Planetary Astronomy in the Development of Western Thought* (Cambridge, Mass.: Harvard University Press, 1957), 1, 66, 79, 91, 185; Peter Gay, *The Enlightenment: A Comprehensive Anthology* (New York: Simon & Schuster, 1973), 13.

2. Kuhn, *Copernican Revolution*, 42, 47, 50, 64, 71–72, 75, 138–40.

3. Kuhn, *Copernican Revolution*, 42, 72, 117, 143, 146–47.

4. Kuhn, *Copernican Revolution*, 200–201, 206–8.

5. Kuhn, *Copernican Revolution*, 130–31, 211–12.

6. Kuhn, *Copernican Revolution*, 146–47, 162–63, 179, 230.

7. Kuhn, *Copernican Revolution,* 219–25; Colin A. Ronan, *The Astronomers* (London: Evans Brothers, 1964), 150.

8. Stillman Drake, *Galileo at Work: His Scientific Biography* (Chicago: University of Chicago Press, 1978), 365–66; Kuhn, *Copernican Revolution*, 83, 86, 117–18, 121, 238–39.

9. Dudley Shapere, *Galileo: A Philosophical Study* (Chicago: University of Chicago Press, 1974), 135–36.

10. Kuhn, *Copernican Revolution*, 254.

11. Jacob Bronowski, *Science and Human Values*, 2d ed. (New York: Harper & Row, 1965), 15, 33; Kuhn, *Copernican Revolution*, 256–57; Ronan, *Astronomers*, 163–65, 169; Jon Butler, *Awash in a Sea of Faith: Christianizing the American People* (Cambridge, Mass.: Harvard University Press, 1990), 28; Henry F. May, *The Enlightenment in America* (Oxford: Oxford University Press, 1976), 6.

12. Kuhn, *Copernican Revolution*, 121, 261, 263; W. S. Fowler, *The Development of the Scientific Method* (New York: Penguin, 1962), 48, 51, 55–56.

13. Robert S. Lopez, *The Commercial Revolution of the Middle Ages, 950–1350* (Cambridge: Cambridge University Press, 1976), 39–40, 43–47, 56, 70–73, 77, 125, 157.

14. Lopez, *Commercial Revolution of the Middle Ages*, 95–99, 109, 157.

15. Andre Gunder Frank, *World Accumulation, 1492–1789* (New York: Monthly Review Press, 1978), 25, 36, 44, 50–53, 97, 110, 122, 213.

16. J. D. Chambers and J. E. Mingay, *The Agricultural Revolution, 1750–1880* (London: B. T. Batsford, 1966), 2, 4, 6, 9, 12, 34–36, 40, 54–57, 61, 63, 66–70.

17. Howard Mumford Jones, *Revolution and Romanticism* (Cambridge, Mass.: Harvard University Press, 1974), 128.

18. Maryanne Cline Horowitz, "The Stoic Synthesis of the Idea of Natural Law in Man: Four Themes," *Journal of the History of Ideas* 35 (January–March 1974):6, 9–10, 12–15.

19. Augustine, *On Free Choice of the Will*, trans. Anna S. Benjamin and L. H. Hackstaff (New York: Bobbs-Merrill, 1964), 49, 155.

20. Thomas Aquinas, *Summa Theologica*, trans. Fathers of the English Dominican Province, 3 vols. (New York: Benziger Brothers, 1947), vol. 1, 1, 398–99, 422–23, 851, 989; Alister McGrath, *The Intellectual Origins of the European Reformation* (Oxford: Basil Blackwell, 1987), 140.

21. Martin Luther, "Preface to the Epistle of St. Paul to the Romans," 1522, in *Martin Luther: Selections from His Writings*, ed. John Dillenberger (Garden City, N.Y.: Doubleday, 1961), 20; John Calvin, *Institutes of the Christian Religion*, trans. Henry Beveridge, 2 vols. (Grand Rapids, Mich.: Eerdmans, 1970), vol. 1, 64, 72; William J. Bouwsma, *John Calvin: A Sixteenth-Century Portrait* (Oxford: Oxford University Press, 1988), 139, 142, 147–48, 155.

22. Thomas Hobbes, *Leviathan, Parts I and II* (New York: Bobbs-Merrill, 1958), 120, 131; Paul K. Conkin, *Self-Evident Truths* (Bloomington: Indiana University Press, 1974), 88–89.

23. Conkin, *Self-Evident Truths*, 92, 95; Paul A. Rahe, *Republics, Ancient and Modern: Classical Republicanism and the American Revolution* (Chapel Hill: University of North Carolina Press, 1992), 509.

24. John Locke, *An Essay Concerning Human Understanding*, ed. A. D. Woozley (New York: Penguin, 1964), 12, 16–20, 89.

25. Alexander Pope, *Poems*, ed. John Butt (New Haven, Conn.: Yale University Press, 1963); Peter Gay, *The Enlightenment: An Interpretation*, 2 vols. (New York: Alfred A. Knopf, 1967, 1969), vol. 1, 142; vol. 2, 27, 272; Richard Steele, *The Tatler*, ed. Donald F. Bond, 3 vols. (Oxford: Clarendon Press, 1987), no. 25, vol. 1, 192–95; Joseph Rykwert, *The First Moderns: The Architects of the Eighteenth Century* (Cambridge, Mass.: MIT Press, 1980), 1–19, 288–326; Conkin, *Self-Evident Truths*, 100; May, *Enlightenment in America*, 118. Adam Smith is discussed more fully in chapter 5.

26. John Adams, diary, January 1759, in *The Diary and Autobiography of John Adams*, ed. L. H. Butterfield, 4 vols. (Cambridge, Mass.: Harvard University Press,

1961), vol. 1, 73; Richard M. Gummere, *The American Colonial Mind and the Classical Tradition: Essays in Comparative Culture* (Cambridge, Mass.: Harvard University Press, 1963), 110, 115; Jefferson to Henry Lee, May 8, 1825, in *The Writings of Thomas Jefferson*, ed. Albert Ellery Bergh and Andrew A. Lipscomb, 20 vols. (Washington, D.C.: Thomas Jefferson Memorial Association, 1903), vol. 16, 118–19.

27. James Wilson, "The Law of Nature," in *The Works of James Wilson*, ed. Robert Green McCloskey, 2 vols. (Cambridge, Mass.: Harvard University Press, 1967), vol. 1, 132–33, 145–46; James Wilson, "The Law of Nations," in *The Works of James Wilson*, ed. McCloskey, vol. 1, 164–65; James Wilson, "Man as Member of Society," in *The Works of James Wilson*, ed, McCloskey, vol. 1, 237; Rahe, *Republics, Ancient and Modern*, 564.

28. Richard M. Gummere, *Seven Wise Men of Colonial America* (Cambridge, Mass.: Harvard University Press, 1967), 74–75; Benjamin Rush, "The Influence of Physical Causes upon the Moral Faculty," 1786, in *The Selected Writings of Benjamin Rush*, ed. Dagobert Runes (New York: Philosophical Library, 1947), 181–82; Thomas Paine, "Examination of Prophecies, " 1804, in *The Writings of Thomas Paine*, ed. Moncure Daniel Conway, 4 vols. (New York: AMS Press, 1967), vol. 4, 410–11.

29. Jefferson to Peter Carr, August 10, 1787, in *The Papers of Thomas Jefferson*, ed. Julian P. Boyd, 26 vols. (Princeton, N.J.: Princeton University Press, 1950), vol. 12, 15; Jefferson to John Adams, August 22, 1813, in *The Adams–Jefferson Letters: The Complete Correspondence between Thomas Jefferson and Abigail and John Adams*, ed. Lester J. Cappon, 2 vols. (Chapel Hill: University of North Carolina Press, 1959), vol. 2, 368; Jefferson to Adams, October 14, 1816, in *The Adams–Jefferson Letters*, ed. Cappon, vol. 2, 492; Adams to Jefferson, September 14, 1813, in *The Adams–Jefferson Letters*, ed. Cappon, vol. 2, 374; Adams to Jefferson, May 3, 1816, in *The Adams–Jefferson Letters*, ed. Cappon, vol. 2, 471; Jefferson to Benjamin Waterhouse, June 26, 1822, in *The Writings of Thomas Jefferson*, ed. Bergh and Lipscomb, vol. 15, 385; Thomas Jefferson, in *The Complete Jefferson: Containing His Major Writings, Published and Unpublished, Except His Letters*, ed. Saul K. Padover (New York: Duell, Sloan, and Pearce, 1943), 1104; John Adams, diary, August 7, 1796, in *The Diary and Autobiography of John Adams*, ed. Butterfield, vol. 3, 239; John Adams, diary, August 13, 1796, in *The Diary and Autobiography of John Adams*, ed. Butterfield, vol. 3, 240.

30. Marie Kimball, *Jefferson: The Road to Glory, 1743–1776* (New York: Coward-McCann, 1943), 115.

31. Charles Page Smith, *James Wilson: Founding Father, 1742–1798* (Chapel Hill: University of North Carolina Press, 1956), 330–33.

32. Benjamin Franklin, *Benjamin Franklin: The Autobiography and Other Writings*, ed. L. Jesse Lemisch (New York: Penguin Books, 1961), 94–105.

33. G. E. R. Lloyd, *Greek Science after Aristotle* (New York: W. W. Norton, 1973), 40–50, 92–95, 100–6.

34. Henry C. Montgomery, "Washington the Stoic," *Classical Journal* 31 (March 1936): 371–72; James Thomas Flexner, *George Washington*, 4 vols. (Boston: Little, Brown, 1965–1969), vol. 1, 241.

35. Jefferson to Peter Carr, August 10, 1787, in *The Papers of Thomas Jefferson*, ed. Boyd, vol. 12, 16.

36. Peter Shaw, *The Character of John Adams* (Chapel Hill: University of North Carolina Press, 1976), 35.

37. Zoltan Haraszti, *John Adams and the Prophets of Progress* (Cambridge, Mass.: Harvard University Press, 1972), 60; Shaw, *Character of John Adams*, 272; Franklin, *Benjamin Franklin*, ed. Lemisch, autobiography, 95.

38. Thomas Jefferson to Charles Thomson, January 9, 1816, in *Jefferson's Extracts from the Gospels*, ed. Dickson W. Adams (Princeton, N.J.: Princeton University Press, 1983), 365; Jefferson to William Short, October 31, 1819, in *The Writings of Thomas Jefferson*, ed. Bergh and Lipscomb, vol. 15, 219, 223–24.

39. Jefferson to Robert Skipwith, August 3, 1771, in *The Papers of Thomas Jefferson*, ed. Boyd, vol. 1, 80; Jefferson to Peter Carr, August 19, 1785, in *The Papers of Thomas Jefferson*, ed. Boyd, vol. 8, 407; Jefferson to William Short, October 31, 1819, in *The Writings of Thomas Jefferson*, ed. Bergh and Lipscomb, vol. 15, 219–20; Jefferson to Charles Thomson, January 9, 1816, in *Jefferson's Extracts from the Gospels*, ed. Adams, 365.

40. Thomas Jefferson, A Bill for the Establishment of Religious Freedom, 1779, in *The Papers of Thomas Jefferson*, ed. Boyd, vol. 2, 545; Jefferson to John Adams, April 11, 1823, in *The Adams–Jefferson Letters*, ed. Cappon, vol. 2, 591, Adams to Jefferson, September 14, 1813, in *The Adams–Jefferson Letters*, ed. Cappon, vol. 2, 374; Jefferson to Benjamin Waterhouse, June 26, 1822, in *The Writings of Thomas Jefferson*, ed. Bergh and Lipscomb, vol. 15, 384–85; Edwin S. Gaustad, *Faith of Our Fathers: Religion and the New Nation* (San Francisco: Harper & Row, 1987), 76–77, 90; Franklin, *Benjamin Franklin*, ed. Lemisch, 92.

41. Jefferson to Miles King, September 26, 1814, in *The Writings of Thomas Jefferson*, ed. Bergh and Lipscomb, vol. 14, 197; Jefferson to John Adams, August 22, 1813, in *The Writings of Thomas Jefferson*, ed. Bergh and Lipscomb, vol. 13, 349; Thomas Jefferson, *Notes on the State of Virginia*, ed. William Peden (Chapel Hill: University of North Carolina Press, 1955), 159; Jefferson to John Adams, August 15, 1820, in *The Adams–Jefferson Letters*, ed. Cappon, vol. 2, 569; Jefferson to John Adams, April 8, 1816, in *The Adams–Jefferson Letters*, ed. Cappon, vol. 2, 468; Jefferson to John Adams, April 11, 1823, in *The Adams–Jefferson Letters*, ed. Cappon, vol. 2, 592.

42. Jefferson to Joseph Priestley, April 9, 1803, in *The Writings of Thomas Jefferson*, ed. Bergh and Lipscomb, vol. 10, 374; Jefferson to Benjamin Rush, April 21, 1803, in *The Writings of Thomas Jefferson*, ed. Bergh and Lipscomb, vol. 10, 383; Jefferson to John Brazier, August 24, 1819, in *The Writings of Thomas Jefferson*, ed. Bergh and Lipscomb, vol. 15, 210; Jefferson to William Short, October 31, 1819, in *The Writings of Thomas Jefferson*, ed. Bergh and Lipscomb, vol. 15, 220; Jefferson to Robert Skipwith, August 3, 1771, in *The Papers of Thomas Jefferson*, ed. Boyd, vol. 1, 80; Jefferson to John Adams, July 5, 1814, in *The Adams–Jefferson Letters*, ed. Cappon, vol. 2, 433.

43. Jefferson to Benjamin Waterhouse, June 26, 1822, in *The Writings of Thomas Jefferson*, ed. Bergh and Lipscomb, vol. 15, 385; Jefferson to Benjamin Rush, April 21, 1803, in *The Writings of Thomas Jefferson*, ed. Bergh and Lipscomb, vol. 10, 384; Jefferson to William Short, August 24, 1820, in *The Writings of Thomas Jefferson*, ed. Bergh and Lipscomb, vol. 15, 257; Jefferson to John Adams, April 11, 1823, in *The Adams–Jefferson Letters*, ed. Cappon, vol. 2, 594.

44. Jefferson to John Adams, July 5, 1814, in *The Adams–Jefferson Letters*, ed. Cappon, vol. 2, 432–33; Jefferson to William Canby, September 18, 1813, in *The Writings of Thomas Jefferson*, ed. Bergh and Lipscomb, vol. 13, 378; Jefferson to Benjamin Rush, September 23, 1800, in *The Writings of Thomas Jefferson*, ed. Bergh and Lipscomb, vol. 10, 175; Jefferson to Joseph Priestley, March 21, 1801, in *The Writings of Thomas Jefferson*, ed. Bergh and Lipscomb, vol. 10, 228; Jefferson to Charles Thomson, January 9, 1816, in *The Writings of Thomas Jefferson*, ed. Bergh and Lipscomb, vol. 14, 385–86; Jefferson to William Short, October 31, 1819, in *The Writings of Thomas Jefferson*, ed. Bergh and Lipscomb, vol. 15, 219–20; Jefferson to Short, August 4, 1820, in *The Writings of Thomas Jefferson*, ed. Bergh and Lipscomb, vol. 15, 258; Jefferson to Benjamin Waterhouse, June 26, 1822, in *The Writings of Thomas Jefferson*, ed. Bergh and Lipscomb, vol. 15, 385.

45. Gaustad, *Faith of Our Fathers*, 105.

46. Jefferson to John Adams, August 15, 1820, in *The Adams–Jefferson Letters*, ed. Cappon, vol. 2, 568–69; Jefferson to John Adams, October 12, 1813, in *The Adams–Jefferson Letters*, ed. Cappon, vol. 2, 385; Jefferson to John Adams, April 11, 1823, in *The Adams–Jefferson Letters*, ed. Cappon, vol. 2, 594; Jefferson to Augustus B. Woodward, March 24, 1824, in *The Writings of Thomas Jefferson*, ed. Bergh and Lipscomb, vol. 16, 18; Jefferson to Benjamin Rush, April 21, 1803, in *The Writings of Thomas Jefferson*, ed. Bergh and Lipscomb, vol. 10, 380.

47. Gaustad, *Faith of Our Fathers*, 102–3.

48. Gaustad, *Faith of Our Fathers*, 107.

49. Jefferson to John Adams, October 12, 1813, in *The Adams–Jefferson Letters*, ed. Cappon, vol. 2, 384; Jefferson to William Short, August 4, 1820, in *The Writings of Thomas Jefferson*, ed. Bergh and Lipscomb, vol. 15, 257–60; Jefferson to Short, October 31, 1819, in *The Writings of Thomas Jefferson*, ed. Bergh and Lipscomb, vol. 15, 220; Gaustad, *Faith of Our Fathers*, 102.

50. Jefferson to Peter Carr, August 17, 1785, in *The Papers of Thomas Jefferson*, ed. Boyd, vol. 8, 407.

51. Jefferson to Maria Cosway, October 12, 1786, in *The Papers of Thomas Jefferson*, ed. Boyd, vol. 10, 449–51.

52. Gaustad, *Faith of Our Fathers*, 61, 63–66; May, *Enlightenment in America*, 126–27, 129; Franklin to Ezra Stiles, March 9, 1790, in *Benjamin Franklin*, ed. Lemisch, 337; Max Farrand, ed., *The Records of the Federal Convention of 1787*, 3d ed., 4 vols. (New Haven, Conn.: Yale University Press, 1966), vol. 1, 451–52.

53. Gaustad, *Faith of Our Fathers*, 56–57.

54. Gaustad, *Faith of Our Fathers*, 76–79.

55. Gaustad, *Faith of Our Fathers*, 88–96; John Quincy Adams to John Adams, January 3, 1817, in *The Selected Writings of John and John Quincy Adams*, ed. Adrienne Koch and William Peden (New York: Alfred A. Knopf, 1946), 292.

56. Jefferson to Maria Cosway, October 12, 1786, in *The Papers of Thomas Jefferson*, ed. Boyd, vol. 10, 451; Haraszti, *John Adams and the Prophets of Progress*, 302.

4

THE ORIGINS AND
VARIETIES OF REPUBLICANISM

Humanism not only influenced the religious and philosophical beliefs of eighteenth- and nineteenth-century Americans, but also shaped their political theories. The confidence with which Americans advanced their often conflicting views stemmed from a strong belief in the power of human reason to uncover universal laws of politics, just as Newton had uncovered the physical laws of the universe.

Just as the Protestant Reformation had inaugurated an intense theological debate throughout the Western world, the American founders' need to justify resistance to British taxation and, ultimately, to construct a new republic, initiated a similar debate concerning political theory. Just as Protestants in Europe and America had fashioned ingenious arguments from materials afforded by the venerable Judeo-Christian tradition to address their most pressing concerns, the founders cleverly applied the equally revered classical political heritage to their own problems. The founders' common political terminology and common interpretation of the American Revolution created the illusion of consensus. They could agree that they were all "republicans" who endorsed popular sovereignty, natural law, mixed government, and a pastoral lifestyle. But after the Revolution, once the powerful enemy had been defeated, the illusion of consensus quickly evaporated. The founders began to realize, often to their horror, that they differed from one another fundamentally concerning the practical meaning of popular sovereignty and natural law. Furthermore, while some began transferring their allegiance from mixed government to representative democracy, others turned from the pastoral lifestyle that classical theorists had considered the foundation of republican government and advocated a new industrial order. Members of each side saw the other as betraying the core of republicanism, while considering their own departure from the classical orthodoxy a minor deviation.

POPULAR SOVEREIGNTY

The theory of popular sovereignty holds that a society's form of government must be based on popular consent. Popular sovereignty should not be confused with democracy. While popular sovereignty allows the people to choose their own form of government, democracy, or majority rule, is merely one possible choice. It is perfectly consistent with popular sovereignty for the people to choose a monarchical, oligarchic, or mixed form of government.

The concept of popular sovereignty can be traced back to ancient Greece and Rome. The Stoics placed a particular emphasis on the idea that all political authority derived from the people. Even the edicts of the Roman emperors were considered law not merely because they represented the will of the emperor, but also because the people had supposedly consented to that particular mode of legislation. The Roman jurist Ulpian declared, "The will of the prince has the force of law because the people conferred on him all its power."[1]

The Right of Rebellion

But the widespread acceptance of popular sovereignty left open the question of the conditions under which a people might justly rebel against a government. In a famous passage in his letter to the Romans (13:1–4), Paul contended that nothing could justify popular rebellion. Rulers were the agents of God and could not be forcibly deposed. But other Pauline passages (such as 1 Cor. 7:23) suggested that while the Christian must be prepared to endure oppression patiently for the sake of Christ, he must disobey any orders to renounce his religion or to engage in immoral acts. In other words, while the Christian must endure injury to himself patiently, he must absolutely refuse to commit any injury against either God or his fellow human beings. Peter agreed. While denying the right of rebellion against rulers (1 Pet. 2:7, 13–14), he also refused to obey laws against the preaching of Christianity, declaring: "We ought to obey God rather than men" (Acts 5:29). Similarly, Augustine argued that the Christian's duty to obey government was second only to his duty to obey God. In cases of conflict between the two he must disobey secular authority, but he must not commit violence against it.[2]

Ambrose began an alternate tradition that made obedience dependent on just rule, a view that acquired much force after the conquest of western Europe by the Franks, whose customs of royal election and contractual obligation left them ill disposed to absolute rule. Thomas Aquinas argued that resistance to tyranny was justified in those rare cases when the tyranny was so great that the horrible violence and chaos normally produced by rebellion would not be worse. Unjust laws were "acts of violence rather than laws . . . wherefore such laws do not bind in conscience." Aquinas added that, under certain circumstances, the Catholic Church could depose a ruler. Nevertheless, Aquinas cautioned against the constant changing of laws, much less rulers, because it diminished respect for law in general.[3]

While the Protestant reformers followed Paul in denying the right of rebellion to citizens acting alone, they asserted the right of lower magistrates to lead popular rebellions against higher magistrates. Martin Luther prohibited individual Christians from taking it upon themselves to employ force against their prince, while at the same time absolving them of any duty to follow him into unjust wars or other immoral acts. Like Jesus standing before Pontius Pilate, Christians must accept the unjust ruler's power while also rebuking him for his tyranny. Luther wrote: "Christians fight for themselves not with the sword and gun, but with the cross and suffering, just as Christ, our leader, does not bear a sword, but hangs upon the cross. . . . There is a big difference between suffering injustice and keeping still. We should suffer. We should not keep still.

The Christian must bear testimony for the truth and die for the truth." Luther's solution to the turmoil of the Reformation period was to have each prince select the *outward* religious practices of his kingdom (no one could dictate inner beliefs) in the interest of social unity; dissenters must then either immigrate to a region that conformed to their beliefs or remain silent. On the other hand, Luther contended that lower magistrates, such as the Protestant princes of Germany, had the right to lead their subjects into rebellion against higher magistrates, such as the Catholic Holy Roman Emperor. Likewise, while John Calvin chose flight to Geneva as the only proper response when persecuted in Catholic France, once in Geneva he fully expected the Protestant magistrates of that town to help him expel those who refused to conform to the Protestantism that prevailed there. Bad rulers were God's chastisement for human sin and must be obeyed, except when they commanded immoral acts. Calvin wrote: "In that obedience which we hold to be due to the commands of rulers, we must always make the exception, nay, must be particularly careful that it is not incompatible with obedience to Him to whose will the wishes of all kings should be subject. . . . If they command anything against Him let us not pay the least regard to it, nor be moved by all the dignity which they possess as magistrates—a dignity to which no injury is done when it is subordinated to the special and truly supreme power of God." But, while the individual Christian was obliged to disobey "the impious and wicked edicts of kings," the right of active resistance was confined to lower magistrates. The people should never take it upon themselves to inaugurate and lead a rebellion, however justified, but should follow the lead of magistrates.[4]

By stressing the sinfulness of popularly led rebellions, the Protestant reformers probably prevented more insurrections than they caused. Luther bitterly opposed a peasants' rebellion in Germany in 1524–1525. While rebuking the German princes for their abuse of the poor, Luther argued that if each man took matters into his own hands there would be "neither authority nor order, but only murder and bloodshed." Rebellion only replaced tyranny with anarchy and mob rule. Luther called rebellion "an unprofitable method" of redressing grievances that "never brings about the desired improvement [and] generally harms the innocent more than the guilty." He added: "No insurrection is ever right, no matter how right the cause it seeks to promote." Luther noted that the "Peasants' War" produced atrocities on both sides. Likewise, Calvin refused to sanction a Huguenot revolt against the French king Henry II (1547–1559).[5]

Calvin's Scottish disciple John Knox, the founder of the Presbyterian Church, was one of the few Protestant reformers who dissented from the view that average citizens had no right to lead a rebellion against tyrannical rule. Knox wrote treatises claiming that rebellion against ungodly monarchs like the English queen Mary Tudor was not only a right but a duty.[6]

In opposition to popular sovereignty, monarchists Jean Bodin and Thomas Hobbes argued that once the people relinquished their sovereignty to a ruler, they could not recover it. Conversely, German Protestant Johannes Althusius contended that sovereignty always rested with the people, although the people could delegate specific powers to a ruler under a compact. Popular sovereignty was inalienable. Even a people depraved enough to relinquish it could never do so. This was also the Puritan position. Algernon Sidney was the first prominent author, however, to take the radical view that a change in the system of government need not be dependent on unjust rule. Sidney argued for a continuous process of changing the covenant. John Locke was more conservative, arguing that only great and persistent tyranny justified a change in government form.[7]

The Means of Establishing Popular Consent

Theorists also disagreed about the proper means of establishing popular consent. Before the Puritans, consent had never implied participation. Popular consent was demonstrated by the mere absence of rebellion. But the Puritans decided that popular consent for the form of government could be established beyond doubt only through the drafting of written compacts, signed by every adult male. The first written constitution was the Fundamental Orders of Connecticut (1639). The written constitution is perhaps America's greatest contribution to political science. This distinctively American process for establishing consent underwent numerous revisions in the last quarter of the eighteenth century, a period in which Americans drafted and ratified twenty-five state and two federal constitutions. Americans eventually determined that consent must be established through drafting conventions, popular ratification of the constitution (or ratification conventions), and amendment procedures (or reconvention provisions). The drafting convention was a special convention whose delegates were elected for no other purpose than to draft a constitution. Hence it was a more progressive means of establishing popular consent than having legislatures, interested parties whose members had been elected for other reasons, draft constitutions. Direct popular ratification (or special ratification conventions) ensured that the constitution was approved by a majority of the citizens. Amendment procedures (or reconvention provisions) created a mechanism for peaceful change of the government form. In 1780 Massachusetts became the first state to provide for all three of these means of establishing consent for a constitution.[8]

The Shattering of the Illusion of Consensus Regarding Popular Sovereignty

But the early republican period revealed that the apparent consensus among patriots during the American Revolution concerning the right to rebel and the proper means of establishing consent was an illusion. In the 1790s members of the Democratic-Republican Party defended the French Revolution and the Whiskey Rebellion, insurrections the Federalists denounced. These disputes were preceded by a bitter controversy concerning methods of establishing consent for the U.S. Constitution. While all agreed that the Constitution was superior to the Articles of Confederation, the nation's first constitution, in its provisions for establishing popular consent, Antifederalists were infuriated by the extreme difficulty in amending the new Constitution, especially since they believed it granted the federal government too much power. Under the new Constitution, two-thirds of both houses of Congress had to propose an amendment, and three-quarters of the states had to approve it. Indeed, Thomas Jefferson continued to argue that a constitutional convention should be held every nineteen years to draft a new compact, which would again be submitted for popular approval. Only in this way could the consent of the governed be assured. Most Americans, including James Madison, the other leader of the Democratic-Republican Party, disagreed, considering so constant a process of constitutional change too destabilizing.[9]

Furthermore, the Constitution was deliberately vague ("we the people") regarding whether sovereignty was held by the people of the nation as a whole or by the people of the individual states separately. As a result of this vagueness, Jefferson and Madison felt justified in espousing the nullification doctrine, the theory that states, as the proper interpreters of the Constitution, could nullify federal laws they considered unconstitutional. (Madison later claimed he had been misinterpreted, but his assertion that states could "interpose their authority" between the federal government and the people clearly suggested some brand of nullification.) Although John Marshall was successful in substituting the Supreme Court's power of judicial review for the nullification doctrine—that is, substituting the federal courts for the states as the proper interpreters of the Constitution—antebellum southerners, led by John C. Calhoun, continued to issue eloquent defenses of the doctrine. Indeed, the very need for vagueness in the Constitution reveals the depth of sectional differences over the nature of popular sovereignty at the birth of the Republic.[10]

By the antebellum period most northerners, believing that the Constitution had created a system of national sovereignty, would argue that the federal Congress possessed complete power to prohibit slavery in the territories, while most southerners, believing it had created a system of state sovereignty, would declare that the Fifth Amendment protected any citizen's right to bring his property (slave) into any territory. In Thomas Hart Benton's phrase, these competing theories of sovereignty were the two blades of a pair of shears that would eventually sever the bonds of the Union.[11]

NATURAL LAW

Like popular sovereignty, natural law was an element of the republican tradition that evoked both reverence and contention. As we have seen, while nearly all theists and humanists shared a belief in natural law, orthodox theists believed that original sin prevented humans from fully comprehending it and, therefore, considered Scripture a preferable ethical guide. Though humanists shared a confidence in the human ability to understand natural law, they disagreed with one another concerning the method of comprehension. Some favored reason and experience, others intuition, most a combination of both.

Natural Rights

Western theorists disputed the content of natural law. Like nearly all who followed them, the Greeks rejected the notion of an absolute right to life. They approved of capital punishment for the most serious crimes. Liberty was equally circumscribed. Nearly all of the Greek city-states practiced military conscription and slavery. Indeed, in a famous passage, Aristotle suggested that some men were suited to be masters and others to be slaves (*Politics*, 1.2.1252). Neither Plato nor Aristotle recognized individual ownership of property as an inalienable right.[12]

Christian theologians agreed that rights were limited. Relying on Genesis 9:6 ("Whoever sheds man's blood, by man shall his blood be shed"), Augustine supported capital punishment and believed that killing was permissible in a "just war," though military victors were obligated to behave humanely. Augustine no more recognized an absolute right to death than an absolute right to life. He flatly condemned suicide, claiming that even Judas had been wrong to kill himself. Like Job, "who endured dreadful evils in his body rather than deliver himself from all torment by self-inflicted death," Judas should have trusted in God's mercy.[13]

Medieval theologians defined liberty as the individual's right to occupy his proper place in society. Complete liberty, like complete equality, was impossible. Men were spiritually equal, but since they were far from intellectually equal, they might legitimately opt for a system of political inequality. Slavery was justified only in cases in which the only alternative was death, as with some criminals or prisoners of war. Despite its own collectivized monasteries, the Catholic Church considered private property, like government itself, a regrettable necessity resulting from original sin. For most men private property was a necessary incentive to work, just as punishment was a necessary disincentive to crime. But wealth was a trust from God, not an end in itself, and should be shared. In times of dire need, the hungry could steal food without fault. Drawing on Scripture (Luke 6:35), on Augustine, and on other early church writers, most medieval theologians condemned the charging of interest on loans. Yet, under increasing pressure from bankers, the church eased its restrictions on usury in the late Middle Ages.[14]

Protestants were also restrictive in their definition of the right of property. Luther condemned the charging of interest except in rare cases, such as when elderly people with no other means of support lent out their money; even then no one should charge more than 6 percent (a sizable interest rate then). Calvin only grudgingly accepted the Genevan practice of charging 5 percent interest on loans. Early American Puritans expected their governments to set prices and prohibit usury. American colonists justified the seizure of Native American lands with the argument that the right to ownership of land was reserved for those who put it to productive use—a self-serving limitation on property rights, to be sure, but a limitation nonetheless.[15]

John Locke distinguished between "real property" and "artificial property." "Real property" was access to land and one's produce from it. Since the fruits of one's labor represented years of hard work, the right to their enjoyment was an extension of one's right to life. "Artificial property" included all other possessions, such as monetary wealth. While artificial property might be recognized and protected by societies for purposes of convenience, its possession did not constitute a natural right.[16]

During the American Revolution, the patriots were unanimous in denouncing the threat to their property posed by parliamentary taxation without representation and the danger to their liberty posed by the Intolerable (or Coercive) Acts. They cheered John Dickinson's rousing declaration in the *Letters from a Farmer in Pennsylvania* (1767–1768): "Let these truths be indelibly impressed upon our minds: that we cannot be happy without being free; that we cannot be free without being secure in our property; that we cannot be secure in our property if, without our consent, others may, as by right, take it away." They agreed that property rights were important not only in themselves but also as general measures of liberty; any government powerful enough to arbitrarily infringe on them was powerful enough to infringe on the individual's right to life and liberty as well. The patriot consensus was also expressed in the Declaration of Independence, which identified the three natural rights as "life, liberty, and the pursuit of happiness." (Jefferson's substitution of "pursuit of happiness" for "property" held little significance. It was an attempt to use the broadest possible language to define natural rights, not an attempt to extinguish the natural right of property. Jefferson copied the phrase from George Mason's Virginia Declaration of Rights, written earlier the same year.) Finally, the patriot consensus manifested itself in the drafting of state and federal bills of rights. Patriots often placed their bills of rights in the preambles of the state constitutions, which could not be amended, since natural rights were considered inalienable. When delegates to the Constitutional Convention omitted a bill of rights, partly because they feared any listing would be insufficient, the outcry was so great that supporters of the Constitution were forced to promise that a bill of rights would follow ratification of the Constitution as a set of amendments.[17]

The ten amendments that comprise the Bill of Rights were largely the work of James Madison, who was influenced by the English Bill of Rights and the Virginia Declaration of Rights. These amendments defined natural rights as freedom from a national religious establishment, freedom of speech and of the press, the right to assemble peaceably, the right to petition government, the right to bear arms, freedom from the quartering of soldiers in one's home without one's consent, freedom against unreasonable searches and seizures, freedom from arrest without stated cause, freedom from self-incrimination, the right to due process of law, the right to compensation for public use of one's property, the right to a speedy and fair trial by an impartial jury of one's peers, the right to confront witnesses against oneself, the right to an attorney, and freedom from cruel and unusual punishment. Since even this extensive list of rights was considered insufficient, the Ninth Amendment stated, "The enumeration in the Constitution, of certain rights, shall not be construed to deny or disparage others retained by the people." This amendment was a loophole designed to calm those who worried that any natural right overlooked in the Bill of Rights would be subject to perpetual infringement by the federal government.[18]

The Shattering of the Illusion of Consensus Concerning Natural Rights

But the illusion of consensus soon gave way to bitter disputes about the precise nature of these natural rights. While strict civil libertarians like Jefferson and Madison sought complete governmental impartiality concerning religion, others interpreted the right of religious freedom differently. While president, Jefferson even refused to issue broadly worded thanksgiving proclamations and to appoint days of prayer. He spoke of "a wall of separation between Church and State." Madison opposed the appointment of chaplains for Congress and the army. The Kentucky Bill of Rights of 1792 excluded clergy from office. Yet many state constitutions continued to employ religious language, and Massachusetts retained its establishment clause until 1830. Delaware and Maryland required that officeholders express a belief in Christianity, Pennsylvania and Tennessee that they express a belief in God, the afterlife, and the divine inspiration of Scripture. New Jersey, Georgia, South Carolina, Massachusetts, and New Hampshire allowed only Protestants to hold office. States continued to penalize blasphemy and violations of Sunday closing laws.[19]

Similar controversies swirled around freedom of speech. In 1798, during a period of hysteria caused by an undeclared naval war with France, a Federalist Congress passed the Sedition Act, which defined as seditious libel any "false, scandalous, and malicious" writings against the U.S. government. Federalists denied that the law violated the First Amendment, which stated that Congress could not "abridge" the right of free speech. They argued that by allowing truth as a defense in seditious libel cases, the act actually expanded free speech. (During the colonial period even truthful speech against the government had been defined as seditious. Since the sole intent of such laws had been to prevent insurrection, the truthfulness of seditious speech had been considered irrelevant, though, in practice, juries had often ignored the law, taken truth into account, and acquitted defendants.) Only fourteen Democratic-Republicans (mostly editors of extremely partisan and genuinely slanderous newspapers) were prosecuted, and only ten convicted, under the Sedition Act, and those convicted were mostly fined. Even the imprisoned editors continued to slander the government from prison. Many Americans continued to believe that the government had not only a right but an obligation to fine or imprison irresponsible editors. As president a few years later, Thomas Jefferson encouraged the governor of Pennsylvania to prosecute slanderous editors of the opposition party. Jefferson believed that states had the authority to punish slanderous editors but the federal government did not. But a growing number of Americans, outraged by government officials' employment of force against political opponents, began to define free speech more broadly.[20]

Conflicts concerning the right of property continued as well. Thomas Jefferson attempted to persuade the House of Burgesses to grant each Virginian fifty acres as a birthright. Although his interpretation of the right of property was clearly defeated, it continued to arise in the guise of various calls for land redistribution.[21]

The most serious dispute regarding natural rights concerned slavery. The realization that slavery constituted a monumental violation of the natural right of liberty caused a great deal of anxiety among both northern and southern leaders. During the early republican period American political leaders were content to abolish slavery in the northeastern states and in the Northwest Territory and to end the foreign slave trade. But it was not long before a vocal minority in the North challenged slavery in the South as well.[22]

MIXED GOVERNMENT

The consensus in favor of mixed government that had prevailed during the American Revolution collapsed in the early republican era as well. Mixed government had a long and venerable history. In the fifth century B.C. the Greek historian Herodotus (*Histories*, 3.80–82) alluded to three forms of government: monarchy, aristocracy, and democracy—rule by the one, the few, and the many. In the following century Plato (*Laws*, 756e–757a, 832c; *Politicus*, 291d–303c) claimed that each of these forms degenerated over time: monarchy into tyranny, aristocracy into oligarchy, and democracy into ochlocracy (mob rule). He suggested that the best form of government would be a mixed government, one that balanced the power of the three orders of society. (The theory represented a marked departure from the oligarchy of "guardians," led by a philosopher-king, that Plato had advocated in the *Republic* more than a decade earlier.) Aristotle then immortalized mixed government theory, making it the centerpiece of his *Politics* (3.7), in which he cited numerous examples of mixed government in the ancient world.

In the second-century B.C. the Greek historian Polybius presented the Roman republic as the most outstanding example of mixed government. He claimed that the Roman constitution, which had been constructed slowly through trial and error and had reached perfection at the time of the Second Punic War (218–201 B.C.), was the secret of Roman success. The interdependence between the one, the few, and the many minimized internal strife. The consuls (in this case, the "two" rather than the "one"), the aristocratic senate, and the popular assembly had balanced each other perfectly. Presented with the need to explain to his dazed and defeated compatriots among the Greeks how a group of western "barbarians" had managed to conquer "almost the whole inhabited world" (the Mediterranean basin), the historian understandably turned to a well-established Greek theory.[23]

But such was the beguiling clarity and simplicity of Polybius's analysis that he convinced many of the Romans themselves that their complex system of balances was the chief cause of their success. Cicero (*Republic* 2.23–30) seized upon Polybius's theory to thwart the increasing efforts of ambitious Romans to consolidate their own power at the republic's expense. Even the Roman emperors in the age that followed cloaked their edicts in the language and forms of the republic. Of course, modern historians note that the Roman republic, like many of the other highly touted examples of mixed government, was actually closer to an oligarchy than to a mixed government. The immense power of the senate overshadowed that of the consuls and the people.[24]

Nevertheless, mixed government theory dominated Western political thought for millennia, winning the support of such disparate theorists as Aquinas, Calvin, and Niccolò Machiavelli. The dominance of the mixed government tradition in Western political thought was not challenged until the rise of absolutism in the seventeenth century. Absolute monarchists Jean Bodin, Robert Filmer, and Thomas Hobbes, who were as revolutionary in their own way as latter-day democrats, attacked the hallowed theory of mixed government with great zeal. Bodin denied the possibility of such a thing as mixed government, arguing that the Roman republic had been a simple democracy. Since the only real choice lay between the simple systems, and since monarchy was the best of these systems (Bodin agreed with his opponents that democracy was the worst), reasonable men had no choice but to support monarchy. Filmer concurred, contrasting the paltry 480 years of the Roman republic with the millennia of ancient Near Eastern monarchies. Even during that time, the Roman republic's restlessness demonstrated its inability to find a decent form of government. Filmer argued that "Rome began her empire under Kings and did perfect it under Emperors; it did only increase under the popularity." Contending that effective government demanded the concentration of sovereignty in a monarch, Filmer concluded that mixed government was a vain "fancy." Similarly, Hobbes assaulted the traditional system of classical education that instilled the absurd belief in mixed government. He faulted Greek and Roman aristocrats for exaggerating the tyranny of monarchs and introducing the chimera of mixed government in order to restore an aristocratic form of government.[25]

English republicans responded to these unprecedented assaults on mixed government both by reasserting classical arguments against the simple systems and by adding Great Britain to their list of successful mixed governments. The king, the House of Lords, and the House of Commons joined the Roman government in the pantheon of mixed government theorists. Seventeenth-century Englishman James Harrington was the most important of these modern advocates of mixed government. It was Harrington who contributed a concept essential to any American adaptation of mixed government theory, the concept of "natural aristocracy." Even in a new country without a titled aristocracy, like his fictional utopia Oceana, certain men would possess greater talent than others. In any free society this natural difference in talent would produce unequal wealth. Unequal wealth would, in turn, produce class conflict. Mixed government, combined with a few laws limiting the size of landholdings, was the only means of preventing violent struggles between the classes and the tyranny that inevitably followed these civil wars. Hence Oceana's government consisted of a senate that represented the natural aristocracy, a huge assembly elected from the common people, and an executive to provide a balancing center of power. Harrington believed that such a system would produce good laws, which would, in turn, produce good men. Algernon Sidney shared Harrington's respect for mixed government. Mixed government theory was used to justify both the British system of government and the American colonial governments, which generally consisted of a royal governor, a small senate or upper house, and an assembly elected by the colonists.[26]

The Founders and Mixed Government

The founders of the United States had access to every level of this mixed government tradition. Hence it was only natural that, when confronted by unprecedented parliamentary taxation during the 1760s and 1770s, they should turn to the most ancient and

revered of political theories to explain this perplexing phenomenon. Patriot leaders such as Richard Henry Lee, Samuel Adams,
and John Adams ascribed the new tyranny to a degeneration of
the mixture of the English constitution. Although the form of the
British government remained the same, King George III had destroyed its delicate balance by using his patronage powers to buy
the House of Commons and to pack the House of Lords. This
corruption had then seeped into colonial governments, where
royal governors generally possessed the power to appoint the upper branch of the legislature. As in the nations of antiquity, the
source of tyranny was an inadequate mixture.[27]

The framers of the new state constitutions that emerged from
the American Revolution never doubted that their governments
should be mixed. Rather, their dilemma was how to mix them in a
society that no longer possessed a monarch and that had never possessed a titled aristocracy. The framers decided that these essential
roles should be played by an elected governor and by a senate consisting of Harrington's "natural aristocracy." Ten of the thirteen
states created a senate, nearly all of them establishing property qualifications for senate candidates that exceeded those for members of
the lower house. North Carolina and New York even established
special property qualifications for their senates' electors, a practice
that won James Madison's approval as late as 1788. Maryland went
even further, establishing an electoral college to select its senators.
When Virginia chose to have its upper house elected in the same
manner as its lower assembly, and when Pennsylvania decided to
eliminate its upper branch altogether, the resultant furor engulfed
both states. Unmollified by the creation of a long-termed Council
of Censors (based on the Spartan ephors and the Roman censors)
to monitor the single, democratic assembly, obstructionists finally
crippled the Pennsylvania Constitution, forcing the drafting of a
new constitution that replicated the mixture of the other state governments. Americans had decided that since education and talent
often accompanied wealth, and since wealth (unlike either talent or
virtue) could be easily quantified, property was the most appropriate criterion for identifying the "natural aristocracy" that would
provide their governments with the necessary senatorial stability.

The state senates were generally smaller than the lower houses, and senators generally served longer, staggered terms to diminish their vulnerability to popular pressure.[28]

Even Thomas Jefferson, the future champion of representative democracy, embraced mixed government theory during the Revolution. Young Jefferson had devoted more space in his legal and political commonplace book to the Baron de Montesquieu, the most famous modern advocate of mixed government, than to any other author. In 1776 Jefferson argued that "the wisest men" should be selected to the Virginia Senate and should be, "when chosen, perfectly independent of their electors." Experience taught Jefferson "that a choice by the people themselves is not generally distinguished for its wisdom," a sentiment echoed in his literary commonplace-book quotations. Hence he disliked the Virginia Constitution's provision for the direct election of senators. The first draft of his own proposed constitution established a nine-year, nonrenewable term, so that senators would not always "be casting their eyes forward to the period of election (however distant) and be currying favor with the electors, and consequently dependent on them." Jefferson could even accept Edmund Pendleton's suggestion "to an appointment for life, or to any thing rather than a mere creation by and dependence on the people." In 1782 Jefferson was still complaining about the Virginia Senate. He noted, "The purpose of establishing different houses of legislation is to introduce the influence of different interests or different principles." But since both of Virginia's houses were elected in the same manner, Virginia could not derive "those benefits" of a mixed system that compensated for its inconvenience. Jefferson also deplored the weakness of Virginia's governor, remembering his own troubles as governor during the Revolutionary War. Jefferson's proposal for a new Virginia constitution the following year favored the indirect election of senators and the elimination of all previous restrictions on the senate's power to originate or amend any bill. He added that the governor should appoint the state's judges, in order to make the jurists "wholly independent of the Assembly—of the Council—nay, more, of the people."[29]

John Adams was the most visible and most persistent proponent of mixed government in America. As early as 1763 he claimed, in "An Essay on Man's Lust for Power": "No simple Form of Government can possibly secure Men against the Violences of Power. Simple Monarchy will soon mould itself into Despotism, Aristocracy will soon commence on Oligarchy, and Democracy will soon degenerate into Anarchy, such an Anarchy that every Man will do what is right in his own Eyes, and no Man's life or Property or Reputation or Liberty will be safe." In 1772 he contended: "The best governments of the World have been mixed. The Republics of Greece, Rome, and Carthage were all mixed Governments." In 1776 Adams published *Thoughts on Government*, a series of essays urging the Virginia and North Carolina legislatures to establish mixed governments in their new constitutions. The pamphlets exerted a tremendous influence upon the framers of the state constitutions. In 1780 Adams played a leading role in drafting the Massachusetts Constitution, then widely considered the best of all the state constitutions. Under the Massachusetts Constitution representation in the senate was based upon the amount of taxes paid by each district. A higher property qualification was required for the senators' electors than for the representatives' electors. The governor was a limited, elective monarch who possessed the veto power, a fixed salary, and broad powers of appointment.[30]

In 1787 Adams wrote *A Defence of the Constitutions of Government of the United States of America*, which remains the fullest exposition of mixed government theory by an American. Adams summarized the genesis of the theory in Plato's work and its development by Aristotle, Polybius, and Cicero. While respecting later writers, such as Machiavelli, Harrington, Sidney, Locke, and Montesquieu, Adams considered these theorists overrated, emphasizing that "the best part" of their writings came directly from the ancients. Indeed, Machiavelli's shady reputation and Harrington's support for "agrarian acts" (land redistribution laws) tempered the conservative New Englander's admiration for both of these modern republicans.[31]

But Adams and the other founders did appreciate Montesquieu's greatest contribution, his popularization of the theory of the separation of powers, which held that the executive, legislative, and judicial functions of government should be separated into distinct branches. Adams considered the separation of powers necessary to a proper mixture in government. In his *Defence*, the first volume of which was circulated at the Constitutional Convention, Adams claimed that since the time when Lycurgus (now considered a mythical figure) first instituted mixed government in Sparta in the eighth century B.C., only three improvements had been made in the science of government: representation, the separation of powers, and the granting of the veto power to all three orders of society. Adams was particularly emphatic about the necessity of a high degree of separation of powers in a mixed government:

> If there is one certain truth to be collected from the history of all ages, it is this: That the people's rights and liberties, and the democratical mixture in a constitution, can never be preserved without a strong executive, or, in other words, without separating the executive power from the legislative. If the executive power, or any considerable part of it, is left in the hands of either an aristocratical or democratical assembly, it will corrupt the legislature as necessarily as rust corrupts iron, or as arsenic poisons the human body; and when the legislature is corrupted, the people are undone.[32]

Indeed, though Adams received both his general political theory and his principal supporting examples for that theory from the ancients, it was a theory substantially altered by the modern innovations Adams listed. Representation removed the people from direct participation in government. Based upon a suspicion of government alien to the ancients, Montesquieu's separation of powers balanced government branches rather than social orders. (Classical political theorists had not feared government power in general, only the excessive accretion of authority by its monarchical, aristocratic, or democratic branch. While they had strenuously denounced ambitious individuals or groups who attempted to seize too much power, as citizens of small societies possessing participatory government, they would not have understood the modern fear of "government encroachments on the people"—a formulation comprehensible only to modern republicans living in large societies and alienated from distant centers of power.) Based on the same suspicion of government, federalism, the balance between federal and state governments soon incorporated into the U.S. Constitution, was also largely a modern innovation, though the founders studied the few, surviving details concerning ancient Greek confederacies. Furthermore, the executive veto injected a greater degree of monarchical power into modern republics than had existed in the ancient republics. Most significant, although it failed to make Adams's list of modern innovations, was Harrington's concept of natural aristocracy, a concept essential to the American adaptation of mixed government. The eventual replacement of England's hereditary king and aristocrats by the United States with an elective monarch and an assembly of wealth necessarily increased the nation's distance from the classical republics.

The U. S. Constitution was as much a product of mixed government theory as the state constitutions. At the Constitutional Convention James Madison, the "Father of the Constitution," argued for a nine-year term for senators, declaring: "Landholders ought to have a share in the government to support these invaluable interests and to balance and check the other [the many]. They ought to be so constituted as to protect the minority of the opulent against the majority. The senate, therefore, ought to be this body; and to answer these purposes, they ought to have permanency and stability. Various have been the propositions; but my opinion is, the longer they continue in office, the better will these views be answered." It was useless to deny the existence of an American aristocracy, though there were no "hereditary distinctions," and though inequalities of wealth were minor by comparison with Europe. Madison continued: "There will be debtors and creditors, and an unequal possession of property, and hence arises different views and different objects in government. This, indeed, is the ground work of aristocracy; and we find it blended in every government, both ancient and modern." Madison concluded that even in his own day, America could not be regarded as "one homogeneous mass," and that there were recent "symptoms of a leveling spirit" which he feared might lead to "agrarian acts." Four years earlier, when Madison had chaired a committee to recommend books for congressional use, he had placed Aristotle's *Politics* at the top of his list of works on political theory.[33]

In *Federalist* 63 Madison asserted that "history informs us of no long-lived republic which had not a senate." He then related how the Spartan, Roman, and Carthaginian senates, whose members possessed lifetime terms, had acted as an "anchor against popular fluctuations." Madison further argued that the danger of a republic's being corrupted was "greater where the whole legislative trust is lodged in the hands of one body of men than where the concurrence of separate and dissimilar bodies is required in every public act." The operative word here is "dissimilar." Madison did not consider the U.S. Senate a mere redundancy, a democratic body that existed only to block any hasty legislation that might proceed from the other democratic body, the House of Representatives. Rather, it was obvious from the Senate's different manner of selection (it was to be selected by the state legislatures) and much longer term of office that it would house a natural aristocracy. Thus, Madison took care to assuage fears that the Senate would convert the government into an oligarchy by demonstrating that in Sparta, Rome, and Carthage, it was encroachment by the representatives of the people, and not by the senate, that had corrupted the republic. He concluded, "It proves the irresistible force possessed by that branch of a free government which has the people on its side." Evidently, the U.S. Senate was not that branch intended to "have the people on its side." In his notes for the essay Madison cited Aristotle, Polybius, and Cicero as his sources. In the previous essay he had also referred to "the dissimilarity in the genius of the two bodies" that were to form the U.S. Congress. Madison warned Thomas Jefferson: "Wherever the real power in Government lies, there is the danger of oppression. In our Governments the real power lies in the majority of the Community, and the invasion of private rights is chiefly to be apprehended not from acts of Government contrary to the sense of its constituents, but from acts in which the Government is the mere instrument of the major number of the constituents."[34]

Alexander Hamilton advocated mixed government as well. Hamilton's outline for a speech given at the Constitutional Convention on June 18, 1787, a speech in which he advocated lifetime terms for both the president and the Senate, included these statements:

> Here I shall give my sentiments of the best form of government—not as a thing attainable by us, but as a model which we ought to approach as near as possible. British constitution best form. Aristotle—Cicero—Montesquieu—Neckar. Society naturally divides itself into two political divisions—the few and the many, who have distinct interests. If a government [is] in the hands of the few, they will tyrannize over the many. If [it is in] the hands of the many, they will tyrannize over the few. It ought to be in the hands of both; and they should be separated.

He added that the voice of the people was not the voice of God. Hamilton concluded: "Nothing but a permanent body [a lifetime senate] can check the imprudence of democracy." Eight days later, Hamilton opposed Roger Sherman's measure to reduce the senators' term of office, reminding him that the House of Representatives would act as "the democratic body." Hamilton further noted that the absence of legal distinctions in America between citizens did not mean that American society was homogeneous. Inequality of property still constituted "the great & fundamental distinction in Society." At the New York ratifying convention Hamilton declared: "There are few positions more demonstrable than that there should be, in every republic, some permanent body to correct the prejudices, check the intemperate passions, and regulate the fluctuations, of a popular assembly."[35]

Other Federalists endorsed the Constitution because it established a mixed government. Gouverneur Morris, George Wythe, and John Dickinson all championed mixed government at the Constitutional Convention. Morris warned of the usual "encroachments of the popular branch of Government" and suggested an absolute veto by the president as the remedy. Wythe echoed Morris's concern. Dickinson insisted that the Senate "should consist of the most distinguished characters, distinguished for their rank in life and their weight of property, and bearing as strong a likeness to the House of Lords as possible," a body that would combine "the families and wealth of the aristocracy" in order to "establish a balance that will check the Democracy." To ensure that the Senate possessed such a character Pierce Butler and John Rutledge opposed the payment of salaries to its members. In a subsequent pamphlet Dickinson argued that the ambitions of the popular branch were most to be feared, having killed the republics of Carthage, Rome, and Athens. Noah Webster claimed that there were a thousand examples of the failure of "pure democracy," contended that the Roman masses had "extorted" powers from the senate, and concluded that the U.S. Constitution was similar, though superior, to the illustrious mixed constitutions of Britain and Rome.[36]

James Wilson was yet another Federalist advocate of mixed government. He recognized that the Constitution would not establish mixed government in a strict classical sense; no branch of the government would be the province of a hereditary aristocracy. But Wilson also recognized that the Constitution did not propose a democracy, either. The indirect election and lengthy term of the senators would ensure that a natural aristocracy would dominate the Senate. Hence, Wilson concluded: "What is the nature and kind of that government which has been proposed for the United States by the late Convention? In its principle, it is purely democratical. But the principle is applied in different forms, in order to obtain the advantages, and exclude the inconveniences, of the simple modes of government." Having defined mixed government narrowly, Wilson was left without a label for the new government, a predicament he might have avoided by simply calling it a new type of mixed government. Numerous other Federalists supported the Constitution on that very basis.[37]

The Antifederalist Counterattack

Recognizing that mixed government theory provided the theoretical foundation for the Constitution, most Antifederalists either assaulted it vigorously or denied its applicability to the American context. In a fashion ironically similar to that of the seventeenth-century monarchists, the Antifederalist essayist "Centinel" denied that such a thing as mixed government had ever existed. (Centinel was certainly correct concerning Great Britain. Even as he wrote, George III's mental illness was undermining the British monarchy. In addition, the House of Commons remained a misnomer until the mid-nineteenth century as a result of high property qualifications for voting. Great Britain might more aptly have been termed a simple oligarchy than a mixed government.) Furthermore, Centinel argued, even if mixed government was possible, it would promote a lack of responsibility, since the various branches would blame one another for government incompetence or corruption. By contrast, the most responsible government would have a simple structure consisting of one legislative body chosen for a short term. The federal government under the Articles of Confederation, which the Federalists were seeking to displace, was, of course, just such a government. Unlike Centinel, James Monroe accepted the Roman and British governments as models of mixed government but maintained that the American context was entirely different, necessitating government founded on "different principles."[38]

But whatever disagreements existed among Antifederalists over the possibility of mixed government in the abstract, all agreed that the Constitution would not establish one. Rather, the Antifederalists claimed it would produce an oligarchy. As proof of that assertion, Antifederalists generally cited the small number of delegates to be elected to the House of Representatives and, hence, the large size of their electoral districts. As William Grayson of Virginia put it: "If we look at the democratic branch, and the great extent of the country . . . it must be considered, in a great degree, to be an aristocratic representation." He feared that the House "might unite with the other two branches" against the people. Samuel Chase of Maryland agreed. He asserted: "I object [to the Constitution] because the representatives will not be the representatives of the people at large, but really of a few rich men. . . . In fact, no order or class of the people will be represented in the House of Representatives—called the Democratic branch—but the rich and wealthy. They will be ignorant of the sentiments of the middling (and much more of the lower) class of citizens." The large size of the House of Representatives' districts was proof, Antifederalists felt, that the proponents of the Constitution were merely utilizing mixed government theory as a respectable cloak for shameless oligarchical schemes.[39]

The Epicurean Humanism of Both Sides in the Debate

The debate between the Federalists and Antifederalists over mixed government reveals their shared Epicurean humanism. Both sides agreed that humans had acted in a depraved fashion in the past, and both sought to prevent future depravity through a rational rearrangement of the environment. While most Antifederalists believed they could create a virtuous society through proper education accompanied by majority rule, most Federalists believed they could create such a society through a balance in government among the three orders.

John Adams expressed the latter view well. While far from deeming a nation's educational system irrelevant, he argued: "Millions must be brought up, whom no principles, no sentiments derived from education, can restrain from trampling on the laws: orders of men, watching and balancing each other, are the only security; power must be opposed to power, and interest to interest. . . . Religion, superstition, oaths, education, laws, all give way before passions, interest, and power, which can be resisted only by passions, interest, and power." Having reviewed the horrors of the Peloponnesian War, Adams concluded: "Such things ever will be, says Thucydides, so long as human nature continues the same. But if this nervous historian had known a balance of three powers, he would not have pronounced the distemper so incurable, but would have added—so long as parties in cities remain unbalanced." Thus, even so pessimistic a man as John Adams—the same man who charged Polybius with excessive optimism for assuming that the first generation to acquire power would not be corrupted by it—could write that it was possible for a constitution to last forever, if it only possessed the proper balance between the orders. Adams explained: "The best republics will be virtuous and have been so; but we may hazard a conjecture that the virtues have been the effect of the well-ordered constitution, rather than the cause: and perhaps it would be impossible to prove that a republic cannot exist even among highwaymen, by setting one rogue to watch another; and the knaves themselves may, in time, be made honest by the struggle."[40]

The Democratic-Republican Party's Rejection of Mixed Government Theory

In the 1790s Madison, Jefferson, and other Democratic-Republicans clearly distanced themselves from mixed government theory. As early as 1788 Madison began expressing ambivalence concerning the theory. Though taking a clear mixed government position at the Constitutional Convention and in *Federalists* 47, 62, and 63, Madison's *Federalist* 10 proposed a different solution to the problem of majority tyranny. Madison suggested that, unlike the ancient republics, a modern commercial nation like the United States possessed more than two factions, "the few" and "the many." For instance, planters and merchants, though both wealthy, possessed different interests. Furthermore, Madison recognized that not only economic, but also religious and ideological, considerations would create factions. Hence the number of factions in the United States would be so great that majorities must be weak coalitions, incapable of prolonged tyranny. (Representation would enhance this effect by preventing majorities from acting on sudden impulse.) As the years passed, Madison clung ever more fervently to this solution to the problem of majority tyranny, a solution that not only seemed more appropriate to the American situation but also justified a form of government more popular with the public.[41]

Madison's opposition to mixed government theory hardened as a result of Hamilton's fiscal measures, such as the national debt-funding plan, the national bank, and the protective tariff, policies that Madison believed were designed to create an oligarchy. In a 1792 *National Gazette* essay Madison attacked mixed government theory. Of the British model of mixed government, he wrote,

"Those who ascribe the character of the British Government to the form alone in which its powers are distributed & counterpointed forget the changes which its form has undergone." The simple oligarchy of feudal England had lasted longer than its newly balanced government had thus far. The form of government was less important than public opinion, which determined the form. (Public opinion was itself influenced by the form of government but not entirely.) Madison added: "If the nation [Britain] were in favour of absolute monarchy, the public liberty would soon be surrendered by their representatives. If a republican form of government were preferred, how could the monarch resist the national will?" A month earlier he had declared, "Public opinion sets bounds to every government, and is the real sovereign in every free one." Madison seemed not to consider that if he were correct, his own favorite institutional checks, such as the separation of powers and the balance between federal and state governments, were equally futile.[42]

When arranging his notes on the Constitutional Convention for posthumous publication, in 1821, Madison clearly repudiated mixed government theory. He admitted that he had been wrong to support a property qualification for the electors of the House of Representatives, since such a qualification would enable the propertied to oppress those without property, who must one day be the majority. He added that an alternate plan to confine the right of suffrage for one branch to the propertied and for the other branch to the poor was also a bad idea, because "the division of the State into the two Classes, with distinct & independent Organs of power, and without any intermingled Agency whatever, might lead to contests & antipathies not dissimilar to those between the Patricians and Plebeians at Rome." Madison now believed that the division between the propertied and those without property need not overshadow all others and, in so doing, endanger the republic. But to separate the two into distinct branches would be to highlight the distinction. It would be much better to allow these two large groups to fragment on the basis of other considerations. This statement, of course, represented a marked departure from his position at the Constitutional Convention, when he had urged the creation of a "body of the opulent" to protect the propertied from "agrarian acts."[43]

Thomas Jefferson, the other leader of the Democratic-Republican Party, also shifted his support from mixed government to representative democracy in the 1790s. Jefferson's support for the U.S. Constitution had been lukewarm at best; he told James Madison, its leading drafter, that he considered it an interesting first effort but not the best constitution the nation could obtain. By 1790 he had turned against the revered Montesquieu, repudiating the Frenchman's "falsehoods" and "heresies." In 1816 Jefferson expressed his new attitude concerning ancient political theory: "The introduction of this new principle of representative democracy has rendered useless almost everything written before on the structure of government; and, in a great measure, relieves our regret, if the political writings of Aristotle, or of any other ancient, have been lost, or unfaithfully rendered or explained to us." This opinion constituted a significant change from 1787, when Jefferson had sent Madison copies of Polybius's *Histories* at the Constitutional Convention.[44]

PASTORALISM AND REPRESENTATIVE DEMOCRACY

But Jefferson and most other Democratic-Republicans did not base their endorsement of representative democracy on Madison's theory regarding the advantages of modern commercial republics. Rather, most Democratic-Republicans sought the support of the classical pastoral tradition, a heritage as ancient and revered as mixed government theory. Democratic-Republicans comforted themselves with the notion that the United States could safely adopt a democracy, however vilified by classical political theorists, partly because it would feature such "modern improvements" as representation and the separation of powers, but largely because the abundance of land in the United States would allow a citizenry of virtuous farmers. When cutting the trusty anchor of mixed government theory, Democratic-Republicans assuaged their anxiety by fastening the anchor of classical pastoralism with even greater firmness. However ingenious they might be, theories concerning the superiority of modern institutions were, by their very nature, untested, and hence lacked the authority required to reassure a generation raised on ancient verities. Just as the old myth of mixed government had proven a necessary catalyst for the new reality of the U.S. Constitution, so the ancient legend of classical pastoralism proved essential to creating the new reality of representative democracy.

No theme was more ubiquitous in classical literature than that of the moral superiority of the rural, agricultural existence, a lifestyle wedged comfortably between the extremes of "savage" and "sophisticated." The theme began as the motif of such Greek poets as Hesiod and Theocritus and then became the central theme of Virgil and Horace, the leading poets of Rome's Augustan Age. Convinced that farmers were the backbone of Rome, Virgil (*Georgics*, 2.458–474) exhorted his fellow Romans to regenerate the community after a century of civil war by returning to the plow. Virgil claimed that the farmer's lifestyle was the source of republican virtue.[45]

The pastoral theme was as much a staple of classical political theory and history as of Greek and Roman poetry. Aristotle argued that the best republics were predominantly agricultural. The classical historians considered Sparta and republican Rome models not merely because they had possessed mixed governments, but also because they had been agricultural societies. The historians attributed the triumph of Sparta and Rome over their vice-ridden, commercial adversaries, Athens and Carthage, as much to their pastoral virtues as to their government forms. Both produced virtue, the agricultural life by fostering frugality, temperance, and independence, the balanced constitution by requiring moderation, cooperation, and compromise. Furthermore, classical historians attributed the fall of the Roman republic to "the Punic Curse," the commercialization of Rome that had resulted from the republics' conquest of the Carthaginian Empire. The curse of commercial wealth had transformed Rome from a modest village into an imperial city. Whether by choice or necessity, farmers had abandoned the soil for the iniquitous life of the city. Deprived of the dignity afforded by an independent means of sustenance, these former bastions of republicanism had become the clients of dictators, prepared to sell the once-glorious republic for the paltry price of bread and circuses. Disgruntled by their forced subservience to emperors, the aristocratic poets and historians who painted this compelling portrait idealized an epoch that their class had dominated, though their own luxurious lifestyles would hardly have suited them to the rustic existence their works immortalized. Like most worshipers of agriculture who succeeded them, the Roman pastoralists lived a life distant from the manual labor they extolled. Far less romantic about their lot, many of the farmers the pastoralists glorified preferred the freedom from "noble toil" that life in the city afforded. As in the case of mixed government, these Roman aristocrats offered an ideal whose simple beauty remains powerful, however unreflective of reality and however self-interested in origin.[46]

As with mixed government, the founders derived the pastoral tradition both directly from the ancients, who formed the core of the classical curriculum, and through the medium of modern authors. Having spread throughout the Middle Ages and the Renaissance, pastoralism achieved a virtual cult status in seventeenth- and eighteenth-century England and France. James Harrington praised farmers for their love of liberty, moderated by a stability that he found lacking in the city-dwellers of Athens. An enthusiastic supporter of agriculture, King George III was fond of his nickname "Farmer George." Both Farmer Georges, the king and the rebel Washington, corresponded with Arthur Young, one of the high priests of the eighteenth-century pastoral movement. Young declared, "Perhaps we might, without any great impropriety, call farming the reigning taste of the present times."[47]

Thomas Jefferson cherished the pastoral tradition. His favorite books on agriculture were Columella's *De re rustica* and Adam Dickson's *Husbandry of the Ancients*. Like other Virginia aristocrats, Jefferson designed his estate to resemble the Roman villas Pliny and Varro had described. He also planned the inscription of a passage from Horace extolling the joys of the rural life (*Epodes*, 2.1–4, 7–8, 23–34, 39–40, 43–48, 61–66) near a small temple that he hoped to build on his burial ground. As the historian Gilbert Chinard noted, Jefferson removed from the text of Horace's epode those parts that described elements absent from eighteenth-century Virginia life (shrill war clarions and vineyards, for example). By condensing a poem of seventy-two lines into thirty-two, he presented a picture, however idealized, of his own time and place.[48]

In a famous passage in his *Notes on the State of Virginia*, Jefferson glorified agriculture in a manner reminiscent of the *Georgics*: "Those who labor in the earth are the chosen people of God, if ever he had a chosen people, whose breasts He has made His peculiar deposit for genuine and substantial virtue. . . . The mobs of great cities add just so much to the support of pure government as sores do to the strength of the human body. It is the manners and spirit of a people which preserve a republic in vigor." The secret to republican success was pastoral virtue. Jefferson later wrote: "Cultivators of the earth are the most valuable citizens. They are the most vigorous, the most independent, the most virtuous, and they are tied to their country and wedded to its liberty and its interests by the most lasting bonds." Hence Jefferson predicted: "I think our governments will remain virtuous for many centuries; as long as they are chiefly agricultural; and this will be as long as there shall be vacant lands in any part of America."[49]

Ironically, the same pastoralism that elicited dread and sorrow from Jefferson's favorite classical poets and historians inspired hope and confidence in the Virginian. Jefferson expected that centuries must pass before the vast lands of the West were fully settled. Thus, the same ideology that evoked nostalgia from the imperial literati of Rome could be a source of encouragement to an American sitting on the edge of a fertile and lightly settled continent.

Jefferson's passionate embrace of the pastoral tradition colored his perceptions of the world. So determined was he to perpetuate the agricultural character of the United States that he was willing to violate strict construction of the Constitution, one of the core principles of the Democratic-Republican Party, in order to purchase Louisiana. When the absence of a constitutional provision allowing Jefferson to buy territory threatened the future of the Republic's agricultural base, and hence its virtue and longevity, Jefferson reluctantly sacrificed his constitutional scruples to extend the life of the

Republic. The Virginian frequently compared the British commercialism he detested with that of the Carthaginians, implying an analogy between the United States and the frugal Roman republic.[50]

Even the sober Madison occasionally fell into this romanticism regarding agriculture. In 1792 he declared that virtue was the "patrimony" of farmers, who were "the best basis of public liberty and the strongest bulwark of public safety." If Madison differed from Jefferson in placing a greater reliance on the balancing of interests as the favored remedy in combating the decay that had claimed all previous republics, it was because he was haunted by a specter that seemed to Jefferson but a distant cloud. From the time of the Constitutional Convention, if not before, Madison feared and prepared for the day when the continent would be filled, and the numbers of the landless would exceed those of the landed. What else but a balance of interests would then save the Republic from destruction by social vice? While Madison's belief in pastoral virtue separated him from most Federalists, his tendency to place greater reliance upon institutional checks as a republican preservative separated him from most of his fellow Democratic-Republicans.[51]

THE DIVISION OF THE CLASSICAL REPUBLICAN LEGACY

It was as if pure classical republicanism died in the 1790s, and its heirs divided the intellectual legacy. The Federalists retained custody of mixed government theory, while the Democratic-Republicans kept the classical pastoralism. Each party became half-classical, half-modern: The Democratic-Republicans remained pastoral but embraced the new democracy; the Federalists remained aristocratic but embraced the new industry. Hamilton envisioned a wealthy and powerful republic populated by entrepreneurs. A strong central government would unite the nation and ensure prosperity for all its citizens by its wise measures. Its best citizens would be the knowledgeable, the cultured, and the enterprising. Although both the Jeffersonian and the Hamiltonian philosophies were revised during the antebellum period (*all* political parties would soon be forced to adopt a more democratic tone), the vision of the Jacksonian Democrats greatly resembled that of the Jeffersonian Democratic-Republicans, Henry Clay's Whigs that of the Hamiltonian Federalists.[52]

THE MODERN AMERICAN SYSTEM: A HYBRID

Faced with the increasing unpopularity of mixed government theory among the reigning Democratic-Republicans, John Adams became increasingly pessimistic. By the first decade of the nineteenth century he had come to the terrifying conclusion that the mixed government established by the Constitution of 1787 was being transformed, in substance if not in form, into a simple democracy, a form of government he equated with majority tyranny. Divisions between political parties were replacing the intended division between branches. In 1806 Adams declared: "I once thought our Constitution was quasi or mixed government, but they have now made it, to all intents and purposes, in virtue, in spirit, and effect, a democracy. We are left without resources but in our prayers and tears, and having nothing that we can do or say, but the Lord have mercy upon us." By "they," Adams meant the Democratic-Republicans, and particularly Jefferson, whose administration he considered subversive of the intent of the drafters of the Constitution. Ironically, since Jefferson had quickly reinterpreted the Constitution as having established a representative democracy, he had come to the same conclusion about Adams. Jefferson had himself complained, in the 1790s, that Adams's administration of the government was subversive of the spirit of the document. It was of little consolation to Adams that his interpretation of the intent of the drafters was more accurate than Jefferson's. It was Jefferson's that prevailed.[53]

Nevertheless, Adams's judgment was overly pessimistic. The modern American political system is a hybrid of democracy and mixed government. The rise of political parties, combined with other developments, democratized American politics. (These other developments include the linkage of the selection of the electoral college with the popular vote, accomplished before

Adams's death in 1826, and the ratification of the Seventeenth Amendment, which provided for the direct election of senators, in 1913.) Yet elements of mixed government remain. The justices of the Supreme Court, whose power has grown steadily, are still appointed for life by the president, who is still indirectly elected. The senators' larger electoral districts still foster a more aristocratic representation than the House of Representatives (it requires a great deal more money to run for the Senate), while the equality of states in the Senate favors small states. Hence the passage of congressional legislation requires more than simple majority support. Ironically, in their effort to emulate the systems of Sparta, Rome, and Great Britain, whose status as mixed governments was dubious at best, the founders of the United States may have created the first real mixed government in history—though mixed in a modern sense.

Classical mixed government, as defined by purists like Adams, was more the victim of its own fundamental inadequacy than of latter-day changes. The rise of political parties so soon after the establishment of the new government, parties that failed to follow class lines and received support from each branch of government, was proof that Adams's understanding of the interests that divided the United States was too simplistic. Adams failed to see that mixed government, in its rigid Polybian form, was unsuited to a modern commercial nation like the United States. James Madison was correct in noting that modern commercial nations were heterogeneous, possessing more than Polybius's two interests, the few and the many.

THE CIVIL WAR: A FAILURE
OF MIXED GOVERNMENT

The Civil War was, in large part, a product of the failure of American mixed government. When the South became too much of a minority to retain its senatorial and presidential veto powers, and the northern majority refused to obey the Supreme Court's *Dred Scott* decision, which prohibited the abolition of slavery in the territories, many southerners feared they had lost their ability to defend themselves against all manner of northern legislation (not only antislavery laws, but also high protective tariffs on manufactured goods which taxed the South for the benefit of northern factory owners). Many southerners felt that they were faced with a choice between submission to majority tyranny and secession. (Of course, these same southern whites were practicing a more severe form of majority tyranny against the slave population.) They chose secession. Yet, though a minority, the southern white population was large enough and concentrated enough to prosecute a war that inflicted more American casualties than all of the nation's other wars combined.[54]

By the early republican period the word "republicanism" evoked such contrary images in each political party it is no wonder that each thought the worst of the other. Here are men going around calling themselves "republicans" and exalting popular sovereignty and natural law while advocating measures inimical to both, it was frequently said. The same men have the gall to call themselves republicans while also repudiating either mixed government or the pastoral lifestyle. The opposition must, therefore, be liars and conspirators, plotting the downfall of the "republic." The tendency to claim for one's party the exclusive right to employ terminology considered nearly sacred greatly exacerbated tensions—especially when combined with a system of education that socialized young children in the works of classical and British Whig historians who maintained that cunning individuals were constantly plotting against liberty. When confined to political parties, these factors resulted only in overheated rhetoric and improbable conspiracy theories. But when further intensified and employed by the leaders of geographical sections, they resulted in a national tragedy.

Like the blind men in the fable, Americans were all feeling the same great elephant of republicanism. Some had hold of a trunk, others a leg. When all began pulling on their own end, they tore the living organism apart in a bloody civil war. It was finally reassembled, though into a different organism, when one party was able to force the other to concede its image of what an elephant should be.

NOTES

1. Frederick B. Artz, *The Mind of the Middle Ages, A.D. 1200–1500: An Historical Survey*, 3d ed. (New York: Alfred A. Knopf, 1962), 271; H. Outram Evennett, *The Spirit of the Counter-Reformation* (Cambridge: Cambridge University Press, 1968), 91.

2. Elaine Pagels, *Adam, Eve, and the Serpent* (New York: Random House, 1988), 118.

3. Paul K. Conkin, *Self-Evident Truths* (Bloomington: Indiana University Press, 1974), 4; Thomas Aquinas, *Summa Theologica*, trans. Fathers of the English Dominican Province, 3 vols. (New York: Benziger Brothers, 1947), vol. 1, 1020, 1023; Artz, *Mind of the Middle Ages*, 290.

4. Martin Luther, *The Freedom of a Christian*, 1520, in *Martin Luther: Selections from His Writings*, ed. John Dillenberger (Garden City, N.Y.: Doubleday, 1961), 78; Martin Luther, *Secular Authority*, 1523, in *Martin Luther*, ed. Dillenberger, 78, 366, 373, 379, 388, 399; Roland H. Bainton, *Here I Stand: A Life of Martin Luther* (New York: Abingdon-Cokesbury, 1950), 188–89, 206, 212, 243–45, 274; Mark U. Edwards Jr., *Luther's Last Battles: Politics and Polemics, 1531–1546* (Ithaca. N.Y.: Cornell University Press, 1983), 24–25, 30–31, 52; Steven Ozment, *The Age of Reform, 1250–1550: An Intellectual and Religious History of Late Medieval and Reformation Europe* (New Haven, Conn.: Yale University Press, 1980), 271, 357, 367, 372, 419; John Calvin, *Institutes of the Christian Religion*, trans. Henry Beveridge, 2 vols. (Grand Rapids, Mich.: Eerdmans, 1970), vol. 2, 653, 659, 673, 675–76; William J. Bouwsma, *John Calvin: A Sixteenth-Century Portrait* (Oxford: Oxford University Press, 1988), 206, 209, 217.

5. Ozment, *Age of Reform*, 270, 280–81, 427; Bainton, *Here I Stand*, 274, 280–81.

6. Ozment, *Age of Reform*, 421–22.

7. Conkin, *Self-Evident Truths*, 13–14, 19–23, 28.

8. Conkin, *Self-Evident Truths*, 30, 50–51, 54, 59; Perry Miller, *The New England Mind*, 2 vols. (New York: Macmillan, 1939; Cambridge, Mass.: Harvard University Press, 1953), vol. 1, 409.

9. Stanley Elkins and Eric McKitrick, *The Age of Federalism* (Oxford: Oxford University Press, 1993), 313–17, 354–57, 464–67; Herbert J. Storing, ed., *The Complete Antifederalist*, 7 vols. (Chicago: University of Chicago Press, 1981), vol. 4, 213; Jonathan Elliot, ed., *Debates in the Several State Conventions on the Adoption of the Federal Constitution*, 4 vols. (Philadelphia: Lippincott, 1888; reprint, New York: Burt Franklin, 1968), vol. 2, 113; vol. 3, 568; Drew R. McCoy, *The Last of the Fathers: James Madison and the Republican Legacy* (Cambridge: Cambridge University Press, 1989), 54–55.

10. Marvin Meyers, ed., *The Mind of the Founder: Sources of the Political Thought of James Madison* (New York: Bobbs-Merrill, 1973), 301–4; Conkin, *Self-Evident Truths*, 68–70; John C. Calhoun, *A Disquisition on Government and Selections from the Discourse*, ed. C. Gordon Post (Indianapolis: Bobbs-Merrill, 1953), xiv.

11. David M. Potter, *The Impending Crisis, 1848–1861* (New York: Harper & Row, 1976), 54, 59–60, 62.

12. Paul A. Rahe, *Republics, Ancient and Modern: Classical Republicanism and the American Revolution* (Chapel Hill: University of North Carolina Press, 1992), 71, 115.

13. Augustine, *The City of God*, trans. Marcus Dods (New York: Modern Library, 1950), 22, 26–27, 29, 123, 481–82; Augustine, *On Free Choice of the Will*, trans. Anne S. Benjamin and L. H. Hickstaff (New York: Bobbs-Merrill, 1964), 9.

14. Jeffrey Burton Russell, *A History of Medieval Christianity: Prophecy and Order* (New York: Thomas Y. Crowell, 1968), 86; Conkin, *Self-Evident Truths*, 83–84; Artz, *Mind of the Middle Ages*, 275–76; Bainton, *Here I Stand*, 237.

15. Bainton, *Here I Stand*, 237; Ozment, *Age of Reform*, 266, 374; Miller, *New England Mind*, vol. 1, 429; Gary B. Nash, *Red, White, and Black: The Peoples of Early North America*, 3d ed. (Englewood Cliffs, N. J.: Prentice-Hall, 1992), 79.

16. John Locke, *Two Treatises of Government* (Cambridge: Cambridge University Press, 1960), 326–44.

17. Conkin, *Self-Evident Truths*, 102, 113, 124–26, 131; Paul Leicester Ford, ed., *The Political Writings of John Dickinson, 1764–1774* (Philadelphia: Historical Society of Pennsylvania, 1895; reprint, New York: Da Capo Press, 1970), 400.

18. McCoy, *Last of the Fathers*, 89; Conkin, *Self-Evident Truths*, 126.

19. Edwin S. Gaustad, *Faith of Our Fathers: Religion and the New Nation* (San Francisco: Harper & Row, 1987), 45–46, 53–54, 114–17; Henry F. May, *The Enlightenment in America* (Oxford: Oxford University Press, 1976), 249.

20. Elkins and McKitrick, *Age of Federalism*, 592–93, 700, 703, 706, 710–11; Conkin, *Self-Evident Truths*, 128, 134–36; Larry D. Eldridge, *A Distant Heritage: The Growth of Free Speech in Early America* (New York: New York University Press, 1994).

21. Conkin, *Self-Evident Truths*, 113.

22. Potter, *Impending Crisis*, 52–53; McCoy, *Last of the Fathers*, 268.

23. F. W. Walbank, *A Historical Commentary on Polybius*, 2 vols. (Oxford: Oxford University Press, 1957), vol. 1, 635–746.

24. Conkin, *Self-Evident Truths*, 146; H. H. Scullard, *From the Gracchi to Nero: A History of Rome from 133 B.C. to A.D. 68* (London: Merithen, 1959), 18–21, 27.

25. Conkin, *Self-Evident Truths*, 146; Calvin, *Institutes*, vol. 2, 656–57; Niccolò Machiavelli, *The Discourses of Niccolò Machiavelli*, trans. Leslie J. Walker, 2 vols. (New Haven: Yale University Press, 1950), vol. 1, 212–15; vol. 2, 7–12, 271–315; Jean Bodin, *Method for the Easy Comprehension of History*, trans. Beatrice Reynolds (New York: W. W. Norton, 1945), 179–87, 267, 282; Peter Laslett, ed., *Patriarcha and Other Political Works of Sir Robert Filmer* (Oxford: Basil Blackwell, 1949), 85–87, 91, 93; Thomas Hobbes, *Leviathan, Parts I and II* (New York: Bobbs-Merrill, 1958), 175.

26. J. G. A. Pocock, ed., *The Political Works of James Harrington* (Cambridge: Cambridge University Press, 1977), 459, 607; Conkin, *Self-Evident Truths*, 147; Algernon Sidney, *Discourses Concerning Government* (London: A. Millar, 1751; reprint, London: Gregg International Publishers, 1968), 130, 139–40, 434.

27. Gordon S. Wood, *The Creation of the American Republic, 1776–1787* (Chapel Hill: University of North Carolina Press, 1969), 201–2, 211.

28. Wood, *Creation of the American Republic*, 203, 208, 213–14, 232–33.

29. Wood, *Creation of the American Republic*, 201, 213, 215, 436; Douglas L. Wilson, ed., *Jefferson's Literary Commonplace Book* (Princeton, N.J.: Princeton University Press, 1989), 11; Joyce Appleby, *Liberalism and Republicanism in the Historical Imagination* (Cambridge, Mass.: Harvard University Press, 1992), 295; Bernard Bailyn, *The Ideological Origins of the American Revolution*, 2d ed. (Cambridge, Mass.: Harvard University Press, 1992), 293.

30. John Adams, "An Essay on Man's Lust for Power," August 29, 1763, in *The Papers of John Adams*, ed. Robert J. Taylor, 6 vols. (Cambridge, Mass.: Harvard University Press, 1977), vol. 1, 83; John Adams, "Thoughts on Government," 1776, in *The Papers of John Adams*, ed. Taylor, vol. 4, 88; John Adams, diary, spring 1772, in *The Diary and Autobiography of John Adams*, ed. L. H. Butterfield, 2 vols. (Cambridge, Mass.: Harvard University Press, 1961), vol. 2, 58; Wood, *Creation of the American Republic*, 434.

31. John Adams, *A Defence of the Constitutions of Government of the United States of America*, 2 vols. (London, 1787–1788; reprint, New York: Da Capo Press, 1971), vol. 1, xxi, 169–82, 209, 325; Richard M. Gummere, "The Classical Politics of John Adams," *Boston Public Library Quarterly* 9 (October 1957): 172.

32. Adams, *Defence of the Constitutions*, vol. 1, i–iii, xii–xiii.

33. Max Farrand, ed., *The Records of the Federal Convention of 1787*, 3d ed., 4 vols. (New Haven, Conn.: Yale University Press, 1966), vol. 1, 422–23, 431; James Madison, Report on Books, January 23, 1783, in *The Papers of James Madison*, ed. Robert Rutland et al., 15 vols. (Chicago: University of Chicago Press, 1962–1977; Charlottesville: University Press of Virginia, 1977), vol. 6, 76–77.

34. Alexander Hamilton, John Jay, and James Madison, *The Federalist: A Commentary on the Constitution of the United States* (New York: Random House, 1941), no. 63, 410–11, 415; James Madison, Additional Memoranda on Confederacies, November 30, 1787, in *Papers of James Madison*, ed. Rutland, vol. 10, 274; Wood, *Creation of the American Republic*, 410, 559.

35. Farrand, *Records of the Federal Convention*, vol. 1, 299–300, 308, 424, 432; Wood, *Creation of the American Republic*, 557–58.

36. Farrand, *Records of the Federal Convention*, vol. 2, 299; Herbert W. Benario, "The Classics in Southern Higher Education," *Southern Humanities Review* 11 (1977): 16; Gordon S. Wood, *The Radicalism of the American Revolution* (New York: Alfred A. Knopf, 1992), 292; Wood, *Creation of the American Republic*, 554; Paul Leicester Ford, ed., *Pamphlets on the Constitution of the United States: Published During Its Discussion by the People* (New York: Lenox Hill, 1888; reprint, New York: Burt Franklin, 1971), 34, 43, 57–58, 65, 189–90.

37. Elliot, *Debates in the Several State Conventions*, vol. 2, 434, 474, 523–24; James Wilson, "Of Government," in *The Works of James Wilson*, ed. Robert Green McCloskey, 2 vols. (Cambridge, Mass.: Harvard University Press, 1967), vol. 1, 303.

38. Storing, *Complete Antifederalist*, vol. 2, 138–39; Elliot, *Debates in the Several State Conventions*, vol. 3, 218.

39. Elliot, *Debates in the Several State Conventions*, vol. 3, 421; Storing, *Complete Antifederalist*, vol. 5, 89–90. For other references to the Antifederalist fear that the

Constitution would create an oligarchy see Ford, *Pamphlets on the Constitution*, 4; Bailyn, *Ideological Origins of the American Revolution*, 293; Farrand, *Records of the Federal Convention*, vol. 1, 48–49; Kate M. Rowland, *The Life of George Mason*, 2 vols. (New York: Putnam, 1892), vol. 2, 390.

40. Adams, *Defence of the Constitutions*, vol. 1, vi, 99, 181–82, 322–24; vol. 3, 505.

41. Hamilton, Jay, and Madison, *Federalist*, no. 10, 58–59. Madison makes a similar argument in no. 51.

42. James Madison, "For the *National Gazette*," December 19, 1791, in *Papers of James Madison*, ed. Rutland, vol. 14, 170; Madison, "For the *National Gazette*," January 28, 1792, in *Papers of James Madison*, ed. Rutland, vol. 14, 201.

43. Meyers, *Mind of the Founder*, 507.

44. Richard K. Matthews, *The Radical Politics of Thomas Jefferson: A Revisionist View* (Lawrence: University Press of Kansas, 1984), 77; Appleby, *Liberalism and Republicanism in the Historical Imagination*, 295; Thomas Jefferson to Isaac Tiffany, August 26, 1816, in *The Writings of Thomas Jefferson*, ed. Albert Ellery Bergh and Andrew A. Lipscomb, 20 vols. (Washington, D.C.: Thomas Jefferson Memorial Association, 1903), vol. 15, 66; Richard M. Gummere, *The American Colonial Mind and the Classical Tradition: Essays in Comparative Culture* (Cambridge, Mass.: Harvard University Press, 1963), 174.

45. A. Whitney Griswold, "Jefferson's Agrarian Democracy," in *Thomas Jefferson and American Democracy*, ed. Henry C. Dethloff (Lexington, Mass.: D. C. Heath, 1971), 40.

46. Rahe, *Republics, Ancient and Modern*, 414.

47. Rahe, *Republics, Ancient and Modern*, 414; Griswold, "Jefferson's Agrarian Democracy," 40–42.

48. Douglas L. Wilson, "The American Agricola: Jefferson's Agrarianism and the Classical Tradition," *South Atlantic Quarterly* 80 (summer 1981): 347–54; Karl Lehmann, *Thomas Jefferson: American Humanist* (Chicago: University of Chicago Press, 1964), 181; Gilbert Chinard, ed., *The Literary Bible of Thomas Jefferson: His Commonplace Book of Philosophers and Poets* (Baltimore: Johns Hopkins University Press, 1928; reprint, New York: Greenwood, 1969), 32.

49. Griswold, "Jefferson's Agrarian Democracy," 46–47.

50. Jefferson to John Langdon, March 5, 1810, in *Writings of Thomas Jefferson*, ed. Bergh and Lipscomb, vol. 12, 375; Jefferson to William Duane, November 13, 1810, in *Writings of Thomas Jefferson*, ed. Bergh and Lipscomb, vol. 12, 433; Jefferson to Francis C. Gray, March 4, 1815, in *Writings of Thomas Jefferson*, ed. Bergh and Lipscomb, vol. 14, 271; Jefferson to John Wayles Eppes, September 11, 1813, in *Writings of Thomas Jefferson*, ed. Bergh and Lipscomb, vol. 13, 361; Jefferson to Albert Gallatin, October 16, 1815, in *Writings of Thomas Jefferson*, ed. Bergh and Lipscomb, vol. 14, 365.

51. Matthews, *Radical Politics of Thomas Jefferson*, 109–10; Wood, *Creation of the American Republic*, 503.

52. Conkin, *Self-Evident Truths*, 115, 190; Daniel Walker Howe, *The Political Culture of the American Whigs* (Chicago: University of Chicago Press, 1979), 96–122.

53. John Adams to Benjamin Rush, September 9, 1806, in *The Spur of Fame: Dialogues of John Adams and Benjamin Rush, 1805–1813*, ed. Douglass Adair and John A. Schutz (San Marino, Calif.: Huntington Library, 1966), 66–67; Gummere, "Classical Politics of John Adams," 179.

54. Potter, *Impending Crisis*, 281–84, 419.

5

ECONOMIC THEORIES

The ratification of the U.S. Constitution transformed American political debate from a dispute concerning fundamentals into a disagreement about constitutional interpretations. American political debate was no longer a search for truth, with the history of nations as the guide, but a search for legitimacy, with the hallowed Constitution as the authority. Since most Americans agreed that the structure of the government created by the Constitution was nearly perfect, debate over fundamentals shifted to economics, where the same humanist passion for uncovering universal laws received free play. American economists responded to the turmoil produced by the Industrial Revolution in the same fashion that American theologians and political theorists had responded to the Protestant Reformation and the American Revolution: by adapting European theories to their own context in imaginative ways.

THE INDUSTRIAL REVOLUTION

Although the Industrial Revolution that began in the early nineteenth century laid the foundations for U.S. world power in the twentieth and twenty-first centuries, it also divided the nation into three sections, each with its own distinctive economy, and, in so doing, helped cause the Civil War. Increasingly, while the Northeast exchanged its manufactured goods for northwestern grain, the

South was drawn into a separate commercial orbit, exchanging its cotton for British and French manufactured goods. By the 1830s 75 percent of American cotton was exported to foreign countries, more than half to Britain. The limited extent of Southern trade with the North encouraged Southern secession in 1860–1861.[1]

The Industrial Revolution was itself the product of various revolutions in agriculture, transportation, and manufacturing. The invention of the cotton gin (1793), the mechanical reaper (1833–1834), and the steel plow (1837) not only dramatically increased American cotton and grain production but also accelerated the settlement of the West, as did the invention of the steamboat, the construction of a vast railroad network, and the digging of canals. In addition, the invention of various steam-powered spinners and looms counteracted chronic shortages of factory labor, thereby allowing the establishment of textile mills, largely concentrated in the Northeast.[2]

The Industrial Revolution altered American society. One of its effects was urbanization. Port cities like New York, Philadelphia, Baltimore, Boston, and New Orleans expanded tremendously. (New York City had one million inhabitants by 1860.) As a result of the steamboat, inland cities also sprouted along the Ohio River (Pittsburgh, Cincinnati, and Louisville), the Mississippi River (St. Louis), and the Great Lakes (Buffalo, Cleveland, Detroit, Chicago, and Milwaukee).[3]

The second effect of the Industrial Revolution was increased immigration. Glowing reports of plentiful industrial jobs and cheap farmland linked to growing cities by railroads and steamboats attracted many European immigrants, particularly Irish and Germans. More than five million immigrants entered the United States between 1819 and 1860, more than half of these during the 1850s. By 1860 one of every seven Americans was foreign-born. Seeking to escape chronic economic depression and the disastrous potato famine of the 1840s, 1.7 million Irish immigrated to the United States. German immigration peaked in the 1840s and 1850s as well. Between 1848 and 1860 over one million Germans, some of them refugees from the failed revolutions of 1848, immigrated to the United States.[4]

A third effect of the Industrial Revolution was the organization of labor. The first labor unions were formed not by factory workers but by skilled artisans who were being displaced by the new machinery. Unions tended to be local, temporary, and largely social organizations confined to a single craft, though they sometimes struck. The largest strike was that of twenty thousand shoe workers in February 1860. By the 1830s "workingmen's" political parties controlled the local governments of major cities, forcing the two major parties to address their demands for universal manhood suffrage, public schools, the abolition of imprisonment for debt, and the ten-hour workday.[5]

CLASSICAL ECONOMICS

The Physiocrats' Attack on Mercantilism

The turmoil produced by the Industrial Revolution sparked an intense debate between classical and Whig economists, whose theories greatly influenced the policies of the early national period. The first classical economists, the French physiocrats of the mid-eighteenth century, assaulted mercantilism, the prevalent European economic theory of the seventeenth and eighteenth centuries. Mercantilists believed that nations could secure wealth and power only through a favorable balance of trade. A favorable balance of trade could be achieved only through government action: through tariffs to protect domestic industry from foreign competition; through subsidies to keep vital industries afloat; and through territorial expansion to create an ever larger, more diverse, and more self-sufficient empire. Mercantilists measured a nation's wealth by the amount of specie (gold and silver) it possessed; specie must be drawn into the empire through exports and prevented from flowing out via imports.[6]

By contrast, the physiocrats opposed tariffs, subsidies, expansionist wars, and other policies that favored manufacturing and commerce over agriculture, arguing that such measures hindered productivity and progress. The physiocrats contended that agriculture was the only truly productive enterprise. Manufacturing and commerce, which could not exist without agriculture, were useful only to the extent that they allowed farmers to produce more by freeing them from the need to make their own tools and other manufactured goods.[7]

Adam Smith (1723–1790)

Influenced by the physiocrats he met while traveling on the European continent, the British economist Adam Smith published *The Wealth of Nations*, one of the most influential books in Western history, in 1776. Smith contended that material progress was inevitable if government avoided interference in the economy. Since people possessed an insatiable appetite for consumer goods and a love of trade, the individual pursuit of self-interest was both natural and good for the economy (if not always for society as a whole), leading inevitably to specialization and mechanization, which, in turn, produced ever greater efficiency and prosperity. The market was self-regulating, provided that government protected private property and enforced contracts in order to maintain the incentives for production. In a free economy the law of supply and demand determined market prices: If the supply of an item decreased or the demand for it increased, the price of the item rose, providing an incentive for increased production of the item, thus creating a greater supply and reducing the price back to its "natural level" (the cost of its production plus a reasonable profit). Government had no "duty of superintending the industry of private people, and of directing it towards the employments most suitable to the interest of the society," since a free market performed that function far more efficiently than any government ever could. Smith wrote: "No regulation of commerce can increase the quantity of industry in any society beyond what its capital can maintain. It can only divert a part of it into a direction into which it might not otherwise have gone; and it is by no means certain that this artificial direction is likely to be more advantageous to society than that into which it would have gone of its own accord." Smith liked the American colonies, where there were no feudal restrictions on land use or apprenticeship laws to artificially restrict the flow of labor and channel it into unproductive areas. Smith was optimistic that, freed from government restrictions, markets would expand, specialization would increase, and prosperity would reign.[8]

The Wealth of Nations was a devastating attack on mercantilism. Smith's detailed understanding of economic growth separated him sharply from most mercantilists, who paid little heed to that concept. Mercantilists often wrote as though the economic pie remained the same size and only a nation's share of it changed from time to time. While mercantilists generally concerned themselves with the mere transfer of wealth from one nation to another or from one sector of the economy to another, Smith concerned himself with the creation of wealth. He defined a nation's wealth as "the value of the annual produce of its land and labour"—not, in mercantilist fashion, as "the quantity of the precious metals which circulate within it," since gold and silver were mere commodities, whose value rose and fell like that of any other commodity. Unlike the mercantilists, who considered economics a form of struggle between nations, Smith viewed international trade and investment as a source of universal benefit, because expanded markets led to greater specialization and efficiency. In contrast to the mercantilists, he denounced both imperialism and slavery as counterproductive. The seizure and maintenance of colonies required high taxes, which served as a disincentive to production at home and caused capital to move abroad, and slavery left so little incentive to the worker that it was, in the end, the most expensive form of labor. (Smith explained, "A person who can acquire no property can have no interest but to eat as much, and to labour as little, as possible.") He argued that Great Britain should let the American colonies go. He also opposed a national debt, because it allowed politicians to finance senseless wars. Throughout the eighteenth century, Britain had racked up an appalling debt waging a long series of wars against France.[9]

Smith contended that overtaxation for the purpose of funding government waste was perhaps the only policy that could destroy a free-market economy. Of bureaucrats he wrote: "The whole, or almost the whole public revenue is in most countries employed in maintaining unproductive hands. . . . Such people, as they themselves produce nothing, are all maintained by the produce of other men's labour. When multiplied, therefore, to an unnecessary number, they may in a particular year consume so great a share of this produce as not to leave a sufficiency for maintaining the productive labourers." If government drains too much capital from producers, "all the frugality and good conduct of individuals may not be able to compensate for the waste and degradation of produce occasioned by this violent and forced encroachment." Nevertheless, Smith marveled at the productivity of individuals in a free economy:

> The uniform, constant, and uninterrupted effort of every man to better his condition, the principle from which public and national, as well as private, opulence is originally derived is frequently powerful enough to maintain the natural progress of things toward improvement in spite of both the extravagance of government and of the greatest errors of administration. Like the unknown principle of animal life, it frequently restores health and vigour to the constitution in spite, not only of the disease, but of the absurd prescriptions of the doctor.

This last sentence was a sly shot at mercantilist "doctors" whose government regulations harmed the economy while claiming to cure its ills. Smith added that, as much as possible, the recipients of each government service should pay the taxes required to finance it, to prevent the establishment of needless services, and that the level of payment for government services should be based on the quality of their performance, as in the private sector. Taxes should not be significantly redistributive or constitute a significant disincentive to individual effort, on which the health of the economy depended.[10]

Smith did favor government spending in several areas, however. Uncommonly for his day, Smith was a proponent of public education, since he believed that the spread of knowledge fostered economic growth and since he worried that the repetitiveness of work caused by ever-increasing specialization would turn workers into dull simpletons, robbing them of intelligence, judgment, emotion, and courage. He also endorsed government expenditures on roads and canals, which increased economic growth by reducing the cost of transportation ("the greatest of all improvements"), and on a sufficient but not lavish national defense.[11]

Smith divided revenue into three categories: rent, obtained through the ownership of land; wages, obtained by labor; and profit, obtained by the risk of capital (which was itself a store of past labor). The greatest competition was between profit and wages. Greedy merchants and manufacturers conspired secretly to keep wages low and demanded government intervention (corporate monopolies and mercantilist measures) to increase their profits at the expense of economic growth. Smith wrote of manufacturers, "To narrow the competition is always the interest of the dealers"—the precise opposite of society's interest. Manufacturers sought to defeat their competitors through government action, rather than through honest competition, thus imposing "an absurd tax upon the rest of their fellow-citizens." Smith concluded: "The proposal of any new law or regulation of commerce which comes from this order ought always to be listened to with great precaution, and ought never to be adopted till after having been long and carefully examined, not only with the most scrupulous, but with the most suspicious attention. It comes from an order of men whose interest is never exactly the same with that of the public, who have generally an interest to deceive and oppress the public, and who accordingly have upon many occasions both deceived and oppressed it." Smith believed that agriculture was the most, though not the only, productive sector of the economy, in part because nature labored to aid humans.[12]

The publication of *The Wealth of Nations* marked the birth of modern economics. Smith's detailed understanding of economic growth, the importance of specialization and technology, the universal benefits conferred by international trade and investment, the role of supply and demand in the regulation of price, the true source of national wealth (production), the impact of the fluctuations of currency, the hidden (or not-so-hidden) economic costs of imperialism and slavery, and the contribution of improvements in education and transportation to economic growth, was astonishing for the late eighteenth century. The year 1776 was revolutionary in more than one sense.

Thomas Malthus (1766–1834)

In *An Essay on the Principle of Population* (1798), Thomas Malthus advanced a pessimistic version of Smith's theory. While endorsing Smith's classical (laissez-faire) economics, Malthus predicted diminishing returns rather than inevitable progress. He claimed that while population increased geometrically, agricultural production increased only arithmetically. Explosive population growth could be kept in check only by late marriage, war, disease, and famine. In a truly vicious cycle, increases in the food supply caused earlier marriages and lower child mortality, leading to population growth, which led to increased famine and disease, thus bringing population back into line with available resources. In this manner agricultural improvements created their own demand. All that responsible people could do was to marry later and save money to see them through the inevitable contractions. Malthus learned from Benjamin Franklin's statistics concerning America that in a society relatively unfettered by the population-thinners of war, famine, and disease, the population would double every twenty-five years. Government spending on the poor would only worsen matters, increasing their population without giving them the ultimate means to sustain themselves. Malthus opposed government subsidization of manufacturing as equally harmful.[13]

In later years (in *Principles of Political Economy*, 1820) Malthus modified his opposition to government intervention in the economy. Though still convinced that government should intervene as little as possible, he argued that, during periods of economic depression, government could spur demand through deficit spending. In this the later Malthus anticipated the twentieth-century "demand-side" economist John Maynard Keynes. Malthus contended that while personal saving was laudable, an unusually high savings rate could produce an excess of supply over demand, leading to a glut of commodities and a prolonged depression—one such as had been afflicting Britain since the end of the Napoleonic Wars in 1815. Consumers did not always spend on other items the money they saved from the falling prices of some items caused by new machinery; when they failed to do so, those workers left unemployed by the machinery could not find new jobs. In such an instance, government spending was needed to increase the aggregate demand and bring it back into line with the aggregate supply. For this reason Malthus took issue with Smith's criticism of wealthy landowners for employing numerous household servants who produced nothing of permanent value; to Malthus, the service sector of the economy was crucial precisely because it added nothing of permanence that might glut the market. Malthus wrote: "It is necessary that a country with great powers of production should possess a body of consumers who are not themselves engaged in production. . . . There must therefore be a considerable class of persons who have both the will and power to consume more material wealth than they produce, or the mercantile classes could not continue profitably to produce so much more than they consume." While Malthus urged governments to "avoid all wars" and to spend as little as possible while at war, he opposed too severe a reduction of government expenditures or a retiring of national debt immediately following a war, since the restoration of full production tended to create a glut that could be eliminated only by government-inspired demand. Governments should avoid "convulsion in the state of demand at the termination" of wars by employing the poor in the construction of roads and other useful public works.[14]

Yet Malthus's economic theory remained distinctly classical. He still praised those who saved their money and acknowledged "that there is hardly a country in the four quarters of the globe where capital is not deficient." Since gluts caused by excessive supply or deficient demand were fairly rare, so was the need for government action. He contended that even "the most judicious taxation might ultimately be so heavy as to clog all the channels of foreign and domestic trade and almost prevent the possibility of accumulation." He added, "Taxation is a stimulus so liable in every way to abuse, and it is so absolutely necessary for the general interests of society to consider private property as sacred, that no one would think of trusting to any government the means of making a different distribution of wealth, with a view to the general good." He continued to deny "that restrictions upon commerce and heavy taxation are beneficial to a country" in general, while supporting a few tariffs, such as that on foreign grain. Though he advocated deficit spending in time of severe depression, he noted, "I am very far, however, from being insensible to the evils of a great national debt." Though such a debt might spur economic activity, it was "a very cumbersome and very dangerous instrument," sometimes leading to overtaxation and the redistribution of wealth from average citizens to wealthy bondholders. Malthus declared, "Taxes should never be imposed to a greater amount than the necessity of the case justifies . . . [and] every effort should be made . . . to prevent a scale of expenditure so great that it cannot proceed without ruin and cannot be stopped without distress." Deficit spending was "like the unnatural strength occasioned by some violent stimulant which, if not absolutely necessary, should be by all means avoided, on account of the exhaustion which is sure to follow it." Malthus concluded regarding government intervention in the economy, "The ablest physicians are the most sparing in the use of medicine, and the most inclined to trust to the healing power of nature." He endorsed Smith's maxim "that the wealth of nations is best secured by allowing every person, as long as he adheres to the rules of justice, to pursue his own interest in his own way."[15]

Nor did Malthus abandon his belief in long-term diminishing returns. He still insisted: "Whatever fanciful suppositions we may make about sudden improvements in [soil] fertility, nothing of this kind which we have ever seen or heard of in practice approaches to what we know of the power of population to increase up to the additional means of subsistence. Improvements in agriculture, however considerable they may finally prove, are always found to be partial and gradual." Such improvements led only to increased population and the cultivation of less fertile lands, thus bringing population back into equilibrium with the food supply. Though Malthus was now forced to make the significant concession that "the increased productiveness of the powers of labour . . . [can offset] the effect of taking poorer land into cultivation . . . for some centuries to come," this admission of the possibility of short-term relief did not alter his view that population growth would always eventually press upon the food supply. Nevertheless, the idea that there might be short-term situations in which supply actually outstripped demand—in opposition to the long term, in which demand constantly pressed supply—was what spurred Malthus to his theory concerning the need for government measures to increase demand in such instances.[16]

The flaws in Malthus's reasoning concerning diminishing returns are now obvious, if wholly understandable for an economist writing in 1820. Malthus underestimated the power of technology to provide a long-term food surplus and could not foresee that the widespread use of contraceptives would reduce the rate of population growth in industrialized nations. Nevertheless, Malthusian theory has been revived in recent years, though on a different basis. Modern Malthusians are pessimistic not so much because they doubt the ability of agricultural production to keep up with population growth as because they believe that economic growth comes at great cost to the environment. According to modern Malthusians, it is not food production, but the environment as a whole, that is the limiting factor.

David Ricardo (1772–1823)

In *Principles of Political Economy and Taxation* (1817), David Ricardo also espoused a pessimistic form of classical economics. Borrowing heavily from Malthus, Ricardo prophesied that the size of the rent sector of the economy would grow indefinitely at the expense of the other sectors and at the expense of economic growth, since fertile land would grow ever scarcer relative to the population. As the population grew, as fertile soil gradually became sapped of its nutrients, and as less fertile soils were cultivated, the greatly increased demand for food would outstrip the slightly increased supply that resulted from improvements in husbandry and machinery. The increasing demand for food would drive rent steadily upward, eating into the wages of tenant farmers and factory workers and the profits of factory owners until they reached the minimum level required to sustain labor and risk-taking. Like

Malthus, Ricardo was not oblivious to the possibilities of new technology but felt that the increased returns it offered would not be sufficient to offset the diminishing returns in agriculture resulting from soil exhaustion and population growth.[17]

Ricardo attacked the "poor laws," Britain's rudimentary, locally operated welfare system of Elizabethan origin. He wrote:

> The clear and direct tendency of the poor laws . . . is not, as the legislature benevolently intended, to amend the condition of the poor, but to deteriorate the condition of both poor and rich; instead of making the poor rich, they are calculated to make the rich poor; and whilst the present laws are in force, it is quite in the natural order of things that the fund for the maintenance of the poor should progressively increase till it has absorbed all the net revenue of the country, or at least so much of it as the state shall leave us, after satisfying its never-failing demands for the public expenditure. . . . The comforts and well-being of the poor cannot be permanently secured without some regard on their part, or some effort on the part of the legislature, to regulate the increase of their numbers, and to render less frequent among them early and improvident marriages. The operation of the system of poor laws has been directly contrary to this. They have rendered restraint superfluous, and have invited imprudence by offering it a portion of the wages of prudence and industry.

After crediting Malthus with demonstrating "the pernicious tendency of these laws," Ricardo concluded regarding the poor laws: "Every friend to the poor must ardently wish for their abolition. . . . By gradually contracting the sphere of the poor laws; by impressing on the poor the value of independence; by teaching them that they must look not to systematic or casual charity, but to their own exertions, for support, that prudence and forethought are neither unnecessary nor unprofitable virtues, we shall by degrees approach a sounder and more beautiful state." Nevertheless, the poor laws must be reformed gradually, not immediately, since "the habits of the poor have been so formed upon their operation." Ricardo claimed that the only reason the poor laws had not yet bankrupted Britain was that the welfare system was decentralized:

> Each parish raises a separate fund for the support of its own poor. Hence it becomes an object of more interest and more practicability to keep the

rates low than if one general fund were raised for the relief of the poor of the whole kingdom. A parish is much more interested in an economical collection of the rate and a sparing distribution of relief. . . . It is to this cause that we must ascribe the fact of the poor laws not having absorbed the net revenue of the country. . . . If by law every human being wanting support could be sure to obtain it, and obtain it in such a degree as to make life tolerably comfortable, theory would lead us to expect that all other taxes together would be light compared with the single one of poor rates. The principle of gravitation is no more certain than the tendency of such laws to change wealth and power into misery and weakness . . . until at last all classes should be infected with the plague of universal poverty.

Fortunately, the British economy was still growing. But Ricardo added, "If our progress should become more slow . . . then will the pernicious nature of these laws become more manifest and alarming; and then, too, will their removal be obstructed by many additional difficulties."[18]

Like Smith, Ricardo opposed protective tariffs, arguing that free trade caused nations to specialize in what they produced most efficiently. Free trade led to "the best distribution of the labour of the world . . . and the greatest abundance of the necessaries and enjoyments of human life." Ricardo claimed: "The sole effect of high duties . . . is to divert a portion of capital to an employment which it would not naturally seek. It causes a pernicious distribution of the general funds of society—it bribes a manufacturer to commence or continue in a comparatively less profitable employment. It is the worst species of taxation." Mercantilist restrictions on colonial trade were "not less injurious to the mother countries themselves than to the colonies." If consumers could buy cheaper goods from the colonies or from another country, the whole society benefited; the excess capital consumers saved would be employed either in investment or in the purchase of domestic goods, thereby creating jobs.[19]

Ricardo opposed excessive taxation, since taxes "will necessarily fall on capital, that is to say, they will impair the fund allotted to productive consumption." He contended: "There are no taxes which have not a tendency to lessen the power to accumulate. . . . Some taxes will produce these effects in a much greater degree than others; but the great evil of taxation is to be found, not so much in any selection of its objects, as in the general amount of its effects taken collectively." Ricardo quoted Smith: "They are all more or less unthrifty taxes that increase the revenue of the sovereign, which seldom maintains any but unproductive labourers, at the expense of the people, which maintains none but productive." Particularly foolish were taxes on the transfer of property, such as the sale of land. Ricardo wrote, "For the general prosperity there cannot be too much facility given to the conveyance and exchange of all kinds of property, as it is by such means that capital of every species is likely to find its way into the hands of those who will best employ it in increasing the productions of the country." If taxes were so exorbitant as to prevent exchanges of property, they became detrimental to economic growth. Ricardo noted that taxation "very frequently operates very differently from the intention of the legislature by its indirect effects."[20]

Ricardo opposed other mercantilist policies as well. He opposed the national debt, arguing that it made government officials and citizens less efficient by blinding them to their nation's real financial situation. The ability to borrow would lead to runaway spending and to wars. Ricardo wrote concerning government officials, "To keep them peaceable you must keep them poor." Ricardo opposed subsidies since they drained the treasury without even giving any long-term benefit to producers of the favored goods; by encouraging production of the goods, subsidies resulted in a greater supply, leading, in turn, to falling prices. The greater the subsidy the government paid producers to compensate for falling prices, the more they caused prices to fall even further by spurring even greater production.[21]

Ricardo anticipated the Federal Reserve system of the modern United States, arguing that the power to increase the money supply through credit should be left in the hands of expert commissioners, appointed by the government but "made totally independent of the control of ministers." Politicians with direct control over the money supply would abuse that power for partisan purposes.[22]

Ricardo attempted to reassure those who feared that the new technology of the Industrial Revolution would cause massive unemployment. He noted that though new machinery caused short-term unemployment, the capital saved was subsequently expended in a new business, thus creating new jobs. If a nation discouraged machinery, capital would move out of the country in the form of investments in foreign countries that encouraged machinery and in the form of purchases of their cheaper goods. He concluded, "The gains of stockholders are national gains and increase, as all other gains do, the real wealth and power of the country."[23]

Later Ricardians, responding to certain intimations of the economist himself, argued that excessive wages obtained through labor unions were as damaging to the economy and, thus, to workers' long-term interest, as excessive profits obtained by mercantilist means. They contended that when labor unions succeeded in obtaining higher wages absent economic growth, it was always at the expense of either profits or the real wages of other workers. If manufacturers swallowed the higher wages in decreased profits, they would have too little capital for reinvestment, which would destroy their firms' competitiveness and lead to worker unemployment in the long term. If, on the other hand, manufacturers passed on the higher wages in the form of higher prices, other workers, as consumers, would suffer a loss in their spending power. Hence both wages and profits should only increase naturally, through economic growth, not artificially, at the expense of one another. Workers and manufacturers must both be patient and await the growth of the pie, rather than using labor unions or government intervention to grab a bigger piece. (Modern conservatives have used the same argument against corporate taxes, alleging that corporations will either pass such taxes on to the consumer in higher prices or swallow them, leading to lower rates of investment and employment.)[24]

But the Ricardians' chief villain was the large landholder. While the manufacturer earned a share of the profits of his firm by risking capital, the landlord collected rent merely for possessing access to nature. John Stuart Mill, a follower of Ricardian economics, wrote that landlords grew richer "in their sleep, without working, risking, or economizing." Ricardo himself noted that the interest of landlords was to raise the price of rent and, hence, the cost of grain, an interest directly opposed to the public interest, since such increases taxed the wages of laborers and the profits of capitalists. He refuted Smith's assertion that agriculture was more productive than manufacturing.[25]

Even more than Smith and Malthus, the Ricardians were full of confidence in the power of human reason to uncover "iron laws" of economics. In less sober moments Ricardo himself stated that some economic "laws" were "as certain as the principle of gravitation," and Mill argued that the social sciences should be followed "after the model ... of the more complex physical sciences," as though humans were as predictable as atoms. By contrast, Malthus wrote: "We should fall into a serious error if we were to suppose that any propositions, the practical results of which depend upon the agency of so variable a being as man, and the qualities of so variable a compound as the soil, can ever admit of the same kinds of proof, or lead to the same certain conclusions, as those which relate to figure and number.... The science of political economy bears a nearer resemblance to the science of morals and politics than to that of mathematics.... We cannot make a science more certain by our wishes or opinions."[26]

John Taylor of Caroline (1753–1824)

The author of a series of books on economics published between 1814 and 1823, a Virginian named John Taylor adapted the theories of the French physiocrats and British classical economists to the American setting. Like Smith, Taylor considered agriculture more productive than industry and commerce. Like most other American classical economists, Taylor much preferred Smith's optimistic version of the theory to Malthus's and Ricardo's pessimistic brand. Taylor believed that free trade would produce unlimited growth through increased demand (e.g., northerners acquiring a taste for tropical fruit) and specialization. Such optimism was typically American. By 1815 the United States had one of the highest living standards in the world, owing to abundant, cheap land, populated by a hard-working, frugal, literate citizenry free from feudal restrictions on the pursuit of wealth. It was difficult for Americans to conceive of land and other natural resources as finite, as Malthus and Ricardo did.[27]

A Democratic-Republican, Taylor opposed the neomercantilist fiscal program of Alexander Hamilton and the Federalists, whom he considered representatives of the modern "aristocracy of paper and patronage" that had replaced the old aristocracy of priests, warriors, and titled landlords. He opposed Hamilton's national debt-funding plan as the plot of "capitalists" against the rest of society. Bondholding capitalists would subsist on the annual interest collected from the taxes of farmers and other laborers, a redistribution of income from the poor to the wealthy that could last for generations (until the principal was paid). Taylor, a slaveholder himself, considered this nothing less than a form of slavery. He contended that corrupt public officials allied with the bondholders wasted public money on standing armies and wars to keep the debt high.[28]

Taylor also opposed the national bank, which he considered a scheme to lend federal funds (taxpayer money) to capitalists without interest. (Private stockholders in the bank received dividends from the bank's profit, which was partly based on the interest accrued by federal deposits.) Taylor failed to note, however, that the stockholders had provided 80 percent of the national bank's initial capital.[29]

But Taylor hated protective tariffs more than any of Hamilton's other proposals. Taylor considered protective tariffs an attempt by northeastern capitalists to enslave southern and western farmers. Tariffs on British and French manufactured goods would impoverish the South by forcing southerners to buy higher-priced, northeastern goods and by leaving the British and French less money (from the sale of their goods) to buy southern cotton. The agricultural West would also face higher prices and the loss of southern markets for their grain, since an impoverished South would be forced to turn to subsistence farming. The tariffs were part of a conspiracy to drive southern and western farmers off their land and force them into the northeastern factories to work for subsistence wages. Taylor believed that, in the long term, tariffs would impoverish the whole nation, since they hurt agriculture, the most productive portion of the economy, and encouraged inefficiency in industry. Protected industries would have no incentive to become more efficient.[30]

Taylor also opposed federally funded transportation improvements, since they unfairly favored particular regions and industries, while the tax burden was shared equally. With its internal river systems, the South needed fewer internal improvements than the North, which desired railroads and canals to connect the northwestern farms to the northeastern cities. Furthermore, federal spending on internal improvements would increase the federal government's need for revenues, leading to higher tariffs.[31]

WHIG ECONOMICS

The chief opponent of classical economics in America was Whig economics, named after the Whig Party, which pursued a program similar to the neomercantilist policy of the Federalists. Although most nineteenth-century economics professors were classical economists, a sizable number of popular economists were Whigs. Economics had not yet rigidified into a professional discipline, complete with dogmas, so that publications featured a wide variety of opinions.[32]

Daniel Raymond (1769–1849)

A native of New England, Daniel Raymond published his *Thoughts on Political Economy* in 1820. Though it failed to sell well, Raymond's work won accolades from aging Federalists, such as John Adams, John Jay, and John Marshall. Raymond believed that although Whig programs involved a short-term redistribution of wealth, they promoted the long-term interest of society as a whole. A national debt, though redistributive, would benefit society, if it was not excessive and if the extra revenue was spent on education and internal improvements, both of which spurred economic growth. Deficit spending must also be employed to create demand in time of depression. Raymond wrote, "If there be a sur-

plus of the product of industry, it is as much the duty of the legislator to make provision, if possible, for its immediate consumption
as it would be to adopt measures for the purpose of supplying the
nation with food in case it should be in want." Raymond denied
that the United States was "ever likely to be oppressed with a public debt of any inconvenient magnitude." The national bank,
though somewhat redistributive, would benefit society by allowing the federal government to regulate the money supply, thereby
moderating the extremes inherent in the recurrent cycles of boom
and bust. These extremes of inflation and depression resulted from
the lack of federal control over irresponsible state banks. State
banks routinely lent too much money and kept too little in reserve, thus spurring false booms that inevitably turned into severe
depressions when debtors defaulted on their debts. By contrast, the
more cautious loans made by the national bank would spur steady
economic growth without the destructive extremes of boom and
bust. A national bank would also provide those who could not operate businesses of their own with a secure place of investment for
their savings, a rarity at that time.[33]

Above all, Raymond contended that a protective tariff,
though redistributive, was necessary to protect infant American
industries from cutthroat British competition. (The British were
purposely selling their goods below cost in the United States in
order to destroy their American competitors, a practice now called
"dumping." The British also possessed the advantages of being
more advanced in manufacturing and of paying much lower
wages.) Although Raymond conceded that tariffs constituted a
short-term tax on consumers, he believed that they would ultimately reduce prices by saving American industries from extinction, thereby increasing the long-term number of suppliers. If tariffs were not imposed, British manufacturers would undersell their
American competitors, drive them out of business, and then take
advantage of their monopoly to increase prices dramatically. In the
long term, tariffs actually encouraged competition and reduced
prices by ensuring the survival of a larger number of competitors.
Furthermore, tariffs would foster national self-sufficiency, an argument even James Madison and Thomas Jefferson came to accept

after the War of 1812. Just as manufacturing predominated too greatly over agriculture in Britain, agriculture predominated too greatly over manufacturing in the United States. Raymond argued, "In both cases ought the government to interpose to restore the equilibrium." The Whig emphasis on a well-balanced economy for reasons of national self-sufficiency and security conflicted with the classical economists' emphasis on specialization as the key to greater efficiency and economic growth.[34]

Raymond also contended that tariffs would provide jobs for women, children, and immigrants and markets for agricultural products, particularly northwestern grain. Taylor had been wrong to conclude that the Northwest would be hurt by tariffs. The Northwest would benefit from the huge new grain market created by the growth of industrial cities in the Northeast. Agriculture and manufacturing were compatible. Raymond denied that agriculture was any more productive than manufacturing or commerce. He declared:

> It is the duty of the legislator to find employment for all the people, and if he cannot find them employment in agriculture and commerce, he must set them to manufacture. It is his duty to take special care that no other nation interferes with their industry. He is not to permit one half of the nation to remain idle and hungry in order that the other half may buy goods where they may be had cheapest. . . . Every man is to be left free to engage in what business he pleases, but he ought not to be allowed patronage and support to the industry of foreigners when his own fellow-citizens are in want of it.

(Raymond's enormous exaggeration of the unemployment rate undercut his argument needlessly.) Raymond denied that tariffs were intended for the benefit of wealthy factory owners; rather, they were "for the benefit of the labouring classes." He contended that the higher cost of consumer goods caused by a tariff was "more than counterbalanced to the labourer by the great demand it creates."[35]

Raymond argued that tariffs were preferable to other forms of taxation, because they were indirectly applied (the foreign exporter paid them and passed the cost on to the domestic consumer) and thus less apt to excite popular anger and opposition. (This was an odd argument since the purpose of his protective tariffs was not to raise revenue but to discourage the purchase of foreign goods altogether; the more successful Raymond's tariffs were in achieving that goal the less revenue they would have raised.) Raymond was such a fan of tariffs that he declared: "The most general rule on this subject is that a tariff ought not to be reduced, although it may frequently require to be raised. . . . The reduction of a tariff is one of the harshest and most violent measures that a government can possibly adopt." It is impossible to find a starker contrast to Ricardo's antitariff rhetoric.[36]

Raymond defended welfare programs like the Elizabethan Poor Laws against the attacks of Malthus, Ricardo, and others. Raymond argued that the fundamental reason for poverty was not laziness but a shortage of jobs: "We see multitudes of instances every day of men who are able and willing to work but who cannot obtain work." Sometimes these workers lacked the necessary skills for the type of labor currently in demand; at other times, there was simply not enough aggregate demand in the economy for full employment. In such instances, rather than let people starve, government had an obligation to provide some sort of assistance to the unemployed. Raymond added, "It is not true that the poor will voluntarily place their dependence for support upon public charity; the great mass of mankind have an innate feeling of independence and pride which scorns to receive charity as long as they have the power of maintaining themselves." The number of those "so lost to all sense of shame as to be willing to subsist upon charity . . . is comparatively small, and the vigilance of those who act as almoners to the public will always be able to prevent any great imposition being practiced on the public by such persons." But Raymond preferred tariffs and public works programs to poor laws, since the former encouraged work, the latter sloth.[37]

Henry Carey (1793–1879)

A prolific Irish-American economist, Henry Carey wrote numerous works on Whig economics from the 1830s until his death in 1879. Carey turned Malthus on his head, contending that food production increased geometrically relative to human population growth. He argued that humans had always begun farming on the worst soil, because it was the soil best suited to their primitive tools and skills, and had continually moved "down from the hills" to better soil, as their technology had improved. This thesis was an attempt to counter the Malthusian theory that humans would be forced to cultivate soil of worse and worse quality as the best soil was eroded.[38]

Carey's theory was hardly irrefutable, but what mattered most was its underlying premise: Technology would increase the food supply geometrically. The greater the population, the greater the number of minds working together to advance technological progress (better techniques, machines, and transportation) and, thus, the more the food supply would outstrip the population—a direct inversion of Malthus. As a result of technology spawned by increased human interaction, the poorest soil of tomorrow would grow more food than the richest of today. Carey imagined that even the best fields of his day were "not worked to one tenth of their powers." In a virtuous cycle, population growth spawned prosperity, which spawned more population growth. Carey noted triumphantly what even Malthus himself was occasionally forced to concede: that rent, wages, and profits had all been rising, not declining, for centuries—in fact, increasing so rapidly as to outstrip population growth. (Malthus considered this trend a temporary aberration.) When Malthus saw people, he saw only their mouths; when Carey saw them, he saw only their brains. Carey concluded, "Labour is daily more productive—the labourer's power to accumulate capital is daily increasing . . . and thus he is enabled to have better food, better clothing, better shelter, and to obtain with a constantly decreasing quantity of labour the means of support when old age should have disabled him for exertion." Work was becoming less onerous and more profitable for the laborer, thus providing a greater incentive for work.[39]

While it was true that the same mechanization that produced a "constant improvement in the general standard of living" also demanded a more skilled workforce, Carey looked on this chal-

lenge positively, as a chance to improve the intellectual tenor of society. He predicted that economic improvement would lead to both intellectual and moral improvement. As humans became wealthier and less desperate, they would have more time for learning and would "no longer experience a necessity for plundering their fellow men." There would be a decrease in crime and war. Thus, wealth would contribute to a better democracy, just as democracy contributed to greater wealth. Democracy was good for an economy, because the majority demanded internal improvements that spurred economic growth for all, rather than useless palaces enjoyed only by a few aristocrats.[40]

Carey acknowledged that despotic government, insecurity of property, overtaxation, restrictions on the flow of capital and labor, and senseless wars might prevent the increasing returns he envisioned as otherwise inevitable. He also worried that the improper use of land might threaten long-term prosperity. Although in the 1830s he concluded that "the powers of the earth to afford food . . . probably are absolutely incalculable," a few decades later he was not so sure. Carey criticized southern cotton planters, who mined the soil for immediate gain. Nature would wreak its vengeance upon them. Carey doubted the moral superiority of farmers, disdaining the agricultural romanticism of Jefferson and most classical economists.[41]

Carey's optimism was the opposite of Smith's. While Smith argued that progress was inevitable if government left the economy alone, Carey argued that progress was inevitable if government intervened to prevent society's raw materials from being wasted. Carey was one of the first ecologists. He wrote, "That man shall be enabled to pay the debt he contracts toward his great mother earth, when taking from the elements which enter into the commodities required for his support . . . is the condition upon which alone progress can be made." He argued that waste must be recycled. Hence manufacturing, the conversion of raw materials into finished products, must be performed in the United States, so that Americans could recycle their waste. Tariffs were thus necessary to sustain domestic industries. Carey's Irish background no doubt contributed to his belief that classical economics was a weapon of British imperialists to secure American raw materials, which Americans must defend at all costs. Raw materials, once lost, were lost forever. They were the basis for power.[42]

But Carey was not content that there be one center of American industry, located in the Northeast. Much waste of energy and money (from middlemen) would occur in transporting raw materials from the rural areas to the Northeast, and these areas would simply become colonies of New York rather than colonies of London. Carey argued that manufacturing should be decentralized and located near the farms and mines, so that raw materials could be recycled locally. He advocated local as well as national self-sufficiency, yet he endorsed continued specialization among individuals as essential to progress. Carey also supported government intervention, through a national bank, to increase the money supply steadily in order to spur growth.[43]

Carey was disappointed by post–Civil War developments. Government was not intervening properly to ensure long-term growth. Southerners continued to rape the soil through reckless cotton production, the West joined in with the wasteful cattle industry, manufacturing continued to be concentrated in the Northeast, and his own Republican Party (the new Republican Party of Abraham Lincoln) was restricting the money supply.[44]

SIMILARITIES AND DIFFERENCES BETWEEN CLASSICAL AND WHIG ECONOMICS

Similarities: Capitalism and Optimism

Despite their disagreement over the level of government intervention necessary to sustain economic growth, both classical and Whig economists agreed on a free-market model that left most property in the hands of individuals. Equally remarkable was the consensus of optimism among the American supporters of both economic philosophies, in marked contrast to the brooding pessimism of Malthus and Ricardo. Living in a prosperous country blessed with abundant, cheap, fertile land and hard workers, American economists did not become pessimistic until after the Civil War. The age of humanism was at its peak.

Differences: Advantages and Disadvantages of Each Policy

Based on conflicting values, classical and Whig economics each possessed its own set of advantages and disadvantages. Designed to maximize individual liberty, classical policies spurred economic growth, but at the expense of social stability. Classical economists generally failed to appreciate humans' intense desire for stability and security and, hence, the political dangers inherent in an unrestrained economy. They failed to acknowledge that some form of safety net, whether public or private, was needed, if only to prevent the people from being led by fear and anxiety into casting aside the whole free enterprise system. However limited its economic effects, Franklin Roosevelt's moderate New Deal created a sense of security amid the despair of the Great Depression of the 1930s that may well have prevented the overthrow of capitalism in the United States. When asked if Roosevelt had carried out his party's program, socialist leader Norman Thomas replied that he had—"on a stretcher."[45]

Designed to combine a degree of liberty with a degree of stability, Whig economics also spurred a measure of economic growth, but at the expense of fiscal responsibility and individual self-reliance. Whig economists generally failed to appreciate both the tenacity with which special interests would cling to government support long after its original purpose had been achieved and the extent to which government bureaucracies would entrench themselves and grow well beyond their original size and mission. The Whigs also naively assumed that, once given power over the economy, government officials would always behave wisely and ethically.

THE FAILURE OF THE RADICAL ALTERNATIVES

Socialism

The fact that the vast majority of Americans limited themselves to these two schools of capitalist theory reveals much about American culture. The historian Louis Hartz once contended that the absence of a feudal tradition in America and the abundance of land in the New World worked together to foster American individualism and to prevent the development of influential socialist and other radical traditions. He argued that because America never had feudal barons, it never produced a Karl Marx. Whatever the cause, it is clear that America never possessed the strong socialist tradition that developed in Europe. Though Socialist Party candidate Eugene V. Debs received nearly one million votes (approximately 6 percent of the vote) in 1912, the party's coalition fell apart soon after, as a result of World War I and the fear of communism precipitated by the Bolshevik Revolution in Russia.[46]

Whether because of the inherent inefficacy of socialism (as conservatives allege) or because of the unique cultural context in America (as Hartz claimed), none of the major socialist experiments in American history succeeded. When the Virginia Company attempted communal ownership of land at Jamestown, it found that its settlers were "bowling in the streets" even while food was in perilously short supply. Since each colonist was fed whether or not he worked, each waited for someone else to do the work. This "starving time" ended only when the company changed its policy and distributed land among individual settlers. Encouraged to work for themselves, the colonists began to do so, especially when they discovered the export possibilities of tobacco. After 1617, lethargy gave way to frantic activity, as settlers used every available plot of land, even growing tobacco in the streets.[47]

Though famed for their selflessness and their work ethic, the Pilgrims had a similar experience with communal ownership of land, nearly starving within three years' time. The sober William Bradford recorded that collectivism "was found to breed much confusion and discontent and retard much employment that would have been to their benefit and comfort." He explained: "For the young men that were most able and fit for labour and service did repine that they should spend their time and strength to work for other men's wives and children without any recompense. . . . This was thought injustice." Women who worked harder than others complained as well. As a result, diligence soon declined, creating a crisis. According to Bradford, the Pilgrims then "began to think how they might raise as much corn as they could and obtain a better crop than they had done, that they might not still thus languish in misery." He related: "At length, after much debate of things . . . [they] so assigned to every family a parcel of land, according to the proportion of their number. . . . This had very good success, for it made all hands very industrious, so as much more corn was planted than would have been by any means the Governor or any other could use. . . . The women now went willingly into the field . . .which before would allege weakness and inability; whom to have compelled would have been thought great tyranny and oppression." Bradford concluded: "The experience that was had in this common course and condition, tried sundry years and that amongst godly and sober men, may well evince the vanity of that conceit of Plato's and other ancients, applauded by some of later times: that the taking away of property . . . would make them happy and flourishing. . . . Let none object this is man's corruption. . . . I answer, seeing all men have this corruption in them, God in His wisdom saw another course fitter for them." The failed colonial experiment with communal ownership of land repeated itself in antebellum utopian communities, nearly all of which failed within a few years.[48]

Agrarianism

Agrarianism, the belief that everyone has the right to access to land, also failed to attract a large number of adherents. Harking back to the land redistribution schemes of Plato and of the Gracchi brothers of the late Roman republic and to Locke's writings on the natural right to access to land, modern agrarians like Thomas Skidmore proposed societal ownership, but individual control, of land and the taxation of inheritance. Under Skidmore's proposed state constitution, the government of New York would confiscate all property in the state, including land, money, and movable items, and divide it equally among citizens, both male and female, over the age of eighteen. A citizen could sell his lifetime control of his plot of land, but not the land itself, which belonged to society and would revert to it, along with the rest of the citizen's property, upon his death. Inheritance was the great evil to Skidmore and the other agrarians, because it based one's fate upon whether one's ancestors had been long-lived or short-lived, chaste or prolific, wise or foolish, frugal or lavish, fortunate or unfortunate—or too frequently in corrupt capitalist society, on whether they had been unscrupulous enough.[49]

A disciple of Skidmore, George Henry Evans realized that Skidmore's scheme could never be introduced without violent opposition from landholders. As a result, Evans proposed leaving eastern landholdings as they were, while putting agrarianism into operation in the western territories. Evans's National Reform Association (1845) demanded that the federal government provide free but inalienable plots of 160 acres, while limiting the size of landholdings. With the help of influential newspaperman Horace Greeley, the National Reform Association secured the passage of the Homestead Act (1862), which granted 160-acre homesteads to western settlers for a nominal registration fee. But the act lacked the crucial nonalienation clause. Homesteaders, not society as a whole, owned the plots and could dispose of the land in any manner they wished.[50]

Though agrarianism survived the Civil War, the agrarians never achieved their goals. In *Progress and Poverty* (1869), Henry George proposed the confiscation of rent—that is, all profit from land above that which resulted from the owner's own labors. By removing all incentive to monopolize land or to drive up its price through speculation, the taxing of rent would free the land for those willing to farm it. It would also destroy the parasitic, industrial capitalists, whose wealth came from a monopolistic access to natural resources that rightly belonged to all and from the labor of others.[51]

Even the so-called robber baron Andrew Carnegie, whose genius at cutting costs had made him the emperor of iron and steel, favored the taxation of inheritance on a scale that rivaled that of the agrarians. Although Carnegie differed fundamentally from the agrarians in perceiving the new industrialized society and its resultant inequalities of wealth as beneficial to society, he shared their desire for equal opportunity through the elimination of inheritance. Carnegie carried the principle of meritocracy to what he considered its logical conclusion. While he had only disdain for the desire of some agrarians to dismantle industry in order to return to a mythical past, he adapted the agrarian concept of equal opportunity to an industrialized society. Like Marx, he recognized that industrialization was an indispensable source of material progress. But while Marx favored state ownership and control of industry in order to produce equality of condition, Carnegie advocated societal ownership, but individual control, to produce equality of opportunity. But he was no more successful than the traditional agrarians. His only influence was to encourage private philanthropy.[52]

Agrarianism flourished briefly at Vanderbilt University during the 1930s. A group of professors there published *I'll Take My Stand*, a manifesto of southern agrarianism. The authors argued that the northeastern-dominated Republican Party had taken advantage of the Civil War to foist capitalism on the nation. The end result of this corrupt economic system was the Great Depression. The authors called for the return of the land to small farmers. Like previous agrarians and other radicals, they failed to secure the enactment of their program.[53]

THE TRIUMPH OF WHIG ECONOMICS

The Civil War settled the economic dispute in favor of Whig economics. The classical economics that had prevailed throughout most of the early republican period was one of the chief casualties of the war. The Democratic Party of the defeated South was the party of classical economics, while the new Republican Party of the victorious North was the party of Whig economics. As soon as Southern congressmen left Washington when their states seceded from the Union, the Republicans passed legislation increasing the nation's tariffs and funding a transcontinental railroad. The war itself raised the national debt. Only two Democratic presidents were elected between 1860 and 1932. Tariffs remained high during that period, though partly because the tariffs of foreign competitors remained high. In the early twentieth century presidents like Theodore Roosevelt and Woodrow Wilson proposed laws that instituted the first government regulation of big business. In 1913 the Federal Reserve Act created a national banking system. The Progressive Era, based on the belief that big government was necessary to balance big business, had arrived.[54]

Although the Great Depression led to the reduction of tariffs, when many observers realized that the Smoot-Hawley tariff of 1930 had greatly worsened the global depression, it also produced the welfare state. Lyndon B. Johnson's "Great Society" programs expanded the New Deal agencies enormously and supplemented them with a large number of new agencies. The story of the past century is largely the story of the creation of new federal agencies and the expansion of older agencies in an effort to solve a host of problems (the rise of big business monopolies, poverty, two world wars, the Cold War, and racial discrimination).[55]

Contrary to popular belief, social spending has hardly slowed since "the conservative 1980s." In that decade federal spending on income support rose 6 percent above the level of inflation, on health 63 percent above inflation, and on housing 65 percent above inflation. Essentially, Republican presidents and Democratic congresses agreed to spend lavishly on both domestic and defense programs. In the 1990s, though the deficit was reduced partly through economic growth and partly by dramatically reducing the rate of growth of the defense budget, both entitlement and discretionary spending continued to rise rapidly. Domestic spending increased both in real terms and as a percentage of gross domestic product. These figures are all the more remarkable in light of the Republican control of Congress throughout the second half of that decade. While George W. Bush has succeeded in enacting tax cuts consistent with classical economics, he has simultaneously signed bills that have funded both military and domestic programs on a lavish scale. The passage of this Reaganesque combination of classical and Whig proposals by a Republican Congress demonstrates the continued popularity of certain aspects of both economic philosophies.[56]

Nevertheless, the enactment of tax cuts does not negate the existence of an apparent national consensus on the role of government in American life. The continuous and prodigious growth of government over the past half century is clear evidence that the Whig concept of government as the necessary regulator of the economy has prevailed. Although laissez-faire arguments are still invoked in favor of tax cuts and free trade and in order to oppose specific government projects and practices, they are but daggers salvaged from the hull of the scuttled battleship of classical economics. Most Americans now accept a level of government intervention in the economy that surpasses the darkest nightmares of Adam Smith and the brightest dreams of Daniel Raymond.

NOTES

1. George Rogers Taylor, *The Transportation Revolution, 1815–1860* (New York: Rinehart, 1951), 186.

2. Taylor, *Transportation Revolution*, 33, 52, 57–58, 63, 227; Constance Green, *Eli Whitney and the Birth of American Technology* (Boston: Little, Brown, 1956), 45–48; Stuart Bruchey, *Enterprise: The Dynamic Economy of a Free People* (Cambridge, Mass.: Harvard University Press, 1990), 139, 142–43, 154, 221, 230, 237; W. Elliot Brownlee, *Dynamics of Ascent: A History of the American Economy* (New York: Alfred A. Knopf, 1974), 106, 116, 119–20, 135–36; Lawrence F. Abbott, *Twelve Great Modernists* (New York: Doubleday, Page, 1927), 174–75; Walter Licht, *Working for the Railroad: The Organization of Work in the Nineteenth Century* (Princeton, N.J.: Princeton University Press, 1983), 10.; Thomas Dublin, *Women at Work: The Transformation of Work and Community in Lowell, Massachusetts, 1826–1860* (New York: Columbia University Press, 1979), 9, 16–19, 59.

3. Brownlee, *Dynamics of Ascent*, 88–89, 136, 149–52, 155–58; Bruchey, *Enterprise*, 148; Taylor, *Transportation Revolution*, 384.

4. Brownlee, *Dynamics of Ascent*, 100, 112–13; William V. Shannon, *The American Irish* (New York: Macmillan, 1963), 28; Carl Wittke, *Refugees of Revolution: The German Forty-Eighters in America* (Philadelphia: University of Pennsylvania Press, 1952), 43.

5. Joseph G. Rayback, *A History of American Labor* (New York: Macmillan, 1959), 17, 54–55, 59, 65–68, 70, 76, 89, 95; Sean Wilentz, *Chants Democratic: New York City and the Rise of the American Working Class, 1788–1850* (Oxford: Oxford University Press, 1984), 203, 213–14, 223, 290, 385.

6. Brownlee, *Dynamics of Ascent*, 63–67.

7. Paul K. Conkin, *Prophets of Prosperity: America's First Political Economists* (Bloomington: Indiana University Press, 1980), 18–19.

8. Adam Smith, *The Wealth of Nations* (New York: Penguin Books, 1970), 22, 28, 44–48, 54–58, 61, 76–79, 81, 117, 126, 172–73, 197–98, 223, 466.

9. Smith, *Wealth of Nations*, 81, 135, 172, 440, 488–89; Brownlee, *Dynamics of Ascent*, 63; Thomas Sowell, *Classical Economics Reconsidered* (Princeton, N.J.: Princeton University Press, 1974), 11–13, 24–25; Robert Middlekauff, *The Glorious Cause: The American Revolution, 1763–1789* (Oxford: Oxford University Press, 1982), 57.

10. Smith, *Wealth of Nations*, 78, 442–43.

11. Smith, *Wealth of Nations*, 77–78, 81–82, 251.

12. Smith, *Wealth of Nations*, 229–32, 356–59, 371, 462.

13. Thomas Robert Malthus, *An Essay on the Principle of Population* (New York: W. W. Norton, 1976), xiv, 21–22, 35–39, 43–44, 47, 53, 56.

14. Thomas Robert Malthus, *Principles of Political Economy*, 2d ed. (Clifton, N.J.: August M. Kelly, 1974), vii–viii, 6–7, 315–16, 323, 354, 360, 398–401, 418, 422, 429, 436; Smith, *Wealth of Nations*, 430, 447.

15. Malthus, *Principles of Political Economy*, 6, 16, 328, 410–11, 418, 427, 434–35.

16. Malthus, *Principles of Political Economy*, 160–62, 195–96.

17. David Ricardo, *Principles of Political Economy and Taxation* (London: J. M. Dent and Sons, 1943), 35, 37, 40–42, 52, 57–58, 65, 67, 69, 71, 75, 222.

18. Ricardo, *Principles of Political Economy and Taxation*, 61–63.

19. Ricardo, *Principles of Political Economy and Taxation*, 210, 212–14, 227.

20. Ricardo, *Principles of Political Economy and Taxation*, 94–97, 157.

21. Ricardo, *Principles of Political Economy and Taxation*, 205; Sowell, *Classical Economics Reconsidered*, 26, 67–68.

22. Ricardo, *Principles of Poltical Economy and Taxation*, 245.

23. Ricardo, *Principles of Political Economy and Taxation*, 266, 271, 289.

24. Conkin, *Prophets of Prosperity*, 36–37, 132.

25. Sowell, *Classical Economics Reconsidered*, 16; Ricardo, *Principles of Political Economy and Taxation*, 225, 292.

26. Sowell, *Classical Economics Reconsidered*, 118, 137; Malthus, *Principles of Political Economy*, 1, 432.

27. Conkin, *Prophets of Prosperity*, 3–4, 52, 56, 61–62, 71.

28. Conkin, *Prophets of Prosperity*, 57.

29. Conkin, *Prophets of Prosperity*, 59.

30. Conkin, *Prophets of Prosperity*, 61–78.

31. Conkin, *Prophets of Prosperity*, 61–78.

32. Conkin, *Prophets of Prosperity*, 171–72.

33. Daniel Raymond, *The Elements of Political Economy*, 2 vols. (New York: August M. Kelley, 1964), vol. 1, i–ii, 50, 123; vol. 2, 4, 96, 103, 129–32, 146–47, 155–62, 261, 274–76, 310. Raymond's book, *Thoughts on Political Economy*, was later retitled, as indicated above.

34. Raymond, *Elements of Political Economy*, vol. 1, 219–20; vol. 2, 196–97, 200, 242, 245–49; A. Whitney Griswold, "Jefferson's Agrarian Democracy," in *Thomas Jefferson and American Democracy*, ed. Henry C. Dethloff (Lexington, Mass.: D. C. Heath, 1971), 49–50; Drew R. McCoy, *The Last of the Fathers: James Madison and the Republican Legacy* (Cambridge: Cambridge University Press, 1989), 94–95.

35. Raymond, *Elements of Political Economy*, vol. 1, 205–7, 216, 375–76, 392; vol. 2, 230–31, 240–44.

36. Raymond, *Elements of Political Economy*, vol. 2, 247–48, 296, 304.

37. Raymond, *Elements of Political Economy*, vol. 2, 32, 49–51, 71, 76–77, 80–81, 96, 103.

38. Henry C. Carey, *Principles of Social Science*, 3 vols. (Philadelphia: J. B. Lippincott, 1858), vol. 2, 180, 235; Conkin, *Prophets of Prosperity*, 271–72, 281–82.

39. Henry C. Carey, *Principles of Political Economy*, 3 vols. (New York: August M. Kelley, 1965), vol. 1, 160, 166, 171–74, 185, 191, 212, 309, 340; vol. 3, 9, 12.

40. Carey, *Principles of Political Economy*, vol. 1, 341; vol. 2, 8, 464–66; vol. 3, 51, 246, 249.

41. Carey, *Principles of Political Economy*, vol. 1, 171, 340; vol. 2, 462–63; vol. 3, 62; Carey, *Principles of Social Science*, vol. 2, 202, 253; Conkin, *Prophets of Prosperity*, 283, 294.

42. Carey, *Principles of Social Science*, vol. 1, 273–83, 286–88, 387–88, 407, 427, 448; vol. 2, 177–81, 272–74.

43. Conkin, *Prophets of Prosperity*, 265–67, 280, 283–95, 300–301.

44. Conkin, *Prophets of Prosperity*, 281, 304–6.

45. Kenneth S. Davis, *FDR, the New Deal Years, 1933–1937: A History* (New York: Random House, 1979), 647, 674–75.

46. Louis Hartz, *The Liberal Tradition in America* (New York: Harcourt-Brace, 1955), 3, 5, 18; H. Wayne Morgan, *Eugene V. Debs: Socialist for President* (Syracuse, N.Y.: Syracuse University Press, 1962), 138, 142.

47. Bruchey, *Enterprise*, 1.

48. William Bradford, *Of Plymouth Plantation, 1620–1647* (New York: Random House, 1981), 132–34; Ronald G. Walters, *American Reformers, 1815–1860* (New York: Hill & Wang, 1978), 48–71.

49. Paul A. Rahe, *Republics, Ancient and Modern: Classical Republicanism and the American Revolution* (Chapel Hill: University of North Carolina Press, 1992), 71, 139; H. H. Scullard, *From the Gracchi to Nero: A History of Rome from 133 B.C. to A.D. 68* (London: Merithen, 1959), 18–21, 27; J. G. A. Pocock, ed., *The Political Works of James Harrington* (Cambridge: Cambridge University Press, 1977), 459, 607; John Locke, *Two Treatises of Government* (Cambridge: Cambridge University Press, 1960), 327–44; Paul K. Conkin, *Self-Evident Truths* (Bloomington: Indiana University Press, 1974), 113; Thomas Skidmore, *The Rights of Man to Property* (New York: Burt Franklin, 1964).

50. Rayback, *History of American Labor*, 70; Wilentz, *Chants Democratic*, 340–42; David M. Potter, *Division and the Stresses of Reunion, 1845–1876* (Glenview, Ill.: Scott, Foresman, 1973), 200.

51. Henry George, *Progress and Poverty* (New York: Robert Schalkenbach Foundation, 1940), xi, 6–8, 10, 263, 287, 328–29, 369–74, 405, 460–61.

52. Andrew Carnegie, *The Gospel of Wealth and Other Timely Essays*, ed. Edward C. Kirkland (Cambridge, Mass.: Harvard University Press, 1962), xvii–xviii, 15–29.

53. Twelve Southerners, *I'll Take My Stand* (New York: Peter Smith, 1951), x, xiii, xvii–xx, 16–25.

54. Potter, *Division and the Stresses of Reunion, 1845–1876*, 200–202; Eliot Jones, *The Trust Problem in the United States* (New York: Macmillan, 1929), 326–29, 333–71; Arthur S. Link, *Woodrow Wilson and the Progressive Era, 1910–1917* (New York: Harper & Row, 1954), 52–53.

55. L. Ethan Ellis, *Republican Foreign Policy, 1921–1933* (New Brunswick, N.J.: Rutgers, 1968), 21–22.

56. Ed Rubenstein, "Decade of Neglect," *National Review*, August 31, 1992, 38. Rubenstein cited the Congressional Research Service as his source. With regard to the 1990s see Robert J. Samuelson, "The Peace Dividend," *Newsweek*, January 26, 1998, 49.

6

REVIVALISM, REFORM, AND ROMANTICISM IN THE ANTEBELLUM PERIOD

By the antebellum period humanism had transformed American Christianity, yet in so gradual and informal a fashion as to arouse little notice. Formerly orthodox Christians either openly or tacitly abandoned the crucial doctrine of original sin for an optimistic conception of human nature and a resultant belief in the possibility of lasting social and moral progress. Ironically, while alarmed by certain elements of eighteenth-century humanism—the emphasis on cold reason and the rejection of the supernatural—many antebellum Christians adopted a doctrine of perfectionism that was just as inconsistent with orthodox theism. Meanwhile, some romantic literary figures, such as the transcendentalists, substituted Platonic humanism for Christianity entirely. By then, all classes and regions were united by a common nationalism that may, in itself, have constituted a form of humanism.

REVIVALISM

The Second Great Awakening

In the early nineteenth century the United States was engulfed by a second wave of religious revivals. Like the Great Awakening, the Second Great Awakening was, in part, a reaction against the religious rationalism and materialism of an increasingly prosperous society. A group of religious rationalists boldly attacked Christian orthodoxy, eventually seceding from the Congregational

Church to form the Unitarian Church. Mostly affluent, they were called Unitarians because they rejected the Holy Trinity, including the divinity of Jesus, for the belief in a single, unitary God. Thomas Paine went even farther in his assault on the Bible, declaring in *The Age of Reason*, "It is a book of lies, wickedness, and blasphemy, for what can be more blasphemous than to ascribe the wickedness of man to the orders of the Almighty?" Such provocative declarations evoked great fear at a time when Americans were breathlessly considering reports of the abominations of the French Revolution, including Robespierre's pagan temples to Reason. At the same time universalism thrived among less affluent Americans. Universalists believed that every individual would *eventually* be saved, after doing penance for his sins in the afterlife, a doctrine that contradicted numerous biblical passages. While Unitarians believed that humans were too good to be damned, universalists held that God was too good to damn them. These movements were relatively small, but they were alarming to orthodox Christians already disturbed by the social instability and materialism produced by the Industrial Revolution. Lighting a match to this volatile mixture, revivalist ministers set the country ablaze.[1]

The Second Great Awakening began in central Kentucky. James McGready and four Presbyterian colleagues, joined by a Methodist preacher, spearheaded a series of summer revivals that began in 1795 and reached its climax in 1800–1801. Like most revivalists of both the first and second Great Awakenings, McGready contrasted the wrath of God toward unrepentant sinners with His love and mercy for those who repented, put their faith in Christ, and asked for forgiveness. As the historian John Boles puts it:

> Much of the emotive content of the sermons was not aimed at forcing the sinner in the audience to come to God in fear. Rather, it was evidenced when the deeply religious minister described the moving panorama of Jesus Christ's spiritual agony and physical suffering. Such a momentously poignant story of suffering and love, guilt and forgiveness, elicited the innermost feelings from the faithful both behind and in front of the pulpit. . . . It was this juxtaposing of fear and anxiety with love and security that made evangelical preaching so convincingly effective.

The destruction of complacency through terror was but the first step in the conversion process and was itself loving in intent.[2]

Indeed, McGready's revival improved the moral climate of Kentucky. One observer found Kentuckians "now as distinguished for sobriety as they had formerly been for dissoluteness; and indeed, I found Kentucky the most moral place I had ever been in; a profane expression was hardly heard, a religious awe seemed to pervade the country, and some deistical characters had confessed that, from whatever cause the revival might originate, it certainly made the people better." McGready's revival soon spread throughout the South and into Ohio, western Pennsylvania, and New York.[3]

The Second Great Awakening gave birth to a new institution, the camp meeting, at which Christians gathered for conversion and inspiration. The largest camp meeting occurred in August 1801 at Cane Ridge in Bourbon County, Kentucky. Attendance probably reached ten thousand one Sunday, twenty thousand over the six days of continual preaching. For Methodists and some Presbyterians, camp meetings became annual, standardized affairs.[4]

The eastern United States participated as fully in the Second Great Awakening as the West. In 1795 Timothy Dwight, the grandson of Jonathan Edwards, became president of Yale. By then only four or five students there professed orthodox Christianity. Dwight stirred Yale to a religious fervor that produced six revivals in the next twenty-five years. The famous revival preacher Lyman Beecher was one of his students. In 1808 Jedediah Morse, another prominent Congregationalist minister, established Andover Theological Seminary to counter Unitarian Harvard. Andover played a leading role in establishing other seminaries and colleges throughout the North. After 1810 missionaries were dispatched to India and Africa.[5]

Western New York blazed with such religious fervor that modern historians have dubbed it the "Burned-Over District." In 1821 a twenty-nine-year-old lawyer named Charles G. Finney had a conversion experience there. Finney announced soon after, "I have a retainer from the Lord Jesus Christ to plead his case." Ordained a Presbyterian minister in 1824, Finney rode from town to town preaching. Graceful in motion, with a voice of great clarity, tone, and power, Finney spoke logically but with wit, verve, and informality. He always preached from the church floor, disdaining the pulpit. He denounced excessive commercialism: "O this money that destroys a man's spirituality and endangers his soul! . . . The whole course of business in the world is governed by the maxims of supreme and unmixed selfishness." Finney employed newspaper advertising and door-to-door announcements to spread his message. He wrote manuals that taught preachers the new revival methods. He was the first nationally known American minister.[6]

In 1835 Finney became president of the new Oberlin College in Ohio, where he wrote theological tracts. Oberlin was one of the few American colleges to admit African Americans. It became a hotbed of antislavery activity. Although Finney advocated the use of persuasion to get slaveholders to free their slaves rather than the legal abolition of slavery, his students included prominent abolitionists.[7]

Finney ridiculed those who argued that revivalism contradicted predestination. Why couldn't God use revivals as His predestined means of causing repentance and saving souls? Finney complained, "Generation after generation have gone down to hell while the church has been dreaming and waiting for God to save them without the use of means."[8]

Like his predecessors, Finney hoped to precipitate a national Pentecost that would baptize America in the Holy Spirit. There were certainly enough preachers to do the physical baptizing; between 1776 and 1845 the number of American ministers per capita tripled.[9]

Effects of the Second Great Awakening

One effect of the Second Great Awakening was the emergence of new denominations. The most exotic and unorthodox of these new sects was the Church of Jesus Christ of Latter-day Saints, more popularly known as the Mormon Church. The Mormons soon suffered persecution for several reasons. First, many

Americans considered the addition of a new book to the sacred Scriptures a blasphemous act. Mormons accepted the *Book of Mormon*, revealed to church founder Joseph Smith Jr. in the 1820s, as such an addition.[10]

Second, many Americans were horrified by rumors of polygamy among the Mormon leadership. In 1841 Smith married the second of his nearly forty wives, some of whom were already married to other men, though the *Book of Mormon* had specifically condemned marriage to more than one wife. Smith based the practice of polygamy on a revelation but shared the revelation with, and encouraged the practice among, only a few trusted friends. Nevertheless, Mormon dissidents learned of the practice and informed Smith's enemies outside the sect.[11]

Third, many Americans were appalled by other Mormon doctrines. In his later years Smith advanced a polytheistic religion, in which both Jesus and Lucifer were sons of the ruling deity, Elohim. According to Smith, none of the numerous gods in existence had created the universe, which was eternal, though Jesus had organized the earth from preexisting matter at the instigation of Elohim, a coveted assignment that had so filled Lucifer with envy that he had rebelled against Elohim. The gods had once been like humans, and some humans would one day be gods. A popular Mormon phrase declared: "As man is God once was; as God is man may become." Devout Mormons could expect to reach godhood, the power to organize and people worlds, in the next life, as they assumed many other races on other planets had already done. (Non-Mormons would receive a lesser glory in the afterlife, but only the very worst would suffer eternal torment.) Mormons depicted Elohim, Jehovah (next in power to Elohim), Jesus, Lucifer, and the numerous other gods as separate entities, each composed of matter. Elohim had literally begotten his son through Mary in the same manner that humans beget their children. In fact, all of the gods were married and had children. Mormons also practiced posthumous baptism as a means of saving their ancestors, a doctrine that would later make Utah a center for genealogical research.[12]

Fourth, many Americans were suspicious of the Mormons' strict cohesion and incautious rhetoric about establishing a government that would rule the world one day. Shortly before his death in Carthage, Illinois, in 1844, Smith even established a secret council as a sort of world-government-in-waiting. His attempt to run for president of the United States in 1844 intensified suspicions. When Mormon dissidents published reports of Smith's secret practice of polygamy and plans for world government, Smith shut down their press, but not before the local authorities were aroused to arrest Smith on the charge of treason. While in prison, Smith and his brother were killed by a mob.[13]

After Smith's death, Brigham Young assumed leadership of most of the Mormons, ultimately guiding them to the Great Salt Lake (1846–1848). Isolated by mountains and desert, but fed by mountain streams of melted snow and close enough to the Oregon Trail for trade purposes, Utah proved an excellent location for a Mormon settlement.[14]

A smaller group of Mormons rejected the practice of polygamy, falsely attributing it to Young and not Smith. (Though Young always defended polygamy, he admitted that when Smith had initially introduced the practice, "It was the first time in my life that I desired the grave, and I could hardly get over it for a long time.") The smaller group remained in the Midwest, where their Reorganized Church of Jesus Christ of Latter-day Saints, headquartered at Independence, Missouri, is now known as the Community of Christ.[15]

The Republican platform of 1856 denounced "the twin relics of barbarism, slavery and polygamy." Although Utah possessed a population larger than that required for statehood, Congress delayed its entrance until 1896, six years after Mormon president Wilford Woodruff finally agreed to abolish polygamy on the basis of another revelation. By 1997 successful missionary efforts had made the Mormon Church the sixth largest Protestant denomination in the United States, with four million members (and an additional five million members abroad).[16]

Another group of denominations, the Adventist sects, formed in the "Burned-Over District" in the 1840s. Adventists believed that Christ was going to return soon (William Miller even proposed the year 1843, and then 1844, both of which elapsed without incident). The Seventh Day Adventists advocated a return to the celebration of the Sabbath on Saturday. (The seventh day of the week, on which God rested, according to the Book of Genesis, is Saturday. Jews have always observed the Sabbath on that day. The transfer of the Sabbath to Sunday was a Christian innovation, commemorating the day of Jesus's resurrection. Constantine then established Sunday as a day of rest as well as a day of worship.) Seventh Day Adventists also rejected the doctrine of separable, immaterial souls, arguing that individuals had no consciousness between death and the resurrection on Judgment Day. Based on the same materialist conception of reality, these Adventists also replaced eternal punishment of the damned with physical punishment of a limited duration followed by a second, permanent death. Other new sects included the Disciples of Christ and Churches of Christ, which formed around the desire to restore first-century Christianity.[17]

The Second Great Awakening also increased the popularity of certain older sects. The Methodist Church's emphasis on an emotional attachment to Christ was perfectly suited to the revivalism of the age. The founder of Methodism, John Wesley, was journeying to Georgia in 1735 to convert Native Americans to Christianity when a fierce storm pounded his ship. Deeply moved by the faith of the ten Moravian missionaries who sang psalms throughout the ordeal, Wesley contrasted their fervor with the cold rationalism then seeping into his own Anglican Church. He then determined to reform the Church of England. Wesley's followers emphasized free will. There was a method to salvation, one emphasizing faith, and a method to sanctification (purification) that included a variety of means.[18]

Not even Wesley's unpopular Tory views seemed capable of halting the expansion of Methodism in America. (Wesley urged the American colonists to submit to British rule.) In 1784, after the Revolutionary War, the Methodist Episcopal Church of America split from the Anglican Church. As a result of a sustained missionary effort, African American membership in the Methodist Church increased from 1,890 in 1786 to 209,836 in 1861. By 1800, 20 percent of the Methodists in the United States were

African Americans. Some Methodists, like Wesley himself, were initially opposed to slavery and even denied church membership to slaveholders.[19]

American Methodist bishops were chosen by a general conference of ministers (a bottom-up system Wesley detested), and the prevailing liturgy was a much simplified version of the Anglican form. This substantial reduction in the hierarchical and formalistic elements of Anglicanism, combined with the circuit system, in which frequently rotated preachers served large areas, increased Methodism's appeal in the frontier regions of both the North and the South. By 1850 the Methodist Church was the largest Christian denomination in the United States.[20]

Composed largely of Calvinists who practiced adult baptism by immersion, the various Baptist sects also spread rapidly in the early republican and antebellum periods. Some consider Roger Williams to have been the first Baptist minister in America. By 1700 there were ten Baptist congregations scattered throughout New England. In the 1750s New England Baptists sent missionaries into western Virginia and North Carolina, where they were frequently assaulted by Anglican mobs, jailed, and fined.[21]

Most Baptists favored a congregationalist structure, religious toleration, and an emotional style of preaching. Until the Revolutionary War, many were pacifists. Some opposed slavery. Baptists devoted much attention to converting slaves. There were approximately 18,000 black Baptists by 1793, 468,000 by 1859 (2.7 million by the 1900s). In fact, by the Civil War, 90 percent of African American Christians were either Baptist or Methodist. The closing years of the eighteenth century and the early decades of the nineteenth century witnessed an unprecedented spread of Christianity among African Americans.[22]

If Methodist and Baptist ministers were generally less educated than their Episcopalian, Presbyterian, and Congregationalist counterparts, they made up for it in numbers, in devotion, and in the ability to relate to the concerns of their congregations. By 1855 nearly 70 percent of all American Protestants, white and black, were either Methodist or Baptist. The substitution of the evangelical emphasis on the conversion experience for the Anglican emphasis on ritual and the Puritan emphasis on theological instruction helped to attract both blacks and poor whites to the Methodist and Baptist churches.[23]

Another effect of the Second Great Awakening was the growth of even greater religious toleration among Protestant denominations. As Protestants participated in an increasing number of interdenominational revivals and reform societies, all of which emphasized moral concerns over sectarian dogma, their ecumenism grew. The need for unity was one of the chief themes of revival preachers. James McGready warned his congregation, "Contention is one of the most subtle and effective engines of hell." Charles Finney advised that converts "should not be taught to dwell upon sectarian distinctions, or to be sticklish about sectarian points." A visiting Parisian pastor was surprised at the degree of religious harmony, considering the unprecedented number of denominations in America. Though Protestants might quarrel, they did not exclude one another from the Christian community. There were even numerous instances of different denominations sharing a single church building.[24]

Yet the same evangelical Protestants most eager to put aside doctrinal differences with their fellow Protestants in order to form a general movement for reform were most apt to engage in virulent attacks on Catholics. In 1834 Lyman Beecher's vicious and paranoid speech against Catholics in Boston helped cause the burning of a convent in Charlestown the following evening. Though Beecher repudiated the barbaric attack, he continued to provoke such violence with fantasies of Catholic conspiracies to enslave the United States. Evangelicals were prominent figures in the "nativist" movement that sought to extend the naturalization periods of Irish and German Catholics and exclude Catholics from political office.[25]

Nevertheless, there was more religious toleration in the antebellum United States than in any other nation in the world, and this religious freedom proved crucial to the survival of American Christianity. Many evangelicals were pleasantly surprised to discover that the religious toleration that had come to full fruition in the late eighteenth century actually benefited religion. Having fought to save the establishment of the Congregationalist Church in Connecticut, Lyman Beecher found that disestablishment was "the best thing that ever happened to the State of Connecticut." He explained, "It cut the churches loose from dependence on state support. It threw them wholly on their own resources and on God." When the clergy and the laity could no longer sit back and expect the government to promote religion, they were forced to do so themselves, and the crusade imparted a new vitality to their churches. Furthermore, once the church was separated from the state, the inevitable periodic surges of popular anger against the latter no longer spilled over onto the former. The historian Garry Wills has argued persuasively that the separation of church and state is one of the principal reasons why Christianity survived in America while becoming almost extinct in western Europe, where religious establishments continued long after they had been dissolved in the United States. The state-supported churches of western Europe became corrupt and apathetic political institutions devoid of inspiration—just another despised government bureaucracy.[26]

Yet another effect of the Second Great Awakening was a growing belief in free will. Methodists, who had inherited the free-will position from the Anglican Church, disseminated it throughout the United States. Most revivalists implied that Christians could receive grace through a willful acceptance of Christ as their lord and savior. In a virtuous cycle, grace, the action of the Holy Spirit, then increased the faith initiated by the believer. "New School" theologians like Nathaniel Taylor so revised the Calvinist doctrine of predestination as to render it meaningless, a reinterpretation supported by many prominent Calvinist ministers. By the mid-nineteenth century most Protestant Americans had abandoned predestination, even while continuing to use, in a significantly modified form, Pauline rhetoric.[27]

Finally, and most significantly, the Second Great Awakening spread postmillennialism, the doctrine that Christ would return after humans had created the utopian millennium prophesied in the Bible. Antebellum postmillennialism contradicted the orthodox Christian doctrine of original sin that underlay premillennialism, the belief that Jesus's return and rule were necessary to inaugurate the millennium, since humans were too sinful to save themselves, much less to create an earthly utopia. Postmillennialism flatly contradicted the numerous biblical passages concerning the end-times, both in the Old and New Testaments, all of which portrayed the Messiah as entering a world plagued by bloody wars, rampant immorality, and natural disasters. Nevertheless, in 1835, Charles Finney declared that "the millennium can come in three years" if Americans simply "do their duty." He added, "The world is not growing worse but better."[28]

The popularity of postmillennialism in antebellum America can be attributed to a growing belief in perfectionism. Influenced by a series of tracts written by John Wesley, beginning in 1741 and culminating in his *Plain Account of Christian Perfection* (1766), Methodists argued that an individual's decision to accept Jesus's atonement for humanity's sins won him the grace of the Holy Spirit. Grace, in turn, produced in the individual both gratitude to God and discontent with his remaining inclination to sin. Through faith, good works, earnest prayer, fasting, and obedience to God's commandments, this discontent could be followed by a second stage producing complete love of God and perfection of the soul. Though a person so fully sanctified might still make moral mistakes through ignorance, his intentions would always be pure. Though temptation would never cease (a logical problem if the soul is truly perfect), and "backsliders" might even lose the grace they had received through neglect of prayer and good works, the fully sanctified individual could live without committing any intentional offenses against God. Indeed, Wesley claimed that such an individual would be "in such a sense perfect, as . . . to be freed from evil thoughts and evil tempers." There was no theoretical reason why all who accepted Christ should not achieve complete sanctification, though in practice some would probably never achieve it. Though original sin had made it impossible for people to avoid impure thoughts and intentional offenses against God before the atonement of Christ, the possibility of grace now saved Christians from the necessity of sin. Wesley was not deterred from this view by the fact that even the greatest disciples, Peter and Paul, had sinned. Wesley wrote: "No necessity of sin was laid upon them. The grace of God was sufficient for them. And it is sufficient for us at this day."[29]

Wesley explicitly assaulted the theology of both Calvinists and Roman Catholics, who agreed with one another that the effects of original sin were never completely eliminated until death. (Nevertheless, Wesley may have drawn upon a Catholic strain of perfectionism latent in monasticism. He read and admired the medieval mystic and perfectionist Thomas á Kempis.) By 1762 even Wesley expressed concern that some Methodists were going "from house to house to persuade people to believe they are perfect when God hath not persuaded them," and that others "believe that they cannot err ... [or that] it [is] impossible for them to sin and fall." Wesley's perfectionism—ignored by many Methodists since the late nineteenth century—went beyond the classic free-will doctrine and approached the perfectionism of the Gnostics, who had challenged the doctrine of original sin in the early church. As late as 1852 the Methodist General Conference declared: "The crowning work of the Spirit of holiness is to sanctify believers wholly—their whole spirit, soul, and body—and to preserve them blameless until death. We would, therefore, exhort you, dear brethren, that the doctrine of entire sanctification or entire holiness be not confined to our standards, but that it may be a matter of experience in our hearts and may be constantly practiced in our lives."[30]

Even Lyman Beecher and Charles Finney, ordained ministers in Calvinist congregations, advanced competing doctrines of perfectionism that reflected popular optimism about the achievement of an earthly utopia. Beecher suggested that the triumph of American-style representative democracy and freedom of thought and expression around the world would bring on the millennium. Finney insisted that those who had achieved grace would "habitually live without sin and fall into sin only at intervals so few and far between that, in strong language, it may be said in truth that they do not sin." Finney claimed that man could learn "to prefer the glory of God and the interest of His kingdom to his own selfish interests" and that "the perfect control of this preference over all the moral movements of the mind brings a man back to where Adam was previous to the fall and constitutes perfect holiness." He predicted, "As the millennium advances, it is probable that these periodical excitements [revivals] will be unknown," because they will become unnecessary. He explained: "Children will be trained up in the way they should go, and there will be no such torrents of worldliness, and fashion and covetousness, to bear away the piety of the church as soon as the excitement of a revival is withdrawn." Such a view presupposed the complete annihilation of original sin by grace.[31]

Many antebellum Americans substituted for traditional Christian pessimism about the earthly life a conception of social progress that was even more optimistic than that of Epicurean humanists. While Epicurean humanists stated only that the "blank slate" of the infant's mind rendered earthly progress a possibility, many antebellum Americans considered such progress inevitable.

REFORM

The increasing popularity of postmillennialism produced an almost feverish desire for social reform to hurry the Second Coming of Christ. Most reformers worked for more than one organization, considering them all part of a general and united effort to destroy evil. So genuine was the commitment of the reform leaders that, though they must have been perpetually tempted by the millions of dollars in contributions that passed through their hands, there is only one known instance of theft from a reform organization in the antebellum period. Postmillennialism spawned so many reform societies that by 1835 one foreign observer noted in his diary, "Americans are Society mad."[32]

Yet, although southerners were as evangelical and postmillennialist as northerners, few southerners participated in the antebellum reform movements, except for a mild effort at temperance. Southern evangelicals were more individualistic than their northern counterparts; they generally called individual persons to account for their transgressions, not society as a whole. It should also be noted that the Whig Party and its successor, the new Republican Party of Abraham Lincoln, included in its ranks more reformers than the

Democratic Party, whose social philosophy, like its economic philosophy, tended toward laissez-faire.[33]

Though it is true that the antebellum mania for reform arose from the displacement of Christian orthodoxy by a strain of humanist perfectionism, this is not to suggest that orthodox theism and reform are mutually exclusive. Humanist reformers differ from theist reformers only in purpose. While humanists believe that the purpose of reform is to achieve lasting social and moral progress, orthodox theists believe that the struggle for moral improvement, though ultimately futile in a world crippled by original sin, is a noble effort, pleasing to God. (While eliminating God from the picture, many modern existentialists have adopted the same Augustinian position.) Furthermore, to the orthodox theist, reform might be necessary just to keep human society from regressing. One does not cease cleaning his house altogether merely because it will soon become dirty again. Just as continual effort is needed merely to keep a house in a livable condition, reform may be needed just to keep society in a livable condition. Although periods of intense reform (like periods of intense housecleaning) cannot be sustained, and invariably lapse into periods of apathy and inaction, they are still necessary to prevent the complete collapse into barbarism toward which the human race inclines. This was the theist's conception of reform.

The Public Education Movement

But while the postmillennialist reformers of the antebellum era agreed on the possibility of progress, some differed (as humanists still do) concerning the correct means of achieving it. Many reformers viewed public education as the chief path to the millennium. Partly as a result of the elimination of property qualifications for voting, the number of public schools increased greatly during the antebellum period. Most Americans accepted the Jeffersonian view that progress could be achieved through majority rule combined with public education.

Massachusetts lawyer, legislator, and educational reformer Horace Mann considered public education the greatest tool in the struggle against poverty. He called education "the great equalizer of the condition of men," and added that it "does better than disarm the poor of their hostility toward the rich; it prevents [their] being poor." A good public school system would also make students of all economic classes virtuous. Mann wrote, "Our system inculcates all Christian morals." He supported Bible-reading in the public schools, though he resisted all efforts to teach specific sectarian doctrines. He sponsored many reforms, including state boards of education (he himself was appointed the first secretary of education of Massachusetts in 1837), teacher-training institutes, and a minimum school year of six months.[34]

From 1800 to 1850 the amount of time the average American child spent in school doubled. By 1860, 320 high schools (more than half concentrated in Massachusetts, New York, and Ohio) began filling the great void of secondary education in the United States. As the number of public schools increased, and the supply of available male teachers decreased owing to other professional opportunities, women filled the gap. Teaching became one of the few professions open to women, though they were paid considerably less than their male counterparts.[35]

Other new educational opportunities for common people included the lyceum lectures (an impressive lecture circuit that featured prominent politicians and literary figures), cheap Bibles (including foreign-language Bibles for immigrants) distributed by the American Bible Society (1816), Sunday schools supplied with materials by the American Sunday School Union (1824), inexpensive sermons and essays distributed by the American Tract Society (1825), public libraries, and new (largely denominational) colleges. The American Educational Society aided indigent college and seminary students who proved themselves serious, well-behaved, and pious.[36]

The Temperance Movement

Others saw intemperance as both the chief cause of poverty and the greatest hindrance to social progress. Antebellum Americans drank enormous amounts of alcohol. The census of 1810 reported approximately fifteen thousand distilleries producing over twenty-two million gallons of distilled liquor per year. This figure does not include beer, wine, cider, or the millions of gallons of liquor produced by illegal stills. So many frontier farmers converted their grain into whiskey, to reduce the bulk and make it easier to transport over difficult roads and mountains, that whiskey became a sort of currency in frontier areas. Even clergymen were paid with it. Lyman Beecher recalled an ordination in 1811 at which a large group of ministers engaged in excessive drinking and smoking.[37]

Alarmed by the increase in alcohol consumption, as many as one million Americans took some sort of temperance pledge. Temperance advocates ranged from Abraham Lincoln to numerous southerners. Factory owners supported temperance—for their workers at least. With their rigid schedules and dangerous machinery, the new factories, trains, and steamboats required a greater degree of sobriety.[38]

Supporters of temperance argued that a reduction in alcohol consumption would decrease poverty and crime, create a more wholesome environment for children in the home, and save souls. The *Baptist Register* of Utica, New York exulted, "The glorious cause of temperance and religion . . . march with correspondent steps onward to perfection." More than one in every eight novels published in the United States in the 1830s dealt with temperance. Temperance advocates' favorite among these novels was Timothy Shay Arthur's *Ten Nights in a Barroom* (1853), a melodramatic work in which nearly every character is killed in a barroom fight. In 1826 a group of Boston ministers established the American Society for the Promotion of Temperance. On their pledges not to drink distilled liquor the ministers placed a T (for "total abstinence") beside their signatures. Hence leaders of the movement for abstinence became known as "teetotalers." By 1831 the society possessed 170,000 lay members and 2,000 local chapters, nearly all of them associated with a Christian denomination.[39]

In 1833 the United States Temperance Union, soon known as the American Temperance Union, was formed. The organization initially promoted abstinence only from distilled liquor but soon extended it to all forms of alcohol and even advocated legal prohibition, thereby alienating the sizable portion of its membership who had no problem with the moderate drinking of beer or wine. In fact, the leaders of one local temperance society met at a tavern to toast their own moderation. But the more zealous temperance advocates criticized farmers for selling grain to distillers; proposed the denial of the Lord's Supper to the intemperate; suggested removing the wine from the Lord's Supper; and criticized the consumption of tea, coffee, and tobacco as well.[40]

Although temperance reformers failed to secure national or state legislation against alcohol, except for a few temporary laws restricting its sale in parts of New England, New York, and the Northwest, they succeeded in passing fairly permanent prohibition laws in certain localities. More important, by drawing attention to the national drinking problem, they persuaded Americans to reduce their alcohol consumption dramatically.[41]

Aid for the Poor

Antebellum reformers also constructed a large number of almshouses, orphanages, and hospitals for the poor. Home missionary and tract societies found jobs for the poor; distributed food, clothing, and money to them; and resettled destitute children. In 1851 the Young Men's Christian Association was established. The YMCA launched rescue missions in poor areas. Its goal was to help young men grow not only in the love of God and in Christian faith, but also in zeal for human welfare. By 1825 there were over one hundred private relief organizations in New York City alone. These organizations generally distinguished between the "worthy poor"—widows, orphans, the disabled, and others down on their luck—and the "unworthy poor," idlers and criminals. European visitors were astonished at the vast sums the laity contributed to charity, the construction of churches, and the maintenance of reform organizations.[42]

The Prison Reform Movement

Perhaps the best example of antebellum optimism concerning human nature and the possibility for progress was the prison reform movement. Partly on the basis of the Italian Enlightenment philosopher Cesare Beccaria's contention that it was the certainty and duration of punishment, not its severity, that deterred crime, American states had abolished or greatly reduced various forms of physical punishment, including death, whipping, the stocks, and branding, during the decades after the American Revolution, substituting prison sentences for these penalties. Previously, jails had been designed only to hold prisoners until they received their physical punishment. Assuming that human nature was essentially good, prison reformers in a dozen states developed the concept of the "penitentiary," a place where prisoners could repent of their crimes. Reformers insisted that prisoners occupy separate cells and that they be prohibited from speaking to one another or to the outside world. Only then could they enjoy the quiet necessary to reflect upon the folly of their ways and repent. In New York prisoners were allowed virtually no verbal communication, and in Pennsylvania they did not even know the identities of fellow convicts. Like other reformers of the age, prison reformers often saw their favored institution, the penitentiary, as the remedy for all the evils of society. Since crime was produced by a bad environment, not innate flaws in the human character, society might eliminate it through a new environment that would instill self-discipline in prisoners. The penitentiary would reform those few the revival failed to convert. "Reform schools" were first constructed in this period to provide similar discipline for juvenile delinquents.[43]

By the 1820s prison reformers had also achieved success in abolishing imprisonment for debt. Debtors had previously been imprisoned alongside violent criminals. The prison reformers' optimism about human nature was perhaps surpassed only by that of the small anarchist wing of the American Peace Society (1828), who opposed prisons themselves and any other kind of force, including personal self-defense and defensive wars (at least until the Civil War, at which point they endorsed the Union effort).[44]

Asylums for the Mentally Ill

Prison reformers and others also lobbied for the construction of mental institutions. Objects of shame, some sufferers of mental illness had been kept hidden in attics, while others had been held in prisons, cages, stalls, and pens. The mentally ill were often painfully restrained by mechanical contraptions. Even King George III of England was not safe from cruel and unusual (though well-intentioned) "treatments" after he became mentally ill in the 1780s. In 1830, with the help of Horace Mann, the Boston Prison Discipline Society persuaded the Massachusetts legislature to authorize the construction of a hospital for the mentally ill at Worcester. Completed three years later, the hospital became a model for other mental institutions.[45]

The leading crusader for such institutions was Dorothea Dix, a Boston schoolteacher financed by a modest inheritance. Dix was especially opposed to the imprisonment of the mentally ill. She argued that this practice was not only inhumane to the mentally ill, but also constituted cruel and inhuman punishment for other prisoners, who were compelled to listen to their ravings all day. Like some other reformers of her era, she refused to concede anything to biological inheritance; she blamed an alleged increase in insanity completely on the stresses of the new industrial order. Indeed, she expected mental institutions to teach self-control and Christian virtue as much as any school or penitentiary. By the Civil War, the federal government, twenty-eight states, and four cities had constructed mental institutions. Institutions for the deaf and blind also date from this period.[46]

The "Cult of Domesticity" and the Women's Rights Movement

Meanwhile, some women hoped to improve society by clarifying their proper role within it. Many accepted the pervasive system of stereotypes that modern historians have branded "the cult of domesticity." This ideology was perhaps most fully expressed in Catharine Beecher's best-selling book, *A Treatise on Domestic Economy* (1841). Amid the usual advice on home economics, the raising of children, gardening, and health, some of it quite advanced for its day, Beecher claimed that women were inherently different from men: less intellectual, more emotional, and more moral. Because of these inherent differences, the woman's proper sphere was domestic, while the man's proper sphere was public. Women should be concerned with maintaining the household, not with politics, economics, or other public affairs. This conclusion reveals as much about antebellum attitudes toward home and work as it does about beliefs concerning gender differences; public affairs supposedly required more intelligence and less morality than domestic matters.[47]

Beecher did not argue that women were inferior to men. On the contrary, in this supremely moralistic age, to claim moral superiority was to claim a general superiority. Furthermore, Beecher considered the domestic sphere more important and more challenging than the public sphere. What could be more important than establishing the home as a haven from the cold, cruel world? What could be more crucial than raising the next generation? What could be more difficult than satisfying the physical, medical, educational, and spiritual needs of growing children? Although Beecher believed that a woman's place was in the home, she considered her role a vital one and insisted that husbands give their wives equal pay.[48]

Since the role of homemaker was a difficult and crucial job, it should be treated as a profession. Beecher founded women's schools in Connecticut, Ohio, and Wisconsin, schools that boldly departed from the usual emphasis on rote learning while retaining the common focus on religious and moral training. She also established the American Woman's Education Association to promote female education. She believed that extensive training would improve the work and morale of women, by giving them a sense of esprit de corps, and would gain for them the social status they deserved.[49]

Other prominent women shared Beecher's conception of gender roles. Though Louisa McCord, Beecher's southern counterpart, denied that women were intellectually inferior to men, she believed they possessed a different kind of intellect, one that would be wasted in the political arena seeking "the ambiguous honour of the Presidency." The hearth provided enough real challenges for any martyr, philosopher, or saint—all far greater roles than that of politician. Real heroes and heroines did not battle against nature but perfected it. Even the feminist Sarah Grimke once wrote that women were morally superior to men because "the sexual passion in men is ten times stronger than in women," though at another time she wrote, "God has made no distinction between men and women as moral beings." Grimke's ambivalence on the issue of moral equality (she had no such ambivalence in asserting that women were the intellectual equals of men) revealed an enduring tension within feminist thought: the tension between the quest for equality, based on the claim of the sameness of the genders, and the assertion of female superiority, based on the claim of innate differences between them.[50]

The belief in the moral superiority of women was perhaps most clearly enshrined in *Uncle Tom's Cabin* (1852), the first American novel to sell over one million copies. In the novel, by Harriet Beecher Stowe, Catharine Beecher's sister, the female characters must save the souls of their poor, misguided menfolk from the moral evil of slavery. The few moral men in the novel have been made so by their tender wives and sweet old mothers (even Simon Legree feels pangs of guilt at the thought of his saintly mother), and the only immoral woman (Marie St. Clare) remarks that she inherited her proslavery views from her father. The only moral equals of women are children (like little Eva) and slaves (like Uncle Tom), whose worldly powerlessness is exceeded only by their moral purity.[51]

But a vocal minority of women sought progress through equality of the genders. These women rejected the cult of domesticity and the legal and political inequalities that resulted from it. The other antebellum reform movements briefly opened a narrow door into public life for women, leading some to desire greater political participation. Some of these women held a convention at Seneca Falls, New York, on July 19, 1848. Elizabeth Cady Stanton drafted the Declaration of Sentiments, a document based on the Declaration of Independence, which compared wives with slaves and criticized male assaults on female self-confidence and self-respect. The declaration demanded the ballot, greater educational and professional opportunities for women (including clerical ordination), and the repeal of laws granting husbands greater property and custody rights in divorce cases. Despite the reform experience of veterans of the antislavery movement like Stanton, Susan B. Anthony, Sojourner Truth, the Grimke sisters, Lucy Stone, and numerous other suffragettes, the women's rights movement failed to achieve its chief goal until 1920, when the Nineteenth Amendment guaranteed American women the vote.[52]

The antebellum suffragettes were as much a product of the Second Great Awakening as the followers of the cult of domesticity. Stanton's Declaration of Sentiments urged the American woman to "move in an enlarged sphere which her great Creator has assigned her." Sarah Grimke declared that God had created woman as the equal of man, subject only to God. She added, "The lust of dominion was probably the first effect of the fall [of Adam and Eve]; and as there was no other intelligent being over whom to exercise it, woman was the first victim of this unhallowed passion." What is most striking in Grimke's writings is that her plea for the admission of women into politics and the clergy was not so much a demand for equal rights as a demand for equal duties, in stark contrast to the modern, almost universal obsession with rights. She bemoaned the fact that the obstacles to the full participation of women in society prevented them from fulfilling their obligations as moral beings.[53]

The Abolitionist Movement

A growing number of northerners began to believe that slavery was the enemy that must be slain to achieve the promise of progress on which the nation had been founded. As late as 1830, most American emancipation societies were located in the slave states of the South. The American Colonization Society (1816), founded on the view that slaves should be emancipated and colonized in Africa, was the largest antislavery organization. Its members included James Madison, James Monroe, John Marshall, Henry Clay, and Daniel Webster. Some members advocated colonization as a means of Christianizing Africa. Most African Americans opposed colonization from the beginning. America was their native land, and they had earned a place in it. Nevertheless, having purchased land from various West African tribes, the American

Colonization Society created the independent Republic of Liberia. By 1860, only about ten thousand African Americans, a tiny fraction of the South's 3.5 million blacks, had emigrated to Liberia with the help of the society. Putting aside the question of fairness, the colonization of so many people in West Africa would have been impractical even if southern slaveholders had agreed to release their slaves. As it was, some slaveholders supported only the colonization of free blacks, who they feared might incite their slaves to rebel.[54]

The 1830s witnessed a fateful development. The antislavery movement shifted to the North and became much more radical. On January 1, 1831, twenty-six-year-old William Lloyd Garrison established the first antislavery newspaper in America. He began the first issue of the *Liberator* with a fervent attack upon slavery: "I will be as harsh as truth, and as uncompromising as justice. On this subject, I do not wish to think, or speak, or write with moderation. . . . I am in earnest—I will not equivocate—I will not excuse—I will not retreat a single inch—AND I WILL BE HEARD!!!" (And he *was* heard; death threats filled his mail, and a Boston mob nearly lynched him in 1835.) Garrison vehemently denounced those moderate abolitionists who favored gradual emancipation combined with compensation for slaveholders. He asked, "Should a mother gradually extricate her babe from the fire into which she has fallen?" Garrison declared that slavery was opposed to the Bible and to the Declaration of Independence. Southern slaveholders foolishly publicized Garrison's writings by publicly condemning them. Georgia even offered a $5,000 reward for Garrison.[55]

Moderate abolitionists considered Garrison a lunatic whose antics were counterproductive. Garrison advocated northern secession from the corrupt South. (Abolitionist fears of being corrupted by association with southern slaveholders resembled the old Puritan fears of contamination by the Church of England and the old patriot fears of corruption by Great Britain. As nationalism grew, Americans felt greater responsibility for the activities of other sections of the country.) Garrison also denounced the Constitution, because it recognized the legitimacy of slavery.[56]

But, above all, many moderates were irritated by Garrison's vocal demands for greater rights for free blacks in the North. African Americans were disfranchised and segregated in most of the North; some northwestern legislatures would not even allow them to enter their states. In the 1830s Connecticut passed laws that prohibited integrated schools and silenced abolitionist lecturers. In 1836 white mobs in Cincinnati, angered by antislavery agitation, burned down black slums, only the first of many such riots in the city. In 1838 a mob killed abolitionist Elijah P. Lovejoy. Some northerners even opposed the expansion of slavery, not out of sympathy with African Americans, but because they did not wish to come into contact with them in the territories. But, though Garrison never succeeded in converting most northerners to his cause—most opposed the *expansion* of slavery on economic grounds, not the existence of slavery itself on moral grounds—his actions attracted attention and sparked heated debate.[57]

In 1832 Garrison established the New England Anti-Slavery Society. In the following year he joined with New York merchants Arthur and Lewis Tappan to form the American Anti-Slavery Society. With the financial aid of the Tappans, the society filled the mails with 750,000 samples of abolitionist literature by 1838, thereby provoking the fury of white southerners. By that time the society possessed 250,000 members. The organization called for the immediate emancipation of slaves without compensation to slaveowners.[58]

But in 1840 the American Anti-Slavery Society split over women's rights, the question of political action, and Garrison's increasingly virulent attacks on the clergy. Garrison supported equality for women; the Tappan brothers opposed it. Nearly an anarchist, Garrison vehemently denounced any involvement in the new Liberty Party his abolitionist associates had established. Reflecting a Radical Protestant suspicion of politics, Garrison feared that any association with it would corrupt the abolitionist movement, a position that baffled many abolitionists. Meanwhile, Garrison called Baptists who refused to excommunicate proslavery members "sophistical bigots." After the Methodist General Conference criticized radical abolitionism, Garrison called the conference "a cage of unclean birds and a synagogue of Satan." He also declared that antiabolitionist Presbyterian ministers were corrupt and that their Congregationalist counterparts were "clerical despots . . . at the head of the most implacable forces against God and man." Garrison's rhetoric dismayed even many sincere abolitionists, reformers who shared his frustration with clerical inactivity but who did not wish the abolitionist movement to be tarnished as anti-Christian. These dissidents formed the rival American and Foreign Antislavery Society. The road to progress frequently split, compelling each reformer to choose his own path.[59]

Despite Garrison's increasingly strident denunciations of the clergy by the late 1830s, his passionately moralistic rhetorical style and his themes of sin, damnation, and salvation were as evangelical as those of the revivalists, and his unbending opposition to the use of force of any kind (even against criminals and invading armies) clearly showed the marks of perfectionism and postmillennialism. In 1839 Garrison wrote, "Genuine abolitionism . . . is of heaven, not of men."[60]

Most of the other leading abolitionists were also postmillennialist Christians. The "Burned-Over District" became one of the strongholds of antislavery agitation. The abolitionist reformers there were led by Theodore Weld, whose father and older brother were ministers and who had himself attended Lane Seminary in Cincinnati and had worked in the temperance movement. The charismatic Weld had led the students at Lane in revolt against the seminary's administrators when they had tried to squelch his abolitionist activism. He also organized educational opportunities for the African Americans of the city. Often beaten and pelted with rocks, eggs, and vegetables by angry mobs, Weld toured New England, New York, Pennsylvania, and Ohio on behalf of abolitionism. He joined with his wife, Angelina Grimke of South Carolina, to publish *American Slavery As It Is* in 1839. Based on thousands of accounts of slaveholders' cruelties, some taken from southern publications, the book sold a hundred thousand copies in a single year. Harriet Beecher Stowe kept it nearby for source material when writing *Uncle Tom's Cabin*.[61]

Grimke, who had become a Quaker, shared Weld's postmillennial fervor. While she commiserated with the Adventists over the delay in the Second Coming of Christ, she emphasized that "it was not necessary that Christ should be visible to our fleshly eyes in order that He should reign in the world." The millennium would soon begin in people's hearts. She added: "Who cannot see & feel that we have entered upon a new era? ... Truth ... is finding its way into the most secret recesses of Church & State." Grimke rejected the Adventists' premillennialism for the more popular postmillennialism of the age. She trusted that slavery, "a crime against God and man," would soon end. Her sister Sarah declared, "No abolitionism is of any value which is not accompanied with deep, heartfelt repentance."[62]

The Tappan brothers were equally devout. Sizable contributors to nearly every major reform organization in the nation, they made their employees pray every morning and evening and abstain from smoking, drinking, attending plays, and staying out after 10:00 P.M. Lewis Tappan once wrote to his brother Benjamin: "You ask why I cannot keep my religion to myself. Because I see you in danger of eternal damnation. . . . I love you." Arthur Tappan had even tried to bribe Presbyterian churches to deny the Lord's Supper to anyone who made, sold, or drank hard liquor. Gradually, the antislavery movement absorbed most of the reformers and the zeal of the other movements.[63]

The slavery issue caused the fragmentation of churches. The northern and southern branches of the Methodist Church split over the issue in 1844, not to reunite for nearly a century; the largest Baptist denomination divided over it in 1845, never to reunite. The dissolution of these churches was a disaster for national unity. Henry Clay wrote regarding the schism in the Methodist Church, "Scarcely any occurrence has happened for a long time that gave me so much real concern and pain." As they had expanded their membership and had become fully integrated parts of the southern establishment, southern Methodists and Baptists had gradually dropped their early abolitionism and embraced slavery.[64]

ROMANTICISM

Meanwhile, a national literature emerged out of the growing reaction against the rationalism of the Enlightenment. While most

American literary figures, as members of the upper or upper-middle class, were hardly influenced by revival preachers, they shared the preachers' disgust with the Enlightenment's emphasis on reason over intuition and matter over spirit. Most of the American romantics were New Englanders, rebelling against the rational materialism (Epicurean humanism) of their parents. Many of the romantics longed for the spiritualism of their Puritan ancestors, even though they rejected their forebears' Calvinist doctrines. Although he was a prominent minister in the Unitarian Church for three years, Ralph Waldo Emerson felt indebted to "that old religion which, in the childhood of most of us, still dwelt like a sabbath morning in the country of New England, teaching privation, self-denial, and sorrow!"[65]

While American romantics shared a common belief in the existence of human nature, a belief that contradicted the "blank slate" theory of the Epicurean humanists, they differed markedly with one another concerning its characteristics. While the transcendentalists believed that human nature was essentially good, the most gifted novelists and short-story writers, Nathaniel Hawthorne, Herman Melville, and Edgar Allan Poe, believed that it was essentially bad. Ironically, though unorthodox in their religious opinions, the latter three romantics more closely approached the orthodox Christian doctrine of original sin than did the postmillennialist Christian reformers. Indeed, precisely because they were at odds with the prevailing optimism of the age, the works of Hawthorne, Melville, and Poe were far less popular than the novels of Harriet Beecher Stowe, Susan Warner, and other sentimental, postmillennialist authors, and their admission into the American literary canon had to await a more pessimistic age.[66]

The Fiction Writers: Hawthorne, Melville, and Poe

A descendant of one of the judges at the Salem witch trials, Hawthorne published his best novel, *The Scarlet Letter*, in 1850. It was a tale of sin, guilt, and revenge—or, as Hawthorne himself put it, "a tale of human frailty and sorrow." In the novel the Puritan authorities compel adulteress Hester Prynne to wear the scarlet letter A as a badge of shame. But Hester's suffering wins her redemption, while her lover, the Reverend Arthur Dimmesdale, is destroyed by a gnawing guilt, and her husband, Roger Chillingworth, is ruined by his obsession with revenge. Hawthorne carefully balanced his portrayal of Hester's very real sin and the punishment it merited with the self-righteousness of the Puritan leaders who pursued her with relentless vigor.[67]

In Hawthorne's "Earth's Holocaust" (1844), frontiersmen build a bonfire to burn European relics of "oppression," old books and symbols of royalty and aristocracy. Hawthorne concludes with the very Puritan observation that the bonfire had accomplished nothing, since the human heart, the true source of oppression, had remained intact. Melville said of Hawthorne, "The great power of blackness in him derives its force from its appeal to that Calvinistic sense of Innate Depravity and Original Sin, from whose visitations, in some shape or other, no deeply thinking mind is always and wholly free." Hawthorne's heroes inevitably fail in their quest to make reality match their ideals. His moral is always to renounce such intentions and be satisfied with an imperfect world.[68]

Nevertheless, Hawthorne's belief that the strong bonds of sin and suffering united humanity, combined with his conviction that the spiritual life was more real than the material, distinguished him from the realists of the late nineteenth and early twentieth centuries. Hawthorne wrote, "Man must not disclaim his brotherhood, even with the guiltiest, since, though his hand be clean, his heart has surely been polluted by the flitting phantasms of iniquity." His works revealed the beauty and redemptive power of courage, sympathy, and love in the face of adversity. As the literary historian F. O. Matthiessen put it, in his tragic figures "Hawthorne was most able to affirm the warmth and strength of the heart, and so to create a sense not merely of life's inexorability and sordidness, but of its possibilities of beauty and grandeur."[69]

Melville's greatest work, perhaps the greatest of all American novels, was *Moby-Dick* (1851), a novel he spent years writing while working on whaling vessels after his family's fortune had been lost. In the novel Captain Ahab searches for the white whale that caused the loss of his leg. His single-minded desire for revenge ends in the destruction of his ship and the deaths of himself and nearly all of his crew. Ahab's first mate, Starbuck, warns him, "Let Ahab beware of Ahab." But, though tragically aware of his own growing madness, Ahab is unable to alter his course. Ahab's quarrel is not chiefly with Moby Dick, but with God, or whatever consciousness governs the universe with what Ahab regards as an unfathomable coldness. Ahab declares concerning the whale: "I see in him outrageous strength, with an inscrutable malice sinewing in it. That inscrutable thing is chiefly what I hate; and be the white whale agent, or be the white whale principal, I will wreak that hate upon him." The statements of the novel's narrator, Ishmael, reflect a bleak view of human nature and of nature itself:

> Who ain't a slave? . . . Such is the endlessness, yea, the intolerableness of all earthly effort. . . . We are all somehow dreadfully cracked about the head, and sadly need mending. . . . This earthly air, whether ashore or afloat, is terribly infected with the nameless miseries of the numberless mortals who have died exhaling it. . . . We are all killers, on land and on sea; Bonapartes and Sharks included. . . . He [Ahab] piled upon the whale's white hump the sum of all the general rage and hate felt by his whole race from Adam down; and then, as if his chest had been a mortar, he burst his hot heart's shell upon it. . . . All are born with halters round their necks. . . . Oh, horrible vulturism of earth, from which not the mightiest whale is free! . . . There is no folly of the beasts of the earth which is not infinitely outdone by the madness of men. . . . That mortal man who hath more of joy than sorrow in him, that mortal man cannot be true. . . . "All is vanity." All. . . . When beholding the tranquil beauty and brilliancy of the ocean's skin, one forgets the tiger heart that pants beneath it; and would not willingly remember that this velvet paw but conceals a remorseless fang.

Ahab is even more morose:

> Born in throes, 'tis fit that man should live in pains and die in pangs! . . . I am impatient of all misery in others that is not mad. . . . See the omniscient gods oblivious of suffering man. . . . So far gone am I in the dark side of earth that its other side, the theoretic bright one, seems but uncertain twilight to me. . . . Ahab is for ever Ahab, man. This whole act's immutably decreed. . . . Were I the wind, I'd blow no more on such a wicked, miserable world. . . . Towards thee I roll, thou all-destroying but unconquering whale; to the last I grapple with thee; from hell's heart I stab at thee; for hate's sake I spit my last breath at thee.[70]

Yet, though darker even than Hawthorne, Melville was not as relentlessly morbid as many of the later realists. He tempered his understanding of the sufferings of humans with a recognition of "the essential dignity of man." Though Ahab is not purified by his suffering like Hawthorne's Hester, Ishmael at least survives the calamity and acquires wisdom from it. Painfully aware of the dark side of nature, Ishmael nevertheless refers to "that deep blue, bottomless soul pervading mankind and nature," and recognizes that "in many of its aspects this visible world seems formed in love." Even in the center of "the appalling ocean of life" there remained, in "the soul of man," "one insular Tahiti, full of peace and joy."[71]

A native of Boston raised in Virginia, and the inventor of the detective story, Poe believed that the object of literature was beauty, not truth. Poe's poems and stories were purposefully short (he hated novels), so that they could be read at one sitting, since his goal was always to overwhelm the reader with a single emotion (usually horror). Ironically for one of the leading romantics, Poe's essays on composition attacked all of the romantic myths concerning "inspiration" as the source of literary greatness. Poe's works were always rationally conceived and painstakingly crafted to achieve the desired emotional effect. He would have agreed with Thomas Edison that invention was 1 percent inspiration and 99 percent perspiration. The purpose of Poe's greatest poem, "The Raven" was to excite horror. What could be more terrifying, Poe reasoned, than the absolute certainty that one would never again see his beloved? Poe's universe was as haunted as his own tragic life. The dark, mysterious, and often surreal works of Hawthorne, Melville, and Poe were as different from the rationalist literature of the eighteenth century as they were from the other great branch of American romanticism, transcendentalism.[72]

The Transcendentalists: Emerson, Thoreau, and Whitman

The transcendentalists were so named because they sought to transcend reason, relying instead upon intuition. Their philosophy was a modern brand of Platonic humanism. Influenced by the Neoplatonist Plotinus, Emerson claimed that every person was a follower of either Plato or Aristotle—that is, a believer in either intuition or reason, spirit or matter. In tribute to his friend Bronson Alcott, Emerson wrote in his journal, "The Platonic world I might have learned to treat as cloud-land, had I not known Alcott, who is a native of that country, yet I will say that he makes it as solid as Massachusetts to me." The transcendentalists' other intellectual sources besides Platonism included the mystic Emanuel Swedenborg, the British romantic Samuel Taylor Coleridge, Buddhism, early Hinduism, and German idealism (itself indebted to Plato), though the moralistic Emerson was somewhat impatient with the aloof, contemplative stance of the Eastern mystics and the metaphysical wrangling of the German philosophers.[73]

To the Platonic arguments for innate knowledge the transcendentalists added Jean-Jacques Rousseau's belief that it is civilization that corrupts humans. They contended that the clamor of civilization drowned out the whispered truths of the individual's inner voice. By 1836 some of them had formed what became known as the Transcendentalist Club, which met at their homes in Boston and Concord.[74]

The leading transcendentalist was Ralph Waldo Emerson, who was descended from a long line of New England ministers. Emerson achieved lasting fame as an essayist, a poet, and a popular speaker on the lyceum circuit. In his essay "History," Emerson claimed that humans studied history to satisfy themselves that they could have done the same as others. He added that they could have, since humans were all part of the same "universal mind," a timeless entity similar to the Stoic World Soul. Nature was simple. Emerson contended, "Nature is an endless combination and repetition of a very few laws." As a result, the simple understood nature better than the sophisticated. Emerson wrote, "The idiot, the Indian, the child, and unschooled farmer's boy stand nearer to the light by which nature is to be read than the dissector or the antiquary."[75]

In his more famous essay "Self-Reliance," Emerson urged nonconformity. He argued that only by refusing to conform to the absurdities of civilized society could humans find the quiet and peace to listen to their intuition, which connected them to the

universal mind. People who possessed the courage to be nonconformists were ridiculed by their societies but were later called "geniuses," though they differed from others only in daring to follow
their intuition. Emerson wrote: "To believe your own thought, to
believe that what is true for you in your private heart is true for
all men—that is genius. . . . Imitation is suicide." Children were superior to adults because they were the ultimate nonconformists;
they had not yet been taught to "compute the strength" of opposing forces before forming an opinion. Emerson added:

> Infancy conforms to nobody; all conform to it; so that one baby com-
> monly makes four or five out of the adults who prattle and play with it.
> . . . You must court him; he will not court you. But the man is as it were
> clapped into jail by his consciousness. As soon as he has once acted or
> spoken with eclat he is a committed person, watched by the sympathy
> or the hatred of hundreds, whose affections must now enter his account.
> . . . Society everywhere is in conspiracy against the manhood of its mem-
> bers. . . . Whoso would be a man must be a nonconformist. . . . Nothing
> is at last sacred but the integrity of your own mind.

Emerson seemed to present a paradox: He who would be a man
must behave like a child. He ignored all evidence of selfishness and
cruelty among children, Native Americans, and other groups favored for their primitive "innocence." He retorted to those who
said that the impulses of his intuition might be the voice of the
devil, "They do not seem to me to be such; but if I am the Devil's
child, I will live then from the Devil." He added, "I like the silent
church before the service begins better than any preaching." Intuition was a better guide to truth than complex theological doctrines.[76]

Emerson denied the authority of Scripture. He wrote: "The
Greek and Hebrew Scriptures contain immortal sentences that
have been bread of life to millions. But they have no epical integrity; are fragmentary; are not shown in their order to the intellect." Direct inspiration was preferable to any handed down. For
this reason Emerson admired the Quakers, though he could not
hold to their doctrine of direct revelation (or to any theory of
grace), since he considered the ability to discern truth an innate
faculty.[77]

However much the transcendentalists may have rebelled against the rationalism of their eighteenth-century forebears, they shared their disbelief in the divinity of Jesus and in original sin. Emerson contended that Jesus had been the greatest philosopher in history but had been divine only in the sense that all of humanity was divine and had performed miracles only in the sense that the life of all of humanity was miraculous. Emerson criticized Christianity's "noxious exaggeration about the person of Jesus," declaring, "The soul knows no persons." Like Jefferson, Emerson claimed, without historical evidence, that the Gospel writers had misunderstood Jesus's teachings about Himself.[78]

By speaking in terms of absolute nonconformity, Emerson established himself as the quintessential straw man. Several points are in order here. First, in actively avoiding conformity to a given culture, one invariably conforms to an opposing culture. To some extent, all humans seek refuge from a maddening host of daily decisions in the fortress of habit and avoid the loneliness and uncertainty of true nonconformity. Second, those who are determined to avoid any shadow of conformity to a given culture are as enslaved by it as those who conform to it perfectly. Third, Emerson and the transcendentalists were themselves perfect examples of conformity. Each possessed the same northeastern (mostly New England) background and conformed rigorously to the same doctrine of nonconformity. One result of this paradoxical transcendentalist conformity to nonconformity was an almost adolescent desire to shock readers. Other paradoxical results included deliberate and self-conscious attempts at "spontaneity" and the coy pretense of spurning popularity and fame while at the same time seeking publication. When Emerson wrote, "Only what is private & yours & essential should be printed or spoken," it seemed not to occur to him that the recurring act of making public what is private necessarily makes authors more conscious of their audience. All authors are conscious of an imagined audience, whether they seek to please, to displease, or (in the case of the transcendentalists) to please the like-minded by displeasing society at large. If the transcendentalists had not reached out to an audience with that degree of skill that can only result from conscious effort, they would never have had any influence, and no one would remember them today.[79]

Indeed, properly understood, transcendentalism divides people not into conformists and nonconformists, but into different types of conformists. Those who conform to society are led astray. Those who conform to their intuition are joined together by a common connection with the "universal mind," the source of all love, beauty, and truth. They are not scattered, autonomous individuals, receiving conflicting reports. According to Emerson, "geniuses" are misunderstood only by those who conform to the falsehoods of civilized society. Those who have the courage to tap into the universal mind instantly recognize the truths of a genius, not as revelations, but as familiar friends already intuitively known. All have the same potential for genius, though not all are destined to achieve it.[80]

Emerson echoed Cicero and the Stoics concerning natural law. He wrote: "The intuition of the moral sentiment is an insight of the perfection of the laws of the soul. . . . [These laws] are out of time, out of space, and not subject to circumstance. . . . Man fallen into superstition, into sensuality, is never wholly without the visions of the moral sentiment. . . . It is an intuition. It cannot be received at second hand. Truly speaking, it is not instruction, but provocation, that I can receive from another soul. What he announces, I must find true in me." Emerson urged "an ethics commensurate with nature," forgetting that nature is built upon organisms devouring one another.[81]

The transcendentalists even embraced a Stoic fatalism similar to the predestination of their Calvinist ancestors. Sometimes they seemed to suggest, like the Stoics, that few were destined to follow the path of enlightenment, while at other times they were more optimistic. In his more euphoric moments Emerson even suggested that laws and coercive power might one day be unnecessary: "Society can be maintained without artificial restraints as well as the solar system. . . . The private citizen might be reasonable and a good neighbor without the hint of a jail or a confiscation." Refusing to read *Les Misérables*, Emerson declared, "I do not read the sad in literature." For this reason he disliked *The Scarlet Letter* as well, writing, "No one ought to write as Hawthorne has."[82]

Henry David Thoreau attempted to practice the self-reliance Emerson preached. *Walden* (1854) was a personal account of his own ascetic life at Walden Pond from 1845 to 1847. Thoreau echoed Emerson's contempt for materialism, which distracted the individual from his own inner voice. He praised Native American tribesmen (the Mucclasse), who burned their own possessions every few years rather than burdening themselves and their descendants with them. People must own their things; they must not be owned by them. The more numerous the possessions, the more likely they were to control their owner.[83]

Thoreau also assumed Emerson's posture of contempt for formal education as a means of gaining truth, though both were highly educated. Thoreau noted that men drove their fathers deep into debt so that they could go to college to learn economics. Similarly, Emerson wrote: "Shakespeare will never be made by the study of Shakespeare." Rather, Shakespeare made himself by listening to his own inner voice. A skeptic might retort that without someone to teach Shakespeare to think, speak, and write, his "inner voice" would have been mute. Had Shakespeare been raised by wolves, his inner voice would have instructed him to howl at the moon.[84]

After being jailed for one night in 1846 for refusing to pay the poll tax, because he believed that the Mexican War was an unjust attempt by the slaveholding interests of the United States to expand slavery, Thoreau wrote "On the Duty of Civil Disobedience" (1849). In this essay he advocated nonviolent resistance to immoral laws. Thoreau's essay exerted a profound influence upon Mohandas K. Gandhi and Martin Luther King Jr. Nevertheless, the pacifism that the transcendentalists espoused did not prevent them from applauding the violent actions of the radical abolitionist John Brown.[85]

At any rate, in refusing to pay his poll tax, Thoreau was not attempting to lead a social reform movement but simply seeking to avoid participation in evil. Transcendentalist individualism prevented Emerson and Thoreau from actively participating in reform efforts, since they believed that social reform, if at all possible, could only follow individual reform. Unreformed reformers merely replaced one form of tyranny with another. Reform institutions quickly became as corrupt as the institutions they were created to reform. Institutions were themselves the great evil, since they always ossified, deadening the individual in the process. Since the institution of slavery was the mere symptom of a greater illness in the soul of humankind, its abolition, though proper, would accomplish little. Emerson wrote in his journal, "Your true quarrel is with the state of Man." The only real reform must arise from a change in individual thought.[86]

If Emerson and Thoreau were unimpressed by what passed for "reform," they were even less impressed by what passed for "revolution"—mere attempts to redistribute material goods. While in England in 1848, Emerson responded to the excitement caused by the continental revolutions of that year: "There will be no revolution, none that deserves to be called so. There may be a scramble for money." A reorganization of the economy that merely substituted one form of materialism for another was hardly a real revolution.[87]

While supportive of utopian communities founded by like-minded individuals, Emerson and Thoreau declined to participate because they did not think they could subordinate their individuality to communal effort. Neither man allowed his life of contemplation and study to be interrupted, even by his closest friends, for more than an hour or two. Thoreau wrote in his journal, "Friends will be much apart; they will respect more each other's privacy than their communion." Emerson said of Thoreau, "He required no Phalanx, no Government, no society, almost no memory."[88]

A disciple of Emerson, as well as a former schoolteacher, carpenter's helper, and journalist from Brooklyn, Walt Whitman published a collection of poems called *Leaves of Grass* in 1855. Whitman considered his verse a wild new poetry for a wild new country. Its focus on sexuality was too wild for some. (Emerson was distressed by Whitman's use of his private praise of the book as a public endorsement for it, confessing, "There are parts of the book where I hold my nose as I read." Similarly, Thoreau enjoyed the work but contended: "There are two or three pieces in the book which are disagreeable, to say the least; simply sensual. He

does not celebrate love at all. It is as if the beasts spoke.") The poems mingled sensuality with transcendentalist spiritualism. They
strayed dramatically from European forms and praised democracy.
Whitman introduced the rich language of common people into
the stuffy libraries of the aristocrats. Emerson called his style "a remarkable mixture of the Bhagvat-Geeta and the *New York Herald*."
Whitman repeatedly claimed that his poems were the product of
inspiration, not rational effort, declaring, "Intellect is a fiend."[89]

THE RISE OF NATIONALISM

As we shall see, the rise of nationalism in the United States was another manifestation of the triumph of humanism. The underlying
tribalism on which nationalism is based has existed in all cultures.
A fundamental function of the Greek polis was to instill virtue in
its citizens, and patriotism was considered the greatest of virtues.
Especially adept at this type of social conditioning, Sparta possessed the greatest army in Greece (a connection that did not escape the attention of Adolf Hitler in the twentieth century).
Rome rose to new heights of power by tying religion to patriotism. Indeed, there is a sort of natural selection that seems to support nationalism: Nations with a high degree of nationalism are
more likely to prevail on the battlefield.[90]

The decline and fall of the Roman Empire was due largely to
the decline of patriotism and the rise of internationalism. The loyalty
of the citizens had been gradually transferred from Rome itself to the
person of the emperor, a loyalty more apt to fluctuate. Meanwhile,
Christianity, an internationalist religion opposed to tribalism, undermined Roman patriotism. One Roman observer noted that Christians "live in their own countries, but as aliens; . . . every foreign land
is their country, and every country is foreign to them." Throughout
the medieval period, the loyalty of Europeans rested with their local
lords and with the Roman Catholic Church, a multinational institution that emphasized the inclusion of all cultures.[91]

But by the late Middle Ages kingdoms began the gradual
transformation into nation-states organized along ethnic or cultural

lines. Early nationalist stirrings played a large role in bringing about the Protestant Reformation. English, French, German, and Swiss Protestants rebelled against an Italian-controlled papacy that redistributed wealth from northern to southern Europe. The Swiss reformer Ulrich Zwingli was such a nationalist that he translated the opening verses of the twenty-third psalm: "The Lord is my shepherd, I shall not want. He maketh me to lie down in an Alpine meadow." John Calvin wrote: "Love of country, which is, so to speak, our common mother, is naturally planted in us. . . . His native soil is sweet to everyone, and it is sweet to dwell among one's own people." The Protestant majority of England despised English Catholics as traitors for favoring Italian popes over English monarchs and for allegedly conspiring to turn the country over to Catholic Spain. By fragmenting Christians, the Protestant Reformation began the process by which religion became merely one distinguishing feature of nationality. Furthermore, the Protestant emphasis on individual interpretation of the Bible bolstered the vernacular languages, which also distinguished nationalities from one another. The unifying power of Latin was gradually undermined.[92]

By contrast, the Enlightenment produced a degree of cosmopolitanism. Its philosophers were internationalists who argued that everyone possessed the moral sense and the power of reason. Although they believed that some people were more adept at using reason than others, they thought that the difference was based largely on race and gender rather than on nationality. The British playwright Oliver Goldsmith wrote, "The whole world being one city, I do not much care in which of its streets I happen to reside." Thomas Paine declared, "The world is my country; mankind are my brothers."[93]

But the American and French Revolutions helped undermine the internationalism of the Enlightenment. The overthrow of monarchy and aristocracy shifted citizens' loyalty from the king and the lord to the nation-state as a whole. Modern technology allowed tribalists to recruit unprecedented numbers of tribesmen. In republican France cheap newspapers, compulsory public education, and citizen-armies shared in the task of indoctrination. Although the federal government of the decentralized United States possessed less power than the governments of Europe, popular sentiment enforced as great a conformity in support of nationalism as in Europe. Although newspapers and public schools escaped centralized control, they often spoke with a single voice on the subject of the nation's superiority and unique mission. The McGuffey readers, used widely in American schools, were nationalist to the core.[94]

By the antebellum period many Americans believed that the United States was destined by the will of God to expand, so that it might spread the blessings of democracy. Such expansionist sentiment justified the Mexican War, which resulted in the American seizure of over five hundred thousand square miles of Mexican territory. Most Americans saw no contradiction in the use of force to spread democracy. The need to accomplish the mission outweighed all other concerns. Only a fundamental division between North and South concerning the expansion of slavery prevented further attempts at expansion into Latin America and Canada in the 1850s. Even Emerson, a critic of the Mexican War and expansionism, wrote, "The Supreme Being exalts the history of this people." In 1837, in a famous Phi Beta Kappa address, "The American Scholar," at Harvard, Emerson urged Americans to abandon their attachment to European forms and to create a distinctively American literature. Walt Whitman declared: "The Poetry of other lands lies in the past—what they have been. The Poetry of America lies in the future—what These States and their coming men and women are certainly to be." Joseph Smith was so nationalistic he placed the Garden of Eden in America, contending that it was the Great Flood that had carried Noah and his descendants to the Near East. In the United States, England, and France, historians began writing the first national histories, romantic accounts of the struggle of each nation's "great men" to fulfill its divinely inspired mission.[95]

Although sectionalism interfered with nationalism to some extent, the Civil War was itself a testament to American nationalism. Over a million northerners, remembering Daniel Webster's nationalist speeches from their grammar school readers, fought for the Union, as did many southerners. Within a few decades after the war, the South was perhaps more nationalistic (though also retaining a type of "southern nationalism") than any other section of the nation. By the Spanish-American War (1898) southerners occupied key leadership positions in the U.S. Army once again.[96]

In 1926, in the wake of the unprecedented destruction and bloodshed of World War I, a war produced by an epidemic of jingoistic nationalism, Carlton J. H. Hayes, the first historian of nationalism, called it a religion. Hayes believed that nationalism was the prevalent religion around the globe, having supplanted or distorted the "older religions." Hayes used American nationalism as his principal example. The flag, the Liberty Bell, and the Statue of Liberty were U.S. holy icons, "The Star-Spangled Banner" its hymn, the "infallible" Constitution its Scripture, the black-robed judges its high priests (hence the requirement to stand when they entered the courtroom), the Founding Fathers and Abraham Lincoln its demigods, its God a tribal deity especially supportive of American success, its mission a crusade to spread American-style democracy and capitalism, its taxes a tithe, its Pharisees those who only feigned nationalism, and its heretics those who raised any questions concerning the religion. (Hayes considered himself one of the few heretics. He claimed that whenever he related to most people the mere fact that he studied nationalism, it raised the suspicion that he was some sort of Marxist internationalist.) Nationalism's few heretics were neutralized in various ways. Only university professors escaped punishment—and then only because no one took them seriously, anyway. The reign of nationalism was so supreme it surpassed even the Catholic Church's control over medieval life. Hayes noted that the nation-state commemorated each citizen's birth, marriage, children, and death with registration. One was born into the religion of nationalism and could not escape it. By emigrating to another nation, an individual merely changed his denomination, not his religion.[97]

But if nationalism is a religion, it is a humanist one, though by no means one to which all humanists subscribe. Nationalism holds that earthly progress is possible through the triumph of the nation in question. But nationalism is a hollow religion; it cannot exist without attaching itself to another faith. It holds that earthly progress will come through the triumph of national ideals but does not provide those ideals, which can vary greatly from one society to another. In the United States the ideals have been provided by liberal humanism: Earthly progress will come when the American versions of individualism, democracy, and capitalism are universally practiced.

Furthermore, it must be noted that internationalism is as much a religion for some modern Americans as nationalism was for many antebellum Americans. The modern movement for a world government, which began in the late nineteenth century and produced the League of Nations in 1919 and the United Nations in 1945, was, from the outset, bathed in a fervent utopianism. The most zealous of the internationalists today believe that a world government can solve all of humanity's problems. They forget, first, that even the strongest national governments have failed to solve even purely national problems, and second, that any power granted to government to do good things is eventually used to do bad things as well.[98]

ANTEBELLUM HUMANISM
VERSUS TRADITIONAL THEISM

Antebellum revivalism, reform, and romanticism revealed, as much as antebellum economic and political theory, the extent to which American society had been transformed by humanism. Most Americans agreed that progress could be achieved through religious toleration, representative government, and free enterprise, disagreeing merely about the precise nature of the ideal system. American statesmen, economic theorists, preachers, reformers, and literary figures went well beyond mere statements of preference for their favored systems, such as an orthodox theist or skeptic might consistently advance. They placed their faith in human systems—that is, in the power of human reason or intuition to uncover universal laws and to organize the nation's political, economic, and social institutions in a manner consistent with such laws. They considered evil the result of improperly devised systems, not of innate depravity. Their refrain was the classic refrain of humanism: if only. If only we could change the system in question, society might achieve perfection.

American culture has always been amenable to humanism. Nothing has been more peculiarly American than optimism. The intense work ethic of settlers, the abundance of cheap and fertile land, the mild climate, the absence of a feudal tradition, and the lack of threatening neighbors produced a society marked by an unusual degree of freedom, equality, peace, and prosperity. These qualities, in turn, fed a utopian impulse that made Americans a notoriously energetic people. What the ancient Corinthians once said of the Athenians, at the height of their power, might as easily be said of Americans: "It may truly be said that they were born neither to rest themselves nor to allow others any rest" (Thucydides, *History of the Peloponnesian War*, 1.70). How could Americans ever rest when there was a utopia to be built?

To those theists whose orthodoxy survived the age of humanism, the American belief in the inexorable march of progress seemed hopelessly naive. Even a superficial review of history revealed that nearly every political, economic, and social system imaginable had been attempted, and all had foundered on the rock of human selfishness and irrationality. To dismiss all of human history as an aberration seemed illogical. While orthodox theists possessed their own favorite systems, they expected only minor and temporary improvements from them. Any advancement that could be made should be made, but one should have no illusions about any general or lasting social or moral progress. Humanists might ignore original sin, but ignoring it would not abolish it, only allow it to operate unchecked. Original sin was the chief culprit of human misery, not bad systems. Any system, even absolute monarchy or slavery, would be just and good if human nature were just and good. Indeed, the Judeo-Christian conception of heavenly government was the absolute monarchy of a God of absolute justice and goodness. But, in the absence of such a nature, all human systems were corrupt. Hence to argue passionately about the superiority of various human systems was like arguing passionately about which rhinoceros was the prettiest. One might, indeed, be the prettiest (though that was an aesthetic judgment), but none was pretty enough to get excited about. The theist refrain was a slightly revised version of Shakespeare's famous line: The fault, dear Brutus, lies not in our systems, but in ourselves.

This debate between the theist and the humanist was interrupted by the arrival of a new participant. The age of skepticism had arrived.

NOTES

1. Clifford S. Griffin, *Their Brothers' Keepers: Moral Stewardship in the United States, 1800–1865* (New Brunswick, N.J.: Rutgers University Press, 1981), 15, 138; Whitney R. Cross, *The Burned-Over District: The Social and Intellectual History of Enthusiastic Religion in Western New York, 1800–1850* (New York: Octagon, 1981), 17; Paul K. Conkin, *American Originals: Homemade Varieties of Christianity* (Chapel Hill: University of North Carolina Press, 1997), 58, 72, 100–1; Henry F. May, *The Enlightenment in America* (New York: Oxford University Press, 1976), 174, 261–63; Martin E. Marty, *Righteous Empire: The Protestant Experience in America* (New York: Dial, 1970), 106, 109.

2. John B. Boles, *The Great Revival, 1787–1805* (Lexington: University Press of Kentucky, 1972), 47, 55; Paul K. Conkin, *The Uneasy Center: Reformed Christianity in Antebellum America* (Chapel Hill: University of North Carolina Press, 1995), 124.

3. Boles, *Great Revival*, 70, 113–14, 186–87; Cross, *Burned-Over District*, 9.

4. Conkin, *Uneasy Center*, 126–27.

5. Milton Rugoff, *The Beechers: An American Family in the Nineteenth Century* (New York: Harper & Row, 1981), 8–10.

6. Ronald G. Walters, *American Reformers, 1815–1860* (New York: Hill & Wang, 1978), 22; Keith Hardman, *Charles Grandison Finney, 1792–1875: Revivalist and Reformer* (Syracuse, N.Y.: Syracuse University Press, 1987), 43; Cross, *Burned-Over District*, 152–55; William G. McLoughlin, *Revivals, Awakenings, and Reform: An Essay on Religion and Social Change in America, 1607–1977* (Chicago: University of Chicago Press, 1978), 123, 128, 130; Marty, *Righteous Empire*, 109; Rugoff, *Beechers*, 73; Conkin, *Uneasy Center*, 262.

7. Hardman, *Charles Grandison Finney*, 300; Conkin, *Uneasy Center*, 262.

8. Edwin S. Gaustad, *Faith of Our Fathers: Religion and the New Nation* (San Francisco: Harper & Row, 1987), 128.

9. Timothy L. Smith, *Revivalism and Social Reform: American Protestantism on the Eve of the Civil War*, 2d ed. (Baltimore: Johns Hopkins University Press, 1980), 62; Louis Menand, *The Metaphysical Club* (New York: Farrar, Straus & Giroux, 2001), 80.

10. Klaus J. Hansen, *Mormonism and the American Experience* (Chicago: University of Chicago Press, 1981), 2–9, 29; Conkin, *American Originals*, 163–68; Marty, *Righteous Empire*, 72.

11. Hansen, *Mormonism and the American Experience*, 140–41, 155–56, 195–98.

12. Hansen, *Mormonism and the American Experience*, 71–72, 77–81, 169–70; Conkin, *American Originals*, 182, 186–90.

13. Hansen, *Mormonism and the American Experience*, 136; Conkin, *American Originals*, 202–4; Marty, *Righteous Empire*, 72.

14. Leonard J. Arrington and Davis Bitton, *The Mormon Experience: A History of the Latter-Day Saints* (New York: Alfred A. Knopf, 1979), 110–12.

15. Hansen, *Mormonism and the American Experience*, 142, 156–57, 213; Conkin, *American Originals*, 207–9.

16. Hansen, *Mormonism and the American Experience*, xv, 145–46; Conkin, *American Originals*, 162, 220–21.

17. Conkin, *American Originals*, 115, 124–30; *Uneasy Center*, 288, 292, 294; Cross, *Burned-Over District*, 287, 310; Hansen, *Mormonism and the American Experience*, 115; Marty, *Righteous Empire*, 86–87, 124; Henry Chadwick, *The Early Church* (Baltimore: Penguin, 1969), 128.

18. Conkin, *Uneasy Center*, 67, 72; John Wesley, "The Scripture Way of Salvation," 1765, in *John Wesley*, ed. Albert C. Outler (New York: Oxford University Press, 1964), 277.

19. Conkin, *Uneasy Center*, 63, 73, 75–82, 85–86; Albert J. Raboteau, *Slave Religion: The "Invisible Institution" in the Antebellum South* (Oxford: Oxford University Press, 1978), 131, 143, 175; Rhys Isaac, *The Transformation of Virginia, 1740–1790* (Chapel Hill: University of North Carolina Press, 1982), 261; McLoughlin, *Revivals, Awakenings, and Reform*, 95.

20. Conkin, *Uneasy Center*, 63, 73, 79–82, 85; McLoughlin, *Revivals, Awakenings, and Reform*, 134; Smith, *Revivalism and Social Reform*, 23–24.

21. Conkin, *Uneasy Center*, 58–59; McLoughlin, *Revivals, Awakenings, and Reform*, 92.

22. Raboteau, *Slave Religion*, 131, 152, 209; Jon Butler, *Awash in a Sea of Faith: Christianizing the American People* (Cambridge, Mass.: Harvard University Press, 1990), 150; McLoughlin, *Revivals, Awakenings, and Reform*, 134; Isaac, *Transformation of Virginia*, 170; Conkin, *Uneasy Center*, 134.

23. Raboteau, *Slave Religion*, 133; Conkin, *Uneasy Center*, 45, 59, 82; Smith, *Revivalism and Social Reform*, 22; McLoughlin, *Revivals, Awakenings, and Reform*, 134.

24. Boles, *Great Revival*, 134, 138, 146–47; Cross, *Burned-Over District*, 40, 254; Smith, *Revivalism and Social Reform*, 19, 86.

25. Marty, *Righteous Empire*, 128–29; Rugoff, *Beechers*, 152–53.

26. Gaustad, *Faith of Our Fathers*, 120; Garry Wills, *Under God: Religion and American Politics* (New York: Simon & Schuster, 1990), 16, 25.

27. Conkin, *Uneasy Center*, 227; Rugoff, *Beechers*, 21, 23; Boles, *Great Revival*, 41; Cross, *Burned-Over District*, 27; Smith, *Revivalism and Social Reform*, 114–15; McLoughlin, *Revivals, Awakenings, and Reform*, 135.

28. For reference to the numerous biblical passages concerning wars, immorality, and natural disasters during the end-times, see chapter 9. For Finney's statement see McLoughlin, *Revivals, Awakenings, and Reform*, 130.

29. Smith, *Revivalism and Social Reform*, 114–15; John Wesley, "Christian Perfection," 1741, in *John Wesley*, ed. Outler, 257–64; Wesley, "The Scripture Way of Salvation," 274, 278–79; John Wesley, *A Plain Account of Christian Perfection*, 1766, in *John Wesley*, ed. Outler, 284, 286, 288, 294.

30. Smith, *Revivalism and Social Reform*, 128; Wesley, "Christian Perfection," 251–53; John Wesley, "Cautions and Directions Given to the Greatest Professors in the Methodist Societies," 1762, in *John Wesley*, ed. Outler, 305.

31. Daniel Walker Howe, *The Political Culture of the American Whigs* (Chicago: University of Chicago Press, 1979), 157; Charles G. Finney, "What a Revival of Religion Is," 1835, in *The American Intellectual Tradition*, 3d ed., 2 vols., ed. Charles Capper and David A. Hollinger (Oxford: Oxford University Press, 1997), vol. 1, 194; Hansen, *Mormonism and the American Experience*, 61–62.

32. Griffin, *Their Brothers' Keepers*, 78; Walters, *American Reformers*, 33; Marty, *Righteous Empire*, 93.

33. Boles, *Great Revival*, 193–95; Marty, *Righteous Empire*, 64; Conkin, *Uneasy Center*, 118; Walters, *American Reformers*, 7.

34. Walters, *American Reformers*, 207–9; Griffin, *Their Brothers' Keepers*, 138.

35. Stuart Bruchey, *Enterprise: The Dynamic Economy of a Free People* (Cambridge, Mass.: Harvard University Press, 1990), 155–56; Rugoff, *Beechers*, 61.

36. Griffin, *Their Brothers' Keepers*, 76, 94, 213; Thomas Dublin, *Women at Work: The Transformation of Work and Community in Lowell, Massachusetts, 1826–1860* (New York: Columbia University Press, 1979), 81; Conkin, *Uneasy Center*, 145; Boles, *Great Revival*, 191; Smith, *Revivalism and Social Reform*, 36.

37. Walters, *American Reformers*, 124; Cross, *Burned-Over District*, 211; Griffin, *Their Brothers' Keepers*, 13; Rugoff, *Beechers*, 28.

38. Walters, *American Reformers*, 127, 129, 139; Cross, *Burned-Over District*, 136.

39. Walters, *American Reformers*, 127, 132; Cross, *Burned-Over District*, 169; W. J. Rorabaugh, *The Alcoholic Republic: An American Tradition* (New York: Oxford University Press, 1979), 190–93, 199; Howe, *Political Culture of the American Whigs*, 159; Butler, *Awash in a Sea of Faith*, 279.

40. Walters, *American Reformers*, 126–27, 129–30; Cross, *Burned-Over District*, 212–13, 215–16.

41. Walters, *American Reformers*, 136–37; Griffin, *Their Brothers' Keepers*, 133, 224.

42. Walters, *American Reformers*, 174, 195; Smith, *Revivalism and Social Reform*, 38, 51, 167, 175.

43. Cesare Beccaria, *Of Crimes and Punishments*, trans. Henry Paolucci (Indianapolis, Ind.: Bobbs-Merrill, 1963), 46–47; Marcello Maestro, *Cesare Beccaria and the Origins of Penal Reform* (Philadelphia: Temple University Press, 1973), 138–39; Walters, *American Reformers*, 196–98.

44. Walters, *American Reformers*, 115, 117, 119, 175.

45. Walters, *American Reformers*, 200–202, 204; Helen E. Marshall, *Dorothea Dix: Forgotten Samaritan* (New York: Russell & Russell, 1937), 65–66, 71; C. E. Vulliamy, *Royal George* (New York: D. Appleton-Century, 1937), 199–200.

46. Dorothea Dix, "Memorial on Asylums," 1843, in *A More Perfect Union: Documents in U.S. History*, 3d ed., 2 vols., ed. Paul F. Boller Jr. and Ronald Story (Boston: Houghton Mifflin, 1992), vol. 1, 154.

47. Rugoff, *Beechers*, 183; Jeanne Boydston, Mary Kelley, and Anne Margolis, *The Limits of Sisterhood: The Beecher Sisters on Women's Rights and Woman's Sphere* (Chapel Hill: University of North Carolina Press, 1988), 117–22, 130–37.

48. Rugoff, *Beechers*, 185.

49. Rugoff, *Beechers*, 53–59, 173, 193.

50. Louisa McCord, "Enfranchisement of Woman," 1852, in *All Clever Men, Who Make Their Way: Critical Discourse in the Old South*, ed. Michael O'Brien (Athens: University of Georgia Press, 1992), 342–44, 350–51, 353; Sarah Grimke, *Letters on the Equality of the Sexes and the Condition of Woman*, 1838, in *The American Intellectual Tradition*, ed. Capper and Hollinger, vol. 1, 224–25; Hansen, *Mormonism and the American Experience*, 159–60.

51. Harriet Beecher Stowe, *Uncle Tom's Cabin* (New York: American Library, 1966), 44–45, 91–94, 201–3, 240, 282, 382, 398–99, 441–42; Jane Tompkins, *Sensational Designs: The Cultural Work of American Fiction, 1790–1860* (Oxford: Oxford University Press, 1985), 124, 139.

52. Walters, *American Reformers*, 101, 104, 106–8; Butler, *Awash in a Sea of Faith*, 281.

53. Walters, *American Reformers*, 108; Grimke, *Letters on the Equality of the Sexes and the Condition of Woman*, vol. 1, 214–15, 218, 222, 225.

54. Walters, *American Reformers*, 78; Marty, *Righteous Empire*, 31–32, 57; Griffin, *Their Brothers' Keepers*, 41; P. J. Staudenraus, *The African Colonization Movement, 1816–1865* (New York: Columbia University Press, 1961), 70, 107, 174, 183, 187, 245, 251.

55. John L. Thomas, *The Liberator: William Lloyd Garrison, a Biography* (Boston: Little, Brown, 1963), 98–99, 128, 203; Walters, *American Reformers*, 85; William R. Merrill, *Against Wind and Tide: A Biography of William Lloyd Garrison* (Cambridge, Mass.: Harvard University Press, 1963), 54.

56. Walters, *American Reformers*, 92; Smith, *Revivalism and Social Reform*, 215; Thomas, *Liberator*, 330–31.

57. Walters, *American Reformers*, 79, 85; Leon F. Litwack, *North of Slavery: The Negro in the Free States, 1790–1860* (Chicago: University of Chicago Press, 1961), 70–71, 75–87, 97, 114; Rugoff, *Beechers*, 179, 237; David M. Potter, *The Impending Crisis, 1848–1861* (New York: Harper & Row, 1976), 36–37.

58. Walters, *American Reformers*, 80; Thomas, *Liberator*, 173–74.

59. Walters, *American Reformers*, 87, 89–90, 115; Griffin, *Their Brothers' Keepers*, 154, 157–58; Smith, *Revivalism and Social Reform*, 183.

60. Griffin, *Their Brothers' Keepers*, 113; Walters, *American Reformers*, 91, 115; Marty, *Righteous Empire*, 120; Menand, *Metaphysical Club*, 14.

61. Rugoff, *Beechers*, 146, 149–50; Griffin, *Their Brothers' Keepers*, 86–88; Cross, *Burned-Over District*, 196.

62. Rugoff, *Beechers*, 61; Grimke, *Letters on the Equality of the Sexes and the Condition of Woman*, vol. 1, 226; Cross, *Burned-Over District*, 286.

63. Rugoff, *Beechers*, 141; Griffin, *Their Brothers' Keepers*, 38, 102; Walters, *American Reformers*, 33; Cross, *Burned-Over District*, 277.

64. Conkin, *Uneasy Center*, 250, 252, 254; Smith, *Revivalism and Social Reform*, 189.

65. Marty, *Righteous Empire*, 116; Paul K. Conkin, *Puritans and Pragmatists: Eight Eminent American Thinkers* (Bloomington: Indiana University Press, 1968), 154–56; F. O. Matthiessen, *American Renaissance: Art and Expression in the Age of Emerson and Whitman* (Oxford: Oxford University Press, 1941), 7.

66. Tompkins, *Sensational Designs*, 25–26, 32, 148.

67. Nathaniel Hawthorne, *The Scarlet Letter* (New York: W. W. Norton, 1962), 42, 180–86; Matthiessen, *American Renaissance*, 282, 349–50.

68. Herman Melville, "Hawthorne and His Mosses," 1850, in *The American Intellectual Tradition*, ed. Capper and Hollinger, vol. 1, 350; R. W. B. Lewis, *The American Adam: Innocence, Tragedy, and Tradition in the Nineteenth Century* (Chicago: University of Chicago Press, 1955), 13–14; Taylor Stoehr, *Nay-Saying in Concord: Emerson, Alcott, and Thoreau* (Hamden, Conn.: Archon, 1979), 14–15.

69. Matthiessen, *American Renaissance*, 239, 341, 344, 347, 349–51.

70. Herman Melville, *Moby-Dick, or The Whale* (Evanston, Ill.: Northwestern University Press, 1988), 6, 60, 72, 81, 119, 143, 164, 184, 186, 281, 308, 385, 424, 432, 475, 487, 491, 522, 528, 561, 564, 571–72; David K. Kirby, *Herman Melville* (New York: Continuum, 1993), 21–25.

71. Melville, *Moby-Dick*, 159, 195, 274, 571–73; Matthiessen, *American Renaissance*, 403.

72. Julian Symons, *The Tell-Tale Heart: The Life of Edgar Allan Poe* (New York: Harper & Row, 1978), 221; Edgar Allan Poe, *Essays and Reviews*, ed. G. R. Thompson (New York: Library of America, 1984), 13–25; Howard Mumford Jones, *Revolution and Romanticism* (Cambridge, Mass.: Harvard University Press, 1974), 405–7.

73. Perry Miller, *The New England Mind*, 2 vols. (New York: Macmillan, 1939; Cambridge, Mass.: Harvard University Press, 1953), vol. 1, 278; Ralph Waldo Emerson, "The Divinity School Address," 1838, in *The American Intellectual Tradition*, ed. Capper and Hollinger, vol. 1, 279; Jones, *Revolution and Romanticism*, 128; Stoehr, *Nay-Saying in Concord*, 143; Conkin, *Puritans and Pragmatists*, 158, 169, 171, 173, 177, 185.

74. C. E. Vulliamy, *Rousseau* (Port Washington, N.Y.: Kennikat Press, 1931), 117; Paul F. Boller Jr., *American Transcendentalism, 1830–1860: An Intellectual Inquiry* (New York: Putnam, 1974), xiii.

75. Ralph Waldo Emerson, *Essays: First and Second Series* (Mount Vernon: Peter Pauper Press, 1946), "History," 7–8, 11, 13, 25.

76. Emerson, *Essays*, "Self-Reliance," 27–30, 40.

77. Emerson, "The Divinity School Address," vol. 1, 287; Conkin, *Puritans and Pragmatists*, 163–66.

78. Emerson, "The Divinity School Address," vol. 1, 280.

79. Stoehr, *Nay-Saying in Concord*, 37, 40, 149.

80. Emerson, *Essays*, "History" and "Self-Reliance."

81. Emerson, "The Divinity School Address," 278–79; Stoehr, *Nay-Saying in Concord*, 129.

82. Stoehr, *Nay-Saying in Concord*, 129; Conkin, *Puritans and Pragmatists*, 163–65; Boller, *American Transcendentalism*, 145.

83. Henry David Thoreau, *Walden, or Life in the Woods, and "On the Duty of Civil Disobedience"* (New York: New American Library, 1960), 51.

84. Thoreau, *Walden*, 40; Emerson, *Essays*, "Self-Reliance," 45.

85. Stoehr, *Nay-Saying in Concord*, 44; Matthiessen, *American Renaissance*, 116; Henry David Thoreau, "On the Duty of Civil Disobedience," in *Walden*, 222–40; Perry Miller, afterword, in *Walden*, 255; Martin Luther King, Jr., "Pilgrimage to Nonviolence," 1958, in *Words That Made American History*, 2 vols., ed. Richard N. Current, John A. Garraty, and Julius Weinberg (Boston: Little, Brown, 1978), vol. 2, 529.

86. Stoehr, *Nay-Saying in Concord*, 54; Conkin, *Puritans and Pragmatists*, 165, 189.

87. Stoehr, *Nay-Saying in Concord*, 17.

88. Stoehr, *Nay-Saying in Concord*, 71, 76–77, 82, 105.

89. Matthiessen, *American Renaissance*, 523, 526–27, 532, 535, 539, 543; Walt Whitman, *Leaves of Grass* (New York: Vintage Books, 1992); Boller, *American Transcendentalism*, 178–79.

90. Paul A. Rahe, *Republics, Ancient and Modern: Classical Republicanism and the American Revolution* (Chapel Hill: University of North Carolina Press, 1992), 139–85; Mars M. Westinghouse, "Nazi Germany and Ancient Sparta," *Education* 65 (November 1944):153–63; R. H. Barrow, *The Romans* (New York: Penguin, 1949), 14, 24–26.

91. Barrow, *Romans*, 54; E. R. Dodds, *Pagan and Christian in an Age of Anxiety* (Cambridge: Cambridge University Press, 1968), 20; Hans Kohn, *Nationalism: Its Meaning and History* (Princeton, N.J.: D. Van Nostrand, 1955), 13.

92. Roland Bainton, *Here I Stand: A Life of Martin Luther* (New York: Abingdon-Cokesbury Press, 1950), 267; William J. Bouwsma, *John Calvin: A Sixteenth-Century Portrait* (Oxford: Oxford University Press, 1988), 16; A. G. Dickens, *The English Reformation* (New York: Schocken Books, 1964), 108, 262, 311–12; Kohn, *Nationalism*, 14–15.

93. Carlton J. H. Hayes, *Essays on Nationalism* (New York: Macmillan, 1926), 43. For reference to Thomas Jefferson's belief in the intellectual inferiority of blacks and women see Thomas Jefferson, *Notes on the State of Virginia*, ed. William Peden (Chapel Hill: University of North Carolina Press, 1955), 138–43; Jefferson to Maria Cosway, October 12, 1786, in *The Papers of Thomas Jefferson*, 21 vols., ed. Julian P. Boyd (Princeton, N.J.: Princeton University Press, 1950), vol. 10, 450; Jefferson to Anne Willing Bingham, May 11, 1788, in *The Papers of Thomas Jefferson*, ed. Boyd, vol. 13, 151.

94. Kohn, *Nationalism*, 19–29; Stanley W. Lindberg, ed., *The Annotated McGuffey: Selections from the Eclectic McGuffey Readers, 1836–1920* (New York: Van Nostrand Reinhold, 1976), 47–49, 139–40, 147–49, 327–30, 346–48.

95. Potter, *Impending Crisis*, 1, 196-197; Sacvan Bercovitch, *The Puritan Origins of the American Self* (New Haven, Conn.: Yale University Press, 1975), 166; Boller, *American Transcendentalism*, xix; Matthiessen, *American Renaissance*, 543; Hansen, *Mormonism and the American Experience*, 67; David Levin, *History as Romantic Art: Bancroft, Prescott, Motley, and Parkman* (Stanford, Calif.: Stanford University Press, 1959), vii, 25, 28, 80, 82; Thomas B. Macaulay, *History of England: From the Accession of James II*, 4 vols. (London: Dent, 1953); Jules Michelet, *Histoire de France*, ed. Claude Mettra (St. Amand: J'ai Lu, 1963).

96. Emory Thomas, *The Confederate Nation, 1861–1865* (New York: Harper & Row, 1979), 155; Ralph Henry Gabriel, *The Course of American Democratic Thought* (New York: Ronald Press, 1956), 138–39.

97. Hayes, *Essays on Nationalism*, 93–125. See also Carlton J. H. Hayes, *Nationalism: A Religion* (New York: Macmillan, 1960).

98. Sondra R. Herman, *Eleven Against War: Studies in American Internationalist Thought, 1898–1921* (Stanford, Calif.: Stanford University Press, 1969).

III

THE AGE OF SKEPTICISM

7

THE RISE OF MODERN SKEPTICISM

Although theists and humanists had often quarreled due to their conflicting conceptions of human nature, their common belief in a universal moral order had frequently allowed a fair degree of cooperation between them. They had fought the American Revolution together, had established a new constitution together, had promoted the same economic theories, and had joined the same social reform movements. American humanists' willingness to speak of a God, combined with American theists' willingness to deemphasize original sin, had sometimes obscured the differences between them. But neither group was prepared for the appearance of a philosophy that openly, even proudly, denied the existence of any moral order. As a result, the rise of modern skepticism produced an unprecedented psychic crisis.

The opening salvo of the new skepticism was fired by the most reluctant of warriors, a British biologist named Charles Darwin. By positing for humans a common ancestry with the animals, Darwin's theory of natural selection provided the basis for Sigmund Freud's psychological theories. Freud's theories rejected both the Epicurean blank slate and Platonic intuition, the two theories of human nature on which humanist hopes of progress rested. By replacing the "laws" of Newton with mere statements of probability, physicists then undermined confidence in reason as a means of gaining transcendent truth. The new scientific theories devastated the large number of Americans who based their belief in

God on rational proofs and challenged those orthodox Christians whose faith was based on a literal interpretation of the Bible.

DARWIN'S THEORY OF NATURAL SELECTION

Four Preexisting Concepts

Darwin arrived at the theory of natural selection by piecing together four preexisting concepts. The first concept was evolution. As early as the sixth century B.C., after observing the mammalian characteristics of the smooth shark, the Greek philosopher Anaximander argued that all living creatures had come from the water and that humans had evolved from sea creatures. In the eighteenth and early nineteenth centuries numerous philosophers and scientists suggested the possibility of evolution on the basis of the apparent gradations between different species when arranged in a series. But creation remained the dominant biological theory.[1]

The most influential of the evolutionists was Jean Lamarck (*Philosophie Zoologique*, 1809), who maintained that all organisms, including humans, had evolved from simpler organisms. Confronted with the herculean task of classifying the Paris Museum of Natural History's collection of specimens, Lamarck could not decide whether certain specimens represented different species or different varieties of the same species. Such was his difficulty that he finally concluded that there was no such entity as a "species." There was no universally applicable basis for distinguishing a species from a related species. Even the best basis for such a distinction—that members of the same species could produce offspring together—could sometimes be true of what biologists classified as different species. Horses could mate with donkeys to produce mules (though the mules themselves were sterile). Lamarck concluded that each individual organism represented a different point along a spectrum. To cordon off a section of the spectrum and call it a species was an arbitrary practice. The very term "species" was a consequence of the outdated belief in a single creation.[2]

Lamarck's rejection of the term "species" stemmed from his theory of rapid evolution. He claimed that environmental changes caused immediate alterations in organisms. Certain organs grew or diminished because of increased use or disuse. These changes could then be inherited by offspring. By 1889, biologist August Weismann had disproved Lamarck's theory, demonstrating that mice whose tails had been cut off never produced short-tailed offspring. Similarly, if a man with small muscles increases their size through exercise, he will not transmit a propensity for large muscles to his children.[3]

The second concept that led Darwin to his theory was the complete suitability of organisms to their environment. Ironically, the most eloquent proponent of this concept was William Paley (*Natural Theology*, 1802), who employed it to prove the existence of God. Surely, the fact that the traits of scores of animals suited their respective environments perfectly proved the existence of a designer. But Darwin, who had read Paley's book while a student at Cambridge University, soon envisioned a quite different explanation for this phenomenon.[4]

The third concept that led Darwin to the theory of natural selection was the struggle for existence. As we have seen, in 1798, classical economist Thomas Malthus argued that while the human population increased geometrically, the food supply increased only arithmetically. Hence there was a perpetual competition for survival. Darwin read Malthus's essay "for amusement" in 1838.[5]

The fourth concept was an abundance of time. Darwin's natural selection required a tremendous amount of time to produce the earth's staggering variety of species. Charles Lyell provided the time. In his *Principles of Geology* (1830–1833) Lyell laid the foundations for modern geology, contending that changes in geological formations were the result of the operation of natural processes over millions of years. By contrast, the standard Christian chronology, developed by the seventeenth-century archbishop James Ussher, had set Earth's birth date at 4004 B.C. (a calculation based on the Old Testament listing of the generations since Adam). Darwin became such a close friend of Lyell's that he once wrote, "I always feel as if my books came half out of Lyell's brain."[6]

The Theory

Darwin had already been influenced by the first two of these concepts when he embarked on the HMS *Beagle* (1831–1836), a vessel that surveyed various points along both coasts of South America before touring the South Sea Islands and Australia. While serving as the expedition's naturalist, Darwin amassed a large amount of data and several cases full of specimens, whose rich variety he pondered for decades after returning to England. By 1842 Darwin had reached most of his conclusions but held back from publication. Meanwhile, Alfred Russel Wallace came to the theory of natural selection independently of Darwin. After Wallace sent Darwin a paper outlining his own conclusions and requested that Darwin forward the paper to Lyell if he considered it sufficiently important, Darwin coauthored a paper with Wallace. The following year, 1859, Darwin published *The Origin of Species*.[7]

Darwin argued that the reproductive process produced random variations in the traits of organisms. (Even siblings differed significantly from one another, although they had the same parents.) Those organisms best adapted to their environment survived to reproduce and, thus, to bequeath their desirable traits to their descendants. Organisms without these favorable traits died before they could reproduce, since there was not enough food for all to survive. Over the course of millions of years, the small changes in organisms that accrued from these different survival rates produced qualitative change: Species evolved into wholly different species. (Since Darwin's evolution was much slower than Lamarck's, he retained a use for the word "species"; he often used the term to refer to organisms that clustered around a particular point on the spectrum at a particular time.)[8]

Darwin envisioned nature as a great sculptor, molding organisms over time. He wrote that the theory of natural selection "is the doctrine of Malthus applied with manifold force to the whole animal and vegetable kingdoms; for in this case there can be no artificial increase of food, and no prudential restraint from marriage." Since other species could neither farm nor abstain from sexual intercourse, their limited food supply and accelerating numbers produced an even greater struggle for existence than among humans. Simple mathematics taught that there must be a struggle for existence. Each pair of nearly every species produced more than two offspring, yet the overall number of organisms in most species remained remarkably constant. Darwin hypothesized that all living organisms, including humans, had evolved from simple organisms.[9]

What was Darwin's evidence for natural selection? First, he noted that the fossil record revealed that certain species had become extinct and that new species had arisen. This fact could not be explained by the doctrine of a single creation (at least not one lasting six literal days), but could be explained by the theory of natural selection. If a species received a beneficial variation, it would increase its numbers through a greater survival rate. Greater numbers would, in turn, mean the possibility of a larger number of beneficial variations, leading to even greater numbers. Given the limited amount of available food, such success for one species could come only at the expense of another species, which, because of its ever smaller numbers, would possess ever fewer beneficial variations, leading ultimately to extinction. Second, Darwin noted that humans had consciously bred desired qualities into their domesticated plants and animals for centuries, producing remarkable changes in both in the process. Why, then, couldn't nature, with millions of years at its disposal, accomplish even more? Third, like Paley, Darwin related numerous examples of the suitability of organisms to their respective environments. Darwin wrote: "We see this . . . plainly in the humblest parasite which clings to the hairs of a quadruped or feathers of a bird. . . . We see beautiful adaptations everywhere and in every part of the organic world." Fourth, Darwin presented embryology in support of his theory. Darwin claimed that each stage of the embryo mirrored an evolutionary stage in the development of the species. He contended, "Embryology will often reveal to us the structure, in some degree obscured, of the prototype of each great class."[10]

Darwin recognized that his arguments were not, in any real sense, "proof" of natural selection. New species and the suitability of organisms to their respective environments might be attributed to multiple creation or to a single creation process of six phases not corresponding to literal twenty-four hour periods. Although the changes wrought by artificial selection were dramatic, the human breeding of animals was an intentional, intellectual process, not an accidental one, and had only produced new varieties of the same species; it had never converted one species into another, as Darwin claimed natural selection had. Considered in isolation, the embryology argument was rather weak. Even some creationists believed that embryos passed through stages mirroring the "hierarchy" of animals; such development did not necessarily suggest evolution. Finally, since the theory of natural selection did not allow the prediction of specific outcomes, it could not be validated in the same fashion as most other scientific theories.

The only evidence that Darwin believed could validate his theory of natural selection, a fossil record revealing all of the intermediate steps by which aboriginal species had evolved into their modern descendants, did not exist. Hence Darwin devoted a whole chapter of his book to the argument that the fossil record was grossly incomplete, calling it "a history of the world imperfectly kept and written in a changing dialect." He ascribed its incompleteness partly to the fact that formerly contiguous geographical regions were no longer contiguous (Lyell's view).[11]

The Application of the Theory to Human Evolution

In *The Descent of Man* (1871) Darwin hypothesized that, at some point, humans' apelike ancestors had been forced down from the trees by climatic changes. Because they no longer needed their hands for locomotion, their backs straightened and they developed the ability to grasp tools. Their feet flattened to hold the newly erect body and their big toes grew to provide balance. With the development of tools for combat and hunting, their fangs became teeth. The elimination of the muscle at the back of the neck provided room for the brain to expand, though brain size was insufficient, in itself, to explain human intelligence. Here Darwin deferred to the American Chauncey Wright, who contended that the increase in the size of the brain and in the number of its synapses, combined with the development of facial muscles and the larynx, had given humans the power of speech, a tremendous advance that had allowed self-consciousness. Thus, a series of quantitative changes had produced the qualitative difference between human intelligence and that of other animals. Darwin also argued that human moral codes were yet another product of natural selection. The "social instincts," reinforced by reason and language (the use of praise and blame), had developed because they had been necessary to the survival of the species.[12]

Darwin devoted much of *The Descent of Man* to demonstrating the physical and mental similarities between humans and other animals. The bones, muscles, nerves, blood vessels, and brains of humans, as well as their parasites, birth process, and embryonic development (except in its final stages) paralleled those of other animals. Humans were subject to many of the same diseases as other animals and responded similarly to many of the same medicines. To illustrate that men and monkeys possessed similar tastes and nervous systems, Darwin related the story of baboons in northeast Africa that were captured using beer as bait. The next morning the baboons wore pitiful expressions on their faces, held their heads in their hands, and turned away from beer. More important, Darwin claimed that while humans were more intelligent than other animals, the difference between the intelligence of an ape and a fish was far greater than that between a human and an ape. Animals often taught their young and frequently reasoned their way out of difficult situations. Darwin related how monkeys that had been stung by a wasp wrapped in the same cloth as a lump of sugar often held the next cloth offered to them up to their ears, to listen for a buzzing sound, before unwrapping it. Darwin noted that animals possessed a wide range of personalities and emotions, feeling happiness, sadness, curiosity, jealousy, loyalty, courage, and fear. Some animals had an impressive memory capacity, and others dreamed.[13]

The Reaction to Darwin's Theory

Many biologists immediately assaulted Darwin's theory. A shy and sickly man, Darwin left most of the defense of his theory to more pugnacious friends like Thomas H. Huxley (often called "Darwin's bulldog"), a self-educated zoologist and a committed atheist. Creationists like Adam Sedgwick (Darwin's former professor at Cambridge) and Richard Owen (England's greatest anatomist) derided Darwin for bothering the scientific world with his unproven theories. Similarly, Louis Agassiz, the world-renowned Harvard professor of natural history and codiscoverer of the Ice Age, insisted that God had inserted new species at the beginning of each geological age. Agassiz was no more a biblical literalist than Sedgwick or Owen. Rather, he was a deist and a philosophical idealist who believed that every species was a "thought of God" and who contradicted the Book of Genesis, claiming that the human races were different species, created at different times. He considered the structural similarities between species evidence of "associations of ideas in the Divine Mind," rather than proof of common ancestry.[14]

Even fellow evolutionists criticized Darwin. Some rebuked him for using terms like "natural selection" and "competition," which implied a consciousness in nature. Did two seeds actively compete? Others, including Joseph Hooker, who was one of Darwin's chief defenders, criticized Darwin for overemphasizing natural selection. They noted that some mortality was accidental. When some fish eggs were eaten, or some seeds fell upon bad ground, it was not because they were less fit than others; they merely happened to be in the wrong place at the wrong time. Furthermore, some charged that Darwin was too obsessed with finding a use for every trait of every organism. Some traits were neither helpful nor harmful but merely neutral. Finally, the "macromutationist" followers of Lamarck attacked Darwin. They continued to argue that evolution from one species to another could occur within a single generation.[15]

Evolution since Darwin

Evolutionists have since modified Darwin's theory. Darwin had not understood how the random variations in heredity were produced. It was the Austrian monk Gregor Mendel who hypothesized that the combination of parental genes determined traits. Each trait was produced by the complex interrelation of numerous genes within the chromosomes. One did not inherit traits directly, as Darwin had sometimes suggested; one inherited genes, whose interaction determined traits. Mendel's theory was first published in an obscure Austrian journal in 1865 and did not become widely known in western Europe until the early twentieth century. Neither Darwin nor Mendel understood the role played by genetic mutations, seemingly random discrepancies in the copying of genes that occur during cell division, in producing variation, nor the role played by the seemingly random breaks in strands of DNA (deoxyribonucleic acid) that make possible multiple recombinations.[16]

In 1953 James D. Watson and Francis H. C. Crick identified the molecular structure of DNA, a self-replicating substance arranged in a double helix that contains the body's genetic code, the blueprint for amino acids, which produce the body's proteins. It was estimated in 1964, when there were three billion people in the world, that as little as twenty milligrams of DNA had provided the blueprint for every human ever born.[17]

Evolutionists believe that fossil finds in Africa in the last few decades have revealed a pattern of evolution that dates the earliest known hominids at over three million years ago. Although Darwin's gradual process of natural selection has prevailed over Lamarck's doctrine of immediate inheritance, some twentieth-century evolutionists, including Stephen Jay Gould, argued that evolution may require far less time than Darwin supposed.[18]

As proof of the validity of Darwin's theory, modern evolutionists also point to discoveries regarding the intelligence of animals. Wild apes modify stems and sticks to capture and eat insects and use leaves to sop up water they cannot reach with their lips. Some apes have been taught sign language.[19]

Nevertheless, the debate over evolution continues, even within scientific circles. Although the majority of biologists accept Darwin's theory of natural selection, a sizable number have called attention to genuine scientific problems with the theory. Their most effective spokesman is Phillip E. Johnson, who published

Darwin on Trial in 1991. First, Johnson notes that natural selection cannot explain the origins of life, since natural selection could not have occurred before living organisms capable of reproducing existed. In the early 1950s opponents of creation theory thought they had struck pay dirt when the Miller–Urey experiment produced amino acids (not life, but its basis) by sending a spark through a mixture of gases thought to simulate the atmosphere of early Earth. But geochemists now report that the atmosphere of the early planet was quite dissimilar to the mixture employed in the Miller–Urey experiment. Indeed, researchers have become so frustrated at their own lack of success at explaining how life arose from inert matter that Francis Crick resorted to the theory that extraterrestrials had seeded the earth with life, a solution that merely transfers the mystery of life to another planet. Second, Johnson notes that the fossil record is not as supportive of evolution as is commonly believed. Indeed, very few of the vast number of intermediate species (missing links) that must have existed if Darwin's theory is valid have been found, and there are difficulties with each of the few that have been identified. Solly Zuckerman, one of Britain's leading evolutionists and most influential scientists, has expressed concern that the variation among ape fossils is sufficiently great that a scientist whose imagination is fired by the desire to find ancestors can easily pick out some features in an ape fossil and decide that they are "pre-human." Zuckerman compared the professional standards of physical anthropologists to those of parapsychologists, faulting the anthropologists for their reckless speculation. Third, there is the logical problem of how Darwin's micromutations can convert one species into another. Even the simplest organisms depend upon biological systems that are staggeringly complex, consisting of numerous parts that must interact with precision in order for the systems to work at all. Yet Darwin's theory claims that each part of each system arose separately, by chance, and was preserved for long stretches of time, though it could provide no benefit to the organism until all of the other parts were present. (To cite one example: in order to see, a person must possess a lens, a retina, an optic nerve, and complex neurological wiring in the brain to process visual data. The theory of natural selection proposes that each of these parts arose randomly, independently of the others, at a different time, as the result of a micromutation, and was preserved until all of the other parts were present and could work together.) Statisticians have shown that this is highly unlikely. Fourth, biologists have found that most mutations are unfavorable to the organism. Yet, according to modern evolutionists, mutations are the very foundation of evolution. Fifth, recent embryological research has shown that the embryos of different vertebrates are not at all similar in either appearance or genetic makeup in the early stages of development, as Darwin claimed, though some such embryos are similar in appearance (but not in genetic makeup) during the middle stage (the reason the myth of embryo similarity first arose).[20]

FREUDIAN THEORY

In any case, Darwin's theory of natural selection clearly prevailed among the intellectuals of the late nineteenth and early twentieth centuries. Thus, it was only a matter of time before someone developed a Darwinist psychology to replace the Epicurean conception of the blank slate and the Platonic theory of innate goodness.

That psychologist was Sigmund Freud. In the 1890s Freud developed the practice of "psychoanalysis," allowing his patients to speak freely and spontaneously about their innermost thoughts. By 1897 he had formulated the theory of infantile sexuality, which held that sex drives existed even in children, rather than emerging in puberty, as many thought. Humans were sexual creatures from birth to death. In particular, children were troubled by the "Oedipus complex," the subconscious desire to get rid of their parent of the same gender and take that parent's place with their parent of the opposite gender. Parents' love for their children was equally sexual in tone if not in aim.[21]

Freud placed a great deal of emphasis upon dreams (*The Interpretation of Dreams*, 1900) as manifestations of subconscious desires, associated with childhood experiences, that were repressed during conscious life. He wrote, "The interpretation of dreams is the royal road to a knowledge of the unconscious activities of the mind."[22]

The Theory of the Subconscious

In his later works Freud charted the human subconscious. Freud claimed that the subconscious was composed of the id, the ego, and the superego. While the id consisted of amoral, biological desires for sexual gratification and aggression, the superego consisted of the moral imperatives imposed upon the individual by his family and culture, and the ego mediated between the two to form conscious thought. The struggle between the id and the superego was an internal representation of the struggle between individual and societal needs. Freud categorically denied the existence of intuition (conscience), claiming that the moral imperatives of the superego were purely the product of external (societal) forces. He wrote, "We may reject the existence of an original, as it were natural, capacity to distinguish good from bad." Furthermore, Freud contended that human civilization required a balance between the id and the superego. If the id were too powerful, sociopathic behavior would result; if the superego were too powerful, neuroses or depression would result. Freud substituted for the blank slate theory and the belief in innate goodness a psychology based upon Darwin's conception of humans as animals. The seat of human thought and behavior was the subconscious, filled with sensual desires and ultimately beyond the individual's control.[23]

Although Freud located the source of human depravity in an animal origin rather than in original sin, his conception of human nature was as dark and uncompromising as that of John Calvin. Freud wrote: "Men are not gentle creatures who want to be loved. . . . They are, on the contrary, creatures among whose instinctual endowments is to be reckoned a powerful share of aggressiveness." Hence humans enslaved, raped, humiliated, tortured, and killed one another. It was not just that humans used aggression to get what they wanted; aggression *was* what they wanted, and they often employed it without any perceptible gain. Freud wrote that man was a "savage beast to whom consideration towards his own kind is something alien." He cited atrocities committed by the Huns, Genghis Kahn, the Crusaders, and soldiers in World War I. He criticized the naive utopianism of the Marxists, which was based on an "untenable illusion," "an idealistic misconception of human nature." He explained, "Aggressiveness was not created by property. It reigned almost without limit in primitive times, when property was still very scanty, and it already shows itself in the nursery." Therefore, it was "possible to bind together a considerable number of people in love" only when there were "other people left over to receive the manifestations of their aggressiveness." Freud concluded: "There are difficulties attaching to the nature of civilization which will not yield to any attempt at reform. . . . Men have gained control over the forces of nature to such an extent that with their help they would have no difficulty in exterminating one another to the last man."[24]

While, at first glance, the id seemed merely another name for original sin and the superego another name for (an environmentally formed) conscience, Freud's desire for balance distinguished him from orthodox theists, who held that conscience should always prevail over sin (though they recognized that it rarely did so, in practice). Yet Freud leaned in the direction of these moralists when he expressed concern whether the superego, which was instilled from without, could serve as an adequate counterweight to the id, which was innate. He wrote: "Aggression . . . constitutes the greatest impediment to civilization. . . . In consequence of this primary mutual hostility of human beings, civilized society is perpetually threatened with disintegration. Civilization has to use its utmost efforts in order to set limits to man's aggressive instincts. . . . In spite of every effort, these endeavours of civilization have not so far achieved very much." Freud believed that civilization depended on the ability of society to control sexuality, not unleash it, and hoped that psychoanalysis might aid in the task by turning patients from harmful repression to sublimation (the redirection of desire to healthy ends) or conscious choice. Freud's own chaste life and family devotion were models of Victorian morality.[25]

Nevertheless, Freud opposed religion in all forms. He referred to himself, alternately, as "a completely godless Jew" (a contradiction in terms?) and as "a godless medical man." He wrote: "The struggle of the scientific spirit against the religious world view has not come to an end; it is still going on in the present before our eyes. . . . Every scientific investigation of a religious belief has unbelief as its presupposition. . . . Religion alone is the serious enemy." Freud would give the enemy no quarter: "The truth cannot be tolerant; it admits no compromises and reservations." Identifying religion as a "mass delusion," he classed it with alcohol as a form of escape from the harsh reality of existence, whose chief features were pain and death. He boasted, "I am not afraid at all of the Almighty." He declared his own "absolutely negative attitude toward religion, in every form." He compared the rituals of believers with the compulsions of neurotics and attributed the belief that human life must have a purpose to "presumptuousness." He speculated that even the past existence of Jesus might be "a part of mythology." He attributed the idea of hell to an excess of the superego. He declared, "I adhere to the Jewish religion as little as to any other." He would not take his children to synagogue, nor would he allow his wife to observe the Sabbath, calling it "a superstition." In his final book, one of the earliest works of psychohistory, *Moses and Monotheism*, Freud alleged that Moses had been an Egyptian who was murdered by his Jewish followers.[26]

Freud's terse statement regarding his fellow humans—"I can offer them no consolation"—best summarizes the chief difference between theism and skepticism. While both possess pessimistic views of this world, theism offers the consolation of a better and more permanent existence in the afterlife, a consolation skeptics consider a delusion.[27]

The Reaction to Freud

Freud's theories gained wide currency in the United States after World War I, though some psychologists joined his student Carl Jung in deemphasizing the role of sexuality in the formation of personality. (Freud's theory of infantile sexuality had always been the most controversial of his theories. The philosopher William James called Freud a "dirty fellow," and German Marxist Karl Bakhtin wrote, "When one reads Freud, one could think of man as nothing but an appendage to his sexual organs.") Jung also argued that the subconscious contained genetically inherited memories from previous generations. As religious devotion waned in urban areas, as mobility deprived people of their extended families, as industrialization increased the stresses of daily life, and as belief in the power of science and of specialization grew, psychoanalysts took the place of the clergy as the chief advisers and confessors of the urban elite.[28]

THE NEW PHYSICS

The Theory of Relativity

Meanwhile, physicists had begun to challenge the supposedly ageless laws of Newton. In 1905 Albert Einstein published an article entitled, "On the Electrodynamics of Moving Bodies," in which he advanced the special theory of relativity, which applied only to nonaccelerating movement. In 1915, in the general theory of relativity, he broadened the theory to include all forms of motion. Einstein's theory stated that every mass and every acceleration in the universe, however minute, bent space and slowed time. The larger the mass and the greater the acceleration, the more curved the space surrounding it and the slower time proceeded in its vicinity. Time and space were not uniform; measurements of both were relative to mass and to acceleration. (Light traveling to the earth from other galaxies appears to bend near the sun, because the space through which it travels is bent by the sun's mass.) Since acceleration slowed time relative to a nonaccelerating observer, time would proceed much more slowly for one who approached the speed of light than for a stationary observer. Since both the amount of mass and the amount of acceleration in two different vicinities would always differ (however minutely), the degree of curvature of space and the progress of time would always vary from place to place, even across the same room, and would change continuously with changes in mass and acceleration. Thus, none of the rules of Euclidean geometry or Newtonian physics, which were based upon a uniform distribution of space and time, were literally true. There was no such thing as a straight line, since all space was curved, to varying degrees. No clock, even if perfectly constructed, could mark uniform time, since uniform time did not exist. But, though the universe did not conform to the laws of Euclid and Newton, those laws were valid enough to serve as rules of thumb in the completion of human tasks, since the amount of curvature of space or variation in the progress of time in our low-mass solar system was so minute. (Around a black hole, however, space is extremely warped and time proceeds very slowly relative to areas of low mass.) Einstein added that the speed of light was the only constant. In 1907 Einstein also proposed the famous formula $e = mc^2$—energy equals mass times the speed of light squared. Energy and mass were merely two alternate states of existence. This finding, which corresponded to the theory of relativity's equation of mass and acceleration, led ultimately to nuclear power and weapons. A small amount of mass could be converted into a great deal of energy.[29]

The Indeterminacy Principle

Other physicists started a revolution at the micro level equal to Einstein's revolution at the macro level. In 1927, building upon the work of Max Planck and Niels Bohr, Werner Heisenberg proposed the "indeterminacy principle," the theory that no human measurement could determine the position and momentum of a subatomic particle simultaneously. The more precisely a physicist determined the position of a given particle, the less precise would be his measurement of its momentum, and vice versa. Furthermore, physicists could not predict with certainty the future position or momentum of any given particle; they could deal only in probabilities. Heisenberg's theory does not really prove, as some have claimed, that the movement of subatomic particles (and the physical universe that movement creates) is truly random, though Heisenberg and Bohr themselves accepted that conclusion. It proves only that humans are unable to predict it with complete precision, in part because their measuring instruments affect the particles' paths by collapsing their wave functions. As Heisenberg himself emphasized, highly accurate predictions can still be made at the group level of photons. (Einstein was indignant about suggestions of real randomness in the universe, saying, "I cannot believe that God would play dice with the Universe." But it was not merely the imputation of ultimate randomness that bothered Einstein. He was also distressed by the possibility that the universe was impenetrable to human reason. Hence he hoped that quantum physics would later be displaced, a hope Bohr ridiculed as equivalent to the statement, "We may hope that it will later turn out that sometimes 2 x 2 = 5, for this would be of great advantage to our finances.")[30]

Heisenberg finally concluded that minute systems were best explained by quantum probabilities, that medium-sized systems (the vast majority) were best explained by Newtonian laws, and that gigantic systems were best explained by relativity. There was no single set of laws in the universe; each level of phenomena required a different set of explanations, involving a different language and a different manner of thinking. Heisenberg concluded, "Whenever we proceed from the known into the unknown we may hope to understand, but we may have to learn at the same time a new meaning of the word 'understanding.'"[31]

THE RISE OF SKEPTICISM

The Decline in the Belief in Progress

By replacing Newton's "scientific laws" with "statistical probabilities" at the micro level and with relativity at the macro level, modern physicists called into question the very idea of "objective" human knowledge, the idea on which humanist dreams of progress rested. Science had been transformed from a dispenser of truth into a mere pragmatic tool, devoid of transcendent meaning, able to transmit only a shadow of reality. It was ironic that science, the love-child of Epicurean humanists, should dash their hopes by revealing its own limits.

Similarly, Darwin discounted the idea of human progress. The theory that species were becoming ever more complex and ever more suited to their environments held little comfort for humans, who might become extinct as easily as past species. Furthermore, Darwin did not believe that complexity was necessarily superior to simplicity. He noted that while complex organisms were more adaptable, they were also more delicate and more "liable to be put out of order and injured." While reading an 1847 novel about evolution Darwin made a note to himself to "never use the words higher and lower" in reference to animals. Though more complex than other species, humans were not superior; evolution was not a progressive development. In addition, in Darwin's world the environment was as subject to constant change as the organism. How could species become ever more adapted to their environments when their environments were constantly changing? Darwin hypothesized a perpetual cat-and-mouse game between environment and species, both in a constant state of change. There were no fixed points, no standards by which to recognize progress. "Progress" implies movement toward some ultimate end, movement that can at least be recognized, if not precisely measured. Darwin did not envision any end to the flux.[32]

Historical developments helped ensure the acceptance of the theories of Darwin, Freud, and the physicists by raising further doubts about human rationality and potential for progress. When high hopes for successful postwar reconstructions proved unfounded, the unprecedented carnage of the U.S. Civil War and World War I seemed to some to have occurred for naught. The decline of the family farm due to overproduction, the deflation of currency, high protective tariffs, and the monopolistic railroads' high freight rates frightened many Americans who had been raised on the Jeffersonian belief that the success of American democracy depended on pastoral virtue. The Second Industrial Revolution of the late nineteenth and early twentieth centuries produced gross inequalities of wealth, urban slums, and massive immigration, creating a backlash of nativism. In 1890 the U.S. Census Bureau declared that the American frontier no longer existed, causing consternation among those liberal humanists (including disciples of the historian Frederick Jackson Turner) who equated progress with the advancement of American-style democracy and who believed that democracy had been founded on the abundance of cheap land. In short, Darwinism prevailed because it was well adapted to its historical environment.[33]

Darwin and Freud were far more devastating to humanism than to theism. Their theory of human nature, as pessimistic as that of theists, flatly contradicted both Epicurean and Platonic humanism. Darwin devastated the large numbers of Americans who had merged humanism with theism—that is, those who had based their belief in God on such rational proofs as the perfection of natural design. Their despair was reflected in Joseph Wood Krutch's best-selling book, *The Modern Temper* (1929). Krutch argued that Darwin and Freud had destroyed belief in free will and its corollaries: fixed moral standards, romantic love, and heroism. Based on the belief in autonomous individuals freely making choices, these concepts could not survive the evidence that natural selection or the subconscious actually controlled human behavior. Darwin and Freud had removed both the joy and the tragedy that made life meaningful. Krutch concluded, "There is no reason to suppose that human life has any more meaning than the life of the humblest insect that crawls from one annihilation to another." The late nineteenth and early twentieth centuries witnessed a rise in anxiety attacks and suicide, especially among the well-educated.[34]

The Persistence of Humanism

But humanism survived even in the age of skepticism. Orthodox humanists were joined by followers of the Social Gospel movement, Christian humanists who sought progress through a combination of private charity and government action. Unwilling to return to traditional pessimism and premillennialism like most disillusioned Christians of the late nineteenth century, the followers of the Social Gospel movement managed to sustain some of the postmillennialist reform fervor that had pervaded the antebellum period. The movement influenced Woodrow Wilson and other progressives, who sought to regulate big business for the first time and to "make the world safe for democracy" through world government. Though U.S. refusal to join the League of Nations and the league's ultimate failure fostered disillusionment, the creation of the United Nations (1945) restored a sense of hope among internationalists.[35]

The Persistence of Theism

Nor did Darwin's theories destroy theism. Some orthodox theists actually welcomed them. In contending that the universe could be explained without God, he had put forward the question as it really was, as a matter of simple faith. Darwin had separated the proverbial men from the boys, those who had real faith from those who subordinated faith in God to their own flawed reason. Although some ministers, priests, and rabbis spoke out against Darwin, others, like Henry Ward Beecher and Lyman Abbot, accepted his theory completely or modified it to allow more direct divine intervention. The last group advanced the "emergence theory," which held that God had intervened at several crucial points in the evolutionary process, once in order to give humans a leg up on the evolutionary ladder. In fact, Darwin's greatest American exponent, his "American Huxley," Harvard botanist Asa Gray, was a theistic evolutionist who insisted that "order presupposes mind." He believed that God provided the variations in organisms. Until the 1930s most American biologists continued to consider natural selection an insufficient explanation for all of evolution, especially for the origins of human intelligence.[36]

The orthodox theists who were most seriously challenged by Darwin's theory were biblical literalists. Darwin's theory of natural selection conflicted with a literal reading of Genesis 1 and 2, which tell of God's creation of the world in six days. By the early twentieth century, a doctrinally diverse group of biblical literalists had begun calling themselves "fundamentalists" and had formed a coalition. In 1910 the Presbyterian General Assembly identified the five fundamental doctrines of Christianity as the inerrancy of the Bible, the Virgin Birth, the Vicarious Atonement (Jesus's atonement for human sin through the Crucifixion), the Resurrection, and the authenticity of the miracles. (Some fundamentalists later substituted premillennialism for the authenticity of the miracles as the fifth point of fundamentalism, though still believing in the miracles, of course.) These beliefs were further championed in *The Fundamentals* (1910–1915), a twelve-volume series distributed to pastors, missionaries, theology professors and students, the YMCA and YWCA, Sunday school superintendents, and the editors of religious journals. Most fundamentalists also shared an emotional, evangelical style of preaching.[37]

In addition to Darwin, fundamentalists also assaulted "higher criticism," a mid-nineteenth century movement begun in Germany that endorsed nonliteral interpretations of the Bible. Higher critics claimed that the form of Genesis suggested that it was intended as an allegory rather than as a literal account of creation. Genesis was filled with numerical symbolism. The number seven represented completeness. Since the sun had not even been created until the fourth "day" (Genesis 1:16), why should a "day" in Genesis be interpreted as a twenty-four hour period? After all, 2 Peter 3:8 stated, "Do not ignore this one fact, beloved, that with the Lord one day is like a thousand years, and a thousand years are like one day." In a larger sense no one ever really read any extensive written work literally; language was itself a collection of symbols. Symbolism was an inherent part of human communication. What meaningful lesson could one learn from Jesus's admonition to "turn the other cheek" when slapped (Matthew 5:39), or from his parables, if one took them literally? Critics of the fundamentalists were quick to note their torturously nonliteral interpretations of those biblical passages they found unpleasant (e.g., the passage in which Jesus granted Peter the power to "loose or bind sins" [Matthew 16:19] and the passages allowing moderate alcohol consumption).[38]

Fundamentalists feared that once the anchor of biblical literalism was cut, there would be no end to the perversion of Scripture to suit whatever practices were currently fashionable. Biblical teachings would then become meaningless—mere raw materials to bend and

warp into justifications for all manner of selfish and irresponsible behavior. This argument paralleled Thomas Jefferson's argument for
strict construction of the Constitution. If written contracts, whether
religious or political, could be interpreted so loosely as to invalidate
the clearest prohibitions, such contracts would lose all meaning.
While the Bible required, and human reason made possible, some
degree of interpretation, Scripture should be interpreted in as literal
a manner as possible in order to avoid its becoming the mere play-
thing of logical gymnasts bent on affirming their own predilections.[39]

By the mid-1920s the fundamentalist campaign to unseat liberal ministers had failed in all but a few churches, the largest exception being the Southern Baptist Convention. Nevertheless,
fundamentalists succeeded in excluding evolutionary theories
from many schools for another half century. Contrary to popular
belief, the verdict of the famous media circus which became
known as the "Scopes Monkey Trial" (1925) favored the fundamentalists. The governor of Tennessee had signed a law against the
teaching of evolution on the understanding it would not be enforced. But town boosters in Dayton, hoping to get the village on
the map, joined with opponents of the law to engineer a test case.
The defendant was John T. Scopes, a former substitute teacher
who was not even sure he had ever actually taught evolution. Although Scopes's $100 fine was reversed by the state supreme court
on a technicality, the court upheld the constitutionality of the
antievolution statute. The U.S. Supreme Court did not invalidate
such laws until 1968. In 1987 the Supreme Court ruled that
Louisiana could not insist on equal time for creation-science, because it constituted an establishment of religion.[40]

As with Darwin, theists gave Freud mixed reviews. While a
minority of clerics attempted to integrate Freudian theory with
Christian theology, most either ignored or assaulted it. Pope Pius
XII condemned psychoanalysis as a "pansexualist method" that
debased ethics and corroded the soul.[41]

Social Darwinism

Some Americans, later called "Social Darwinists," attempted
to use natural selection to justify beliefs and practices to which

they were already attached. Some appealed to Darwin's theory as evidence for the benefits of classical economics. Competition between individuals was good, since it would lead to the "survival of the fittest," a term coined by the British evolutionist philosopher Herbert Spencer. Government should stay out of the arena, intervening only to ensure that the combatants fought fairly.[42]

But Darwin was far from clear on this matter. Although he used Malthus's theory concerning "the struggle for existence," and although he alluded to the need for some competition within society, it is not clear that he would have endorsed laissez-faire economics. In *The Descent of Man* he wrote that man "manifestly owes this immense superiority to his intellectual faculties, to his social habits, which lead him to aid and defend his fellows, and to his corporeal structure." The second of Darwin's three reasons for human evolutionary success was the instinct for cooperation and mutual aid. As Lester Ward, the author of the first American sociology textbook, put it, even "if nature progresses through the destruction of the weak, man progresses through the protection of the weak." Indeed, some socialists made use of Darwin, claiming that the culmination of evolutionary competition was a cooperative society, and most classical economists of the period borrowed little more from the biologist than a few catch phrases. Though the most famous of these economists, William Graham Sumner, was a fan of Spencer, it was Thomas Malthus who most influenced Sumner.[43]

Others used Darwin to justify racism. As early as the 1860s Darwin's cousin, the accomplished statistician Francis Galton, coined the term "eugenics" to refer to efforts to improve the gene pool of the human race. While Galton confined himself to encouraging early marriage among those whom he considered the genetic elite, later eugenicists were not so restrained. John Fiske contended that the cranial capacity of whites ("the refined and intellectual Teutons") was almost twice that of an inferior race like the Australian aborigines. The eugenics movement influenced such popular works as Madison Grant's book *The Passing of the Great Race* (1916), in which Grant argued that "hordes" of new immigrants were diluting the superior genes of "native Americans," by which he meant the descendants of northwestern Europeans. Grant argued that the "Nordic race" that had established the

United States was being overwhelmed by Slavic and Latin peoples from southeastern Europe. Grant's view received support from Carl C. Brigham's treatise *A Study of American Intelligence* (1923), in which Brigham used U.S. Army IQ scores from World War I to support the claim that Anglo-Saxons were more intelligent than other ethnic groups. The fact that many of the soldiers were recent immigrants who could not read English, the language in which the tests were written, did not dissuade Brigham from his conclusion. Henry Ford's anti-Semitic literature, written at a time when the whole world considered him the very symbol of success, proved an invaluable resource for Nazi propagandists. Pseudoscientific genetic theories helped justify the National Origins Act of 1924, which severely restricted immigration from every part of the globe except northwestern Europe (and Latin America, an interesting loophole), the segregation and disfranchisement of African Americans, and state sterilization laws against the mentally ill and people with mental disabilities (though most such laws were later overturned by the courts).[44]

But Darwin's writings did not support eugenics. When discussing the larger brain size of humans in *The Descent of Man*, Darwin added: "On the other hand, no one supposes that the intellect of any two animals or of any two men can be accurately gauged by the cubic contents of their skulls." He emphasized that what were called "the races" were mere varieties of the same species. Furthermore, one logical deduction from Darwin's theory is that interracial marriage is genetically beneficial. In Darwin's world the greater the intermingling of different varieties of genes the better the chance to profit from a random variation. Spencer came to just such a conclusion, and his American followers supported free immigration and intermarriage with eastern European immigrants as a result, though their racial prejudices still prevented them from advocating intermarriage with people of African or Asian descent. Furthermore, while it is true that Darwin appealed to those with physical or mental disabilities not to reproduce ("Both sexes ought to refrain from marriage if they are in any marked degree inferior in body or mind"), he never advocated the use of coercion against those who rejected his advice. He considered sympathy for the weak a product of natural selection and added, "Nor could we check our sympathy, even at the urging of hard reason, without deterioration in the noblest part of our nature."[45]

Supporters of military and territorial expansion also used Darwin. Alfred T. Mahan (*The Influence of Sea Power upon History*, 1890) used Darwinist language to persuade the American people that the United States must break out of its isolationist shell if it was to avoid defeat in the natural struggle between nations. Mahan contended that a nation's strength and well-being rested primarily on its navy, which required bases and coaling stations. He wrote: "All around us now is strife. 'The struggle of life,' 'the race of life,' are phrases so familiar that we do not feel their significance till we stop to think about them. Everywhere nation is arrayed against nation; our own no less than others." Though Mahan supported a defensive posture and opposed the Spanish-American War (1898), in which the United States acquired Guam, Puerto Rico, the Philippines, and virtual control over Cuba, he endorsed the annexation of these territories once acquired and urged the acquisition of Hawaii and the construction of the Panama Canal. The new imperialist impulse also led the United States into scores of interventions in Latin America.[46]

Racial prejudice was sometimes used to justify imperialism. Some American imperialists agreed with Rudyard Kipling ("The White Man's Burden") that it was the duty of whites to conquer dark-skinned peoples in order to aid in their progress. Yet Darwin himself hardly seems to have been an imperialist, and Spencer declared, "Aggression of every kind is hateful to me."[47]

In short, Social Darwinists of all kinds used Darwin's new theory to claim scientific support for old ideologies and policies. In the process they sometimes damaged the cause of Darwinism itself. For instance, William Jennings Bryan opposed the theory of natural selection not so much because it conflicted with the Book of Genesis as because he was convinced it led to belief "in the merciless law by which the strong crowd out and kill the weak." Bryan blamed Darwin for the growing harshness of society as manifested in eugenics, imperialism, and war— a harshness that reached its height in the paperback shocker

Might Is Right (1896), which declared, "Death to the weaklings, wealth to the strong."[48]

Relativism

While Social Darwinists were applying Darwin's theory to social, economic, and political issues, theorists in a variety of fields began challenging the humanist belief in the existence of "laws" governing human affairs. Though such challenges began well before Einstein proposed his theory of relativity, the new physics accelerated the growth of relativism in the early-to-mid twentieth century. The theories of Einstein and Heisenberg called into question the very idea of objectivity. Humans were fully a part of nature and could never become objective observers of it. They were like rafters plunging down the rapids of a mighty river, able to see only a small part of the swiftly-moving stream—yet flattering themselves that they were detached spectators who could stand above the river and grasp its totality.

Thorstein Veblen attacked the humanist assumption that there were universal laws of economics. Veblen argued that economic institutions were historically and culturally based. In *The Theory of the Leisure Class* (1899), he criticized the "conspicuous consumption" (Veblen coined the term) of the wealthy and their predatory business practices, both of which he considered aristocratic inheritances from a more barbaric age. Sheltered from all want, the rich saw no reason to discard these outdated practices, while the middle class adopted them in emulation of the rich, and the poor were too busy attempting to survive to challenge them. As a result, these practices, which had nothing to do with survival and everything to do with the desire for status, impeded societal evolution. A lifelong socialist, Veblen believed that the values of the leisure class, which reflected the needs of a barbarous past, must be replaced by a frugality and communalism that would satisfy the needs created by the new industrial age.[49]

Similarly, Oliver Wendell Holmes Jr. denied the existence of natural law. Law was not universal but a product of history and culture. Jurists did not deduce law from the workings of the natural world; they created it, in accord with their moral and political beliefs, self-interest, and other factors. The legal reasoning of judges generally followed and justified a decision made on other grounds; indeed, equally valid legal principles could often be cited for opposing decisions. In *The Common Law* (1881) Holmes wrote:

> The life of the law has not been logic; it has been experience. The felt necessities of the time, the prevalent moral and political theories, intuitions of public policy, avowed or unconscious, even the prejudices which judges share with their fellow men, have a good deal more to do than the syllogism in determining the rules by which men should be governed. The law embodies the story of a nation's development through many centuries and it cannot be dealt with as if it contained only the axioms and corollaries of a book of mathematics.

Holmes claimed, "The substance of the law at any given time pretty nearly corresponds, so far as it goes, with what is then understood to be convenient." To call something a "right" was merely to consider it an activity that courts would likely protect from interference. Similarly, Holmes wrote, "A legal duty so called is nothing but a prediction that if a man does or omits certain things he will be made to suffer in this or that way by judgment of the court." He added: "The logical method and form flatter the longing for certainty and repose which is in every human mind. But certainty is generally an illusion, and repose is not the destiny of man." He later wrote, "To have doubted one's own first principles is the mark of a civilized man." In his essay "Natural Law" (1918) Holmes wrote:

> The jurists who believe in natural law seem to me to be in that naive state of mind that accepts what has been familiar and accepted by them and their neighbors as something that must be accepted by all men everywhere. . . . The most fundamental of the supposed preexisting rights—the right to life—is sacrificed without a scruple not only in war, but whenever the interest of society, that is, of the predominant power in the community, is thought to demand it. Whether that interest is the interest of mankind in the long run no one can tell. . . . Certainly we may expect that the received opinion about the present war [World War I] will depend a good deal upon which side wins. . . . Certitude is not a test of certainty. We have been cock-sure of many things that were not so.

Humans must act in spite of the lack of metaphysical certitude. Holmes declared, "That the universe has in it more than we understand, that the private soldiers have not been told the plan of the campaign, or even that there is one, rather than some vaster unthinkable to which every predicate is an impertinence, has no bearing upon our conduct." He added: "That the universe has produced us ... [is] our only but our adequate significance. A grain of sand has the same."[50]

Holmes's criticism of the concept of natural law differed fundamentally from the past criticisms of orthodox theists. Theists did not doubt the existence of a moral order in the universe; they doubted only that humans could either grasp it intuitively or deduce it from nature. Rather, humans required God's direct revelation of the proper morality. But skeptics like Holmes denied the very existence of any universal moral order.

According to Holmes, the history of the law revealed that law was a function of power, not morality. Holmes claimed that the study of the law would benefit "if every word of moral significance could be banished from the law altogether." He denied that life possessed any transcendent meaning, writing, "Life is an end in itself."[51]

Holmes's works were so well-received they eventually won him a position on the Supreme Court. In his tenure there he was unwilling to invalidate laws passed by elected legislatures on the basis of abstract individual rights in which he did not believe. This made him a hero of progressives, whom he despised, since he upheld laws regulating big business, which he admired. He endorsed free speech not as an individual right but as a social good. A wise society permitted free expression because it could achieve satisfactory results only through the sum of all opinions, not because any one person's idea might be "true." Yet society might have a legitimate reason to restrict freedom of speech during a crisis, as when opponents of World War I were imprisoned with Holmes's blessing. In 1927 he voted to uphold a Virginia law permitting the involuntary sterilization of the mentally incompetent. He wrote: "We have seen more than once that the public welfare may call upon the best citizens for their lives. It would be strange if it would not call upon those who already sap the strength of the State for these lesser sacrifices."[52]

Holmes had come to his relativism the hard way. Having served in a regiment that fought in some of the bloodiest battles of the Civil War, Holmes had been wounded three times and had seen numerous friends killed. He had come to blame the unprecedented carnage of the war on the unbending moral certitude of both the abolitionists and the defenders of slavery—on their blind devotion to shadowy and unreal concepts that hardly justified the horrific deaths of so many flesh-and-blood men. He wrote, "It is well that some of us don't know that we know anything." The Civil War had stripped Holmes of his belief in strongly held belief. While there were still a few things for which he was willing to fight, he noted, "Instead of saying that they ought to be I merely say they are part of the kind of world that I like—or should like." Such subjective moral preference "hardly warrants our talking much about absolute truth." As late as the 1930s, shortly before his death, Holmes dissolved in tears when attempting to read a poem about the Civil War. Looking back so many years later, what grieved Holmes deeply was not so much the loss of his close friends as the loss of the innocent, idealistic antebellum world, a world that had bled to death on Civil War battlefields and was now irretrievable. According to a friend, "He told me that after the Civil War the world never seemed quite right again." This sadness no doubt played a role in Holmes's decision not to have children. He claimed, "This is not the kind of world I want to bring anyone else into." Yet the tears demonstrated that behind the cynicism there was still a deep-seated yearning in the heart of the old skeptic for a sense of moral certitude.[53]

Historical writing also reflected the growing pessimism and relativism of the age. In *The Law of Civilization and Decay* (1895), Brooks Adams contended that societies went through cycles of barbarism (dispersed power) and civilization (concentrated power). Since Western civilization had been steadily consolidating power since the Middle Ages, the clear implication was that it was due for a descent into barbarism, a cyclical theory that foreshadowed Oswald Spengler's *Decline of the West*.[54]

Adams's more famous brother Henry shared his pessimism, predicting in 1901 that, at its present rate, "society must break its damned neck" within fifty years through "explosives, or electric energy, or control of cosmic power." Henry Adams's *History of the United States of America during the Administrations of Thomas Jefferson and James Madison* (1889–1891) departed from the old romantic accounts, emphasizing the irony of unintended consequences and the power of uncontrollable social forces. In a slap at the old romantic belief in free will and the power of the individual "great man," Adams wrote that Jefferson and Madison had been "mere grasshoppers kicking and gesticulating on the middle of the Mississippi River" and "carried along on a stream which floated them, after a fashion, without much regard to themselves." History, like nature, did not consult human purposes. Henry was even more pessimistic than Brooks; where Brooks saw cycles, Henry saw only decline. A lapsed Unitarian who had no faith to sustain him after his wife committed suicide in 1885, Henry felt like a mere "bystander" in life. In his bitterness he seemed to relish his own predictions of doom for Western civilization.[55]

Riding this tide of pessimism and relativism, Charles A. Beard (*An Economic Interpretation of the Constitution of the United States*, 1913) gave credence to Holmes's assertion concerning the origins of law. Beard contended that the revered U.S. Constitution, far from being a timeless expression of statesmanship and political wisdom, was an economic document designed to promote the immediate interests of its drafters and supporters.[56]

Nowhere was moral relativism more entrenched than in the new disciplines of anthropology and sociology. The empirical study of countless societies left no doubt that various peoples throughout the world had lived according to different moral standards. To the orthodox theist, this fact presented no problem. It merely meant that some were more right, by the light of revelation and by the grace of God, than others. But the knowledge that large numbers of the world's population disagreed about moral "laws" that were supposed to be accessible to all societies through reason or intuition was devastating to the humanist concept of natural law.

German immigrant Franz Boas, the father of modern anthropology, rejected the terms "higher" and "lower culture," terms that ignored "the relative value of all forms of culture," thereby depriving Westerners "of the benefits to be gained from the teachings of other cultures." He attributed an alleged lack of cultural achievement by other races to Western imperialism and oppression: "The rapid dissemination of Europeans over the whole world cut short all promising beginnings. No race except that of eastern Asia was given a chance to develop a civilization." Intrigued by the diversity of human responses to experience, Boas studied Eskimo and other cultures.[57]

Margaret Mead's famous anthropological work was the descendant of pioneering empirical studies and surveys undertaken by late nineteenth- and early twentieth-century female social scientists. These sociologists hoped to prove that the subordination of women was the product of historical and cultural circumstances, not of biological differences between the genders. In *Coming of Age in Samoa* (1928), Mead captured the American public's attention by celebrating the casual sex she found in these islands. She noted with approval that Samoans did not frown upon homosexuality and "statistically unusual forms of heterosexual activity" and were thus free of harmful guilt. Disagreements between a Samoan male and his wife's seducer could be settled by the latter's payment to the former of "a few fine mats." Mead worried that the attempt by Christian missionaries to encourage "the European standard of sex behavior" in Samoa would cause turmoil in Samoan society. She concluded that "the main lesson" she learned in Samoa was "that adolescence is not necessarily a time of stress and strain, but that cultural conditions [in the West] make it so." The "ever-increasing number of neuroses" in the West was the clear product of a repressive culture. But Mead was confident that the study of other cultures would destroy the "belief in a single [ethical] standard." Mead concluded with an attack on that which conservatives considered the very foundation of civilization, the effort by parents to instill moral values in their children: "The home must cease to plead an ethical cause or a religious belief with smiles and frowns. . . . [Children] must be taught that many ways are open to them, no one sanctioned above its alternative."[58]

Derek Freeman, professor emeritus at Australian National University, has since contended that Mead's conclusions were fatally flawed as a result of inadequate preparation by her mentors (Franz Boas and Ruth Benedict), brief and incompetent fieldwork by Mead herself, her failure to master the Samoan language, and her decision not to live with a Samoan family while in Samoa. Furthermore, Freeman concluded, Mead had been duped by her informants, who told her what she apparently wished to hear. In contrast to Mead's idyllic view of Samoan society, Freeman described that culture as rigidly hierarchical, harsh, repressive, and plagued by violence, especially rape. He contended that the Samoans were both highly competitive and strict with their children. Finally, the Samoans disapproved of premarital sex. A more complete refutation of Mead was hardly possible. Needless to say, Freeman's conclusions are as controversial among anthropologists as Mead's.[59]

While Mead's anthropological work assaulted traditional Judeo-Christian morality, her colleagues attacked modern industrialism. In *Patterns of Culture* (1934), Ruth Benedict contrasted competitive industrial society unfavorably with the cooperative culture of Native American tribes in the southwestern United States. In *Middletown* (1929, 1937), Robert S. Lynd and Hellen M. Lynd found unhappiness and a lack of fulfillment among typical midwesterners. In *Knowledge for What?* (1939), Robert Lynd faulted other social scientists who refrained from cultural criticism and thus neglected their responsibility to point the way toward reconstruction. It was becoming clear that some of the avowed relativists were not relativists at all, but believers in the superiority of non-Western cultures, as they understood them.[60]

Nevertheless, American literary figures espoused a form of relativism as well. The literary historian R. W. B. Lewis has noted that, in the late nineteenth and early twentieth centuries, American literature passed from the "party of hope" (the transcendentalists) and the "party of irony" (the more pessimistic novelists like Nathaniel Hawthorne and Herman Melville) to the "party of tragedy" (which he sometimes called the "party of memory"). The "realists," as this last group was later called, denied sorrow the redemptive power and transcendent meaning the romantic novelists had previously ascribed to it.[61]

The realists transformed American literature in various ways. First, they adopted an earthy style. Determined to shock readers accustomed to the genteel romantic style, the realists relished the exotic dialects and crude behavior of common folk. An easterner who followed the Gold Rush to California, Bret Harte first employed the Western style in *The Luck of Roaring Camp and Other Sketches* (1871). Harte's barroom realism replaced the Jacksonian idealization of the frontiersman. Mark Twain, a southwesterner from Missouri, raised the Western dialect to an art form, shocking many readers with what was then considered profanity.[62]

Second, the realists revolutionized American literature by enveloping their characters and narrators in uncertainty. Influenced by the scientific and philosophical theories of the day, theories that questioned the capacity of humans to decipher the universe, the realists not only made their characters far less assured in their grasp of reality, but also made their narrators (often the characters themselves) far less reliable. They often replaced the romantics' third-person, godlike narrator with either a first-person subjectivism or a dreamlike confusion of causal relationships.

Typical of the self-questioning antiheroes of realist literature were the characters of T. S. Eliot and Ernest Hemingway. The prototypical antihero, Eliot's J. Alfred Prufrock was a realist Hamlet, and the bravado of Hemingway's characters masked a deep confusion. Hemingway remarked concerning the events of his age: "You did not know what it was all about. You never had time to learn. They threw you in and told you the rules and the first time they caught you off base they killed you."[63]

Realist narrators were often unreliable. The reader is not supposed to know for certain whether Henry James's governess in *The Turn of the Screw* (1898) has really seen the ghosts menacing her pupils or suffers from some neurosis. Influenced by the stage, James frequently advanced the plot in a piecemeal fashion, through scattered conversations whose meaning remained always in question. Twain's narrators were equally suspect. Huck Finn is a child, ignorant of the world (though wise after his own fashion).

The narrator of *A Connecticut Yankee in King Arthur's Court* (1889) tells us only what he has read of Hank Morgan's account. The narrator of *The Prince and the Pauper* tells the reader, "It may have happened; it may not have happened; but it could have happened." (Contrast these narrators with Melville's Ishmael, who was somehow able to relate even the thoughts of Captain Ahab with complete confidence.) William Faulkner experimented with a wide variety of narrative techniques, including the use of dreams, fragments of memories, and characters' thoughts, as well as the manipulation of time. Narrator subjectivity reached its peak in Gertrude Stein's "stream of consciousness writing," based on the psychological theories of Freud and William James.[64]

A third innovation of the realists was their use of the symbolism of subconscious desires and fears. Although poets had used symbolism from the very beginning of literature, the realists differed in symbolizing repressed emotions. Even before Freud, the unorthodox poetry of New England recluse Emily Dickinson was filled with symbols of death and sexuality. Although much of Henry James's work also preceded Freud, he frequently made what became known as the "Freudian slip," the unguarded moment or half-spoken word, the climax of his novels. William Faulkner was so enamored of Freudian symbolism that some literary critics have suggested that the Compson family in *The Sound and the Fury* (1929) are the flesh-and-blood equivalents of the id, the ego, and the superego.[65]

Fourth, influenced by the Social Darwinism of their day, many of the realists were genetic determinists who believed that humans were ruled by animal instinct. In Stephen Crane's novel *The Red Badge of Courage* (1895), Henry Fleming runs wildly from battle, caught in the grasp of instinctive fears, but returns and vindicates himself in an equally instinctive act of courage. Jack London blurred the lines between humans and animals in a similar fashion in *The Call of the Wild* (1903). In *The Sea Wolf* (1904), also written by London, Wolf Larsen declares: "Life is a mess. . . . The big eat the little that they may continue to move, the strong eat the weak that they retain their strength. The lucky eat the most and move the longest, that is all." Theodore Dreiser wrote: "We suffer for our temperaments, which we did not make, and for our weaknesses and lacks, which are no part of our willing or doing." To Dreiser, the strong went forward as their instinct compelled them, and the weak either perished or bore life as best they could. H. L. Mencken wrote: "Such is the law of the survival of the fittest, and it stands immutable. . . . The eternal and inexorable law that the strong shall prevail over the weak."[66]

Such cynicism made the realists far less willing than the romantics to accept the possibility of either past or future utopias. A transplanted southwesterner living in Hartford, Connecticut, Mark Twain engaged in a lifelong campaign against romanticism and its worship of the Middle Ages. He believed that southerners' intransigence in support of slavery, an intransigence that had brought destruction upon the South, was the result of their avid reading of Sir Walter Scott's novels. Novels like *Ivanhoe* had dazzled the mind of the Old South with vain notions of an idyllic pastoral society of paternalistic lords and grateful servants. Twain declared, with complete and rare seriousness: "Walter Scott started the Civil War." Using the fable form so treasured by romantics, Twain attacked medieval England in *A Connecticut Yankee in King Arthur's Court* and *The Prince and the Pauper* (1881). Twain's characters lost their innocence through travel: Edward Tudor by switching places with poor Tom Canty and wandering the streets of sixteenth-century London, Hank Morgan through time travel, Americans by traversing Europe (*The Innocents Abroad*), easterners by riding west during the Gold Rush (*Roughing It*), and Huck Finn by rafting the Mississippi River. Twain invites us to join him on a fun-filled voyage, and we go eagerly, little suspecting that he intends to rob us of our illusions. The poverty, destruction, and bitterness wrought by the Civil War had transformed the South from a citadel of romanticism devoted to Walter Scott into a bastion of realism dominated by Twain and Faulkner.[67]

The realists were as skeptical of future utopias as of past utopias. In an early poem Stephen Crane compared the world to a well-crafted ship that had gotten away from God and was now floating on its own, with only the illusion of purpose. In *The Great Gatsby* (1925), F. Scott Fitzgerald attempted to demonstrate the hollowness and futility of the American dream through Jay Gatsby's empty quest for youth and material success. Hemingway's characters are innocents forced to confront the horrors of war, in the process losing all the comforts of religion and tradition and living only for the moment. Hemingway's characters spend much time talking to themselves, disciplining themselves, trying to cope with a reality they cannot understand. John Steinbeck's novel *The Grapes of Wrath* (1939) depicted in graphic detail the horrible waste and human misery of life during the Great Depression. If Eugene O'Neill's relentlessly dismal *Long Day's Journey into Night* was not based on actual events in the playwright's life, it might be considered a satire on realism. In the horrifying play the mother is a morphine addict who dons her wedding dress when stoned, the father is cheap and boorish, and the son is an alcoholic reader of realist literature. All suffer because of a single event. The father, who is miserly as the result of a miserable, poverty-stricken childhood, had employed an incompetent doctor to supervise the birth of the son. The doctor had used morphine as an anesthetic, thereby addicting the mother. Overwhelmed by guilt, the son had then drowned his woes in alcohol. In its most extreme forms the realist corrective to the Polyannish tendencies of some of the romantics perhaps went too far, portraying a world as one-dimensional as the romantic world it sought to displace. Realism had become as unrealistic as the most extreme forms of romanticism.[68]

The voice of the realist age can be heard most clearly in Mark Twain's final short story, "The Mysterious Stranger," various versions of which were published posthumously. Embittered by the death of his daughter, the severe illness of his wife, and bankruptcy caused by poor investments, Twain had grown increasingly disillusioned with the world, writing: "Nature's attitude toward all life is profoundly vicious, treacherous, and malignant. . . . Man has not a single right that is the product of anything but might. There is no such thing as morality." A product of this gnawing anger at the world, "The Mysterious Stranger" was presented in the form of yet another romantic fable. At the very end of the story, the angel tells the boy: "It is true, that which I have revealed to you; there is no God, no universe, no human race, no earthly life, no heaven, no hell. It is all a dream—a grotesque and foolish dream. Nothing exists but you. And you are but a thought—a vagrant thought, a useless thought, a homeless thought, wandering forlorn among the empty eternities!" The boy concludes: "He vanished and left me appalled; for I knew and realized that all he had said was true." Twain's growing skepticism had culminated in solipsism, the belief that nothing exists but oneself.[69]

The literature of "the party of tragedy" resembled that of "the party of irony" in its recognition of the pervasiveness of sorrow in the world. But while the party of irony had ladled the chicken soup of sorrow in moderate portions into elegant bowls, all the while assuring the reader of its healing power, the party of tragedy dumped copious quantities of the scalding liquid into the reader's lap, all the while denying the existence of any balm.

THE IMPACT OF SKEPTICISM

The rise of skepticism in the late nineteenth and early twentieth centuries created disillusionment and consternation throughout the Western world. The doctrine of free will was replaced by the belief that human fate was determined by random variations in gene pools and by the subconscious, neither of which the individual could control. Some forms of theism possessed a determinism of their own, predestination, but in this case, control of human fate had been left to a just God, not to a purposeless nature.

Galileo had written that the universe was a book written by God in the language of mathematics. But the skeptics denied that the book had an author, and, regardless, it was all Greek to them.

NOTES

1. A. R. Burn, *The Pelican History of Greece* (New York: Penguin Books, 1965), 130; Gertrude Himmelfarb, *Darwin and the Darwinian Revolution* (Garden City, N.Y.: Doubleday, 1959), 167, 169; Sir Gavin de Beer, "Biology before the *Beagle*," 1964, in *Darwin: A Norton Critical Edition*, 2d ed., ed. Philip Appleman (New York: W. W.

Norton, 1979), 3; Charles Darwin, "An Historical Sketch of the Progress of Opinion on the Origin of Species," 1861, in *Darwin*, ed. Appleman, 19n1.

2. De Beer, "Biology before the *Beagle*," 4

3. De Beer, "Biology before the *Beagle*," 4–5; Sir Julian Huxley, "Evolution: The Modern Synthesis," 1942, in *Darwin*, ed. Appleman, 247–48; Himmelfarb, *Darwin and the Darwinian Revolution*, 36; Louis Menand, *The Metaphysical Club* (New York: Farrar, Straus & Giroux, 2001), 382.

4. De Beer, "Biology before the *Beagle*," 7–10; Himmelfarb, *Darwin and the Darwinian Revolution*, 43.

5. Thomas Robert Malthus, *An Essay on the Principle of Population* (New York: W. W. Norton, 1976), xiv, 21–22, 35–39, 43–44, 47, 53, 56; Himmelfarb, *Darwin and the Darwinian Revolution*, 157.

6. Himmelfarb, *Darwin and the Darwinian Revolution*, 88, 94, 100, 366; De Beer, "Biology before the *Beagle*," 7; Paul F. Boller Jr., *American Thought in Transition: The Impact of Evolutionary Naturalism, 1865–1900* (Chicago: Rand McNally, 1969), 24.

7. Himmelfarb, *Darwin and the Darwinian Revolution*, 60, 65, 80, 83–84, 192, 233, 237–38, 243; Philip Appleman, preface to *Darwin*, xiv.

8. Charles Darwin, *The Origin of Species*, 1859, in *Darwin*, ed. Appleman, 49–52.

9. Darwin, *Origin of Species*, 87, 115.

10. Darwin, *Origin of Species*, 45–46, 49, 55–56, 66, 81, 86, 114–15, 127, 129; Charles Darwin, *The Descent of Man*, 1871, in *Darwin*, ed. Appleman, 159–60.

11. Darwin, *Origin of Species*, 89–90, 103–8.

12. Darwin, *Descent of Man*, 161–68, 174–76, 199–201.

13. Darwin, *Descent of Man*, 135–40, 155, 177–86.

14. Himmelfarb, *Darwin and the Darwinian Revolution*, 47, 203–4, 252, 258, 264–66; Darwin, *Descent of Man*, 132; Thomas Henry Huxley, "On the Relations of Man to the Lower Animals," 1863, in *Darwin*, ed. Appleman, 231n; Boller, *American Thought in Transition*, 13; Menand, *Metaphysical Club*, 100, 109–13.

15. Himmelfarb, *Darwin and the Darwinian Revolution*, 251; Robert C. Bannister, *Social Darwinism: Science and Myth in Anglo-American Social Thought* (Philadelphia: Temple University Press, 1979), 44.

16. Huxley, "Evolution: The Modern Synthesis," 247–50; John C. Loehlin, Gardner Lindzey, and J. N. Spuhler, "The Context of the Race-IQ Question," in *Darwin*, ed. Appleman, 486; Paul K. Conkin, *When All the Gods Trembled: Darwinism, Scopes, and American Intellectuals* (Lanham, Md.: Rowman & Littlefield, 1998), 27, 32; Himmelfarb, *Darwin and the Darwinian Revolution*, 310–11.

17. Huxley, "Evolution: The Modern Synthesis," 264; Theodosius Dobzhansky, "The Nature of Heredity," 1964, in *Darwin*, ed. Appleman, 267, 269–70, 272.

18. Richard E. Leakey and Roger Lewin, "The Greatest Revolution," 1977, in *Darwin*, ed. Appleman, 280–81; Phillip E. Johnson, *Darwin on Trial* (Downers Grove, Ill.: Intervarsity Press, 1991), 50.

19. Jane Van Lawick-Goodall, "In the Shadow of Man," 1971, in *Darwin*, ed. Appleman, 473, 478–79; Carl Sagan, "Dragons of Eden," 1977, in *Darwin*, ed. Appleman, 482.

20. Johnson, *Darwin on Trial*. See also Jonathan Wells, *Icons of Evolution: Why Much of What We Teach about Evolution Is Wrong* (New York: Regnery, 2000).

21. Sigmund Freud, *Civilization and Its Discontents*, trans. James Strachey (New York: W. W. Norton, 1961), 15, 38; Peter Gay, *"A Godless Jew": Freud, Atheism, and the Making of Psychoanalysis* (New Haven, Conn.: Yale University Press, 1987), 24, 59; Nathan G. Hale Jr., *Freud and the Americans: The Beginnings of Psychoanalysis in the United States, 1876–1917* (New York: Oxford University Press, 1971), 8–11; Sigmund Freud, *The Ego and the Id*, 5th ed., trans. Joan Riviere (London: Hogarth Press, 1949), 40.

22. Harold Bloom, ed., *Sigmund Freud's The Interpretation of Dreams* (New York: Chelsea House, 1987), 2, 77.

23. Freud, *The Ego and the Id*, 15, 29–30, 33, 35, 44, 49, 54-55, 73, 79, 81, 83; Freud, *Civilization and Its Discontents*, 42–43, 55, 59, 71–72, 90.

24. Freud, *Civilization and Its Discontents*, 58–62, 90, 92.

25. Freud, *Civilization and Its Discontents*, 43, 55, 59, 69; Hale, *Freud and the Americans*, 8, 14–15.

26. Gay, *"A Godless Jew"*, vii, 5, 38, 49–50, 73, 79, 111–12, 125–26, 149, 153; Freud, *Civilization and Its Discontents*, 11, 19, 21–28, 38, 89; Freud, *Ego and the Id*, 80.

27. Freud, *Civilization and Its Discontents*, 92.

28. Hale, *Freud and the Americans*, 10, 18, 197, 434; Gay, *"A Godless Jew,"* 39–40; E. A. Bennet, *What Jung Really Said* (New York: Schocken Books, 1967), 121–29; T. Jackson Lears, *No Place of Grace: Antimodernism and the Transformation of American Culture, 1880–1920* (New York: Pantheon, 1981), 10–11, 34–35.

29. Necia H. Apfel, *It's All Relative: Einstein's Theory of Relativity* (New York: Lothrop, Lee & Shepard, 1981), 38–41, 49, 79–82, 98–101.

30. Werner Heisenberg, *Physics and Philosophy: The Revolution in Modern Science* (New York: Harper & Brothers, 1958), 31–33, 43, 46–48, 132, 145, 176; Nick Herbert, *Elemental Mind: Human Consciousness and the New Physics* (New York: Penguin, 1993), 145–47, 172–73.

31. Heisenberg, *Physics and Philosophy*, 176, 201.

32. Darwin, *Origin of Species*, 85; Himmelfarb, *Darwin and the Darwinian Revolution*, 211.

33. David M. Potter, *Division and the Stresses of Reunion, 1845–1876* (Glenville, Ill.: Scott, Foresman, 1973), 187; Robert D. Schulzinger, *American Diplomacy in the Twentieth Century* (Oxford: Oxford University Press, 1984), 123; John D. Hicks, *The Populist Revolt: A History of the Farmer's Alliance and the People's Party* (Lincoln: University of Nebraska Press, 1967), 56–66, 80, 83, 87–95; Alfred Kazin, *On Native Grounds: An Interpretation of Modern American Prose Literature* (New York: Reynal & Hitchcock, 1942), 15; Frederick Jackson Turner, *The Significance of the Frontier in American History* (Ann Arbor, Mich.: University Microfilms, 1966), 199, 221–23.

34. Joseph Wood Krutch, *The Modern Temper: A Study and a Confession* (New York: Harcourt, Brace, 1929), 6–8, 15–23, 48–49; William G. McLoughlin, *Revivals, Awakenings, and Reform: An Essay on Religion and Social Change in America, 1607–1977* (Chicago: University of Chicago Press, 1978), 180; Lears, *No Place of Grace*, 49–50.

35. McLoughlin, *Revivals, Awakenings, and Reform*, 171–72, 177–78.

36. Boller, *American Thought in Transition*, 37–40, 48; Menand, *Metaphysical Club*, 127; McLoughlin, *Revivals, Awakenings, and Reform*, 154–55; Phillip E. Johnson, *Reason in the Balance: The Case against Naturalism in Science, Law, and Education* (Downers Grove, Ill.: Intervarsity Press, 1995), 188.

37. Boller, *American Thought in Transition*, 36; George M. Marsden, *Fundamentalism and American Culture: The Shaping of Twentieth-Century Evangelicalism, 1870–1925* (Oxford: Oxford University Press, 1980), 4, 117–19, 169.

38. Paul K. Conkin, *The Uneasy Center: Reformed Christianity in Antebellum America* (Chapel Hill: University of North Carolina Press, 1995), 269–79.

39. Merrill D. Peterson, afterword to *Jeffersonian Legacies*, ed. Peter S. Onuf, (Charlottesville: University Press of Virginia, 1993), 462.

40. Marsden, *Fundamentalism and American Culture*, 171–84; Johnson, *Reason in the Balance*, 5–6; Garry Wills, *Under God: Religion and American Politics* (New York: Simon & Schuster, 1990), 97–114.

41. Gay, *"Godless Jew,"* 95, 99, 109.

42. Bannister, *Social Darwinism*, 45.

43. Bannister, *Social Darwinism*, 99, 133; William Graham Sumner, "Reply to a Socialist," 1904, in *Essays of William Graham Sumner*, ed. Albert Galloway Keller, 2 vols. (New Haven, Conn.: Yale University Press, 1911), vol. 2, 123–30; "What Makes the Rich Richer and the Poor Poorer," 1887, in *Essays of William Graham Sumner*, ed. Keller, vol. 2, 150–62; "Protectionism: The -Ism which Teaches that Waste Makes Wealth," 1885, in *Essays of William Graham Sumner*, ed. Keller, vol. 2, 365–467; "Laissez-Faire," late 1880s, in *Essays of William Graham Sumner*, ed. Keller, vol. 2, 468–77; Darwin, *Descent of Man*, 161, 207; Menand, *Metaphysical Club*, 303.

44. Bannister, *Social Darwinism*, 165–66, 168–69, 173, 175, 189, 196–98; Madison Grant, *The Passing of the Great Race* (New York: Scribner, 1916); Carl C. Brigham, *A Study of American Intelligence* (Princeton, N.J.: Princeton University Press, 1923); David L. Lewis, *The Public Image of Henry Ford: An American Folk Hero and His Company* (Detroit: Wayne State University Press, 1976), 137, 139, 142–44, 148–50; Keith Sward, *The Legend of Henry Ford* (New York: Rinehart, 1948), 147, 150–51, 159–60; Adolf Hitler, *Mein Kampf* (Boston: Houghton Mifflin, 1939), 929–30; John Higham, *Strangers in the Land: Patterns of American Nativism, 1860–1925* (New Brunswick, N.J.: Rutgers University Press, 1955), 322–24.

45. Darwin, *Descent of Man*, 167, 198, 207; Bannister, *Social Darwinism*, 30, 188–89.

46. Bannister, *Social Darwinism*, 233; Boller, *American Thought in Transition*, 216–18; Schulzinger, *American Diplomacy in the Twentieth Century*, 45–51, 139–41.

47. George Brown Tindall, *America: A Narrative History*, 3d ed., 2 vols. (New York: W. W. Norton, 1992), vol. 2, 917.

48. Bannister, *Social Darwinism*, 201, 244.

49. Thorstein Veblen, *The Theory of the Leisure Class: An Economic Study of Institutions* (New York: B. W. Huebsch, 1922), 188–211; Boller, *American Thought in Transition*, 176, 184, 188–98; Menand, *Metaphysical Club*, 305–6.

50. Oliver Wendell Holmes Jr., *The Common Law* (Cambridge, Mass.: Harvard University Press, 1963), 5; Oliver Wendell Holmes Jr., *The Path of the Law*, 1897, in Louis Menand, ed., *Pragmatism: A Reader* (New York: Vintage Books, 1997), 146, 153–54; Oliver Wendell Holmes Jr., "Natural Law," 1918, in *Pragmatism*, ed. Menand, 173–74, 177; Menand, *Metaphysical Club*, 342–44, 422; Boller, *American Thought in Transition*, 155; Oliver Wendell Holmes Jr., "Natural Law," 1918, in *The American Intellectual Tradition*, 3d ed., 2 vols., ed. Charles Capper and David A. Hollinger (Oxford: Oxford University Press, 1997), vol. 2, 128–29.

51. Boller, *American Thought in Transition*, 148, 164; Morton G. White, *Social Thought in America: The Revolt against Formalism* (New York: Viking, 1949), 65–75.

52. Menand, *Metaphysical Club*, 64–66, 424, 429–31; Boller, *American Thought in Transition*, 165.

53. Menand, *Metaphysical Club*, 3–4, 35, 43, 46–47, 51, 55–56, 61–63, 68–69.

54. Boller, *American Thought in Transition*, 233–35.

55. Boller, *American Thought in Transition*, 237, 242, 244–45.

56. Charles A. Beard, *An Economic Interpretation of the Constitution of the United States* (New York: Free Press, 1986), viii.

57. Lewis Perry, *Intellectual Life in America: A History* (New York: Franklin Watts, 1984), 320–22; George W. Stocking Jr., ed., *The Shaping of American Anthropology, 1893–1911: A Franz Boas Reader* (New York: Basic, 1974), 1, 14–15, 17, 22, 36, 44–45; Menand, *Metaphysical Club*, 386.

58. Margaret Mead, *Coming of Age in Samoa: A Psychological Study of Primitive Youth for Western Civilization* (New York: Dell, 1928), 144–79; Rosalind Rosenberg, *Beyond Separate Spheres: Intellectual Roots of Modern Feminism* (New Haven, Conn.: Yale University Press, 1982), xiii, 139–208.

59. Roy Rappaport, "Desecrating the Holy Woman: Derek Freeman's Attack on Margaret Mead," *American Scholar* 55 (Summer 1986): 313–47.

60. Perry, *Intellectual Life in America*, 323.

61. R. W. B. Lewis, *The American Adam: Innocence, Tragedy, and Tradition in the Nineteenth Century* (Chicago: University of Chicago Press, 1955), 7–10, 197–200.

62. Bret Harte, *The Luck of Roaring Camp and Other Sketches* (New York: P. F. Collier and Son, 1871); Norman Foerster et al., eds., *American Poetry and Prose*, 5th ed. (Boston: Houghton Mifflin, 1970), 826.

63. Foerster, *American Poetry and Prose*, 1101, 1157–59.

64. Foerster, *American Poetry and Prose*, 829, 831, 1097, 1102, 1204; Henry James, *The Turn of the Screw* (New York: Random House, 1930), 8, 44; Mark Twain, *Adventures of Huckleberry Finn* (Indianapolis, Ind.: Bobbs-Merrill, 1967); Mark Twain, *A Connecticut Yankee in King Arthur's Court* (New York: Heritage Press, 1948), 5; Mark Twain, *The Prince and the Pauper: A Tale for Young People of All Ages* (New York: New American Library, 1964), xi; Herman Melville, *Moby-Dick, or The Whale*, ed. Harrison Hayford, Hershel Parker, and G. Thomas Tanselle (Evanston, Ill.: Northwestern University Press, 1988), 186.

65. Foerster, *American Poetry and Prose*, 898, 1021, 1097.

66. Stephen Crane, *The Red Badge of Courage* (New York: D. Appleton, 1895), 57-59, 64–66; Jack London, *The Call of the Wild* (Harmondsworth, England: Puffin Books, 1982); Kazin, *On Native Grounds*, 86, 114; Bannister, *Social Darwinism*, 201, 206.

67. Mark Twain, *Roughing It*, in *The Unabridged Mark Twain*, ed. Lawrence Teacher, 2 vols. (Philadelphia: Running Press, 1979), vol. 2, 551–899; Mark Twain, *The Innocents Abroad, or The New Pilgrim's Progress* (New York: Harper & Brothers, 1911); Kenneth S. Lynn, foreword to *The Prince and the Pauper*, by Mark Twain (New York: New American Library, 1964), 217; Gary Charles Smith, "The Influence of Mark Twain's Journeys on His Work," *Mark Twain Journal* 20 (winter 1979–1980): 10–13.

68. F. Scott Fitzgerald, *The Great Gatsby* (New York: Scribner, 1925); John Steinbeck, *The Grapes of Wrath* (New York: Penguin, 1939); Eugene O'Neill, *Long Day's Journey into Night* (New Haven, Conn.: Yale University Press, 1955); Kazin, *On Native Grounds*, 68–69; Foerster, *American Poetry and Prose*, 1101.

69. Mark Twain, "The Mysterious Stranger," in *The Complete Short Stories of Mark Twain*, ed. Charles Neider (New York: Bantam Books, 1971), 679; Bannister, *Social Darwinism*, 212, 216.

8

PRAGMATISM

Even in an age of crisis, American philosophers managed to formulate a skepticism tinged with optimism. Developed by
William James and John Dewey, pragmatism, the only philosophical school that began in America, differed significantly from the
more pessimistic, Nietzschean brand of skepticism that then prevailed in western Europe and in American realist literature. The
pragmatists' decision to emphasize the natural limits of human reason, rather than innate depravity, as the chief obstacle to social
progress allowed them to maintain a certain degree of optimism.
While belief in the limits of reason raised doubts concerning the
possibility of lasting social progress, it did not preclude the possibility of happiness through the enjoyment of the present moment.

SKEPTICISM FROM THE GREEKS TO NIETZSCHE

Skepticism as a formal philosophy began in ancient Greece,
though it never achieved the popularity of the humanistic
philosophies there. The first skeptic philosopher may have been
Heraclitus (sixth century B.C.), to whom is attributed the famous
statement, "One cannot step into the same river twice," since the
river would not be the same the second time. The universe was in
a constant state of change, and humans were a part of the flux, not
objective observers of it. Hence humans could never fully understand the universe. A wit allegedly replied to Heraclitus that one

could not step into the same river once, since it was changing even while one stepped into it. Similarly, a character in a Greek comedy exploited the Heraclitan doctrine of perpetual change to argue that since he was not the same man he had been yesterday, he should not be required to pay the debts he had then incurred—a view of the rate of change that surpassed even that of Lamarck.[1]

The Sophists of the following century were skeptics as well. Itinerant professors who taught for a fee, they shunned "useless speculation" about the universe and the gods, teaching such "practical" subjects as rhetoric, logic, and statesmanship. One of the leading Sophists, Protagoras of Abdera (in Thrace), declared, "Every man is the measure of all things," a clear declaration of moral relativism and rejection of natural law. He also said, "Of the gods, I cannot say either that they exist or that they do not." Some Sophists taught that human laws were arbitrary and worthy of little respect, a radical break with the Greek reverence for law.[2]

The most famous of the Greek skeptics, the fourth-century B.C. Athenian philosopher Diogenes the Cynic, was the son of a rich banker from Sinope. It was Diogenes who uttered the famous statement, "The love of money is the mother of all evils." He opposed popular customs and values and lived in a large pottery jar, an idea he borrowed from the self-sufficient snail. He also admired dogs ("kunes," whence comes "cynics") for their openness. Once, when Diogenes saw a child drinking from cupped hands, he threw away his cup. His dark view of human nature manifested itself in numerous ways. He wandered the streets of Athens in the daytime carrying a lit lantern, announcing that he was looking for an honest man. When someone asked him why people gave money to beggars but never to philosophers, he replied, "Because they fear that they may become lame or blind one day, but they never expect to become philosophers." Seeing the son of a prostitute throwing rocks at the self-righteous mob that was goading him, Diogenes said, "Careful now, don't hit your father." He also expressed disdain for organized religion. When temple officials arrested a man for stealing a bowl from a temple, Diogenes declared, "The great thieves are leading away the little thief."[3]

Diogenes emphasized the limits of human reason. He said that whenever he saw a steersman, physician, or philosopher at work, he believed that humans were the most intelligent of animals, but when he encountered interpreters of dreams, seers, and conceited and wealthy people, he considered humans the most foolish species. No one impressed him. Having conquered all of Greece, Alexander the Great once searched for the famous skeptic. He finally found Diogenes sunbathing. Standing over Diogenes with his entourage, Alexander asked if there was anything he could do for the philosopher. Diogenes replied, "Yes, you can stand aside and stop blocking my sun." Alexander went away, shaking his head and telling his followers, "If I were not Alexander, I would like to be Diogenes" (Plutarch, *Life of Alexander*, 14). Diogenes agreed with Epicurus that death was nothingness: "How can death be evil when in its presence we are not aware of it?" The Athenian people once punished a boy for destroying the beloved eccentric's pottery jar and gave him a new one. After he died (from eating a raw octopus?), his followers placed the marble statue of a dog on his grave.[4]

Other skeptics expressed despair at the meaninglessness of life and questioned religious truths. Pyrrho of Elis declared, "It matters not whether I live or die." A heckler (heckling philosophers was a favorite pastime of the Greeks) shouted, "Why don't you go kill yourself, then?" After a pause, Pyrrho replied: "Because it matters not." Euhemerus (*Sacred History*) contended that each of the gods had been a human who had served his society so well in some way that the society had deified him after his death.[5]

But, though isolated skeptics have always existed, neither the supernaturalism of the medieval and early modern eras nor the optimism of the late eighteenth and early nineteenth centuries provided skepticism with a congenial environment in which to flourish. For instance, the humanistic optimism of the Enlightenment militated against the widespread acceptance of the philosophy of David Hume, the first great skeptic of the modern age. Hume argued that causation itself might well be an illusion. The relationship between cause and effect could be demonstrated only by experience, which was unreliable. Furthermore, history and culture—that is to say, habit—not reason, ruled humans. Hume often conceded that his views had few converts in the humanistic eighteenth century, though traces of skepticism may also be found in the writings of Voltaire, Edward Gibbon, Lord Chesterfield, and a few other thinkers of that period.[6]

The age of skepticism awaited the age of Darwin, when it was personified by German philosopher Friedrich Nietzsche. In such works as *Thus Spake Zarathustra* (1883), *Beyond Good and Evil* (1886), and *On the Genealogy of Morals* (1887), Nietzsche contended that "the will to power" was the universal force that motivated humans. Less widely noted was his claim that the ultimate form of power was self-discipline. Only the weak sought to control others, as a poor substitute for self-mastery. Contrary to the mythology that soon surrounded Nietzsche, his ideal human, the "overman," was not a general or a dictator, but an artist or philosopher who achieved power by overcoming his own animal nature to create works of beauty, in the process establishing his worth and adding purpose to a purposeless world. Only such a man achieved the happiness that all sought. Though Nietzsche denounced nationalism, militarism, totalitarianism, racism, and anti-Semitism with great vehemence, once even breaking with his sister over her harsh anti-Semitism, and though his overman was a superior individual whose superiority was defined by self-discipline, not a superior race whose superiority was defined by the conquest of other races, his writings were later distorted by Nazi propagandists. The only trait Nietzsche shared with Adolf Hitler was a low opinion of the masses. Nietzsche considered the attainment of the ideal of the overman well beyond the capacity of all but a few and insisted that the gulf separating the overman from ordinary men was greater than that which separated ordinary men from apes. Most humans were cowardly conformists, too weak to challenge the dogmas of their society (unlike Nietzsche himself). As Walter Kaufmann put it, "Men, as Nietzsche saw them, were not naturally equal, did not naturally love one another, and were not naturally free."[7]

Nietzsche attacked both humanism and Christianity. He denied the existence of natural law, claiming that "the thousand and one" moral codes in the world were all expressions of the will to power. Indeed, he praised ancient polytheism for supplying a "multiplicity of norms." He assaulted the theory of progress, arguing that the Greeks and the men of the Renaissance had been superior to modern men. He criticized the Christian emphasis on the afterlife as a concession to the weakness of those who could not achieve self-mastery in this world. Nietzsche pleaded, "I beseech you, my brothers, remain faithful to the earth and do not believe those who speak to you of other-worldly hopes." Nietzsche also rebuked Christianity for repressing animal passions rather than sublimating them (channeling them into creative outlets). A man with strong impulses might become destructive, as had Cesare Borgia, because he had not yet learned to sublimate his impulses, but if he should ever acquire self-control, he might achieve greatness. By contrast, a man whose impulses had been weakened by the repression of Christianity could not become great. Furthermore, Nietzsche contended that Christian morality was the creation of Roman slaves, men who had lacked the mental capacity to appreciate their pagan masters' "freedom from faith" and who had sought to glorify themselves—the "foolish," the "weak," and the "base"—by turning such vices as humility and pity into virtues. (Nietzsche did not explain how "weak" slaves were able to force their ideology on their superior masters.) Christian humility and pity were a slave's ethic, making virtues of necessities. A real friend would help another achieve self-mastery, not impede his doing so by pitying him and indulging him in his weakness. Pity assumed that suffering was bad, rather than a necessary catalyst for strengthening an individual. It was Nietzsche who wrote, "Whatever does not destroy me makes me stronger." He referred to "this queer and sick world to which the Gospels introduce us—a world out of a Russian novel in which the scum of society, nervous diseases, and 'childlike' idiocy seem to give each other a rendezvous." He wrote: "One does well to put on gloves when reading the New Testament. The proximity of so much uncleanliness almost forces one to do this." But worse than Christianity's initial corruption of the superior pagan morality was its subsequent status as a bastion of conformity, a mere handmaiden to the tyrannical state.[8]

Though Nietzsche prophesied that the elimination of any distinction between humans and animals and the death of the belief in God might produce "an age of barbarism" and "wars such as have never happened on earth," he rejected the idea of averting this calamity by a reversion to the "delusions" of either theism or humanism. On the contrary, he declared, "What is falling, that one should also push!" He considered the decline of Christian morality "the most hopeful of all spectacles," since he founded what little hope he had on the creation of a new metaphysics and a new morality. He wrote, "If we cannot discover a new picture of man that will again give him a sense of his essential dignity, the State, in the hands of military despots, will demand that we should yield to it in idolatry; and eventually men will seek only to rob and to exploit one another." But Nietzsche's concept of the overman, his "new picture of man," hardly served his purpose since he himself admitted that it was an ideal approachable only by those few whom he termed "fortunate accidents," the "highest specimens" of humanity. He conceded that the "self-delusion" of theists and humanists engendered "peace of soul" while his own "honest" philosophy was "hostile to life and destructive." He merely argued that "greatness" could not be achieved without "truth," however unpleasant or even socially destructive. Nietzsche wrote, "The strength of a spirit might be measured by how much of the truth he would be able to stand . . . [and] to what degree it would need to be watered down . . . and falsified." He concluded, "The ultimate that can be attained on earth—cynicism."[9]

WILLIAM JAMES (1842–1910)

Pragmatism was a kinder, gentler form of skepticism. Charles S. Peirce first used the term in the 1870s, in a series of philosophical conversations with William James, Oliver Wendell Holmes Jr., and others. He derived the term from Immanuel Kant's reference to "pragmatic belief," a hypothesis that, in the absence of certain knowledge, produces action—like a physician's diagnosis that, however uncertain, leads to a course of treatment. The difference was that while Kant considered pragmatic belief only one of several kinds of belief, Peirce considered it the only kind, since all knowledge was to some degree uncertain.[10]

Born into a chaotic New England family of intellectuals (his brother was the novelist Henry James), William James drifted without an intellectual anchor. His father rejected not only organized religion but all organized institutions of any kind, moving his sons in and out of different schools, so that none could do too much damage. Debate was the bread and butter of the James family dinner table. As a result of this experience, James developed a tolerance for, and a sense of detachment from, all beliefs. Philosophy became for him a pleasant pastime, rather than a guide to transcendent truth.[11]

James's penchant for indecision was almost pathological. Two years into the Civil War he was still fretting about whether or not to enlist in the Union Army. When courting his wife from 1876 to 1878, he sent her conflicting letters every few days. From 1875 to 1881 he changed his mind about a job offer from Johns Hopkins University four times. He spent fifteen years settling on an occupation, never teaching or practicing medicine after receiving his medical degree from Harvard in 1869. He named his youngest son Francis, but when the young boy seemed to dislike his name, he called him John. When the boy was seven, James had his name officially changed to Alexander. When in Europe, he longed for America, and vice versa. In 1903 he began considering retirement from teaching. His diary entries for the last three months of 1905 chronicle a portion of this process: October 26, "Resign!"; October 28, "Resign!!!"; November 4, "Resign?"; November 7, "Resign!"; November 8, "Don't resign"; November 9, "Resign!"; November 16, "*Don't* resign!"; November 23, "Resign"; December 7, "Don't resign"; December 9, "Teach here next year." He retired in 1907. His sister Alice said, "He's just like a blob of mercury." Despite the fact that everyone loved him, James himself wrote, "There is no more miserable human being than one in whom nothing is habitual but indecision."[12]

Indeed, James suffered from a series of emotional problems, such as anxiety attacks and psychosomatic illnesses, that attracted him to psychology. But though James published the much-acclaimed *Principles of Psychology* in 1890, the study of psychology failed to alleviate his suffering, so he turned to philosophy. Since pragmatism was a philosophy concerned with how one might choose in the absence of certain knowledge, it served as a form of therapy for James.[13]

In his philosophical works—*Pragmatism* (1907), *A Pluralistic Universe* (1909), *Essays in Radical Empiricism* (1912), and others—James claimed that reality was the world of "pure experience." Each person's individual experience (raw sensory experience) comprised only a small part of pure experience. Furthermore, the rational concepts humans formed to make sense of individual experience captured only a small part of that experience. Concepts were, by their very nature, abstract and static. Therefore, they could never duplicate reality, which was the many-hued and ever-changing world of pure experience. James claimed, "No abstract concept can be a valid substitute for a concrete reality." One could know about a blue sky or a toothache, but unless he experienced them his knowledge would be shallow and inadequate. Any experience had a multiplicity of facets, most of which humans ignored in order to focus upon what interested them most. Hence there was always a great deal of subjectivity in the concepts one used to characterize an experience. James wrote:

> All these abstract concepts are but as flowers gathered; they are only moments dipped out from the stream of time, snap-shots taken, as by a kinetoscopic camera, of a life that in its original coming is continuous. Useful as they are as samples of the garden, or to re-enter the stream with, they have no value but these practical values. . . . To understand life by concepts is to arrest its movement, cutting it up into bits as with scissors, and immobilizing these in our logical herbarium. . . . What really exists is not things made but things in the making.

James concluded that "thought thus deals solely with surfaces," with the mere relations between experiences rather than with the inner nature of experience. Scientific concepts revealed only the most abstract aspects of reality. The universe they depicted, like that of the Platonic philosophers, resembled more the garden of an aristocrat, "clipped, straight-edged, and artificial," than wild nature. Change was constant. Even the calling forth of a memory represented a new experience; the memory of an occurrence could never fully recapture the original experience of that occurrence. Since change was eternal, static concepts could never encompass it. James declared: "There is no conclusion. What has concluded that we might conclude in regard to it?"[14]

To employ a modern analogy, James's world can be portrayed as a game of Scrabble. The individual receives some letters (individual experience) but not all (pure experience). The individual then uses some but not all of his letters to form words (concepts), in order to reduce his individual experience to some sort of order. The individual can render his experience rationally meaningful only through a process of selection that discards those elements of it that are unsuitable to the chosen concept. The discarded elements are not, in any sense, less real than those retained; if the individual selects a different concept to explain his experience, they may suddenly become crucial (like an otherwise lonely *q* in a Scrabble game). But, in such a case, other elements that suited the previous concept but do not suit the present one will have to be discarded. By their very nature, concepts capture only a tiny fraction of reality.

Worse yet, James noted, most of the small portion of experience that one could capture in a concept was lost in the act of communicating it. Most communication involved language, a system of symbols that could never fully transmit the nuances of one person's concept to another person with a different set of experiences. (The word "grass" evokes a different image in different people, each shaped by the individual's unique experience: the green grass of high noon, as opposed to that colored red by the sunset glow, for instance.) Individual experiences did overlap (otherwise, humans could not communicate with one another at all), but they were never exactly the same for any two people. Cultural and personal biases influenced both the collection and the transmission of all knowledge, including scientific data.[15]

James often criticized Neoplatonic philosophers like Friedrich Hegel. He claimed that they "systematize and classify and schematize and make synoptical tables and invent ideal objects for the pure love of unifying." He concluded: "Too often the results, glowing with 'truth' for the inventors, seem pathetically personal and artificial to bystanders. . . . I feel sure that likes and dislikes must be among the ultimate factors of their philosophy as well as of mine. . . . The 'through-and-through' [Platonic] universe seems to suffocate me with its infallible, impeccable, all-pervasiveness. . . . Philosophy is more a matter of passionate vision than [of] logic . . . logic only finding reasons for the vision afterwards." James's chief frustration was that his opponents would not admit their own subjectivity as freely as he conceded his. But humanists could not make such a concession without threatening the belief in the possibility of objective knowledge that formed the core of humanism.[16]

James attacked the Epicurean humanism of the scientific community even more fervently than the Platonic humanism of the philosophical community. He assaulted the pretensions of scientists to a privileged and exclusive type of truth. His enemy was "a vision of 'Science' in the form of abstraction, priggishness and sawdust, lording it over all." He was incensed by those who claimed scientific authority for their extraneous metaphysical speculations. Just as his father had denounced dogma in religion, James denounced it in science. In his own lifetime James had witnessed the transference of hypnosis, hysteria, and the multiple personality disorder from the realm of "superstition" to the sphere of "science." What then justified haughty scientists in ridiculing and summarily dismissing claims concerning other psychic phenomena? Even if most such claims were "rubbish," as James freely admitted, might not a few be valid, and was it not the job of scientists to test hypotheses rather than to sneer at them? Far from being the province of a godlike objectivity, science had always been advanced most by "the passionate desires of individuals to get their own faiths confirmed." While too much zeal could fatally bias a scientist's conclusions, too little could deprive him of motivation essential to the painstaking work of scientific inquiry. Hence James wrote, "The most useful investigator, because the most sensitive observer, is always he whose eager interest in one side of the question is balanced by an equally keen nervousness lest he become deceived."[17]

James wanted to tame science, to put it in its place. Reason and its product, science, were necessary, since they could uncover enough of reality to aid the survival and increase the comfort of humans, but they should not be considered anything more than useful tools. According to James, reason had "an imperishable use in human life, but that use is not to make us theoretically acquainted with the essential nature of reality." James wrote: "Reality, life, experience, immediacy, use what word you will, exceeds our logic, overflows and surrounds it. . . . Theories thus become instruments, not answers to enigmas in which we can rest. We don't lie back on them; we move forward, and, on occasion, make nature over again by their aid. . . . Ideas (which themselves are but parts of our experience) become true just in so far as they help us get into satisfactory relation with other parts of our experience." Indeed, it was just this power "of translating the crude flux of our merely feeling-experience into a conceptual order" that granted humans their "chief superiority to the brutes."[18]

In acknowledging the need for reason while recognizing its limitations, James resembled his own Puritan forebears. But James's approach to faith was fundamentally different from that of orthodox theists. Although James traveled about assuring Americans that science had not disproved their cherished religious beliefs and that they should keep them, he did not see faith as the Puritans had, as an oracle of truth granted by God. He valued faith only as a therapeutic tool. The psychologist-philosopher worried about the demoralizing effect of science on traditional theists. He noted that, because of science: "The romantic spontaneity and courage are gone, the vision is materialistic and depressing. . . . What is higher is explained by what is lower and treated forever as a case of 'nothing but'—nothing but something else of a quite inferior sort." James considered faith a psychological necessity for many people, providing them with a sense of hope and purpose. He wrote, "The world is the seat of so much unhappiness really incurable in ordinary ways, but cured (in many individuals) by their religious experience." James's conception of faith was as utilitarian as his view of reason: While the proper fruit of reason was technology, the proper fruit of faith was psychological well-being. Neither provided truth. Hence James regarded all religions, all philosophies, even all concepts, with a rough equality: All were "guesses," and any one of them, however scorned, might turn out to be true.[19]

Sometimes James equated truth with hypotheses that were validated by experience, but at other times he defined it as any belief that resulted in the happiness of the individual believer. In the latter vein he wrote: "If theological ideas prove to have a value in concrete life, they will be true, for pragmatism, in the sense of being good for so much. . . . The true is the name of whatever proves itself to be good in the way of belief. . . . I define the true as that which gives the maximal combination of satisfactions, and say that satisfaction is a many-dimensional term that can be realized in various ways. . . . If the hypothesis of God works satisfactorily in the widest sense of the word, it is true." Since there were no conclusive intellectual grounds on which to either validate or reject religious beliefs, and since every individual must decide such momentous questions (even the decision not to choose is a choice), the individual was justified in deciding on emotional grounds. Whatever was better for people to believe was true unless it clashed "with some other vital benefit" conferred by an opposing belief. Hence James consoled his audiences by telling them that their beliefs were valid—whatever they were.[20]

Orthodox theists found James unsatisfying. John Jay Chapman complained that one who possessed James's feeble kind of "faith" would "never convey it—arouse it, evoke it—in another," adding, "This is a somewhat roundabout way of saying that such a man hasn't got faith at all." To James, faith was a pleasant dream that might or might not reflect reality, the important point being that it was very real to the dreamer.[21]

James professed no faith, only a few hypotheses. He hypothesized the existence of a God of finite power and knowledge, a trait that cleared the deity of all charges of responsibility for any evil in the world. James wrote, "If there be a God, he is no absolute all-experiencer, but simply the experiencer of widest actual conscious span." James suspected that when a person died he achieved a union with, and contributed to, the whole, while retaining a separate identity. Unwilling to surrender his individuality, his most precious possession, James could not abide Platonic conceptions of the afterlife involving total absorption into the whole. He confessed that such conceptions made him feel "as if I had to live in a seaside boarding-house with no private bed-room in which I might take refuge from the society of the place."[22]

But James's conceptions of a finite God and an afterlife remained what he called "a working hypothesis," not a faith. He noted:

> The pragmatism or pluralism which I defend has to fall back on a certain ultimate hardihood, a certain willingness to live without assurances or guarantees. . . . I have no living sense of commerce with a God. . . . The Divine, for my active life, is limited to impersonal and abstract concepts. . . . On pragmatic principles we cannot reject any hypothesis if consequences useful to life flow from it. . . . Pragmatism has to postpone dogmatic answer, for we do not yet know certainly which type of religion is going to work best in the long run.

Regarding the afterlife he wrote, "I shan't fret over the event, whatever it turns out to be." He could not pray without feeling "foolish and artificial." When asked whether the Bible was authoritative, he replied: "No. No. No. It is so human a book that I don't see how belief in its divine authority can survive the reading of it." He insisted, "All our thoughts are instrumental and mental modes of adaptation to reality, rather than revelations or gnostic answers to some divinely instituted world-enigma." He dismissed virtually all of traditional Christian theology as irrelevant to the modern age: "The theological machinery that spoke so livingly to our ancestors, with its finite age of the world, its creation out of nothing, its juridical morality and eschatology, its relish for rewards and punishments, its treatment of God as an external contriver, an 'intelligent and moral governor,' sounds as odd to most of us as if it were some outlandish savage religion." He claimed that his own hypothesis of a finite God afforded "a higher degree of intimacy" with the divine than the traditional, "improbable hypothesis" of an absolute God, a being whose complete power, knowledge, and timelessness rendered Him alien to human experience. James noted, "This satisfaction the absolute denies us: we can neither help nor hinder it."[23]

An avowed relativist, James claimed that society ought to reject the fewest possible number of moral claims. Rules should be contextual, not absolute. James minimized the role of reason in ethical discourse, since moral principles had little worth in a shifting context and had to be continually revised.[24]

James's theory of human nature combined nature with nurture. He believed in human instincts, inherited physiological responses to situations. When a person saw a bear, fear did not precede physiological response but accompanied it. But James clearly believed that environmental influences also played a large role in forming human thought and behavior. Less influenced by Darwin than were the European skeptics and American realists, James's conception of human nature contrasted with their more pessimistic view. Indeed, he contended that people were born with a "generous vital enthusiasm about the universe." Children especially, while "in the plastic state," might be taught good habits that would imprint themselves in the nerve cells, fibers, and molecules of the brain.[25]

James's rejection of the notion of social progress rested more on doubts about any transcendent measure of it than on a bleak view of human nature. While theists believed that the way to social progress was clearly defined but obstructed by human nature (original sin), necessitating divine intervention, and humanists believed that it was clearly defined but obstructed by bad systems, skeptics like James denied the existence of any objective standard by which one could measure progress. One's definition of progress depended upon one's values. Since all values were subjective, valid only to the people who held them, there could be no transcendent measure of progress. Furthermore, "progress" implied a procession toward an end to the flux, an end that skeptics did not envision.

James's belief in free will contrasted with Nietzschean skepticism, which tended toward genetic determinism. James did not romanticize free will, as most Christian and humanist believers in free will had; rather he, like Jonathan Edwards, understood it to mean chance. James argued that since humans at least possessed the illusion of making choices, and even of agonizing over decisions, and since determinism could not be proved, belief in free will should take precedence over determinism. But, as James himself understood, this was a purely aesthetic argument: Simplicity must prevail. Predestination disgusted James, because he believed it portrayed God as a bully. Hence James declared, "My first act of free will shall be to believe in free will." James believed that while the human mind was influenced by both genetic inheritance and the environment, there remained a small space left open to chance. If a "God" existed, he was finite and, hence, not responsible for such evils as pain, disease, and natural disasters. James wrote:

> The only difficulties with theism are the moral difficulties and meannesses; and they have always seemed to me to flow from the gratuitous dogma of God being the all-exclusive reality. . . . There is no full consolation. Evil is evil and pain is pain; and in bearing them valiantly I think the only thing we can do is to believe that the good power of the world does not appoint them of its own free will, but works under some dark and inscrutable limitations, and that we by our patience and good will can somehow strengthen his hands.

The universe was largely but not fully completed, and it was the task of humans to aid in its completion. James wrote: "The world really stands malleable, waiting to receive its final touches at our hands. . . . No one can deny that such a role would add both to our dignity and to our responsibility as thinkers. To some of us it proves a most inspiring notion." But the outcome of such a process was by no means certain. James noted: "The being of man may be crushed by his own powers. . . . He may drown in his wealth [of knowledge] like a child in a bathtub, who has turned on the water and who cannot turn it off."[26]

James rejected the claim of extreme skeptics that all causation was an illusion and that the universe was purely random. James repeatedly argued that the relationships between things (the lawfulness of the universe) were not a mere conceptual illusion falsely deduced from experience, but were as much a matter of direct experience as the things themselves. He criticized extreme skeptics for excluding the order of the universe from their philosophy, just as humanists excluded the disorder, though both were equally real. He wrote that causation "lives, apparently, in the dirt of the world as well as in the absolute, or in man's unconquerable mind."[27]

While on his deathbed, James asked his brother Henry to remain in Cambridge, Massachusetts, for six weeks following his death. William would try to communicate with Henry from beyond the grave. Henry never recorded the reception of any transmission from his dead brother. It was a final testimony to William James's open-minded empiricism.[28]

JOHN DEWEY (1859–1952)

The most influential American philosopher of the first half of the twentieth century, John Dewey was born into a poor Vermont family in 1859, the year *The Origin of Species* was published. A prolific writer, he lived ninety-two years, dying in 1952, the year of the hydrogen bomb. He never got over the deaths of two of his sons, one of whom was an uncommonly intelligent toddler. From the time he received a Ph.D. at Johns Hopkins in 1884, Dewey was determined to formulate a complete and systematic philosophy. He achieved this goal with *Experience and Nature* in 1925.[29]

Dewey's philosophy owed much to William James, though Dewey preferred the term "instrumentalism" to "pragmatism." True, Dewey broadened his characterization of reality from James's "pure experience" to "nature," since one could not assume that all aspects of nature were open to human experience. But this was largely a difference in semantics. James did not deny the possibility of phenomena that could not be experienced by humans; he merely concluded that any phenomenon that could not affect humans in some detectable way was neither relevant to humans nor subject to human investigation and, therefore, should not be part of the "universe of philosophic discourse." Dewey agreed, writing: "Philosophy will have to surrender all pretension to be peculiarly concerned with ultimate reality. . . . No theory of Reality . . . is possible or needed."[30]

Like James, Dewey considered reason a necessary but limited tool. Concepts were limited by their static quality and could not depict a rich and changing reality. All of nature was a mixture of repetition and variation, and wisdom was the correct choice and administration of their union. Human inquiry did not begin with thought but with experience. While engaged in activity, a person experienced a feeling of confusion concerning a particular problem. To solve the problem, he formulated and tested various hypotheses. Since both the purpose and the scope of the inquiry were limited by the problem, the answer inevitably raised new questions. Hence the process of inquiry was unending.[31]

For this reason Dewey pitied men like Leon Trotsky who prematurely halted the process of inquiry, declared a hollow victory, and bound themselves to false absolutes. Concerning the "tragic" Trotsky, Dewey sighed, "To see such brilliant native intelligence locked up in absolutes." But Trotsky was no different from most philosophers, who reveled in concepts and neglected experience because "concepts are so clear; it takes little time to develop their implications; experiences are so confused, and it requires so much time and energy to lay hold of them."[32]

Dewey envisioned nature as a three-tiered pyramid. The base of the pyramid was matter; all things consisted of matter. The middle tier of the pyramid was life; while life was dependent upon matter—all life forms were composed of matter—not all matter possessed life. At the top of the pyramid was mind; while all minds were composed of matter and possessed life, not all life forms possessed the power of mind (particularly human intelligence). Since the levels of the pyramid differed in complexity and quality, each level required a different type of explanatory system. Explanations concerning matter had the greatest predictive capacity (though not complete predictive power) but were often the least important to humans, because they ignored the qualities of things to focus exclusively on the quantitative relations between them. Conversely, explanations concerning mind had the least predictive capacity but were often the most important to humans because of their focus on the qualitative. Concepts useful to physics were grossly insufficient to an understanding of the human mind; concepts useful to an understanding of mind were useless to an understanding of physics. Hence to force either an idealist or a materialist explanation on all of nature was to dwarf and distort it. Since humans were fully a part of nature, and humans produced art and moral codes, aesthetic and ethical ideas were no less real or natural than material things. To portray either mind or matter as more real than the other, as the competing idealists and materialists did, was to be guilty of reductionism. Neither the idealists nor the materialists were shy about returning Dewey's fire. Dewey claimed that the advocates of both forms of reductionism turned on him like a fighting husband and wife when a third party intrudes on their argument.[33]

To employ yet another modern analogy, Dewey's view of reality can be likened to a pizza: Although reality is open to consumption, humans can consume it only one slice at a time. The slice must be either long and thin or short and wide. For instance, if a military historian wished to formulate a statement that would apply to every battle ever fought, he would have great difficulty doing so. Perhaps, in the end, all he could say was that in every battle people had attempted to harm one another. Such a slice of reality would be long (it would encompass every battle ever fought) but thin (in richness of meaning). If the historian then lowered his sights and decided to formulate a statement that would apply only to most battles, his slice, though shorter, would widen. At the other end of the spectrum, the historian who described only one particular battle could employ a wealth of vivid details. Such a slice would be extremely short but very wide. Only by sacrificing quantity (the general) could one reach a qualitative understanding of experience (the specific), and vice versa. Hence, while physicists could make more accurate predictions than others, their ability to do so rested solely on their exclusive focus upon the universal aspects of experience and their purposeful neglect of the qualities unique to each individual experience.

While joining James in rejecting reason as an oracle of truth, Dewey went even farther in rejecting faith as such an oracle. In 1908 he called for a moratorium on religious instruction in the public schools, arguing that "the non-supernatural view" should be allowed complete "possession of the machinery of education." While humans had created both religion and science in a futile "quest for certainty," science, however fallible, could at least offer some protection from elemental forces and natural enemies. By contrast, Dewey saw no place for faith in his world, not even as a psychological asset—unless "faith" were defined in purely naturalistic terms, as "allegiance to inclusive ideal ends," such as "affection, compassion and justice, equality and freedom," and "God" were simply employed as a name for those ends. According to Dewey, enormous energy was being wasted on the "rationalization of the doctrines entertained by historic religions." Worse than the absurd beliefs propounded by these religions was their tendency to substitute the authority of revelation for the scientific method as the favored means of acquiring knowledge. While the scientific method could not lead humans to transcendent truth, it was essential to uncovering the smaller truths vital to human survival and comfort. Since the scientific method was "the only method of thinking that has proved fruitful in any subject," it possessed the exclusive right to make cognitive claims.[34]

One of the principal reasons Dewey was so zealous in combating the metaphysical pretensions of science was that he believed such pretensions drove people to the supernatural. When scientists led people to the mistaken belief that nature was a dry, quantitative world, denying to it "the characters which make things lovable and contemptible, beautiful and ugly, adorable and awful," people necessarily rejected it as a cold, emotionally unfulfilling place and retreated to the dream world of the supernatural. Dewey's mission was to call people back from this potentially disastrous revelry in the supernatural to the real world of nature, by showing them that nature itself was rich enough in quality to provide pleasure and meaning. He wrote: "We are no longer compelled to choose between explaining away what is distinctive in man through reducing him to another form of a mechanical model and the doctrine that something literally supernatural marks him off from nature. The less mechanical . . . physical nature is found to be, the closer is man to nature. . . . The change is liberating. It clarifies our ideals, rendering them less subject to illusion and fantasy." Dewey's whole life was devoted to reconciling humans with a mysterious nature, just as Jonathan

Edwards's life had been devoted to reconciling humans with a mysterious God.[35]

Dewey's attacks on religion were partly motivated by moral concerns. Dewey contended that as a result of religion: "Men have never fully used the powers they possess to advance the good in life, because they have waited upon some power external to themselves and to nature to do the work they are responsible for doing." Dewey added, "In the degree in which we cease to depend upon belief in the supernatural, selection is enlightened and choice can be made on behalf of ideals whose inherent relations to conditions and consequences are understood." Like James, Dewey believed that value was based upon experience. Humans valued certain things either because they personally had had good experiences as a result of them, or because their society had had good experiences because of them and, therefore, had socialized its members to consider these things good.[36]

Dewey's conception of ethics was as pragmatic as that of James: Moral inquiry was as much a cognitive process as scientific inquiry, a matter of rationally determining, as best one could, all of the means necessary to achieve the desired experience and all of the consequences that would result from it. Dewey rejected the Platonic idea that ethics arose from innate ideas, siding with Aristotle's view that virtue was an art, a product of training (reason and experience). But unlike Aristotle and other humanists, Dewey rejected the concept of natural law, a universal code of ethics, since "desired experience" might vary from one society to another.[37]

Though his mother had been an evangelical Christian, Dewey also rejected the authority of revealed law as found in religious scriptures. Like natural law, revealed law was static and based upon dubious authority. Religious morality always protected "from inquiry some accepted standard which perhaps is outworn and in need of criticism."[38]

Moral systems, which were merely the wisdom of past experience codified, should be gradually altered to suit new knowledge concerning means, consequences, and experiences. Dewey wrote: "The business of reflection in determining the true good cannot be done once for all. It needs to be done, and done over and over and over again, in terms of the conditions of concrete situations as they arise." The task of determining which values "have become obsolete with the command of new resources" and which "are merely sentimental because there are no means for their realization" was the task of philosophy. Dewey categorically denied that morality was dependent upon religion:

> It is held that relation to the supernatural is the only finally dependable source of motive power; that directly and indirectly it has animated every serious effort for the guidance and rectification of man's life on earth. The other possibility is that goods actually experienced in the concrete relations of family, neighborhood, citizenship, [and] pursuit of art and sciences are what men actually depend upon for guidance and support, and their reference to a supernatural and otherworldly locus has obscured their real nature and has weakened their force.

Dewey subscribed to the latter view.[39]

Dewey offered "art," defined as creative, purposeful activity of nearly any kind, as a less dangerous and equally fulfilling substitute for faith. Dewey wrote, "Many a person is unhappy, tortured within, because he has at command no art of expressive action." Art was not a thing, a product, but the creative process itself, the process of setting goals, planning, and working toward their achievement. Art engaged the mind in solving problems, thereby satisfying the general human impulse for activity while providing a foundation for even greater future enrichment.[40]

Dewey's definition of art was exceedingly broad. For instance, the formulation of a scientific theory was art. (Although religion was also art, it was built on dangerous fantasies.) Dewey detested the false dichotomy of fine arts versus mechanical arts, an ancient distinction he believed had arisen out of aristocratic pretension. The toolmaker was as much an artist as the painter. Indeed, Dewey noted that, simply because of their rarity, antique and foreign tools were collected and prized as fine art by connoisseurs. Even the process of admiring art could involve artistry. In examining a work of art one inevitably reconstructed it. Dewey also rejected the dichotomy of the beautiful versus the useful, since beauty was itself useful in promoting human happiness. Dewey concluded: "The only basic distinction is between bad art and good art. . . . The difference between the ugliness of a mechanically conceived and executed utensil and of a meretricious and pretentious painting is only one of content or material."[41]

Dewey's belief that art was the most enriching experience led him to criticize the two systems he considered the most authoritarian and, therefore, the least artful: American business and American education. Dewey's unique brand of democratic socialism (which he called "functional socialism") was, in a real sense, more radical than that of most socialists (whom he called "state socialists"). His principal desire was not for a more equitable distribution of profits, to enable workers to consume more, but for a major change in the nature of work to make it more fulfilling. His goal was not a planned society—a society devised by a group of intellectuals according to a static plan—but a planning society, a society continually revising itself through the cooperative efforts of average citizens. He defined liberty positively, as the freedom to engage in cooperative and creative action (as the ancient Greeks had defined it), not negatively, as freedom from external control (as many modern republicans had defined it). Modern manufacturing, with its mindless specialization and "stupefying monotony," prevented both the factory owner and the worker from experiencing the joys of art. Creative activity required thought, thought occurred only when habit was disturbed, and the mind-numbing repetition involved in most industrial work formed habit. Exploitation did not flow in a single direction (though Dewey did often refer to management's exploitation of workers): Both owners and workers were exploited by the capitalist system and its obsession with profits. While workers were too specialized and possessed too little control over the manufacturing process to be creative, owners' natural creativity was perverted into the inhumane and unsatisfying habit of devising methods to exploit workers. Denied the joy and pride of creativity, both owners and workers were rewarded with the mere consumption of goods. Dewey's solution was to restore creativity to the production process by giving workers (not government bureaucracies claiming to act on behalf of workers) control of the factories. While Dewey's Puritan ancestors had believed that work was inherently good, Dewey added the caveat, if it is creative.[42]

Similarly, Dewey criticized American education for its lack of artfulness. Students were perceived not as creative beings but as hollow shells to fill with "a mind-crushing load" of unconnected data, rarely relevant to the outer world. Dewey wrote: "No one could construct a house on ground cluttered with miscellaneous junk. Pupils who have stored their minds with all kinds of material which they have never put to intellectual uses are sure to be hampered when they try to think. They have no practice in selecting what is appropriate, and no criterion to go by; everything is on the same dead, static level." As knowledge increased geometrically, the problem of overload would only worsen. Furthermore, the traditional mind-body dualism had led teachers to regard students' natural energy as an enemy to learning, rather than encouraging their pupils to harness that energy, along with their innate curiosity and imagination, for creative activity. The inevitable result was boredom. Just as workers and owners were rewarded with joyless consumption, students were rewarded with joyless grades.[43]

Dewey's solution to the educational problem was the same as his solution to the industrial problem: involvement. Since the best learning occurred when students actively participated in a process from start to finish, teachers should present pupils with problems to solve and encourage them to seek and select the materials required to solve them. Since cooperative skills were essential to society, teachers should encourage students to cooperate in the solution of these problems. The problems teachers presented should not be artificial scholastic problems, but real problems connected to student experience in the outer world. Problems should be new enough to pupils to present a challenge "yet sufficiently connected with existing habits to call out an effective response." Dewey claimed: "Where children are engaged in doing things and in discussing what arises in the course of their doing, it is found, even with comparatively indifferent modes of instruction, that children's inquiries are spontaneous and numerous, and the proposals of solution advanced [are] varied and ingenious. . . . When children have a chance at physical activities which bring their natural impulses into play, going to school is a joy, management is less of a burden, and learning is easier." Such learning—the "how to" kind—resembled students' earliest, most natural, and most enjoyable experiences, learning to walk, talk, skate, and ride a bicycle. Learning should be considered an end in itself, not a means to a more distant end, such as preparation for a job.[44]

Like the distinction between fine and mechanical arts, the dichotomy between liberal and vocational education should be discarded as a relic of the aristocratic past; all learning should be both theoretical and practical. Teachers should use laboratories, shops, gardens, plays, and games to encourage students' active participation in the learning process, not as mere "relief from the tedium and strain of 'regular' school work." Pupils' work should be as enjoyable as their play, their play as intellectually stimulating as their work. The artificial wall between subject areas should be broken down, and the natural connections between them should be made explicit.[45]

The teacher's proper role was that of a helper, not a disseminator of knowledge. The teacher should not so control the process as to prevent the possibility of student mistakes, since learning from mistakes was crucial to intellectual growth. Schools should develop free personalities instead of inhibiting them. Pupils should participate in decision making but should not dictate the subjects taught. The teacher should not indulge a child's every whim, and there should be order in the class, but an order of motion and discussion, not of rigidity and silence—the order of a workshop, not of a prison.[46]

Though Dewey himself had had trouble maintaining order in the classroom while a young high school teacher, and though some of his college students called him "a miserable teacher," his pedagogical theories possessed a solid empirical foundation. In 1896 he began the University Elementary School at the University of Chicago, a primary school that became known as the Laboratory school. Children there were taught in the manner Dewey later suggested in his pedagogical writings. All courses, even carpentry and sewing, were coeducational. The children cooked and served lunch once per week. Dewey found that cooking best fulfilled his ideal of directed, social, relevant activity. Through it, students learned mathematics (measurements), chemistry (the effects of the combination of ingredients), physics (combustion), biology (digestion), and even geography (the origin of ingredients). The children made their own laboratory instruments, including smelters. In his best-selling book about the school, *The School and Society* (1899), Dewey concluded that knowledge was not the product of experience but was experience itself. Thinking and doing were just two names for a single process of adaptation to a contingent universe. Ideas were like hands, instruments for coping. Dewey supervised the University of Chicago's School of Education and Department of Pedagogy, its high school, and its manual training school. He helped establish the American Association of University Professors.[47]

Educational reformers claiming to be followers of Dewey later carried the idea of democracy in the classroom much farther than Dewey himself intended, thereby unfairly bringing his ideas into disrepute. In *Experience and Education* (1938), Dewey attacked some of these reformers, in the process clarifying his own views. He declared that teachers had an obligation to direct their students and ridiculed the idea that such direction constituted an infringement of student freedom. Regarding the notion that teachers should let students do whatever they wanted, Dewey was uncharacteristically blunt: "Such a method is really stupid." Teachers' far greater experience gave them the obligation to direct pupils by stating problems, providing relevant materials for their solution, and suggesting broad courses of action. Even if it were possible to avoid influencing students (it was not), it was incredibly foolish to try. A pupil's freedom should not be interpreted negatively (freedom from teacher influence) but positively (freedom to accomplish things with some degree of aid from the teacher). Children's interests must be developed, not catered to, because their initial interests were too vague, chaotic, and trivial to have much educational value. All projects should have the goal of student mastery of organized subjects. Students should be encouraged to interact with past knowledge, not to flee it, attack it, or parrot it.[48]

Dewey's conception of art was a microcosm of his whole philosophy. To Dewey, the chief importance of industry, education, and every other human endeavor was not the product that resulted from it, but the enjoyment of the creative process, which alone made life worth living. The process of planning and reaching goals was far more important to human happiness than the goals themselves.

Rooted in nature but acting upon it, art was Dewey's substitute for faith, providing humans with a sense of meaning and a richness of experience. Inverting the traditional Christian ethos, in which the present must be marshaled on behalf of a future state of happiness (heaven), Dewey contended that the future (the anticipation of a planned result) must be utilized to create a present state of happiness.

Like James, Dewey believed that genetic inheritance and environment combined to produce human behavior but emphasized the latter factor. He claimed that humans began with "impulses" (instincts, needs, drives), but these were shaped by "habit" (external influences like family and culture). Of the crucial influence of this shaping process Dewey wrote, "Fear may become abject cowardice, prudent caution, reverence for superiors or respect for equals; an agency for credulous swallowing of absurd superstitions or for wary skepticism." Dewey believed that humans' social instinct was their saving grace and should be cultivated above the selfish instinct for individual gratification.[49]

Like James, Dewey denied the possibility of progress, since it implied a final goal, an end to the flux. Dewey did not seek truth, but wisdom, the ability to manage the flux correctly to maximize happiness. The world was a precarious place requiring endless adjustment. Dewey wrote:

> Triumphs are dangerous when dwelt upon or lived off of; successes use themselves up. Any achieved equilibrium of adjustment with the environment is precarious because we cannot evenly keep pace with changes in the environment. . . . Through science we have secured a degree of power of prediction and of control; through tools, machinery, and an accompanying technique we have made the world more conformable to our needs. We have heaped up riches and means of comfort between ourselves and the risks of the world. . . . But, when all is said and done, the fundamentally hazardous character of the world is not seriously modified, much less eliminated.

Happiness was not a final end, a utopia, but a continuous process. Dewey wrote: "The end is no longer a terminus or limit to be reached. It is the active process of transforming the existent situation. Not perfection as a fixed goal, but the ever-enduring process of perfecting, maturing, refining is the aim of living. . . . Growth itself is the only moral end."[50]

Like James, Dewey believed in free will, defined as chance. He believed that the universe, while still possessing a large element of chance, was evolving from a less orderly into a more orderly place, a process humans could assist. Order and disorder were "mixed not mechanically but vitally like the wheat and tares of the parable." Both the "precarious and the assured" were "fundamental features of natural existence." Dewey wrote: "The world is a scene of risk; it is uncertain, unstable. . . . Our magical safeguard against the uncertain character of the world is to deny the existence of chance, to mumble universal and necessary law, the ubiquity of cause and effect, the uniformity of nature, universal progress, and the inherent rationality of the universe."[51]

PRAGMATISM: A KINDER, GENTLER SKEPTICISM

What is most remarkable about the pragmatists is the manner in which they were able to maintain a personal optimism alien to Nietzschean skepticism. Their view of reason and its offspring, science, contrasted greatly with that of the Epicurean humanists. While Epicurean humanists had considered reason the oracle of truth, pragmatists considered it a guide only in the sense that the blind man's walking stick is his guide. It will help him cross the street and will prevent him from falling into an open manhole, but it will not present to him the many dazzling colors of nature. Similarly, while theists saw faith as the oracle of truth, pragmatists viewed it as the blind man's power of hearing. It could provide aesthetic enjoyment, a sense of community with the world, and a feeling of well-being, but its reports might prove illusory.

When combined with their belief in innate animal drives and their belief in a free will defined as chance, the pragmatists' disbelief in any oracle of truth might have produced a brooding pessimism as intense as that of most Nietzschean skeptics of the same period. But James found comfort in the immediacy of experience, Dewey in the joys of the creative process. They preached that life's rewards could be found in its very process, rather than in its products. Heaven was here on earth, not as the permanent utopia humanists hoped for, but in fleeting moments of joy and peace. Even blind men could be happy.

NOTES

1. H. D. F. Kitto, *The Greeks* (New York: Penguin, 1957), 182; A. R. Burn, *The Pelican History of Greece* (New York: Penguin Books, 1965), 204.

2. Kitto, *Greeks*, 167–69; Burn, *Pelican History of Greece*, 249–52. See also Plato's *Protagoras*.

3. Diogenes Laertius, *Lives of Eminent Philosophers*, 6.20, 37, 41, 45, 50, 54, 62, 72.

4. Diogenes Laertius, *Lives of Eminent Philosophers*, 6.24, 43, 56, 68, 76, 78.

5. Vincent C. Horrigan and Raymond V. Schoder, *A Reading Course in Homeric Greek*, 2 vols. (Chicago: Loyola University Press, 1945), vol. 1, 75; Burn, *Pelican History of Greece*, 346.

6. Henry F. May, *The Enlightenment in America* (New York: Oxford University Press, 1976), 113–14, 118–19.

7. Walter Kaufmann, *Nietzsche: Philosopher, Psychologist, Antichrist*, 4th ed. (Princeton, N.J.: Princeton University Press, 1974), 8, 38–39, 41, 43, 45, 63, 66, 164, 170, 189–92, 197, 206, 216, 228, 230, 250, 252, 255, 262, 280–81, 284, 288–89, 293, 295, 297–98, 303, 310, 393, 407.

8. Kaufmann, *Nietzsche*, 103, 125–26, 132, 164, 184, 200, 219–20, 223–24, 227, 231, 233, 277, 308, 312–13, 316, 321, 325, 339–40, 352, 367–68, 371–72, 378.

9. Kaufmann, *Nietzsche*, 98, 109, 167, 329, 355, 358, 361, 364, 409.

10. Louis Menand, *The Metaphysical Club* (New York: Farrar, Straus & Giroux, 2001), 227.

11. Ralph Barton Perry, *The Thought and Character of William James* (New York: George Braziller, 1954), 8, 37, 43; Menand, *Metaphysical Club*, 81, 92.

12. William James, *The Principles of Psychology*, 1890, in *Pragmatism: A Reader*, ed. Louis Menand (New York: Vintage, 1997), 64–65; Menand, *Metaphysical Club*, 75–76, 260; Perry, *Thought and Character of William James*, 112.

13. Perry, *Thought and Character of William James*, 144, 186; Paul F. Boller Jr., *American Thought in Transition: The Impact of Evolutionary Naturalism, 1865–1900* (Chicago: Rand McNally, 1969), 126.

14. William James, *Essays in Radical Empiricism* (Cambridge, Mass.: Harvard University Press, 1976), 4, 18, 21, 46, 121; William James, *Pragmatism* (Buffalo, N.Y.: Prometheus Books, 1991), 19, 26, 79; William James, *A Pluralistic Universe* (Cambridge, Mass.: Harvard University Press, 1977), 94, 105–6, 109–13, 117, 152; Edward C. Moore, *American Pragmatism: Peirce, James, and Dewey* (New York: Columbia Uni-

versity Press, 1961), 136, 138; Perry, *Thought and Character of William James*, 213; Paul K. Conkin, *Puritans and Pragmatists: Eight Eminent American Thinkers* (Bloomington: Indiana University Press, 1968), 289.

15. Conkin, *Puritans and Pragmatists*, 291–92; William James, "The Will to Believe," 1897, in *The American Intellectual Tradition*, 3d ed., 2 vols., ed. Charles Capper and David A. Hollinger (Oxford: Oxford University Press, 1997), vol. 2, 80; James, *Essays in Radical Empiricism*, 40–41.

16. James, *Essays in Radical Empiricism*, 136, 141–43; James, *Pluralistic Universe*, 81; Menand, *Metaphysical Club*, 358.

17. Perry, *Thought and Character of William James*, 38, 204–6, 215; James, "The Will to Believe," vol. 2, 80; Conkin, *Puritans and Pragmatists*, 292.

18. James, *Essays in Radical Empiricism*, 47; James, *Pluralistic Universe*, 96, 98; James, *Pragmatism*, 26;

19. James, *Pragmatism*, 11; Perry, *Thought and Character of William James*, 262.

20. James, *Essays in Radical Empiricism*, 134; James, *Pragmatism*, 35–36, 131; James, "The Will to Believe," vol. 2, 84–85, 88–89; Perry, *Thought and Character of William James*, 260; Moore, *American Pragmatism*, 129.

21. Perry, *Thought and Character of William James*, 213; Moore, *American Pragmatism*, 123.

22. James, *Essays in Radical Empiricism*, 99, 142; James, *Pluralistic Universe*, 57, 141, 143–44; Conkin, *Puritans and Pragmatists*, 340.

23. James, *Pluralistic Universe*, 18, 26, 28, 54, 60; James, *Pragmatism*, 119, 132; Perry, *Thought and Character of William James*, 265–67, 269–70; Menand, *Metaphysical Club*, 358; Boller, *American Thought in Transition*, 141.

24. Perry, *Thought and Character of William James*, 221; Conkin, *Puritans and Pragmatists*, 334–35.

25. James, *Essays in Radical Empiricism*, 71, 75; James, *Pluralistic Universe*, 66; James, *Principles of Psychology*, 65–68; Conkin, *Puritans and Pragmatists*, 287.

26. James, *Pluralistic Universe*, 57, 148; James, *Pragmatism*, 54, 61, 71–72, 83, 112–13; Perry, *Thought and Character of William James*, 168, 379; Conkin, *Puritans and Pragmatists*, 306; Moore, *American Pragmatism*, 116.

27. James, *Essays in Radical Empiricism*, 22–23, 94.

28. Menand, *Metaphysical Club*, 435.

29. John Dewey, *John Dewey: The Essential Writings*, ed. David Sidorsky (New York: Harper & Row, 1977), vii; Robert B. Westbrook, *John Dewey and American Democracy* (Ithaca, N.Y.: Cornell University Press, 1991), 1, 537; Menand, *Metaphysical Club*, 318; Conkin, *Puritans and Pragmatists*, 345, 347, 353.

30. Dewey, *John Dewey*, ed. Sidorsky, xi, xlv, 87–88; Moore, *American Pragmatism*, 184, 205; James, *Essays in Radical Empiricism*, 125; Westbrook, *John Dewey and American Democracy*, 130; John Dewey, *The Need for a Recovery of Philosophy*, 1917, in *Pragmatism*, ed. Menand, 221–22.

31. Dewey, *John Dewey*, ed. Sidorsky, xliii, 32–38, 42, 78, 128.

32. Menand, *Metaphysical Club*, 437; Dewey, *Need for a Recovery of Philosophy*, 228.

33. Dewey, *John Dewey*, ed. Sidorsky, 41, 68, 139, 145–46, 231; Augustine, *On Free Choice of the Will*, trans. Anna S. Benjamin and L. H. Hackstaff (New York: Bobbs-Merrill, 1964), 40; Westbrook, *John Dewey and American Democracy*, 137, 141, 323, 334–35.

34. Dewey, *John Dewey*, ed. Sidorsky, 78, 236, 239–40; Westbrook, *John Dewey and American Democracy*, 142, 418, 424, 427.

35. Dewey, *John Dewey*, ed. Sidorsky, 252–53; Westbrook, *John Dewey and American Democracy*, 326.

36. Dewey, *John Dewey*, ed. Sidorsky, 159–62, 246–47, 253.

37. Dewey, *John Dewey*, ed. Sidorsky, xvii, xxxvi, 69, 156, 165, 170; John Dewey, *Democracy and Education: An Introduction to the Philosophy of Education* (New York: Macmillan, 1916), 412.

38. Dewey, *John Dewey*, ed. Sidorsky, 149–50, 161, 169; Menand, *Metaphysical Club*, 237.

39. Moore, *American Pragmatism*, 256, 265; Westbrook, *John Dewey and American Democracy*, 417.

40. Dewey, *John Dewey*, ed. Sidorsky, 270, 272; Moore, *American Pragmatism*, 230.

41. John Dewey, *Experience, Nature, and Art*, 1925, in *Pragmatism*, ed. Menand, 252, 255; Dewey, *John Dewey*, ed. Sidorsky, 148, 256, 263; Westbrook, *John Dewey and American Democracy*, 339, 395; Dewey, *Democracy and Education*, 159.

42. Westbrook, *John Dewey and American Democracy*, 177–78, 191, 401–2, 435, 453, 456; Dewey, *Democracy and Education*, 159–60, 240, 353, 401; John Dewey, "I Believe," 1939, in *Pragmatism*, ed. Menand, 267–70; Dewey, *John Dewey*, ed. Sidorsky, 201–2, 207; Moore, *American Pragmatism*, 231.

43. Dewey, *Democracy and Education*, 146, 179, 183, 186, 209, 219; Moore, *American Pragmatism*, 249.

44. Dewey, *Democracy and Education*, 79, 129, 144, 161, 181–84, 203, 210, 217, 225–26, 228; Westbrook, *John Dewey and American Democracy*, 169.

45. Dewey, *Democracy and Education*, 190–92, 228, 235, 237, 241–42, 305, 373; Dewey, *John Dewey*, ed. Sidorsky, 233.

46. Dewey, *Democracy and Education*, 187–88, 231; Dewey, *John Dewey*, ed. Sidorsky, xxx–xxxi; Moore, *American Pragmatism*, 250–51.

47. Menand, *Metaphysical Club*, 236, 320, 323–24, 329, 331, 413; Westbrook, *John Dewey and American Democracy*, 8, 378.

48. Westbrook, *John Dewey and American Democracy*, 502–5, 542–43.

49. Westbrook, *John Dewey and American Democracy*, 157–59; Dewey, *John Dewey*, ed. Sidorsky, 212; Moore, *American Pragmatism*, 224–25; John Dewey, "The Influence of Darwinism on Philosophy," 1909, in *The American Intellectual Tradition*, ed. Capper and Hollinger, vol. 2, 174.

50. Dewey, *John Dewey*, ed. Sidorsky, 73, 113, 147; Moore, *American Pragmatism*, 227.

51. Sidorsky, *John Dewey*, ed. Sidorsky, 108, 111–15, 132.

IV

THE AGE OF CONFUSION

9

AMERICAN THOUGHT
SINCE WORLD WAR II

While theism dominated the colonial era, humanism the early republican and antebellum periods, and skepticism the late nineteenth and early twentieth centuries, the era since World War II has been an age of confusion. Sizable numbers of theists, humanists, and skeptics, operating out of what are now well-established traditions, coexist in the tolerant West.

Immediately following World War II, the United States witnessed a resurgence of humanism as a result of the nation's victory over depression and the Axis powers and its uncontested command of the global economy. For the first time in American history the nation's prevalent philosophy no longer paralleled that of Europe; while war-ravaged Europe continued its age of skepticism, marked by such movements as French existentialism, the United States largely reverted to humanism, which had always possessed strong roots in traditional American optimism. In general, the contests of the 1960s represented an internal struggle between humanists: the "conservatives," mostly Epicurean humanists who sought social progress through rational materialism, and the "radicals," mostly Platonic humanists who sought it through intuitive spiritualism. But in the last three decades both theism and skepticism have revived. The existence of large numbers of theists, humanists, and skeptics in the same society has resulted in a "culture war," waged in schools, newspapers, art galleries, and voting booths.[1]

POSTWAR EPICUREAN HUMANISM

In 1945 the United States was unified, confident, and prosperous. As British prime minister Winston Churchill put it: "America stands at this moment at the summit of the world." The misery of the Great Depression seemed but a bad dream, and the outcome of the recent world war appeared to demonstrate the superiority of American institutions. (Russians also perceived the victory as a vindication of their own, very different system.) Since all principal U.S. economic competitors (Germany, Britain, France, and Japan) lay in ruins, the nation was producing nearly half of the world's manufactured goods. Between 1945 and 1966 the nation's gross domestic product nearly tripled. Consumers who had saved billions of dollars during World War II unleashed those savings, purchasing a broad range of appliances: refrigerators, washing machines, sewing machines, vacuum cleaners, freezers, and electric mixers. Automobile registrations rose from twenty-six million to sixty million between 1945 and 1960. Postwar prosperity formed the natural foundation for a resurgence of humanism.[2]

Furthermore, the totalitarian threats posed first by the Axis powers, and then by the Soviet bloc, reinforced the American people's sense of their liberal humanist mission to spread toleration ("human rights"), democracy, and capitalism. This traditional sense of mission was reinforced by two new methods of social conditioning, mass universities and television. In offering veterans a college or vocational education the G.I. Bill (Servicemen's Readjustment Act) of 1944 began the process of transforming American universities from small aristocratic institutions into huge centers for mass education, a trend reinforced by the size and wealth of the baby boom generation and by the Vietnam War. (The surge in enrollment at institutions of higher learning—from 4.7 million to 9.6 million—from 1963 to 1973 was not based solely on demographics or on a greater thirst for knowledge.) Meanwhile, the National Broadcasting Company (NBC) and the Columbia Broadcasting System (CBS), both of which had begun as radio networks, began nationwide television broadcasting after World War II. By 1960 fifty million households, almost 90 percent of

American homes, contained television sets. In these early postwar years both the universities and the television networks tended to promote a sense of national mission.[3]

Postwar humanism assumed a largely Epicurean form. Adolf Hitler had cast a racist pall over the belief in innate human qualities. While genetics continued to be an important field of study, the new "behavioral psychology" of B. F. Skinner challenged the old Freudian theories that had emphasized the role of innate drives in the formation of human thought and behavior. Behavioral psychologists used rewards and punishments to produce desired responses. While, strictly speaking, Skinner did not endorse John Locke's blank slate theory, he argued that humans' innate qualities were so few in number and so neutral in effect as to present no obstacle to behavioral conditioning. Skinner wrote: "We have no truck with philosophies of innate goodness—or evil, either, for that matter. But we do have faith in our power to change human behavior. . . . Men are made good or bad and wise or foolish by the environment in which they grow." Skinner's confidence in the power of behavioral conditioning was so complete that he wrote a novel (*Walden Two*, 1948) about a utopian society that used this method to eliminate not only undesirable behaviors, such as drinking, smoking, gossiping, lying, and promiscuity, but even negative emotions, such as selfishness, competitiveness, hero-worship, jealousy, anger, apathy, boredom, anxiety, fear, hatred, and snobbishness. Skinner failed to explain what would prevent the social scientist dictators of his fictional community, who were not themselves products of systematic conditioning, from using a comprehensive system of conditioning (as well as their control of a command economy) to serve their own selfish ends.[4]

Genuine theism and skepticism remained, of course. From 1940 to 1960 the portion of the American population who belonged to a church or synagogue rose from 50 to 63 percent, and religious films (like *The Ten Commandments*) were enormously popular. This phenomenon has been variously interpreted as a search for community at a time when people were beginning to follow jobs from one region to another and as a Cold War reaction against communist atheism. President Dwight D. Eisenhower himself encouraged the practice of religion, arguing that piety was essential to the survival of American democracy. In 1954 Congress added "one nation under God" to the Pledge of Allegiance. The American Council on Advertising filled the country with bill-boards that stated, "The family that prays together stays together." Catholic priest (later a bishop) Fulton J. Sheen's television program *Life Is Worth Living* was a primetime hit, and the Reverend Billy Graham began filling stadiums.[5]

But other elements of the religious revival movement actually reflected and reinforced Epicurean humanism. Some of the most popular ministers, like the Reverend Norman Vincent Peale (whose book, *The Power of Positive Thinking*, was a best-seller) taught a complacent, feel-good religion that only heightened the materialism of the age.[6]

Critics like Reinhold Niebuhr noted that this brand of religion was more akin to humanism than to orthodox Christianity. By contrast, Niebuhr urged a return to the traditional Christian pessimism concerning human nature. Yet Niebuhr's "neo-ortho-doxy" was no more "orthodox" than it was "new." His description of "God" more closely resembled that of John Dewey than that of any orthodox theologian: "God is not a separate existence but the ground of existence." Niebuhr believed that Christian doctrines expressed only symbolic, not literal, truths.[7]

Meanwhile, a few skeptics challenged the pretensions of scientists to objectivity. In *The Structure of Scientific Revolutions* (1962), Thomas Kuhn argued that it was not evidence that led to the replacement of one scientific paradigm by another, since the new paradigm was generally plagued by as many empirical problems as the old one. Rather, scientists often embraced a new paradigm for personal reasons, including aesthetic taste. Supporters of the new paradigm must "have faith that the new paradigm will succeed with the many large problems that confront it, knowing only that the older paradigm has failed with a few." Kuhn concluded, "A decision of that kind can only be made on faith." Nor were the adherents of the older paradigm any more objective; indeed, it often required the death of a whole generation of scientists for one paradigm to replace another.[8]

Nevertheless, the optimism of Epicurean humanism prevailed. Many Americans assumed that the new prosperity would last forever and would solve all societal problems. While economists convinced the public that they could make recessions disappear permanently, social scientists persuaded Americans that prosperity, combined with government support for the poor and the elderly, would end poverty and crime. Confidence in medicine grew so great, because of the discovery of cures for various diseases, that some began to expect a cure for death itself.[9]

THE REVIVAL OF PLATONIC HUMANISM IN THE 1960s

Similarities between the 1960s Radicals and the Transcendentalists

The 1960s radicals who fought the Epicurean establishment were mostly Platonic humanists. In background and thought they bore an uncanny resemblance to the transcendentalists of the antebellum period. The radicals came mostly from the upper middle class of American society. Their affluent background doomed their communes just as it had doomed the utopian communities established by the transcendentalists and other antebellum reformers. Most commune members lacked the necessary experience with hard labor and with an ascetic, communal life. Members were often reduced to panhandling or going on welfare.[10]

Second, like the transcendentalists, the radicals sought to replace the rational materialism of their parents' generation and the resultant emphasis on science and technology with an intuitive spiritualism. In 1961 *Time* magazine chose fifteen American scientists as its collective "Man of the Year," noting, "Science is at the apogee of its power." But among the radicals science soon fell into disrepute as the handmaiden of a "technocracy" seeking to enslave society and of a "war machine" threatening to destroy the planet. Theodore Roszak expressed the radical program well: "Nothing less is required than the subversion of the scientific world view, with its entrenched commitment to an egocentric and cerebral mode of consciousness. In its place, there must be a new culture in which the non-intellective capacities of the personality—the capacities that take fire from visionary splendor and the experience of human communion—become the arbiters of the good, the true, and the beautiful." Roszak claimed that these "non-intellective capacities" were difficult to describe, precisely because they were nonintellective, but had best been described by "mystics and Romantics." As a result of their rejection of the so-called technocracy, so reminiscent of transcendentalist criticism of the Industrial Revolution, the radicals launched an environmentalist movement whose more extreme proponents went far beyond the traditional conservationism of Theodore Roosevelt to envision a return to a primitive utopia largely devoid of technology.[11]

Third, like the transcendentalists and other Platonic humanists, the radicals claimed that human nature was essentially good. Radicals argued that it was parental and societal brutality that ruined children. They claimed that "evil" was merely a superstitious synonym for "ignorance," an ignorance that could be eradicated by appeals to the inner love and peace that defined humans. Films began to depict children as wiser than their parents, celebrating a human nature "uncorrupted" by civilization. Although some conservatives have blamed Benjamin Spock for the growth of permissive parenting, his wildly popular *Common Sense Book of Baby and Child Care* (1946) criticized only harshness, not strictness.[12]

The civil rights movement both reflected and reinforced the era's optimistic view of human nature. Martin Luther King Jr. frequently appealed to natural law theory, which assumed the ability of humans to deduce a universal code of ethics through reason or intuition. King traced his support for nonviolent resistance to unjust laws to Henry David Thoreau's "On the Duty of Civil Disobedience." Under King's shrewd and inspirational leadership, civil rights advocates managed to secure an end to segregation and disfranchisement through the passage of the Civil Rights Act of 1964 and the Voting Rights Act of 1965. In his famous speech at the March on Washington (1963), King was able to appeal to traditional American egalitarianism, declaring, "I have a dream that one day this nation will rise up and live out the true meaning of its creed: 'We hold these truths to be self evident that all men are created equal.'"[13]

Only a small minority of radicals advocated the use of violence to overturn the capitalist system. Generally Marxist, they represented a brand of Epicurean humanism, promising progress through worker ownership of the means of production. But the Platonic humanists far outnumbered the Marxists within the radical camp.[14]

Fourth, like their transcendentalist forebears, many radicals rejected Christianity, partly on the conviction that it had been compromised by its association with a capitalist establishment and its acquiescence in social evils like racial discrimination. Yet, convinced of the centrality of spirituality to human existence, many radicals turned to alternative faiths that have since become known as "New Age religions." While the transcendentalists had exulted in Indian religious writings, the radicals went beyond the rediscovery of Buddhism and Hinduism to embrace a broad range of spiritual options, including astrology, Native American lore, Taoism, and Druid rites. They understood so little of the complexity and organic unity of each of these ancient traditions, formed over centuries, that they often combined elements of each haphazardly. Even Roszak, a partisan in their cause, complained: "The young do not by and large understand what these traditions are all about. One does not unearth the wisdom of the ages by shuffling about a few exotic catch phrases—nor does one learn anything about anybody's lore or religion by donning a few talismans and dosing on LSD." The defining element in the radicals' conglomeration of beliefs was their rejection of orthodox Christianity. However disjointed the result, the radicals' fascination with alternative religious experiences reflected a distaste for the Christian moralism of the day, which radicals believed emphasized the letter of the law to the exclusion of its spirit. Radicals complained that while Christian ministers preached against drugs, sex, and rock and roll, the poor went hungry. Like some of the ancient Gnostics and the modern antinomians (such as Anne Hutchinson), the radicals argued that intuitive truths transcended traditional moral codes.[15]

Fifth, like the transcendentalists, the radicals embraced a doctrine of absolute nonconformity and rejected what they considered to be the cold materialism of their parents. But in "dropping

out" of the dominant culture, they merely formed a counterculture that was equally conformist in its doctrines and practices. For
men, long hair became as much a requirement for entrance into
the counterculture as was short hair in the dominant culture. Drug
use became a mandatory rite of initiation into the youth culture.
Resistance to the Vietnam War became as much a way of fitting
in as a form of political protest. Even as sympathetic an observer
of the counterculture as Godfrey Hodgson noted: "They allowed
the record industry and the fashion trade to define their collective
personality every bit as rigidly as Detroit had ever done for their
parents. Their long hair, their blue denim, were every bit as much
a uniform as the crew cuts and chinos of the fifties." Furthermore,
the radicals were often inconsistent in their opposition to materialism. Rock and roll groups collected millions of dollars from
songs that denounced "the system" and expressed sympathy for
the poor, while donating very little of the proceeds to charity.
Even as a fugitive, Abbie Hoffman sold the film rights to his letters to his wife.[16]

The Women's Rights Movement

Nevertheless, the radicals succeeded in extending egalitarianism much further than either the transcendentalists or the Epicurean humanists of the Enlightenment, who had often applied
their doctrine of equality only to white males. During World War
II, more than six million women had worked in vital factories because of labor shortages created by the military service of able-
bodied men. The portion of women who worked doubled (from
20 to 40 percent). While some women returned to their homes after the war, others remained on the job; the percentage of women
who worked fell only to 30 percent. Even those who returned to
their homes returned with a new sense of accomplishment and a
taste of independence.[17]

Building on these gains, Betty Friedan published *The Feminine
Mystique* in 1963. Against the old theories of innate gender differences that had barred women from most professions, Friedan asserted "the enormous plasticity of human nature." Though she ad-

mired Freud for seeking to liberate humanity from the Victorian repression of natural impulses, she blamed him for wrapping the revered scientific mantle around the old fallacy that "the identity of woman is determined by her biology." Having documented Freud's belief in the innate intellectual and emotional inferiority of women, Friedan wrote, "Much of what Freud believed to be biological, instinctual, and changeless has been shown by modern research to be a result of specific cultural causes."[18]

Since gender roles were established by culture rather than by innate differences, there was no reason that women should not pursue the same careers as men. Friedan contended that modern technology had rendered housework less than a full-time job for a vigorous person, causing society to underutilize women. She referred to "the emptiness of 'Occupation: house wife'" and to "that ludicrous consignment of millions of women to spend their days at work an eight-year-old could do." She declared: "Women have outgrown the housewife role. . . . The comfortable concentration camp that American women have walked into . . . denies women's adult human identity." She added: "The only kind of work which permits an able woman to realize her abilities fully . . . [is] the life-long commitment to an art or science, to politics or profession." Friedan even blamed clinging housewives for an "ominous" increase in homosexuality among their sons, adding darkly, "Homosexuality . . . is spreading like a murky smog over the American scene."[19]

By 1980 more than half of the nation's wives worked. The entrance of women into the job market led to greater dignity for women and to greater equality within marriage, though it also left many children unsupervised at home.[20]

The Cultural Victory of the Radicals

Despite their political failures, the radicals succeeded in transforming American culture. The most probable reasons for their success are demographic and economic. The traditional strategy of parents in neutralizing adolescent rebellion has always been to "divide and conquer." But the unprecedented size of the "baby boom" generation made containment a virtual impossibility, particularly in an age when radio, film, and television made it clear to each adolescent that he was far from alone in his rebellion. The unprecedented wealth that adolescents had to spend opened the airwaves to them. Their music, films, and corresponding philosophy could not be shut out without denying American business access to the money they generated. In the mid-1960s teenagers bought 53 percent of all movie tickets and 43 percent of all records sold. Teens spent $100 million per year on records in that period. The boomers saved radio, which television had nearly destroyed. American corporations were not dissuaded by the irony of their profiting from the large-scale marketing of songs and films that often attacked commercialism. Furthermore, the unprecedented numbers of boomers who attended college (for the first time, a majority of high school graduates) were able to extend their adolescence into young adulthood, thereby extending the period of rebellion to such a length that it became not just a phase, but a way of life. As Jerry Rubin put it: "We ain't never, never gonna grow up! We're gonna be adolescents forever!" In addition, the sense of the need for rebellion was heightened by a pervasive fear of the draft during the Vietnam War.[21]

THE REVIVAL OF SKEPTICISM

As the baby boomers gradually rose to positions of power within national institutions, especially in the universities and in Hollywood, their influence upon public opinion increased. Henry Louis Gates explained: "After the Vietnam War, a lot of us didn't just crawl back into our library cubicles; we stepped into academic positions. With the war over, our visibility was lost and it seemed for a while—to the unobservant—that we had disappeared. Now we have tenure, and the work of reshaping the university has begun in earnest."[22]

Yet even as the influence of the baby boomers increased, their generation experienced a pronounced intellectual shift toward skepticism. As their hopes for social progress waned in the wake of the Vietnam War, Watergate, and the administrations of Reagan and the senior Bush, skepticism advanced.

Neopragmatism

Richard Rorty led a "neopragmatist" movement. Like William James, Rorty attacked the Epicurean humanist conception of science as an objective arbiter of truth. In "Science as Solidarity" (1986), Rorty noted: "Worries about 'cognitive status' and 'objectivity' are characteristic of a secularized society in which the scientist replaces the priest. The scientist is now seen as the person who keeps humanity in touch with something beyond itself." Rorty added that the idea that "Truth is 'out there' waiting for human beings to arrive at it" was "an unfortunate attempt to carry a religious conception over into culture." He added: "We cannot, I think, imagine a moment at which the human race could settle back and say, 'Well, now that we've finally arrived at the Truth we can relax.'" Rorty declared that in his ideal world, "There would be less talk about rigor and more about originality. The image of the great scientist would not be of somebody who got it right but of somebody who made it new."[23]

There would also be less talk about God, since religion could no more supply transcendent truth than could science. Rorty noted, "Pragmatists would like to drop the idea that human beings are responsible to a nonhuman power." He claimed that society "need be responsible only to its own traditions, and not to the moral law as well." Nothing other than the distinctive historical "loyalties and convictions" that gave a particular group its self-image had any moral claim on the individual. Rorty added: "Most moral dilemmas are thus reflections of the fact that most of us identify ourselves with a number of different communities and are equally reluctant to marginalize ourselves in relation to any of them. The diversity of identifications increases with education, just as the number of communities with which a person may identify increases with civilization."[24]

Yet, like the original pragmatists, Rorty was hardly an extreme relativist; in fact, he referred contemptuously to "the silly and self-refuting view that every belief is as good as every other." The fact that no concept could encompass reality did not signify that all concepts were equally valid.[25]

Similarly, in *The American Evasion of Philosophy* (1989), Cornel West endorsed what he termed "prophetic pragmatism": "Prophetic pragmatism denies Sisyphean pessimism and utopian perfectionism. Rather, it promotes the possibility of human progress and the human impossibility of paradise. This progress results from principled and protracted Promethean efforts, yet even such efforts are no guarantee. And all human struggles—including successful ones—against specific forms of evil produce new, though possibly lesser, forms of evil." Progress involved selecting the right elements from the right traditions, rather than pretending to reject tradition completely, since "all that human beings basically have are traditions." West himself practiced a loose form of Christianity, "stripped of static dogmas and decrepit doctrines," and endorsed religion as a vehicle for both comprehending and influencing the poor and oppressed, who were generally religious.[26]

Deconstructionism

Meanwhile, literary critics, following the lead of Martin Heidegger, Paul de Man, and Jacques Derrida, radically altered the study of texts through "deconstruction," a method of examining texts to uncover the hidden, often subconscious assumptions of their authors. As Jonathan Culler put it, "Literary theory has to a considerable extent assimilated the demonstration that reading should focus on the discrepancies between . . . [texts'] explicit statements and the implication of their modes of utterance." He added, "Deconstruction seeks to undo all oppositions that, in the name of unity, purity, order, and hierarchy, try to eliminate the difference."[27]

In the process deconstructionists sought to reveal the racist, sexist, and homophobic assumptions that lay behind many of the classic texts of the Western canon. Henry Louis Gates maintained regarding his fellow African Americans: "We have been deconstructing white people's languages and discourses since that dreadful day in 1619 when we were marched off the boat in Virginia. Jacques Derrida did not invent deconstruction; we did!" Gates urged the creation of a distinctively black literary theory, arguing that to use only white forms was "the intellectual equivalent of neo-colonialism, placing ourselves in a relationship of discursive indenture." Although he claimed that "the concern of the Third World critic should properly be to understand the ideological sub-texts which any critical theory reflects and embodies, and the relation which the subtext bears to the production of meaning," he added: "We must not succumb . . . to the tragic lure of white power, the mistake of accepting the empowering language of white critical theory as 'universal' or as our own language, the mistake of confusing the enabling mask of theory with our own black faces." Gates confessed: "Much of my early work reflects this desire to out-wit the master by trying to speak his language as fluently as he. Now, we must, at last, don the empowering mask of blackness and talk *that* talk, the language of black difference. While it is true that we must, as [W. E. B.] DuBois said long ago, 'know and test the power of the cabalistic letters of the white man,' we must also know and test the dark secrets of a black and hermetic discursive universe that awaits its disclosure through the black arts of interpretation."[28]

Feminist literary critics engaged in a similar enterprise. Elaine Showalter noted: "Since the 1970s . . . most feminist critics have rejected the concept of the genderless 'imagination,' and have argued from a variety of perspectives that the imagination cannot escape from the unconscious structures and strictures of gender identity." She added that, "In contrast to the hegemony of what it characterized as the arid and elitist 'methodolatry' of patriarchal criticism," feminist literary theory now engaged in "a celebration of an intuitive female critical consciousness in the interpretation of women's texts." Some feminists further identified this female consciousness as including such "matriarchal values" as nurturing, aversion to violence, and "connectedness." (Ironically, this emphasis on intuition and nurturing qualities as the distinctive traits of female consciousness bore no small resemblance to the emphases of the nineteenth-century "cult of domesticity.") Showalter concluded, much like Gates: "Through careful reading of women's texts we will develop a criticism of our own that is both theoretical and feminist. . . . Our enterprise does not stand or fall by proving some kind of parity with male literary or critical 'genius'; even assuming that a female Shakespeare or a female Derrida would be recognized, to question the very idea of 'genius' is part of [Virginia] Woolf's legacy to us."[29]

Most deconstructionists held to the belief that all literature was political, since whoever controlled the language controlled thought, which, in turn, regulated behavior, including power relationships. De Man himself wrote: "It is as a political force that the aesthetic still concerns us as one of the most powerful ideological drives to act upon the reality of history." Gates asked: "How can the use of literary analysis to explicate the racist social text in which we still find ourselves be anything *but* political?" The ultimate effect of these developments was the revival of a relativism reminiscent of that of the late nineteenth and early twentieth centuries.[30]

"Bottom-Up" Historical Writing, Affirmative Action, and Multiculturalism

The egalitarian ethos of the 1960s remained. In historical writing an effort was made to move beyond the traditional equation of history with politics and war in order to give voice to the multitudes of the past who had not been aristocratic, white, or male. Even those historians who studied political and military history began to examine such phenomena as mass voting behavior and the plight of the common soldier rather than dwelling upon the lives of "the great men," the statesmen and the generals. Historians applying quantitative methods to voting records, census data, and other documentary evidence managed to shed some light upon aspects of the lives of ordinary people that had eluded previous historians, who had focused primarily on literary evidence. Simultaneously, academics assaulted what they called the traditional "Eurocentric" bias of academia through the promotion of racial and gender diversity in the hiring of university faculty and the admission of students. They also promoted the study of non-Western cultures in the hope of achieving a global perspective and of making academia more reflective of a nation that was becoming ever more ethnically and culturally diverse and that was growing ever more intertwined in a global economy.[31]

Neorealism

Influenced by the cinematic realism of postwar Italy, the American film industry witnessed the same shift toward skepticism as the universities, as "neorealism" began to dominate the most popular art form of the twentieth century. The quest for realism inevitably led filmmakers to introduce graphic sex and violence into their films. Largely supportive of the trend, film critics began to use the word "dark" as a synonym for "profound." Beginning in the late 1960s a growing number of films dispensed with the usual "happy ending" and put forward a variety of "antiheroes" as protagonists. Portraying self-reflective, self-doubting characters, actors like Dustin Hoffman, Al Pacino, Robert De Niro, and Jack Nicholson replaced the larger-than-life stars of "the golden age of Hollywood," such as Gary Cooper, Clark Gable, and John Wayne. As realists became more concerned with faithfully depicting a reality they considered complex and confused rather than with telling a story, movie plots became less linear.[32]

Television became involved in the neorealist movement more slowly but just as profoundly. A 1992 study found that even Saturday-morning children's programs contained an average of twenty-five violent acts per hour. A 1991 study found that there were thirteen times more references to extramarital sex than to marital sex on television programs. In October of that year six out of seven television pregnancies involved unmarried women. A 1999 survey of 1,351 programs found that 56 percent of all television shows had sexual content, with an average of three sex scenes an hour; the percentage was even higher during prime time. In the scenes depicting or suggesting sexual intercourse, 28 percent of the characters involved knew their sexual partners but had no relationship with them, and another 10 percent had just met their partners. A 2003 study found violence, nudity, and vulgar language at unprecedented levels on the programs of the broadcast networks, even during the "family hour" of viewing (8:00–9:00 P.M.). What struck the author of the study most forcibly was the relative absence of viewer complaints, as compared with a decade earlier.[33]

THE PERSISTENCE OF HUMANISM

The Conservative Counterattack

Yet humanism persisted in both its Epicurean and Platonic forms. Epicurean humanists continued to expect social progress through science, technology, and free markets. Many of the conservative critics of the policies and practices of universities during the 1980s and 1990s were Epicurean humanists who decried the replacement of moral absolutes with relativism. These critics wished to revive some version of the old natural law tradition that had been cast aside by the skeptics. In *The Closing of the American Mind* (1987), Allan Bloom claimed that moral relativism was the central tenet of the modern university and blamed such relativism for numerous social problems, including the enormous increase in divorce since the 1960s. He asserted: "Children may be told over and over again that their parents have a right to their own lives, that they will enjoy quality time instead of quantity time, that they are really loved by their parents even after divorce, but children do not believe any of this. . . . The most important lesson that family taught was the existence of the only unbreakable bond, for better or worse, between human beings."[34]

Other critics of modern academia, including Dinesh D'Souza, charged the universities with suppressing free speech and with presenting a form of multiculturalism that had more to do with advancing a wholly Western, radical agenda than with teaching students about other cultures. D'Souza complained that radical multiculturalists falsely portrayed such works as *I, Rigoberto Manchu*, the account of a Marxist Latin American, as representative of non-Western culture, while systematically excluding the *Koran*, the Indian epic *Ramayana*, the *Analects* of Confucius, and other texts central to non-Western cultures, because these texts endorsed the subordination of women.[35]

The New Age Movement

Meanwhile, a burgeoning New Age movement has arisen among Platonic humanists. Most New Agers embrace a philosophy similar to that of the ancient Stoics, a form of pantheism that conceives of "God" as nothing more than a name for the World Soul, which is the universe itself. Hence most New Agers consider all humans a part of God. They consider humans innately good and contend that sin is nothing more than ignorance. Hence "Christ" is a mere name for a state of enlightenment that any human can achieve through his own effort—by recognizing the reality of pantheism—and "hell" is just another name for an unenlightened state of being. Some New Agers espouse a doctrine of reincarnation: Individual souls lead many lives, transmigrating into many different bodies, a process of "spiritual evolution" that purges souls of bad karma, so that they can finally rejoin the World Soul. Some New Agers dabble in astrology, séances, psychic phenomena, witchcraft, and magic crystals.[36]

By 1987 there were more than twenty-five hundred New Age book stores and more than three thousand publishers of New Age books and journals in the United States alone. New Age gurus have been in demand everywhere, from the Clinton White House to corporate boardrooms, teaching mental exercises designed to increase worldly success. At Stanford Business School, Professor Michael Ray has prepared future captains of industry with tarot cards and chants "to release their deeper selves."[37]

THE PERSISTENCE OF THEISM

Vatican II and the New Catholicism

Yet traditional theism has persisted in many forms, helping to pave the way for the "culture war." The Catholic Church witnessed extensive change as a result of the papacy of John XXIII and the Second Vatican Council (1962–1965). While Pope John XXIII did away with papal seclusion and harshness toward other religions, Vatican II resulted in liturgical changes emphasizing congregational participation, a surge of ecumenism, and a greater emphasis on the right of dissent within the church based on the individual conscience. The Catholic Mass was transformed. It was now recited in the vernacular language, rather than in Latin, and the priest now faced the congregation rather than the wall. The laity were now allowed into the sanctuary, where the altar stood, and were permitted to speak and to sing. The laity also became more involved in decision making at the parish level. A charismatic movement arose within the church, healing services were offered, retreats were organized, religiously mixed marriages were accepted to a greater degree, and marriages were annulled in much larger numbers. Despite these changes, the church reaffirmed its positions against birth control, abortion, the ordination of women, and married priests. The American bishops also spoke out against the death penalty and the nuclear arms race and on behalf of the poor. In *Economic Justice for All: A Pastoral Letter on Catholic Social Teaching and the U.S. Economy* (1986), the bishops wrote: "We are proud of the strength, productivity, and creativity of our economy, but we also remember those who have been left behind in our progress. We believe that we honor our history best by working for the day when all our sisters and brothers share adequately in the American dream. . . . Every economic decision and institution must be judged in light of whether it protects or undermines the dignity of the human person." Nevertheless, increasing numbers of American Catholics began to ignore the teachings of the hierarchy on both social and economic matters.[38]

The Revival of Protestant Fundamentalism

Meanwhile, Protestant fundamentalism revived in the 1970s, and became a powerful political force in the 1980s and 1990s, largely in reaction to what the fundamentalists perceived as a national moral decline resulting from the sexual revolution. In 1980 Jerry Falwell, founder of the Moral Majority organization, expressed an anxiety common to many fundamentalists concerning the growth of gambling, prostitution, pornography, homosexuality, and drug abuse. Falwell claimed, "Our very moral existence is at stake." He contended, "America was born in her churches, and she must be reborn there as well." He added: "I love America not because of her pride, her wealth, or her prestige; I love America because she, above all the nations of the world, has honored the principles of the Bible.

America has been great because she has been good. We have been the breadbasket of the world, we have fed our enemies and canceled their national debts against us." He concluded: "We as American citizens must recommit ourselves to the faith of our fathers and to the premises and moral foundations upon which this country was established. . . . It is time to call America back to her moral roots. It is time to call America back to God."[39]

Fundamentalism also revived in reaction to a growing dissent against biblical teaching on sexual matters within mainline Protestant denominations. By the 1990s some Episcopal bishops began ordaining noncelibate homosexuals, a movement that later culminated in the consecration of the first openly gay bishop. A national committee of Presbyterians condoned teen sex and endorsed a new family structure, including same-sex marriages, and the ordination of practicing homosexuals. The Presbytery of Greater Atlanta refused to revoke the ordination of a transsexual minister. The national synod of the Presbyterian Church and the General Convention of the Episcopal Church rejected resolutions requiring their clergy to honor the biblical injunction against extramarital sex.[40]

Fundamentalist fervor has also been heightened by millennialism, the belief that Christ will return soon. Millennialists like Hal Lindsey, whom *Time* magazine once dubbed "the Jeremiah for this Generation," have sold millions of books. Lindsey's *The Late Great Planet Earth* (1970) was the nonfiction best-seller of the 1970s; by 1990, twenty-eight million copies of the book had been sold. The most revered minister in the United States, Billy Graham, is a cautious millennialist. There are now several weekly television programs, such as *Jack Van Impe Presents*, that correlate current world events with biblical prophecy. Jerry Jenkins's and Tim LaHaye's "Left Behind" series of novels concerning end-time prophecy have become national best-sellers.[41]

Although millennialism has been especially widespread at the close of centuries and millennia, it has hardly been restricted to such times. The heavily symbolic Book of Revelation has always provided abundant raw materials for millennialist claims, and generations have often taken pride in the belief that the events they were witnessing were somehow more significant than those experienced by previous generations. Crusaders saw the recapture of Jerusalem from the Muslims as a sign of the end-times. Later generations made the same claim regarding the Black Death, the Protestant Reformation, the English Civil War, the Great Awakening, the American Revolution, the Napoleonic Wars, and the U.S. Civil War. The Puritan ministers John Cotton and Cotton Mather predicted the return of Christ in specific years. The adventist William Miller convinced over fifty thousand Americans that Christ would return in 1844. Jonathan Edwards was nearly alone in placing the millennium of Christ's rule in the distant future—around the year 2000. More recently, the combination of the ancient doctrine of original sin with modern technological progress has made an apocalypse seem inevitable to many Christians. If science and technology progress geometrically, while human nature remains essentially selfish—if the destructive power of our weapons steadily increases, while our willingness to use them does not abate—an apocalypse would seem the inevitable fate of humankind.[42]

One cannot understand the attitudes of millions of Americans toward Israel, Russia, the European Union, the United Nations, the computer, gun control, and other vital issues without a comprehension of popular millennialist teachings. In recent years, millennialists have hypothesized the following scenario, based upon a combination of literal and allegorical interpretations of the surprisingly numerous biblical passages in both the Old and New Testaments that concern the end-times. Christians will disappear suddenly in the Rapture, taken by Christ into heaven, where they will be spared the tribulations to follow (Matt. 24:30–31; Mark 13:26–27; 1 Cor. 15:51–54; 1 Thess. 1:10, 4:15–17, 5:9). Russia and a confederacy of Muslim allies will invade Israel (Ezek. 38:1–16). God will defeat the invasion force through a great earthquake. The Antichrist, at the head of the European Union (which millennialists identify as the revived Roman Empire discussed throughout Revelation), will broker a seven-year peace agreement with Israel and many other nations (Dan. 9:27). He will rise to world dominance (Rev. 13:7), pretending to bring peace to a war-torn planet. Possessed by Satan, the Antichrist will perform astonishing miracles (2 Thess. 2:9) and will recover from a mortal wound (Rev. 13:12), perhaps even rising from the dead in a gross imitation of Jesus's resurrection. The Antichrist will be opposed by "two witnesses" in Jerusalem, who will preach the truth (Rev. 11:3–7) for three and a half years, inciting his anger. After three and a half years, the Antichrist will violate his treaty with Israel and invade the nation. Having defeated his enemies, the Antichrist will enter Jerusalem in triumph. He will stop the sacrifices and offerings in the Great Temple (yet to be rebuilt), will desecrate it by installing a statue of himself to be worshiped, and will declare himself God (Dan. 9:27, 12:11; Matt. 24:15; 2 Thess. 2:3–4). The Antichrist's worship will be organized by his ally, the "False Prophet," who will either be an apostate Christian religious leader or perhaps even an impostor pretending to be Christ Himself (Rev. 13:11: a being "like a lamb," Christ's symbol, but who "spoke like a dragon," Satan's symbol). The Antichrist will kill the "two witnesses" and leave their bodies to rot in the streets of Jerusalem. But after three and a half days the witnesses will rise from the dead in full view of the world (via satellite?) and ascend into heaven as a sign of God's power (Rev. 11:7–12). The Antichrist will force each citizen to bear a mark on his head or right hand, without which the citizen will not be able to buy or sell (Rev. 13:16–18). The Antichrist will execute large numbers of Christians and Jews who refuse to worship him and bear his mark (Dan. 8:24; Rev. 13:17). The souls of those who resist and refuse to take the mark will be saved; the souls of those who take the mark will be damned. Three and a half years after the Antichrist's desecration of the temple, seven after his treaty with Israel, Christ Himself will return to demolish the Antichrist's armies and those of his allies (Rev. 19:11–21). Christ will then judge humanity (Matt. 25:31–46), separating the saved from the damned. The righteous will go forth into eternal life, the damned into eternal punishment. Christ will then rule the world for one thousand years, followed by the creation of a new heaven and earth that will endure forever (Rev. 20 and 21).[43]

THE "CULTURE WAR": A COMPLEX PHENOMENON

The coexistence of theism, humanism, and skepticism in the same society has produced a culture war. But the war is not a simple conflict with clearly delineated sides. It features loose coalitions of factions that are not always logically consistent. Most people are not rigorous philosophers, obsessed with consistency. Humans are creatures of many competing moods, and each mood contains within itself the germ of a philosophy. So it should be no surprise that most people straddle the lines between philosophical categories. Nevertheless, though only the most committed partisans in a cultural war tend toward consistency, they are generally the most vocal and the most likely to provoke social change (often in ways they later regret).

Animal rights advocates are a good example of the difficulties in categorizing many modern activist groups. They are skeptical in their elimination of the distinction between humans and animals, but humanist in their conception of nature as benevolent. Though annoying to Epicurean humanist scientists who use animals in the hope of saving and improving human lives, animal rights arguments are an extension of the natural law philosophy that has always been a core element of humanism. Animal rights activists speak in the traditional humanist cadence of natural rights. "Humane treatment [for animals] is simply sentimental, sympathetic patronage," claims Michael W. Fox, director of the Center for Respect of Life and Environment at the Humane Society of the United States. "The animal rights philosophy is abolitionist rather than reformist," adds Tom Regan, a leader of the movement. "It's not better cages we work for, but empty cages. We want every animal out." Furthermore, the animal rights advocates' underlying supposition, that nature is good and pain is an aberration caused by cruel (overcivilized) humans, is a central tenet of Platonic humanism since Rousseau.[44]

CONCLUSION

The present age differs from previous eras not in the existence of the three philosophies but in the existence of large numbers of adherents of each philosophy simultaneously. Much of the heated nature of contemporary American political debate stems from fundamental philosophical differences between the combatants.

These differences are far more resistant to resolution than economic, ethnic, and gender differences. But even deep philosophical differences and heated debate need not descend into hostility, much less into violence. Most of us have close friends for whom we would sacrifice our lives but with whom we disagree on fundamental issues. Strongly held beliefs can be compatible with compassion and respect. The battle for the American mind must be fought with ideas, not bullets.

NOTES

1. Reinhold Niebuhr, *Faith and History: A Comparison of Christian and Modern Views of History* (New York: Scribner, 1949), 162; Allan Bloom, *The Closing of the American Mind* (New York: Simon & Schuster, 1987), 379.

2. Godfrey Hodgson, *America in Our Time* (Garden City, N.Y.: Doubleday, 1976), 18–19, 51–52, 155, 466; Robert Lekachman, *The Age of Keynes* (Random House, 1966), 4; George Brown Tindall, *America: A Narrative History*, 3d ed. (New York: W. W. Norton, 1992), 1180; Landon Y. Jones, *Great Expectations: America and the Baby Boom Generation* (New York: Coward, McCann & Geoghegan, 1980), 40; Robert J. Samuelson, "Great Expectations," *Newsweek*, January 8, 1996, 29.

3. Hodgson, *America in Our Time*, 53–54, 70, 76, 142; Jones, *Great Expectations*, 82; Erik Barnouw, *Tube of Plenty: The Evolution of American Television*, 2d ed. (Oxford: Oxford University Press, 1990), 99–148; Samuelson, "Great Expectations," 27.

4. B. F. Skinner, *Walden Two* (New York: Macmillan, 1948), 43–44, 49, 73, 83–93, 104, 115–16, 136, 139–40, 144, 150, 163, 167, 195–97, 222–23, 228.

5. William G. McLoughlin, *Revivals, Awakenings, and Reform: An Essay on Religion and Social Change in America, 1607–1977* (Chicago: University of Chicago Press, 1978), 186–88; Elaine Tyler May, *Homeward Bound: American Families in the Cold War Era* (New York: Basic, 1988), 25–26; Michael Medved, *Hollywood vs. America: Popular Culture and the War on Traditional Values* (New York: HarperCollins, 1992), 50–51; Garry Wills, *Under God: Religion and American Politics* (New York: Simon & Schuster, 1990), 17; Stephen L. Carter, *The Culture of Disbelief: How American Law and Politics Trivialize Religious Devotion* (New York: Basic, 1993), 100.

6. May, *Homeward Bound*, 26–27.

7. Reinhold Niebuhr, *The Children of Light and the Children of Darkness: A Vindication of Democracy and a Critique of Its Traditional Defense* (New York: Scribner, 1944), xii–xiii, xv, 10, 12, 16–17, 24, 41, 59; Niebuhr, *Faith and History*, 4–6, 33–34, 166–68, 179, 214, 237; Robert B. Westbrook, *John Dewey and American Democracy* (Ithaca, N.Y.: Cornell University Press, 1991), 529.

8. Thomas. S. Kuhn, *The Structure of Scientific Revolutions*, 1962, in *The American Intellectual Tradition*, 3d ed., 2 vols., ed. Charles Capper and David A. Hollinger (Oxford: Oxford University Press, 1997), vol. 2, 317–25.

9. Hodgson, *America in Our Time*, 18, 464; Samuelson, "Great Expectations," 26.

10. Laurence Vesey, *The Communal Experience: Anarchist and Mystical Counter-Cultures in America* (New York: Harper & Row, 1973), 196–97, 475.

11. Hodgson, *America in Our Time*, 6, 402–3; Theodore Roszak, *The Making of a Counter Culture: Reflections on the Technocratic Society and Its Youthful Opposition* (Garden City, N.Y.: Doubleday, 1968), 50–51, 54–55, 78.

12. Medved, *Hollywood vs. America*, 148, 155; Benjamin Spock, *Baby and Child Care*, 4th ed. (New York: Hawthorn Books, 1976), 8–11, 13, 17–18, 20–21, 24, 41, 46, 48–49.

13. Martin Luther King Jr., "Letter from the Birmingham Jail," 1963, in *The American Intellectual Tradition*, ed. Capper and Hollinger, vol. 2, 327; Martin Luther King Jr., "Pilgrimage to Nonviolence," 1958, in *Words That Made American History*, 2 vols., ed. Richard N. Current, John A. Garaty, and Julius Weinberg (Boston: Little, Brown, 1978), vol. 2, 529; Hodgson, *America in Our Time*, 157, 184.

14. Roszak, *Making of a Counter Culture*, xii.

15. Roszak, *Making of a Counter Culture*, 51, 82, 131–37, 145, 147; Hodgson, *America in Our Time*, 311; McLoughlin, *Revivals, Awakenings, and Reform*, x.

16. Hodgson, *America in Our Time*, 308–9, 351; Roszak, *Making of a Counter Culture*, 71, 166–69; Bloom, *Closing of the American Mind*, 77; Jones, *Great Expectations*, 112, 268.

17. Jones, *Great Expectations*, 166, 173.

18. Betty Friedan, *The Feminine Mystique* (New York: W. W. Norton, 1963), 79, 103, 106–9, 113, 116, 118, 124–25, 136.

19. Friedan, *Feminine Mystique*, 129, 131, 206, 256, 275–76, 308, 342, 348.

20. Jones, *Great Expectations*, 169, 183–84, 209, 214.

21. Jones, *Great Expectations*, 73, 93–94, 108; Hodgson, *America in Our Time*, 340.

22. Dinesh D'Souza, *Illiberal Education: The Politics of Race and Sex on Campus* (New York: Free Press, 1991), 18.

23. Richard Rorty, "Science as Solidarity," 1986, in *The American Intellectual Tradition*, ed. Capper and Hollinger, vol. 2, 358, 362–63, 367.

24. Rorty, "Science as Solidarity," vol. 2, 363; Richard Rorty, "Philosophy as a Kind of Writing: An Essay on Derrida," 1978–1979, in *Pragmatism: A Reader*, ed. Louis Menand (New York: Vintage, 1997), 313–14; Richard Rorty, "Postmodernist Bourgeois Liberalism," 1983, in *Pragmatism*, ed. Menand, 332–34.

25. Rorty, "Science as Solidarity," vol. 2, 361, 365.

26. Cornel West, *The American Evasion of Philosophy*, 1989, in *Pragmatism*, ed. Menand, 406, 408, 412–13.

27. Jonathan Culler, "Paul de Man's Contribution to Literary Criticism," in *Future Literary Theory*, ed. Ralph Cohen (New York: Routledge, 1989), 268–79.

28. Henry Louis Gates, "Authority, (White) Power, and the Black Critic," in *Future Literary Theory*, ed. Cohen, 324–46.

29. Elaine Showalter, "A Criticism of Our Own: Autonomy and Assimilation in Afro-American and Feminist Literary Theory," in *Future Literary Theory*, ed. Cohen, 347–69.

30. Culler, "Paul de Man's Contribution to Literary Criticism," 271; Gates, "Authority, (White) Power, and the Black Critic," 336.

31. Lee Benson, *The Concept of Jacksonian Democracy: New York as a Test Case* (Princeton, N.J.: Princeton University Press, 1961); Charles Royster, *A Revolutionary People at War: The Continental Army and American Character, 1775–1783* (Chapel Hill: University of North Carolina Press, 1979); Nancy F. Cott and Elizabeth H. Pleck, eds., *A Heritage of Her Own: Towards a New Social History of American Women* (New York: Simon & Schuster, 1979); Elizabeth Fox-Genovese, *Within the Plantation Household: Black and White Women in the Old South* (Chapel Hill: University of North Carolina Press, 1988); Linda Kerber, *Women of the Republic: Intellect and Ideology in Revolutionary America* (Chapel Hill: University of North Carolina Press, 1990); Joan Scott, *Gender and the Politics of History* (New York: Columbia University Press, 1988); Linda Kerber and Jane Sherron De Hart, eds., *Women's America: Refocusing the Past*, 4th ed. (New York: Oxford University Press, 1995); John W. Blassingame, *The Slave Community: Plantation Life in the Antebellum South* (New York: Oxford University Press, 1972); Eugene Genovese, *Roll, Jordan, Roll: The World the Slaves Made* (New York: Pantheon, 1974); Sean Wilentz, *Chants Democratic: New York and the Rise of the American Working Class, 1788–1850* (New York: Oxford University Press, 1984); Leon Fink, *In Search of the Working Class: Essays in American Labor History and Political Culture* (Urbana: University of Illinois Press, 1994); Martin Bernal, *Black Athena: The Afroasiatic Roots of Classical Civilization*, vol. 1, *The Fabrication of Ancient Greece* (New Brunswick, N.J.: Rutgers University Press, 1987); David E. Stannard, *American Holocaust: The Conquest of the New World* (Oxford: Oxford University Press, 1992).

32. Paul Monaco, *Ribbons in Time: Movies and Society since 1945* (Bloomington: Indiana University Press, 1988), 124, 128; Christopher Williams, *Realism and the Cinema: A Reader* (New York: Routledge, 1980), 25, 32.

33. Medved, *Hollywood vs. America*, 108, 112–13, 143, 247; "U.S. TV Soaked in Sex, Study Finds," a Reuters story reproduced by msnbc.com, February 9, 1999; Steven Daly, "Blue Streak," *TV Guide*, August 2–8, 2003, 28–34.

34. Bloom, *Closing of the American Mind*, 118–19.

35. D'Souza, *Illiberal Education*, 1, 11–12, 15, 22, 71–80, 86–89, 100–104, 118, 136–38, 195, 226–27, 239, 248, 254–55.

36. Walter Martin, *The New Age Cult* (Minneapolis, Minn.: Bethany House, 1989), 19, 21, 29–34, 39, 41, 58–59, 61, 65, 70, 76, 79, 81, 84–86, 93, 113–14, 119.

37. Martin, *New Age Cult*, 8; Kenneth L. Woodward, "Soul Searching," *Newsweek*, July 8, 1996, 34; Kenneth L. Woodward, "Deepak's Impact," *Newsweek*, October 20, 1997, 53–54, 56; Kenneth L. Woodward, "Heaven's Gatekeepers," *Newsweek*, March 16, 1998, 64–65.

38. Jay P. Dolan, *The American Catholic Experience: A History from Colonial Times to the Present* (South Bend, Ind.: Notre Dame University Press, 1992), 425–26, 429–36,

439–40, 446, 451–52; U.S. Catholic Bishops, "A Pastoral Message: Economic Justice for All," 1986, in *Religion in American History: A Reader*, ed. Jon Butler and Harry S. Stout (New York: Oxford University Press, 1988), 501–3.

39. Jerry Fallwell, "The Imperative of Moral Involvement," 1980, in *Religion in American History*, ed. Butler and Stout, 505, 510–11.

40. Kenneth L. Woodward and Anne Woodward, "A Bishop in the Dock," *Newsweek*, February 26, 1996, 62; Kenneth L. Woodward, "Sex, Morality, and the Protestant Minister," *Newsweek*, July 28, 1997, 62; Daniel Pedersen, "Crossing Over," *Newsweek*, November 4, 1996, 66; William J. Bennett, *The De-Valuing of America: The Fight for Our Culture and Our Children* (New York: Simon & Schuster, 1992), 222.

41. Paul Boyer, *When Time Shall Be No More: Prophecy Belief in Modern American Culture* (Cambridge, Mass.: Harvard University Press, 1992), ix, 5, 139–40, 144, 203, 264; Hal Lindsey, *The Final Battle* (Palos Verdes, Calif.: Western Front, 1995), xiv; Jerry Jenkins and Tim LaHaye, *Left Behind*, 12 vols. (Wheaton, Ill.: Tyndale, 1995–2004).

42. Boyer, *When Time Shall Be No More*, 50–51, 56, 60–61, 64–65, 68–72, 81, 115, 123, 229, 275.

43. Tim LaHaye, *No Fear of the Storm: Why Christians Will Escape All the Tribulation* (Sisters, Ore.: Multnomah, 1992); Daymond R. Duck, *On the Brink: Easy-to-Understand End-Time Bible Prophecy* (Lancaster, Pa.: Starburst Publishers, 1995); Lindsey, *The Final Battle*.

44. Jerry Adler and Mary Hager, "Emptying the Cages: Does the Animal Kingdom Need a Bill of Rights?" *Newsweek*, May 23, 1988, 59–60; Matt Bai, "Breaking the Cages," *Newsweek*, September 29, 1997, 66.

BIBLIOGRAPHICAL SUGGESTIONS
FOR GENERAL READERS

This list barely scratches the surface of the vast, rich literature concerning the history of American thought. It is intended merely to serve as a starting point for further investigation.

The best collection of documents regarding American intellectual history is Charles Capper's and David A. Hollinger's two-volume set, *The American Intellectual Tradition* (3d ed., Oxford University Press, 1997). Other useful collections include Bernard Bailyn, ed., *Pamphlets of the American Revolution* (Harvard University Press, 1965); Charlene Bangs Bickford, Kenneth R. Bowling, and Helen E. Veit, eds., *Creating the Bill of Rights: The Documentary Record from the First Federal Congress* (Johns Hopkins University Press, 1991); Jon Butler and Harry S. Stout, eds., *Religion in American History* (Oxford University Press, 1988); Robert M. Crunden, ed., *The Superfluous Men: Conservative Critics of American Culture, 1900–1945* (University of Texas Press, 1977); Jonathan Elliot, ed., *Debates in the Several State Conventions on the Adoption of the Federal Constitution* 4 vols., (Burt Franklin, 1968); Max Farrand, ed., *The Records of the Federal Convention of 1787* 3d ed., 4 vols. (Yale University Press, 1966); Paul Leicester Ford, ed., *Pamphlets on the Constitution of the United States* (Burt Franklin, 1971); Louis Menand, ed., *Pragmatism: A Reader* (Vintage, 1997); Michael O'Brien, ed., *All Clever Men, Who Make Their Way: Critical Discourse in the Old South* (University of Georgia Press, 1992); and Herbert J. Storing, ed., 7 vols., *The Complete Antifederalist* (University of Chicago Press, 1981).

Among the many broad works on the history of American thought are A. J. Beitzinger, *A History of American Political Thought* (Dodd, Mead, 1972); Jon Butler, *Awash in a Sea of Faith: Christianizing the American People* (Harvard University Press, 1990); Merle Curti, *The Growth of American Thought* (Harper and Brothers, 1943); Jay P. Dolan, *The American Catholic Experience: A History from Colonial Times to the Present* (University of Notre Dame Press, 1992); Ralph Henry Gabriel, *The Course of American Democratic Thought* (Ronald, 1956); Eugene D. Genovese, *The Southern Tradition: The Achievement and Limitations of American Conservatism* (Harvard University Press, 1994); Louis Hartz, *The Liberal Tradition in America* (Harcourt-Brace, 1955); Richard Hofstadter, *The American Political Tradition* (Vintage, 1948); Michael Kammen, *People of Paradox* (Random House, 1972); Martin E. Marty, *Righteous Empire: The Protestant Experience in America* (Dial, 1970); Leo Marx, *The Machine in the Garden: Technology and the Pastoral Ideal in America* (Oxford University Press, 1964); William G. McLoughlin, *Revivals, Awakenings, and Reform: An Essay on Religion and Social Change in America, 1607–1977* (University of Chicago Press, 1978); Vernon Louis Parrington, *Main Currents in American Thought* (Harcourt, Brace, 1930); Lewis Perry, *Intellectual Life in America: A History* (Franklin Watts, 1984); Stow Persons, *American Minds: A History of Ideas* (Henry Holt, 1958); Henry Nash Smith, *Virgin Land: The American West as Symbol and Myth* (Harvard University Press, 1950); Garry Wills, *Under God: Religion and American Politics* (Simon & Schuster, 1990); and Caroline Winterer, *The Culture of Classicism: Ancient Greece and Rome in American Intellectual Life, 1780–1910* (Johns Hopkins University Press, 2002).

Useful works concerning the Protestant Reformation include Roland H. Bainton, *Here I Stand: A Life of Martin Luther* (Abingdon-Cokesbury, 1950); William J. Bouwsma, *John Calvin: A Sixteenth-Century Portrait* (Oxford University Press, 1988); A. G. Dickens, *The English Reformation* (Schocken Books, 1964); Mark U. Edwards Jr., *Luther's Last Battles: Politics and Polemics, 1531–1546* (Cornell University Press, 1983); G. R. Elton, *Reform and Reformation: England, 1509–1558* (Harvard University Press, 1977); H. Outram Evennett, *The Spirit of the Counter-Reformation* (Cambridge University Press, 1968); Derek Hirst, *Authority and Conflict: England, 1603–1658* (Harvard University Press, 1986); Alister Mc-

Grath, *The Intellectual Origins of the European Reformation* (Basil Blackwell, 1987); Steven Ozment, *The Age of Reform, 1250–1550: An Intellectual and Religious History of Late Medieval and Reformation Europe* (Yale University Press, 1980); and George Huntston Williams, *The Radical Reformation* (Westminster, 1962).

The most insightful book about the Puritans remains Edmund S. Morgan's *The Puritan Dilemma: The Story of John Winthrop* (Little, Brown, 1958). For a more thorough discussion of Puritan thought see Perry Miller's two-volume study, *The New England Mind* (Macmillan, 1939; Harvard University Press, 1953). For a more critical view of the Puritans see Sacvan Bercovitch's *The Puritan Origins of the American Self* (Yale University Press, 1975) and *The American Jeremiad* (University of Wisconsin Press, 1978), as well as Emory Elliott's *Power and the Pulpit in Puritan New England* (Princeton University Press, 1975). The most sensible book on the Salem witch trials is Paul Boyer's and Steve Nissenbaum's *Salem Possessed: The Social Origins of Witchcraft* (Harvard University Press, 1974). Other books concerning the Puritans include Emery Battis, *Saints and Sectaries: Anne Hutchinson and the Antinomian Controversy in the Massachusetts Bay Colony* (University of North Carolina Press, 1962); T. H. Breen, *Puritans and Adventurers: Change and Persistence in Early America* (Oxford University Press, 1980); Charles E. Hambrick-Stowe, *The Practice of Piety: Puritan Devotional Disciplines in Seventeenth-Century New England* (University of North Carolina Press, 1982); Kenneth A. Lockridge, *A New England Town: The First Hundred Years* (W. W. Norton, 1970); Perry Miller, *Errand into the Wilderness* (Harvard University Press, 1956); Edmund S. Morgan, *Roger Williams: The Church and the State* (Harcourt-Brace, 1967); Lee Schweniger, *John Winthrop* (Twayne, 1990); Kenneth Silverman, *The Life and Times of Cotton Mather* (Harper & Row, 1984); Ola Elizabeth Winslow, *John Eliot, "Apostle to the Indians"* (Houghton Mifflin, 1968); and Larzer Ziff, *Puritanism in America: New Culture in a New World* (Viking, 1973).

Works on other Protestant sects in colonial America include Randall Balmer, *A Perfect Babel of Confusion: Dutch Religion and English Culture in the Middle Colonies* (Oxford University Press, 1989); E. Digby Baltzell, *Puritan Boston and Quaker Philadelphia: Two Protestant Ethics and the Spirit of Class Authority and Leadership* (Free Press, 1979); Edwin B. Bronner, *William Penn's "Holy Experiment": The Founding of*

Pennsylvania, 1681–1701 (Greenwood, 1978); John Putnam Demos, *A Little Commonwealth: Family Life in Plymouth Colony* (Oxford University Press, 1970); Melvin B. Endy Jr., *William Penn and Early Quakerism* (Princeton University Press, 1973); Jack D. Marietta, *The Reformation of American Quakerism, 1748–1783* (University of Pennsylvania Press, 1984); and Frederick Woolverton, *Colonial Anglicanism in North America* (Wayne State University Press, 1984).

Books concerning the Great Awakening include: Douglas J. Elwood, *The Philosophical Theology of Jonathan Edwards* (Columbia University Press, 1960); Norman Fiering, *Jonathan Edwards' Moral Thought and its British Context* (University of North Carolina Press, 1981); Rhys Isaac, *The Transformation of Virginia, 1740–1790* (University of North Carolina Press, 1982); George William Pilcher, *Samuel Davies: Apostle of Dissent in Colonial Virginia* (University of Tennessee Press, 1971); and Patricia J. Tracy, *Jonathan Edwards, Pastor: Religion and Society in Eighteenth-Century Northampton* (Hill & Wang, 1979).

The literature on the Founding Fathers is particularly extensive. The best works on their philosophical and religious beliefs are Daniel Boorstin, *The Lost World of Thomas Jefferson* (Henry Holt, 1948); Edwin S. Gaustad, *Faith of Our Fathers: Religion and the New Nation* (Harper & Row, 1987); Zoltan Haraszti, *John Adams and the Prophets of Progress* (Harvard University Press, 1972); Adrienne Koch, *The Philosophy of Thomas Jefferson* (Harvard University Press, 1952); Karl Lehmann, *Thomas Jefferson: American Humanist* (University of Chicago Press, 1964); and Henry F. May, *The Enlightenment in America* (Oxford University Press, 1976).

Useful books on the political philosophy of the founders include Douglass Adair, *Fame and the Founding Fathers* (W. W. Norton, 1974); Joyce O. Appleby, *Capitalism and a New Social Order: The Republican Vision of the 1790s* (New York University Press, 1984); Bernard Bailyn, *The Ideological Origins of the American Revolution* (2d ed., Harvard University Press, 1992); Lance Banning, *The Jeffersonian Persuasion* (Cornell University Press, 1978) and *Conceived in Liberty: The Struggle to Define the New Republic, 1789–1793* (Rowman & Littlefield, 2004); Kenneth R. Bowling and David Kennon, eds., *Inventing Congress: Origins and Establishment of the First Federal Congress* (Ohio University Press, 1999); H. Trevor Colbourn, *The Lamp of Experience: Whig History and the Intellectual Origins of the American Revolution*

(University of North Carolina Press, 1965); Paul K. Conkin, *Self-Evident Truths* (Indiana University Press, 1974); Richard Beale Davis, *Intellectual Life in Jefferson's Virginia, 1790–1830* (University of North Carolina Press, 1964); Henry C. Dethloff, ed., *Thomas Jefferson and American Democracy* (D. C. Heath, 1971); Stanley Elkins and Eric McKitrick, *The Age of Federalism* (Oxford University Press, 1993); Gary L. Gregg II, ed., *Vital Remnants: America's Founding and the Western Tradition* (ISI, 1999); Linda K. Kerber, *Federalists in Dissent: Imagery and Ideology in Jeffersonian America* (Cornell University Press, 1970); Ralph Ketcham, *From Colony to Country: The Revolution in American Thought, 1750–1820* (Macmillan, 1974); Michael Lienesch, *New Order of the Ages: Time, the Constitution, and the Making of Modern American Political Thought* (Princeton University Press, 1988); Richard K. Matthews, *The Radical Politics of Thomas Jefferson: A Revisionist View* (University Press of Kansas, 1984); Drew R. McCoy, *The Last of the Fathers: James Madison and the Republican Legacy* (Cambridge University Press, 1989); Forrest McDonald, *Novus Ordo Seclorum* (University Press of Kansas, 1985); Peter S. Onuf, ed., *Jeffersonian Legacies* (University Press of Virginia, 1993); J. G. A. Pocock, *The Machiavellian Moment: Florentine Political Thought and the Atlantic Republican Tradition* (Princeton University Press, 1975); Paul A. Rahe, *Republics, Ancient and Modern: Classical Republicanism and the American Revolution* (University of North Carolina Press, 1992); Jack N. Rakove, *James Madison and the Creation of the American Republic* (2d ed., Longman, 2002); James H. Read, *Power Versus Liberty: Madison, Hamilton, Wilson, and Jefferson* (University Press of Virginia, 2000); Meyer Reinhold, *Classica Americana: The Greek and Roman Heritage in the United States* (Wayne State University Press, 1984); Carl J. Richard, *The Founders and the Classics: Greece, Rome, and the American Enlightenment* (Harvard University Press, 1994); Jennifer Tolbert Roberts, *Athens on Trial: The Antidemocratic Tradition in Western Thought* (Princeton University Press, 1994); M. N. S. Sellers, *American Republicanism: Roman Ideology in the United States Constitution* (New York University Press, 1994); Peter Shaw, *The Character of John Adams* (University of North Carolina Press, 1976); Gerald Stourzh, *Alexander Hamilton and the Idea of Republican Government* (Stanford University Press, 1970); C. Bradley Thompson, *John Adams and the Spirit of Liberty* (University Press of Kansas, 1998); Garry Wills, *Cincinnatus: George Washington and the*

Enlightenment (Doubleday, 1984) and *Explaining America: The Federalist* (Penguin, 1981); Susan Ford Wiltshire, *Greece, Rome, and the Bill of Rights* (University of Oklahoma Press, 1992); Gordon S. Wood, *The Creation of the American Republic, 1776–1787* (University of North Carolina Press, 1969) and *The Radicalism of the American Revolution* (Alfred A. Knopf, 1992); Jean M. Yarbrough, *American Virtues: Thomas Jefferson on the Character of a Free People* (University Press of Kansas, 1998); and Michael P. Zuckert, *The Natural Rights Republic: Studies in the Foundation of the American Political Tradition* (Notre Dame University Press, 1996).

Among the many histories of American economics and of American economic thought are W. Elliot Brownlee, *Dynamics of Ascent: A History of the American Economy* (Alfred A. Knopf, 1974); Stuart Bruchey, *The Roots of American Economic Growth, 1607–1861: An Essay in Social Causation* (Harper & Row, 1968) and *Enterprise: The Dynamic Economy of a Free People* (Harvard University Press, 1990); Paul K. Conkin, *Prophets of Prosperity: America's First Political Economists* (Indiana University Press, 1980); Robert Lekachman, *The Age of Keynes* (Random House, 1966); Drew R. McCoy, *The Elusive Republic: Political Economy in Jeffersonian America* (University of North Carolina Press, 1980); Thomas Sowell, *Classical Economics Reconsidered* (Princeton University Press, 1974); and George Rogers Taylor, *The Transportation Revolution, 1815–1860* (Rinehart, 1951).

Among the books on the Second Great Awakening are Leonard Arrington and Davis Bitton, *The Mormon Experience: A History of the Latter-Day Saints* (Alfred A. Knopf, 1979); John B. Boles, *The Great Revival, 1787–1805* (University Press of Kentucky, 1972); Paul K. Conkin, *The Uneasy Center: Reformed Christianity in Antebellum America* (University of North Carolina Press, 1995) and *American Originals: Homemade Varieties of Christianity* (University of North Carolina Press, 1997); Whitney R. Cross, *The Burned-Over District: The Social and Intellectual History of Enthusiastic Religion in Western New York, 1800–1850* (Octagon, 1981); Klaus J. Hansen, *Mormonism and the American Experience* (University of Chicago Press, 1981); Keith Hardman, *Charles Grandison Finney, 1792–1875: Revivalist and Reformer* (Syracuse University Press, 1987); Albert J. Raboteau, *Slave Religion: The "Invisible Institution" in the Antebellum South* (Oxford

University Press, 1978); and Milton Rugoff, *The Beechers: An American Family in the Nineteenth Century* (Harper & Row, 1981).

Among the useful works on antebellum reform movements are Jeanne Boydston, Mary Kelley, and Anne Margolis, *The Limits of Sisterhood: The Beecher Sisters on Women's Rights and Woman's Sphere* (University of North Carolina Press, 1988); Clifford S. Griffin, *Their Brother's Keepers: Moral Stewardship in the United States, 1800–1865* (Rutgers University Press, 1981); William R. Merrill, *Against Wind and Tide: A Biography of William Lloyd Garrison* (Harvard University Press, 1963); Timothy L. Smith, *Revivalism and Social Reform: American Protestantism on the Eve of the Civil War* (2d ed., Johns Hopkins University Press, 1980); P. J. Staudenraus, *The African Colonization Movement, 1816–1865* (Columbia University Press, 1961); John L. Thomas, *The Liberator: William Lloyd Garrison, a Biography* (Little, Brown, 1963); and Ronald G. Walters, *American Reformers, 1815–1860* (Hill & Wang, 1978).

Books on American romanticism include Paul F. Boller Jr., *American Transcendentalism, 1830–1860: An Intellectual Inquiry* (Putnam, 1974); Howard Mumford Jones, *Revolution and Romanticism* (Harvard University Press, 1974); David K. Kirby, *Herman Melville* (Continuum, 1993); David Levin, *History as Romantic Art: Bancroft, Prescott, Motley, and Parkman* (Stanford University Press, 1959); F. O. Matthiessen, *American Renaissance: Art and Expression in the Age of Emerson and Whitman* (Oxford University Press, 1941); Taylor Stoehr, *Nay-Saying in Concord: Emerson, Alcott, and Thoreau* (Archon, 1979); Jane Tompkins, *Sensational Designs: The Cultural Work of American Fiction, 1790–1860* (Oxford University Press, 1985); and Edward Wagenknecht, *Edgar Allan Poe: The Man behind the Legend* (Oxford University Press, 1963).

Thoughtful works on nationalism include Carlton J. H. Hayes's *Essays on Nationalism* (Macmillan, 1926) and *Nationalism: A Religion* (Macmillan, 1960) and Hans Kohn's *Nationalism: Its Meaning and History* (D. Van Nostrand, 1955).

Useful books on intellectual life in the late nineteenth and early twentieth centuries include Robert C. Bannister, *Social Darwinism: Science and Myth in Anglo-American Social Thought* (Temple University Press, 1979); Paul F. Boller Jr., *American Thought in Transition: The*

Impact of Evolutionary Naturalism, 1865–1900 (Rand McNally, 1969); Henry Steele Commager, *The American Mind: An Interpretation of American Thought and Character since the 1880s* (Yale University Press, 1950); Paul K. Conkin, *When All the Gods Trembled: Darwinism, Scopes, and American Intellectuals* (Rowman & Littlefield, 1998); Nathan G. Hale Jr., *Freud and the Americans: The Beginnings of Psychoanalysis in the United States, 1876–1917* (Oxford University Press, 1971); John Higham, *Strangers in the Land: Patterns of American Nativism, 1860–1925* (Rutgers University Press, 1955); Gertrude Himmelfarb, *Darwin and the Darwinian Revolution* (Doubleday, 1959); Richard Hofstadter, *Social Darwinism in American Thought* (Beacon, 1992); William R. Hutchinson, *The Modernist Impulse in American Protestantism* (Cambridge University Press, 1976); Alfred Kazin, *On Native Grounds: An Interpretation of Modern American Prose Literature* (Reynal & Hitchcock, 1942); Christopher Lasch, *The New Radicalism in America, 1889–1963: The Intellectual as a Social Type* (Vintage, 1965); T. Jackson Lears, *No Place of Grace: Antimodernism and the Transformation of American Culture, 1880–1920* (Pantheon, 1981); R. W. B. Lewis, *The American Adam: Innocence, Tragedy, and Tradition in the Nineteenth Century* (University of Chicago Press, 1955); George M. Marsden, *Fundamentalism and American Culture: The Shaping of Twentieth-Century Evangelicalism, 1870–1925* (Oxford University Press, 1980); Henry F. May, *The End of American Innocence: A Study of the First Years of Our Own Time, 1912–1917* (Alfred A. Knopf, 1959); Donald B. Meyer, *The Protestant Search for Political Realism, 1919–1941* (University of California Press, 1961); Rosalind Rosenberg, *Beyond Separate Spheres: Intellectual Roots of Modern Feminism* (Yale University Press, 1982); Cynthia E. Russett, *Darwin in America: The Intellectual Response, 1865–1912* (W. H. Freeman, 1976); Daniel Joseph Singall, *The War Within: From Victorian to Modernist Thought in the South, 1919–1945* (University of North Carolina Press, 1982); and Morton G. White, *Social Thought in America: The Revolt against Formalism* (Viking, 1949).

The best book about pragmatism is Louis Menand's Pulitzer-prize-winner, *The Metaphysical Club* (Farrar, Straus & Giroux, 2001). Other notable works include Paul K. Conkin, *Puritans and Pragmatists: Eight Eminent American Thinkers* (Indiana University Press, 1968); Edward C. Moore, *American Pragmatism: Peirce, James, and Dewey* (Columbia University Press, 1961); Ralph Barton Perry, *The Thought and Character of William James* (George Braziller, 1954); and Robert B. Westbrook, *John Dewey and American Democracy* (Cornell University Press, 1991).

Useful books concerning the baby boom generation include Godfrey Hodgson, *America in Our Time* (Doubleday, 1976); Landon Y. Jones, *Great Expectations: America and the Baby Boom Generation* (Coward, McCann, and Geoghegan, 1980); Elaine Tyler May, *Homeward Bound: American Families in the Cold War Era* (Basic, 1988); and Laurence Vesey, *The Communal Experience: Anarchist and Mystical Counter-Cultures in America* (Harper & Row, 1973).

There have been a plethora of books on "the culture war" of the past thirty years, of course. But because partisans in that conflict have written nearly all of these, I consider them "primary sources" rather than "secondary sources," and for this reason I decline to list them here.

INDEX

ABOUT THE AUTHOR

Carl J. Richard is professor of history at the University of Louisiana, Lafayette. His previous books include *The Founders and the Classics* and *Twelve Greeks and Romans Who Changed the World*. He lives near Broussard, Louisiana.